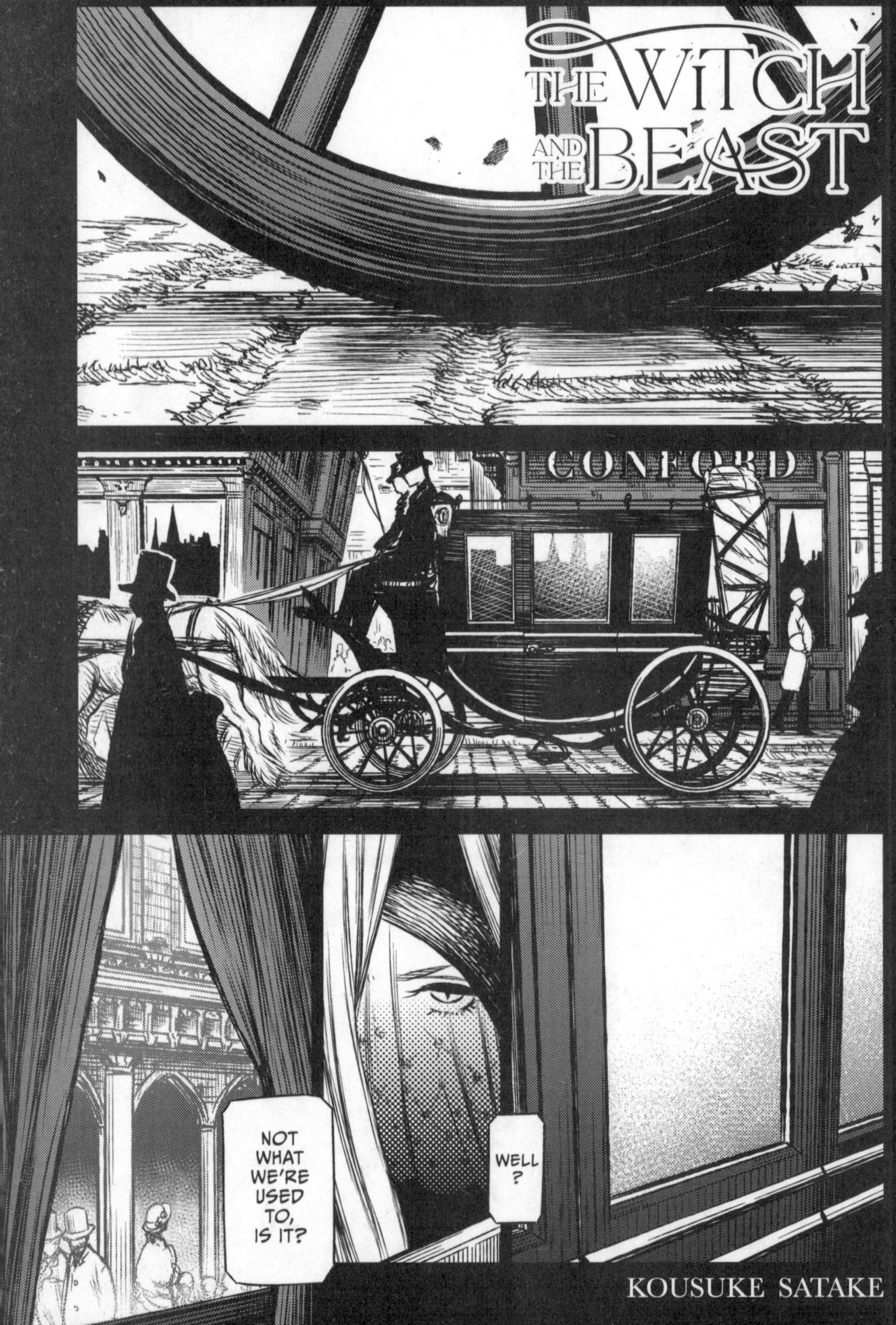
THE WITCH AND THE BEAST
CONFORD
WELL?
NOT WHAT WE'RE USED TO, IS IT?
KOUSUKE SATAKE

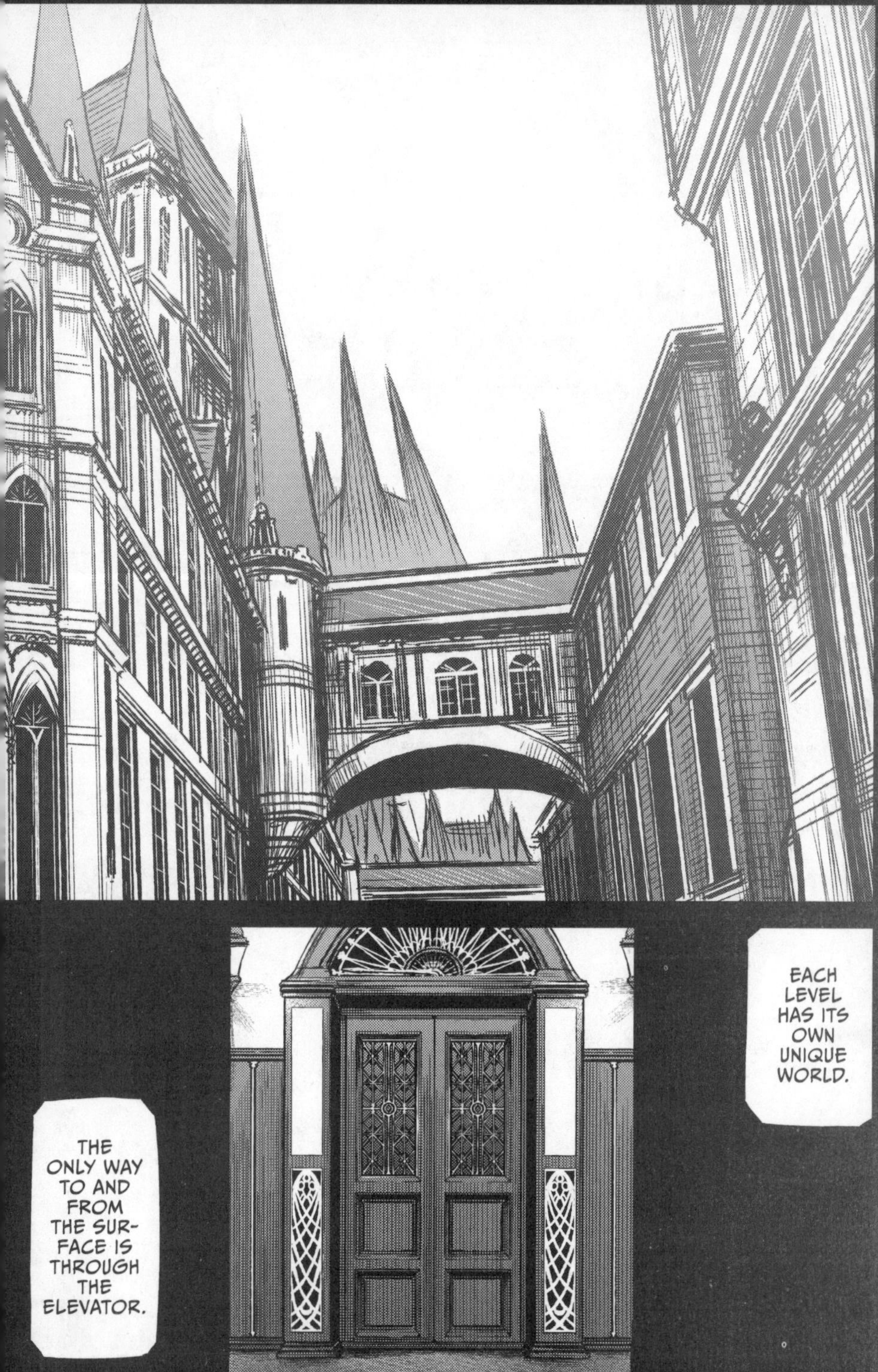
EACH LEVEL HAS ITS OWN UNIQUE WORLD.
THE ONLY WAY TO AND FROM THE SUR-FACE IS THROUGH THE ELEVATOR.

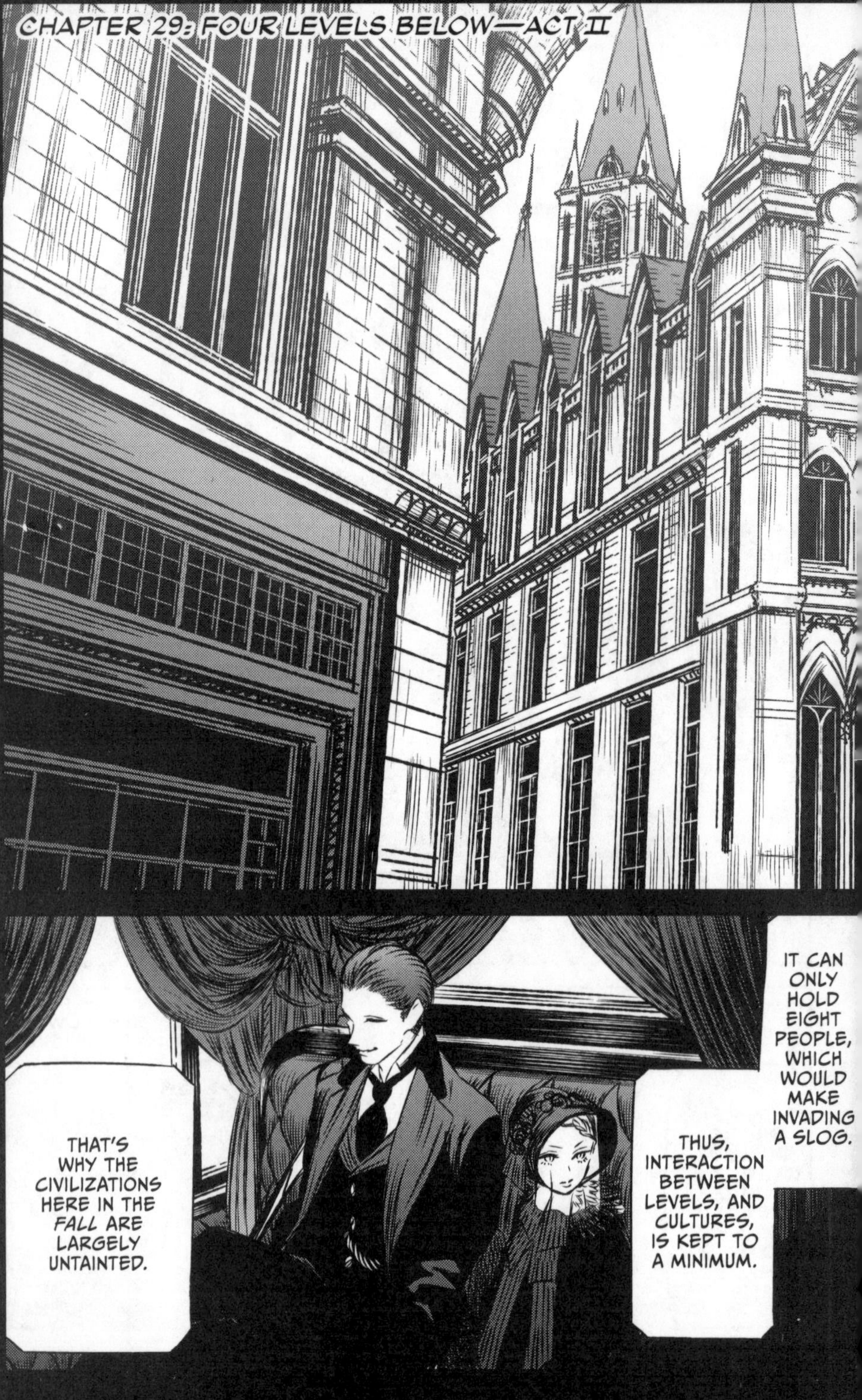
CHAPTER 29: FOUR LEVELS BELOW—ACT II
IT CAN ONLY HOLD EIGHT PEOPLE, WHICH WOULD MAKE INVADING A SLOG.
THUS, INTERACTION BETWEEN LEVELS, AND CULTURES, IS KEPT TO A MINIMUM.
THAT'S WHY THE CIVILIZATIONS HERE IN THE *FALL* ARE LARGELY UNTAINTED.

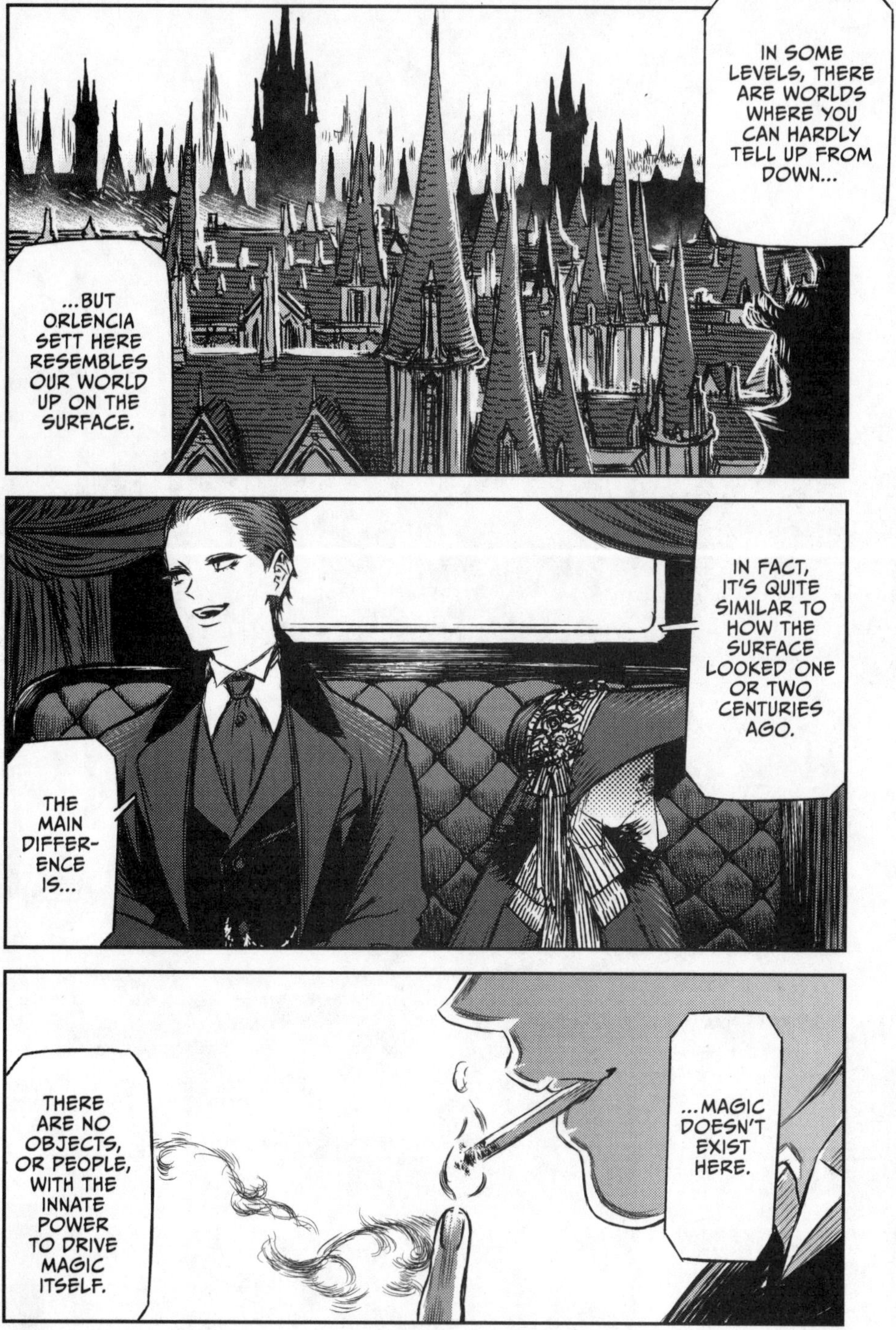
IN SOME LEVELS, THERE ARE WORLDS WHERE YOU CAN HARDLY TELL UP FROM DOWN...
...BUT ORLENCIA SETT HERE RESEMBLES OUR WORLD UP ON THE SURFACE.
IN FACT, IT'S QUITE SIMILAR TO HOW THE SURFACE LOOKED ONE OR TWO CENTURIES AGO.
THE MAIN DIFFER-ENCE IS...
...MAGIC DOESN'T EXIST HERE.
THERE ARE NO OBJECTS, OR PEOPLE, WITH THE INNATE POWER TO DRIVE MAGIC ITSELF.

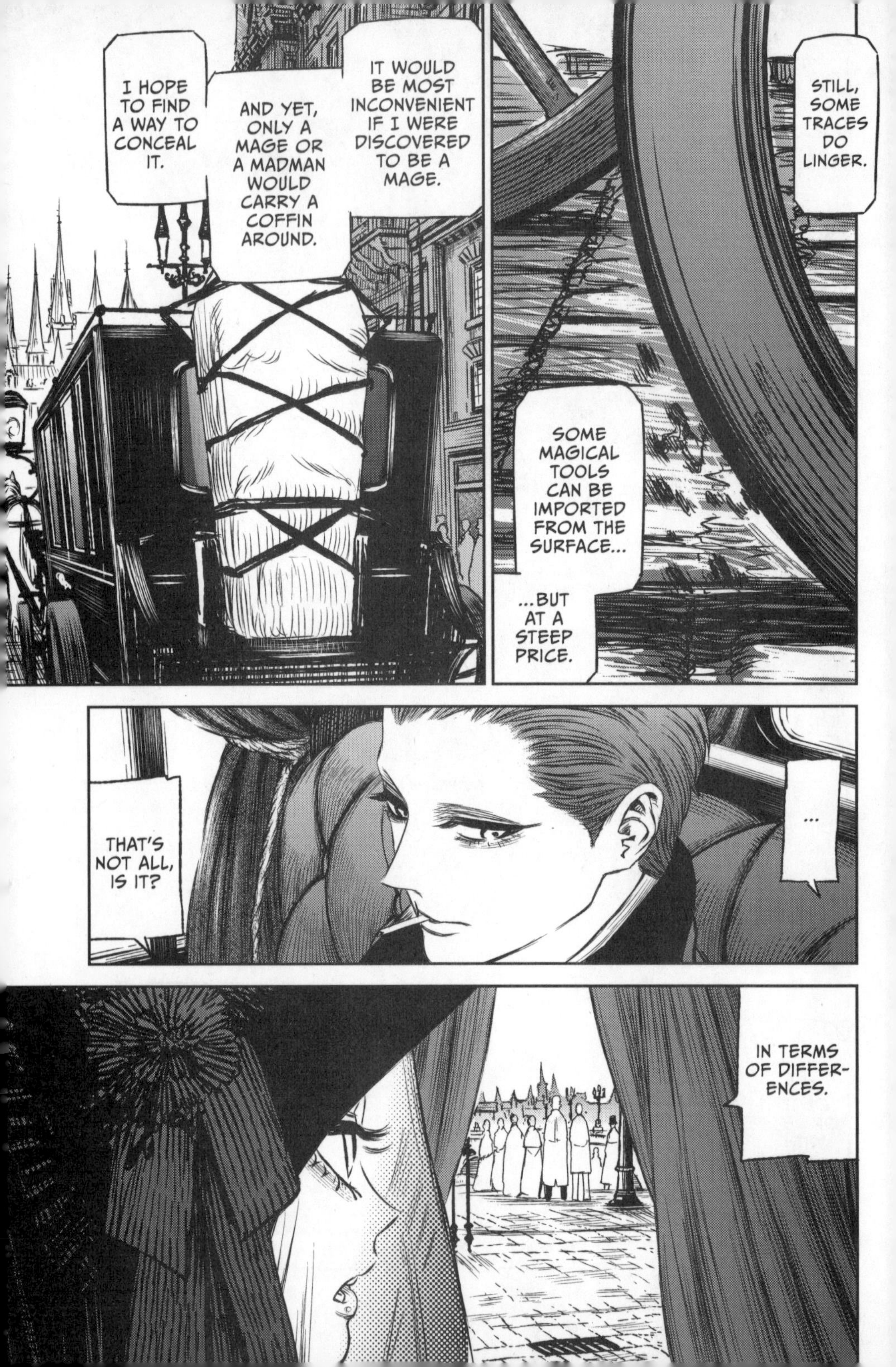

STILL, SOME TRACES DO LINGER.
SOME MAGICAL TOOLS CAN BE IMPORTED FROM THE SURFACE...
...BUT AT A STEEP PRICE.
IT WOULD BE MOST INCONVENIENT IF I WERE DISCOVERED TO BE A MAGE.
AND YET, ONLY A MAGE OR A MADMAN WOULD CARRY A COFFIN AROUND.
I HOPE TO FIND A WAY TO CONCEAL IT.
...
THAT'S NOT ALL, IS IT?
IN TERMS OF DIFFERENCES.

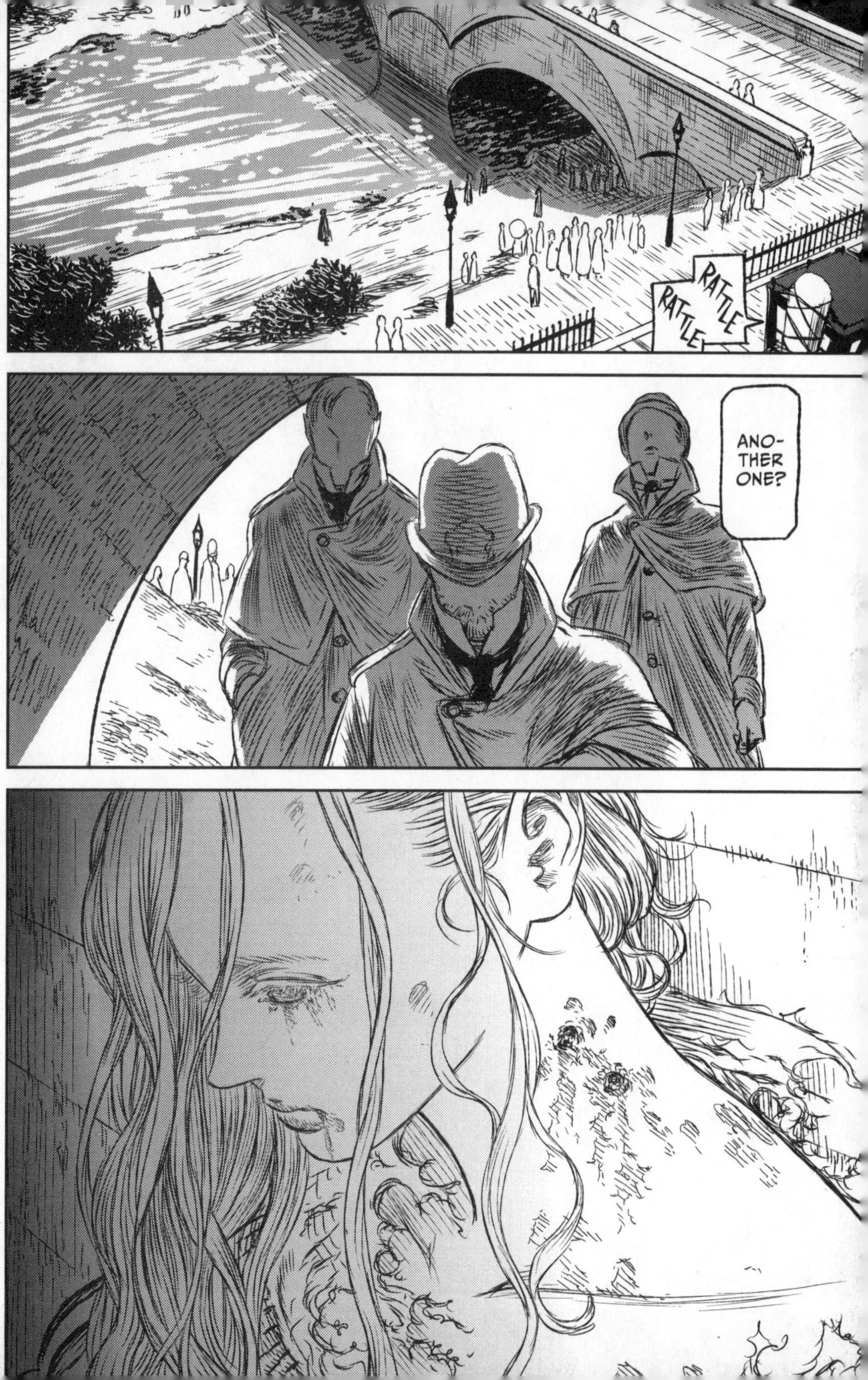
RATTLE
RATTLE
ANO-THER ONE?

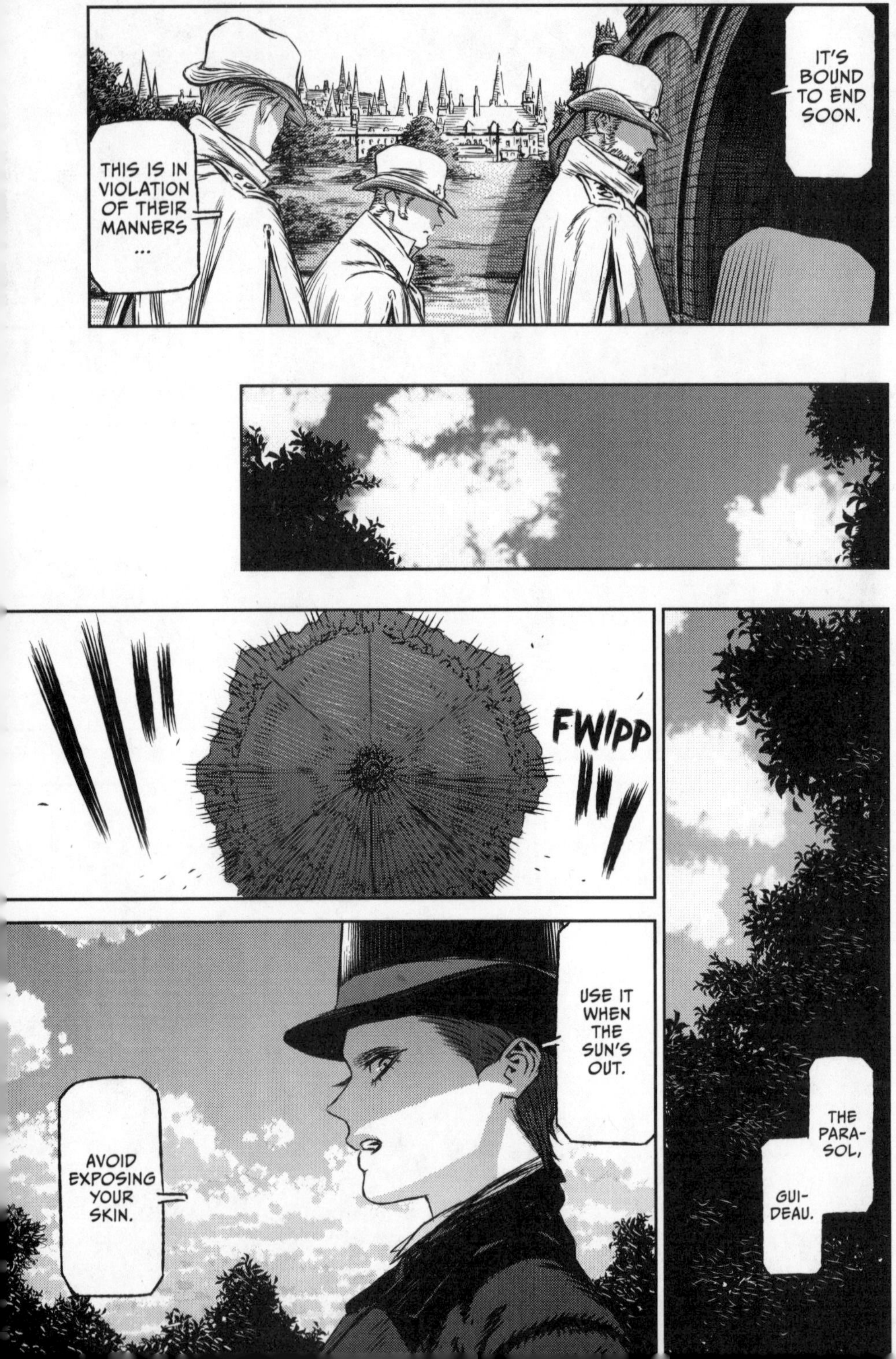
IT'S BOUND TO END SOON.
THIS IS IN VIOLATION OF THEIR MANNERS ...
THE PARA-SOL,
GUI-DEAU.
FWIPP
USE IT WHEN THE SUN'S OUT.
AVOID EXPOSING YOUR SKIN.

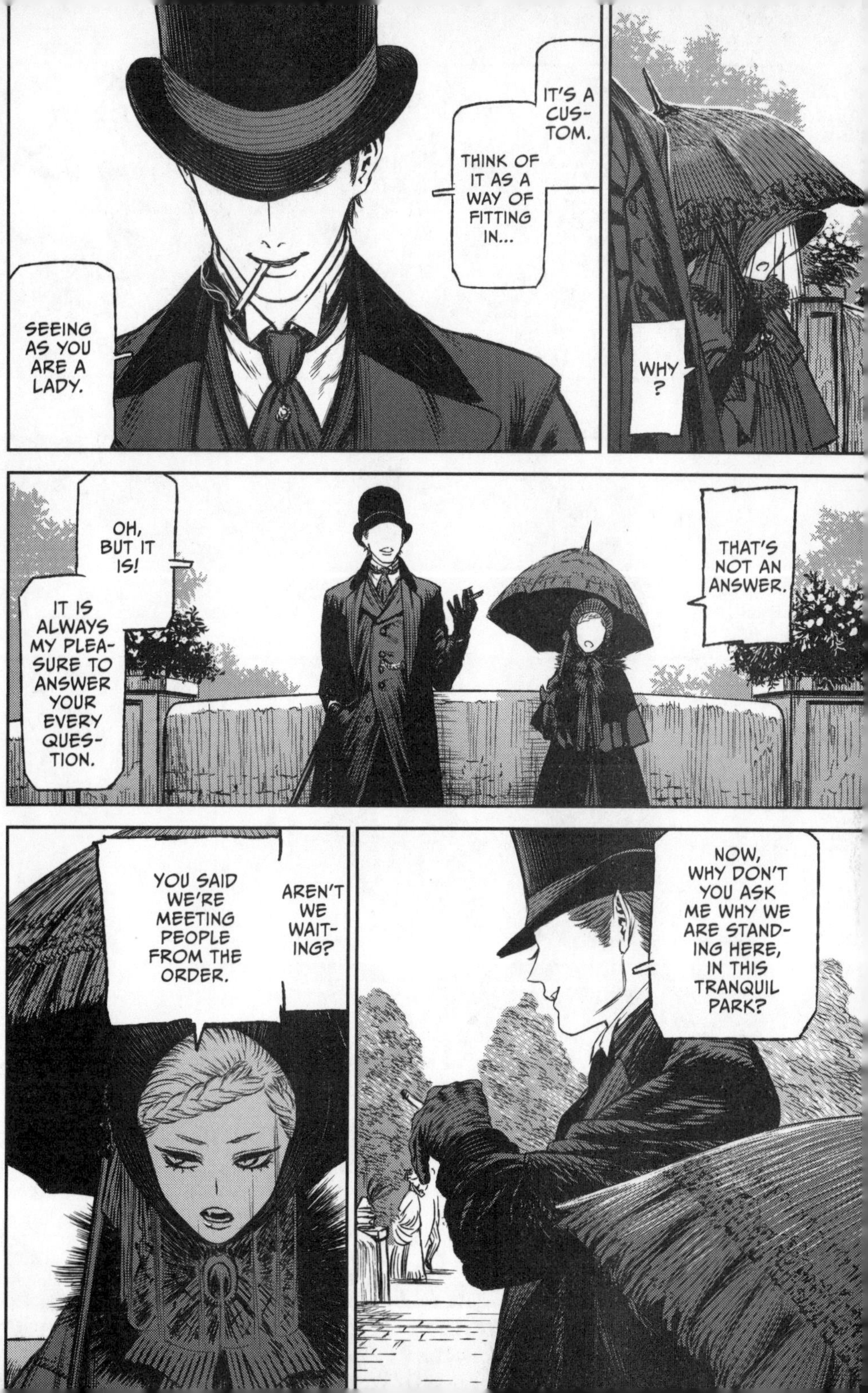
WHY?
IT'S A CUSTOM.
THINK OF IT AS A WAY OF FITTING IN...
SEEING AS YOU ARE A LADY.
THAT'S NOT AN ANSWER.
OH, BUT IT IS!
IT IS ALWAYS MY PLEASURE TO ANSWER YOUR EVERY QUESTION.
NOW, WHY DON'T YOU ASK ME WHY WE ARE STANDING HERE, IN THIS TRANQUIL PARK?
YOU SAID WE'RE MEETING PEOPLE FROM THE ORDER. AREN'T WE WAITING?

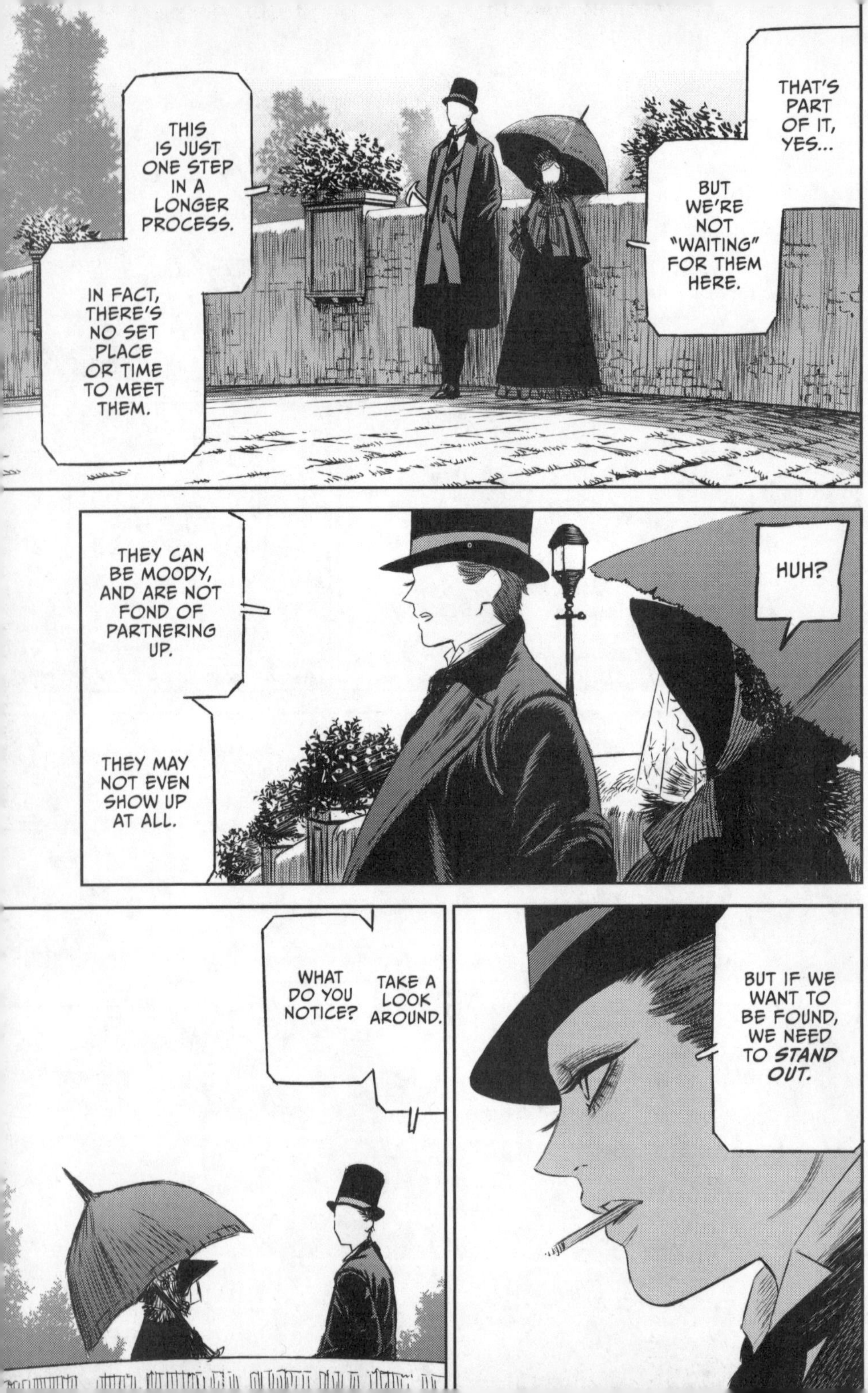
THAT'S PART OF IT, YES...
BUT WE'RE NOT "WAITING" FOR THEM HERE.
THIS IS JUST ONE STEP IN A LONGER PROCESS.
IN FACT, THERE'S NO SET PLACE OR TIME TO MEET THEM.
HUH?
THEY CAN BE MOODY, AND ARE NOT FOND OF PARTNERING UP.
THEY MAY NOT EVEN SHOW UP AT ALL.
BUT IF WE WANT TO BE FOUND, WE NEED TO ***STAND OUT.***
TAKE A LOOK AROUND.
WHAT DO YOU NOTICE?

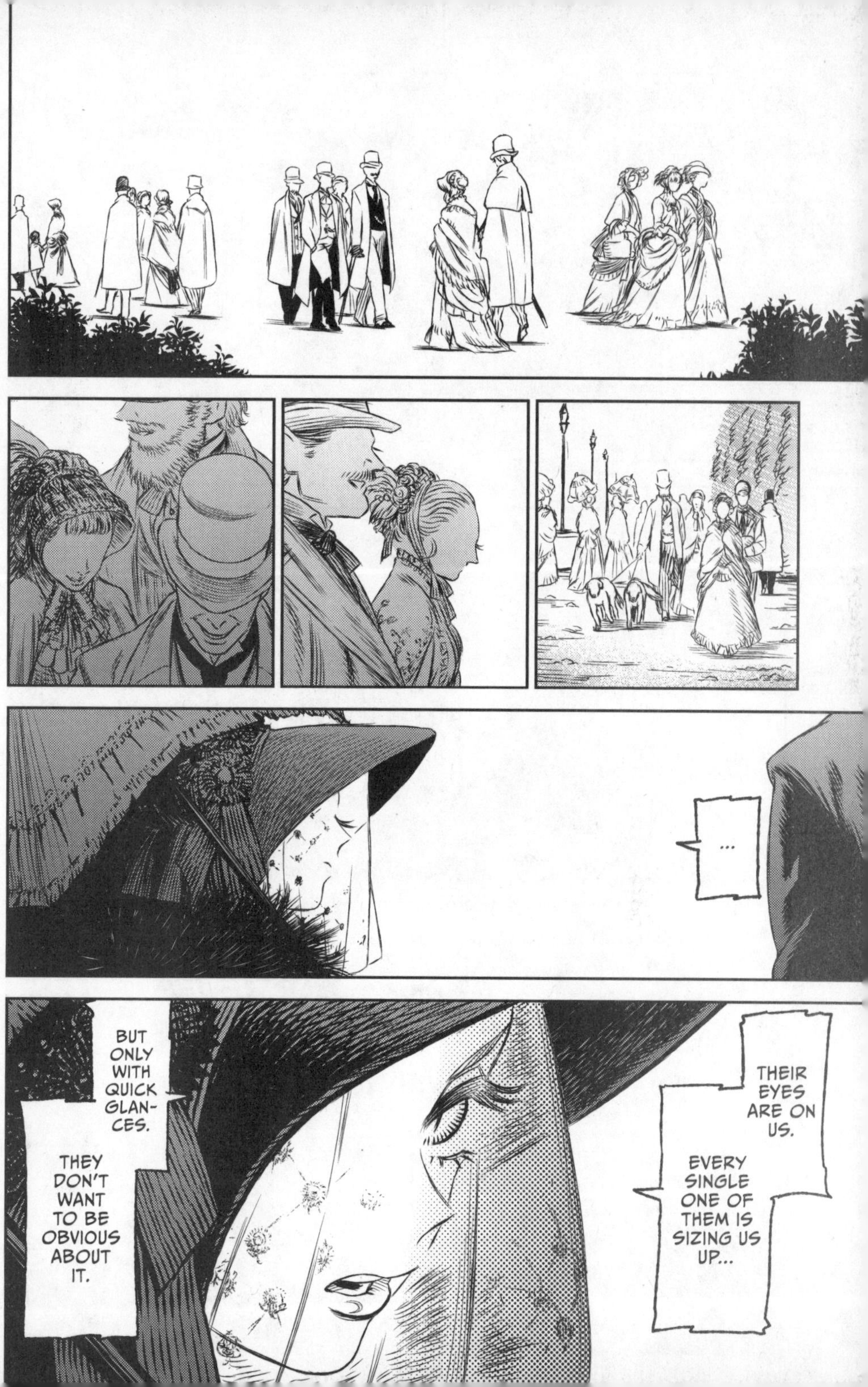
...
THEIR EYES ARE ON US.
EVERY SINGLE ONE OF THEM IS SIZING US UP...
BUT ONLY WITH QUICK GLANCES.
THEY DON'T WANT TO BE OBVIOUS ABOUT IT.

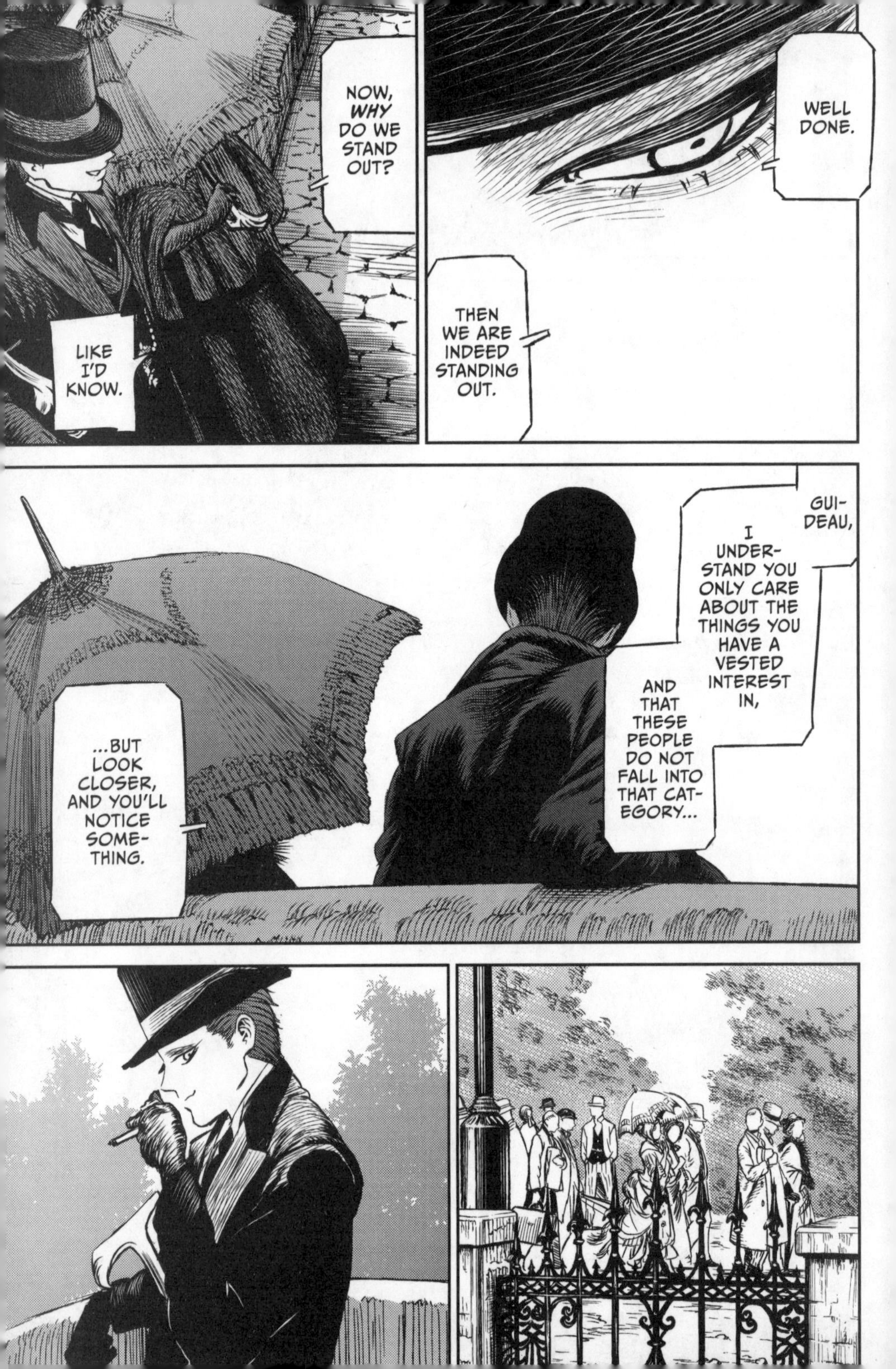
WELL DONE.
THEN WE ARE INDEED STANDING OUT.
NOW, *WHY* DO WE STAND OUT?
LIKE I'D KNOW.
GUIDEAU,
I UNDERSTAND YOU ONLY CARE ABOUT THE THINGS YOU HAVE A VESTED INTEREST IN,
AND THAT THESE PEOPLE DO NOT FALL INTO THAT CATEGORY...
...BUT LOOK CLOSER, AND YOU'LL NOTICE SOMETHING.

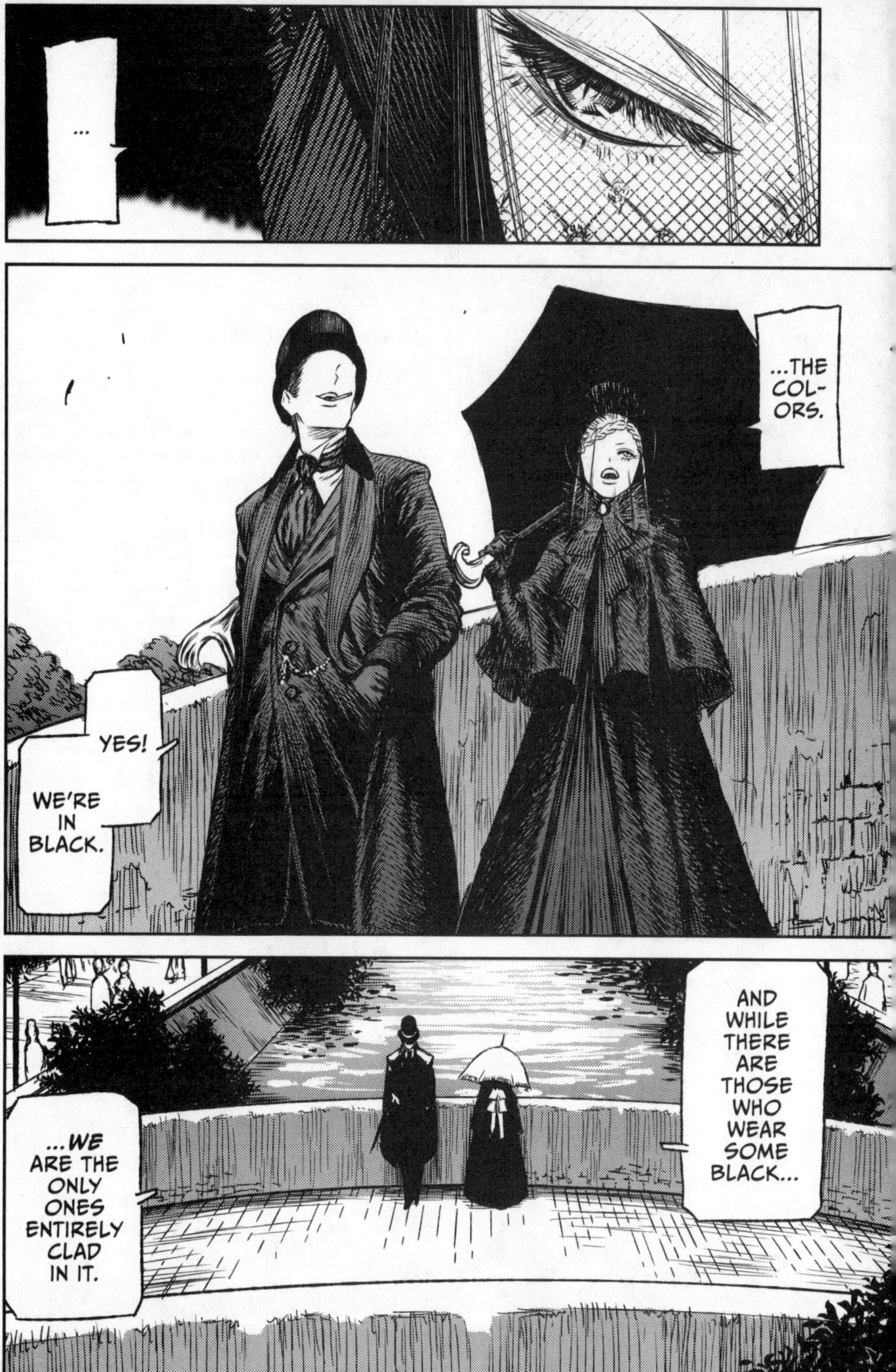
...
...THE COL-ORS.
YES!
WE'RE IN BLACK.
AND WHILE THERE ARE THOSE WHO WEAR SOME BLACK...
...WE ARE THE ONLY ONES ENTIRELY CLAD IN IT.

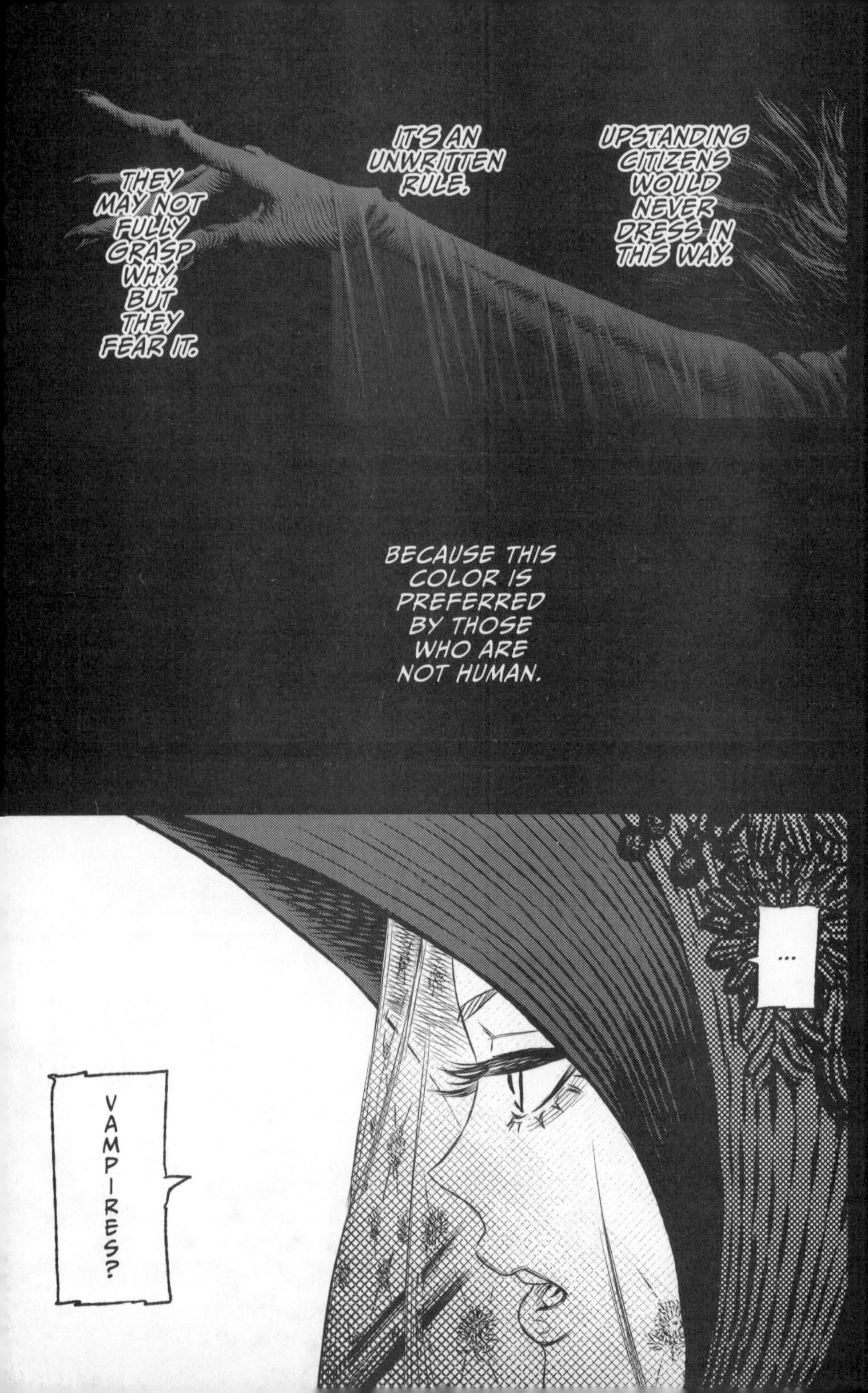
UPSTANDING CITIZENS WOULD NEVER DRESS IN THIS WAY.
IT'S AN UNWRITTEN RULE.
THEY MAY NOT FULLY GRASP WHY, BUT THEY FEAR IT.
BECAUSE THIS COLOR IS PREFERRED BY THOSE WHO ARE NOT HUMAN.
...
VAMPIRES?

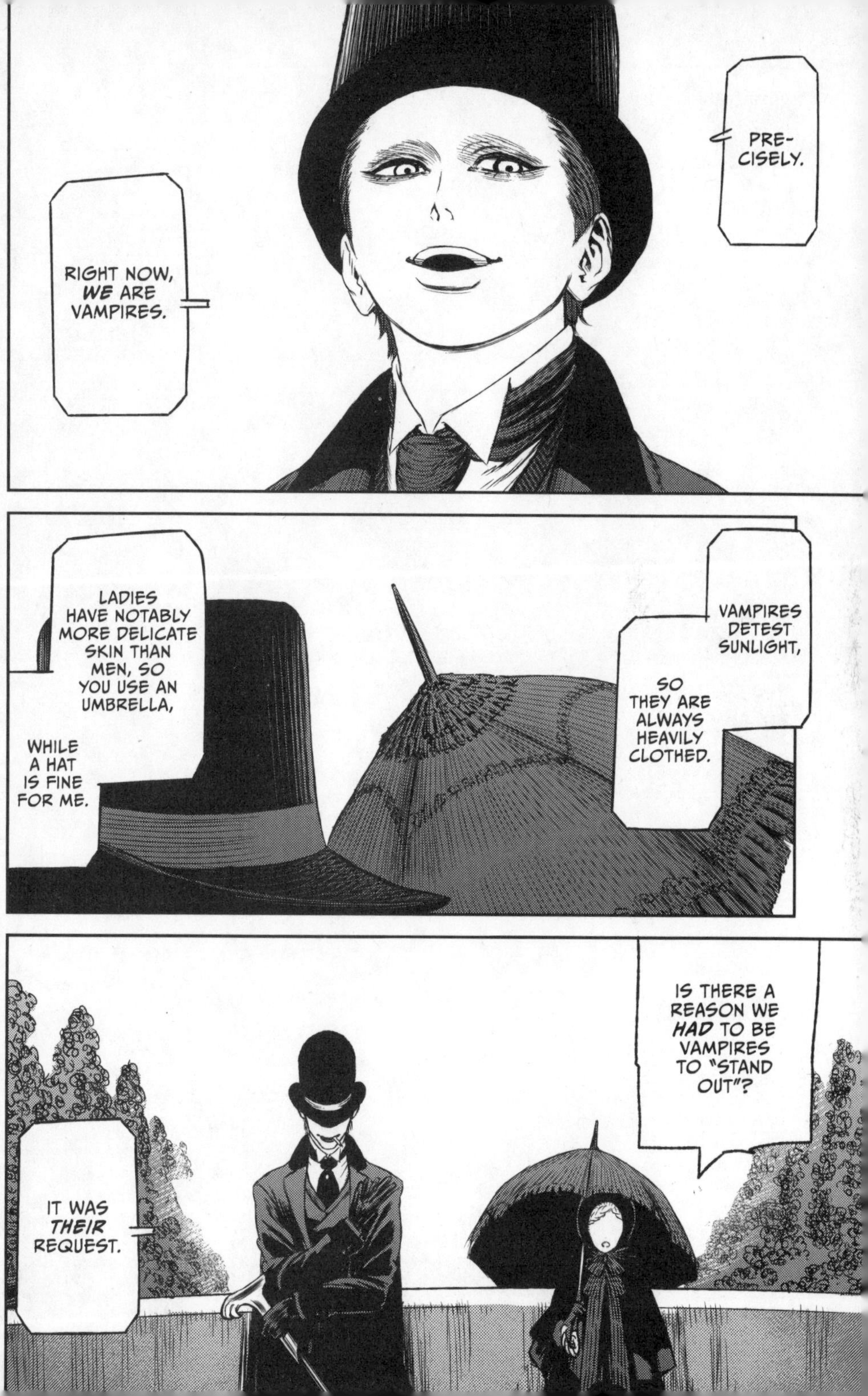
PRE-CISELY.
RIGHT NOW, *WE* ARE VAMPIRES.
VAMPIRES DETEST SUNLIGHT,
SO THEY ARE ALWAYS HEAVILY CLOTHED.
LADIES HAVE NOTABLY MORE DELICATE SKIN THAN MEN, SO YOU USE AN UMBRELLA,
WHILE A HAT IS FINE FOR ME.
IS THERE A REASON WE *HAD* TO BE VAMPIRES TO "STAND OUT"?
IT WAS *THEIR* REQUEST.

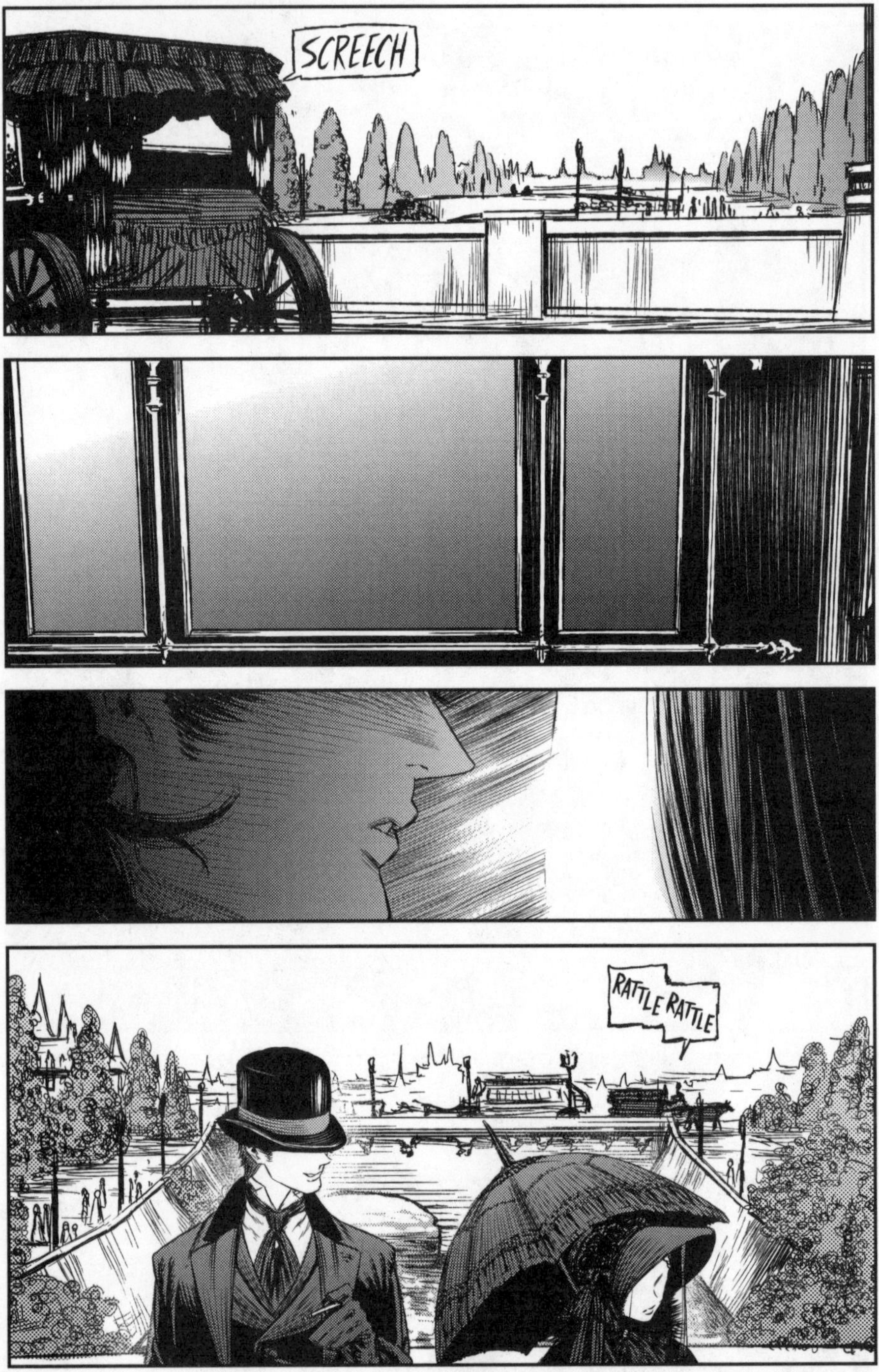
SCREECH
RATTLE RATTLE

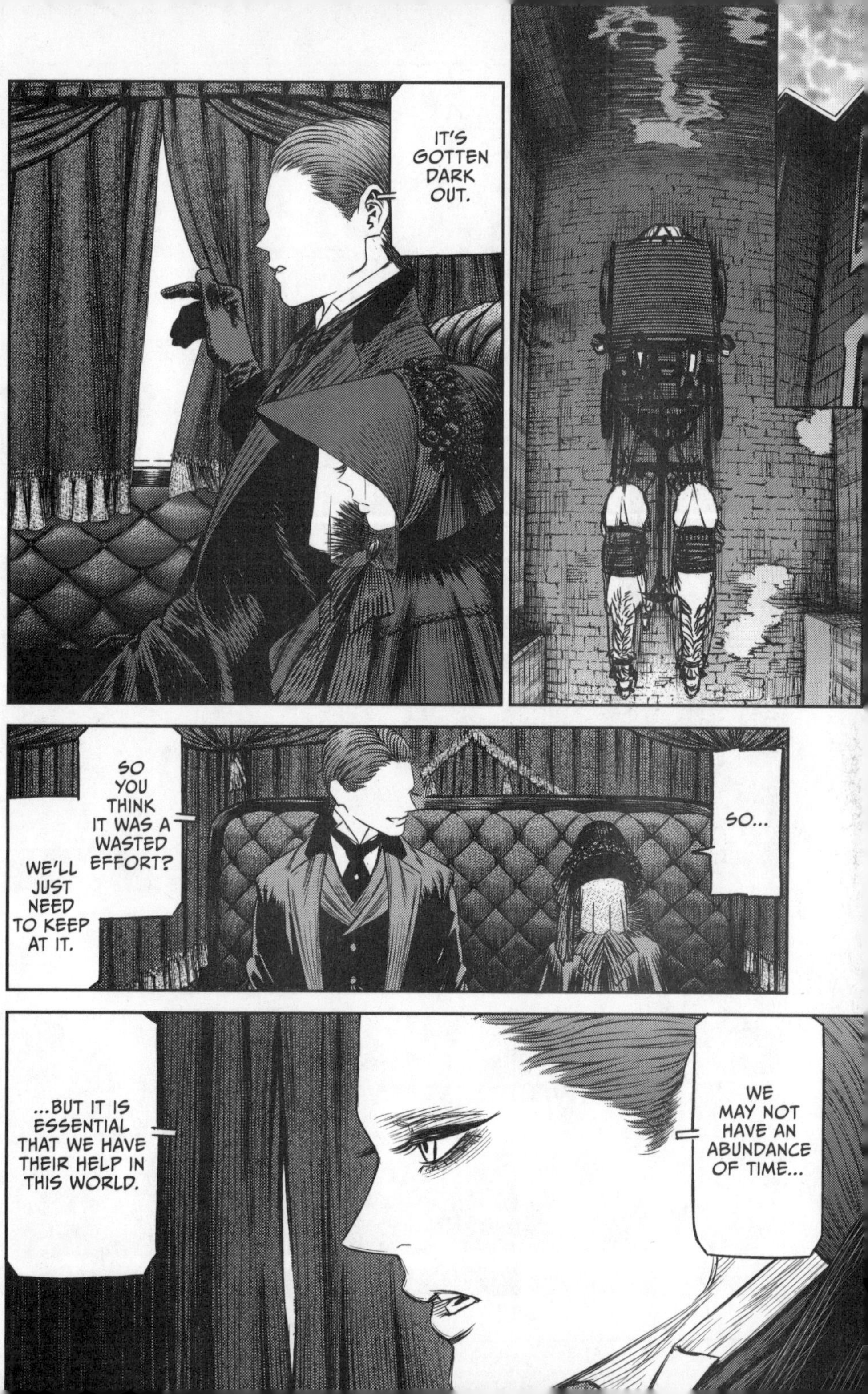
IT'S GOTTEN DARK OUT.
SO...
SO YOU THINK IT WAS A WASTED EFFORT?
WE'LL JUST NEED TO KEEP AT IT.
WE MAY NOT HAVE AN ABUNDANCE OF TIME...
...BUT IT IS ESSENTIAL THAT WE HAVE THEIR HELP IN THIS WORLD.

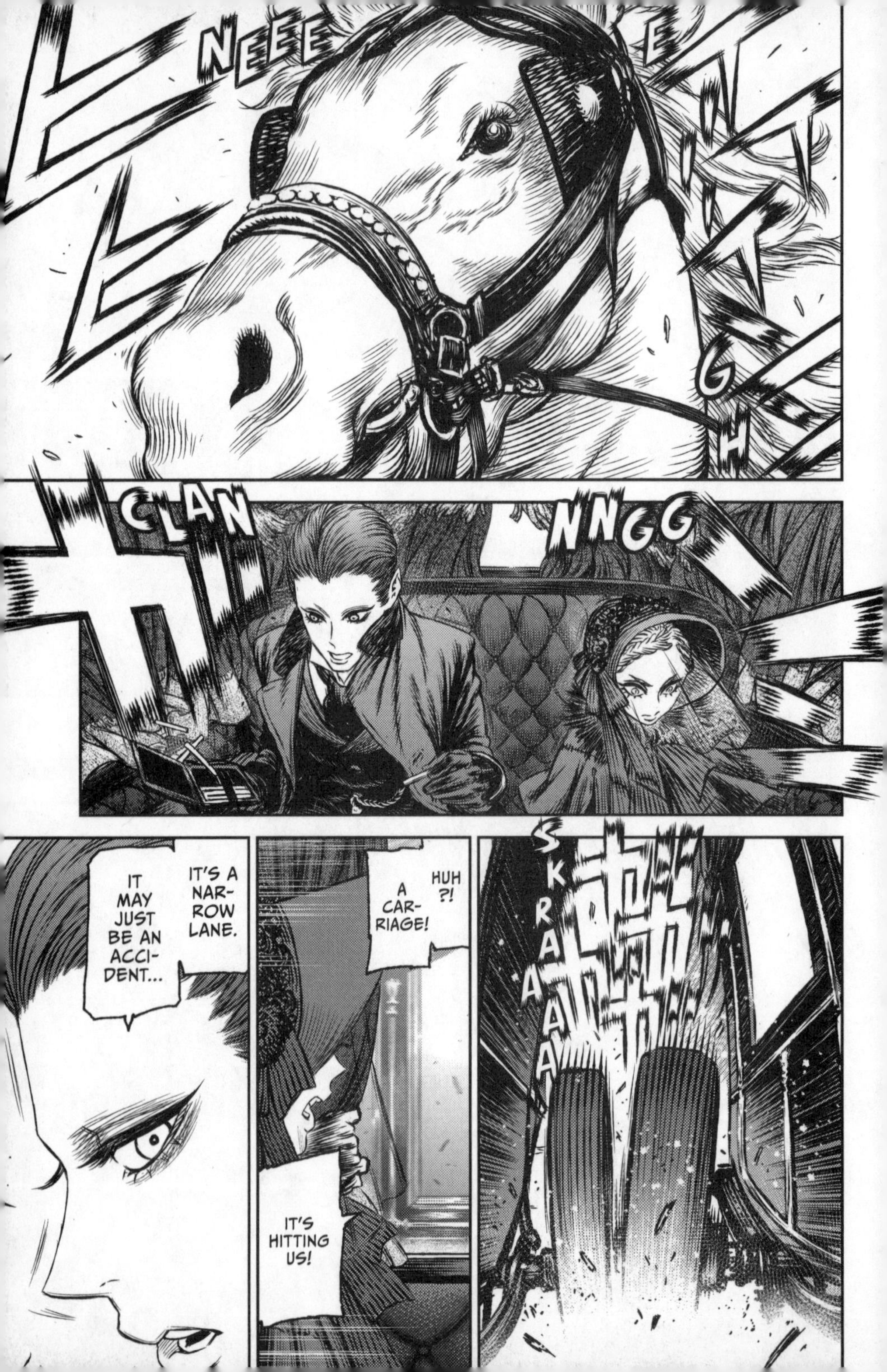

NEEE
E
GH
CLAN
NNGG
SKRAAAA
HUH?!
A CARRIAGE!
IT'S HITTING US!
IT'S A NARROW LANE.
IT MAY JUST BE AN ACCIDENT...

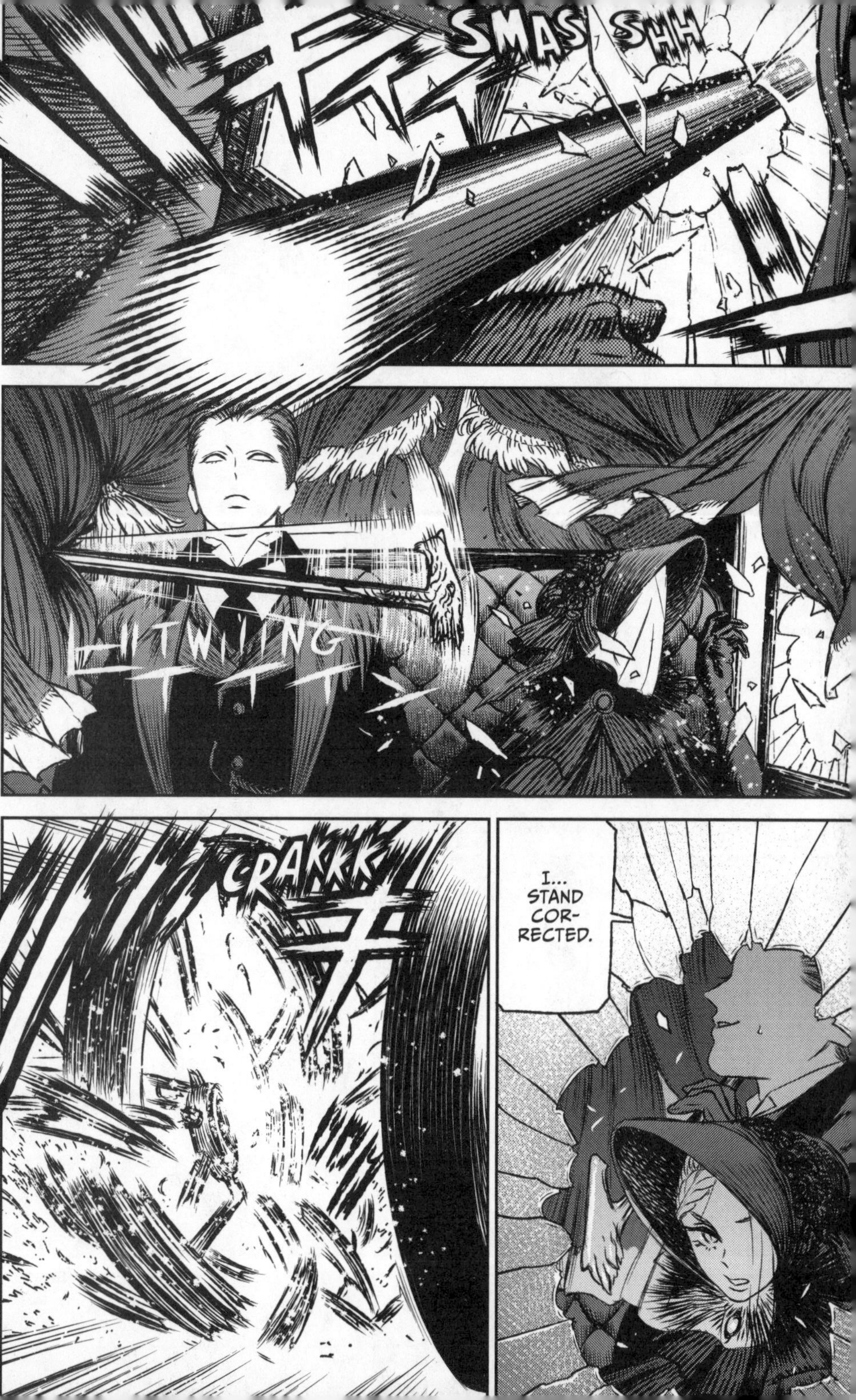
SMASSHH
TWIIING
I... STAND COR-RECTED.
CRAKKK

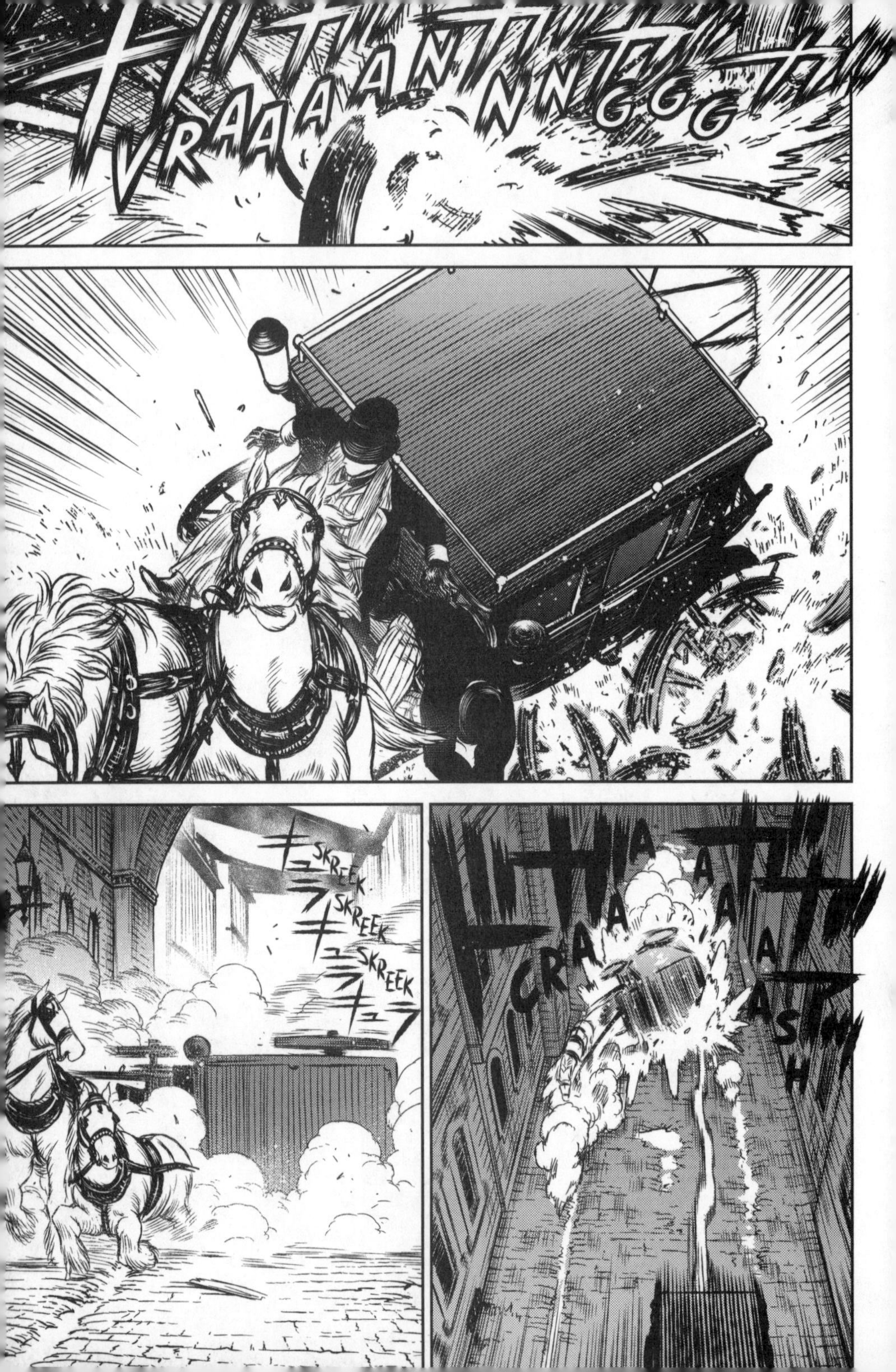
VRAAAANNNGGG
CRAAAAAAASH
SKREEK
SKREEK
SKREEK

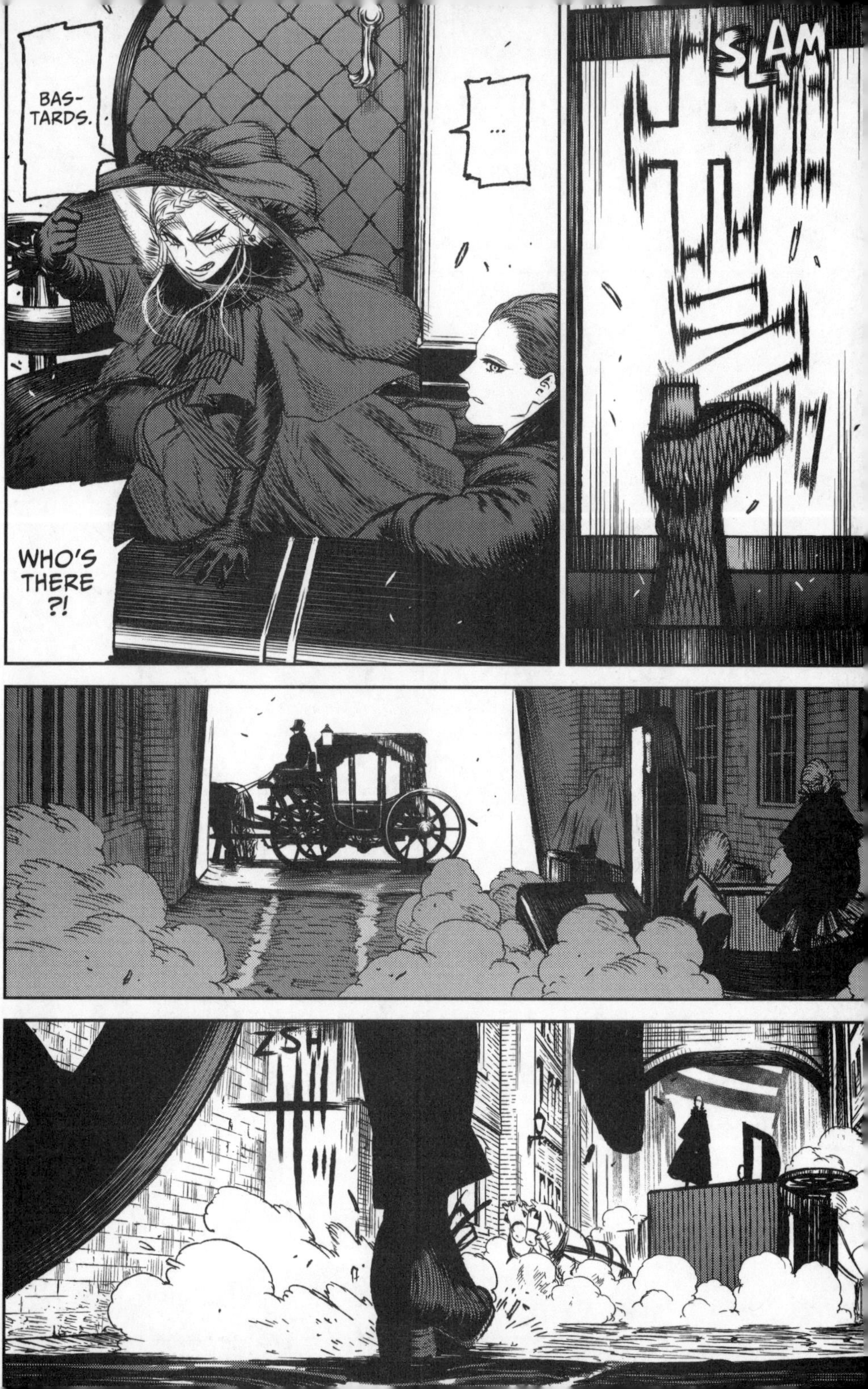
SLAM
...
BAS-
TARDS.
WHO'S
THERE
?!
ZSH

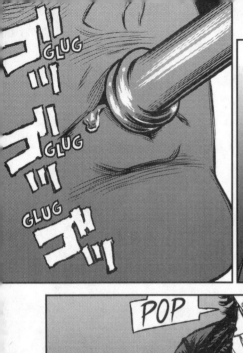

GLUG
GLUG
GLUG

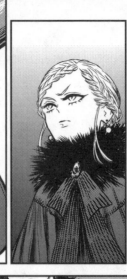

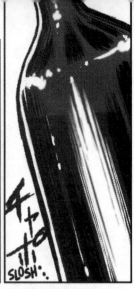

SLOSH

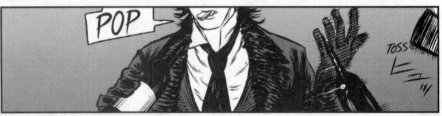

POP

TOSS

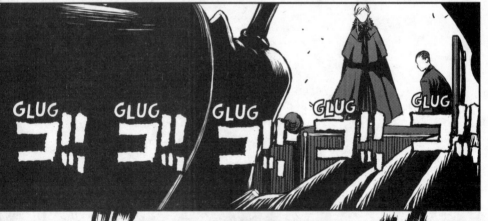

GLUG
GLUG
GLUG
GLUG
GLUG

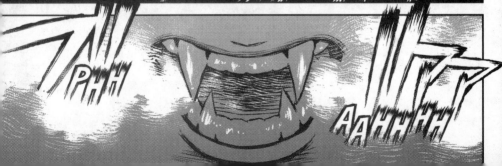

PAH

AAHHHH

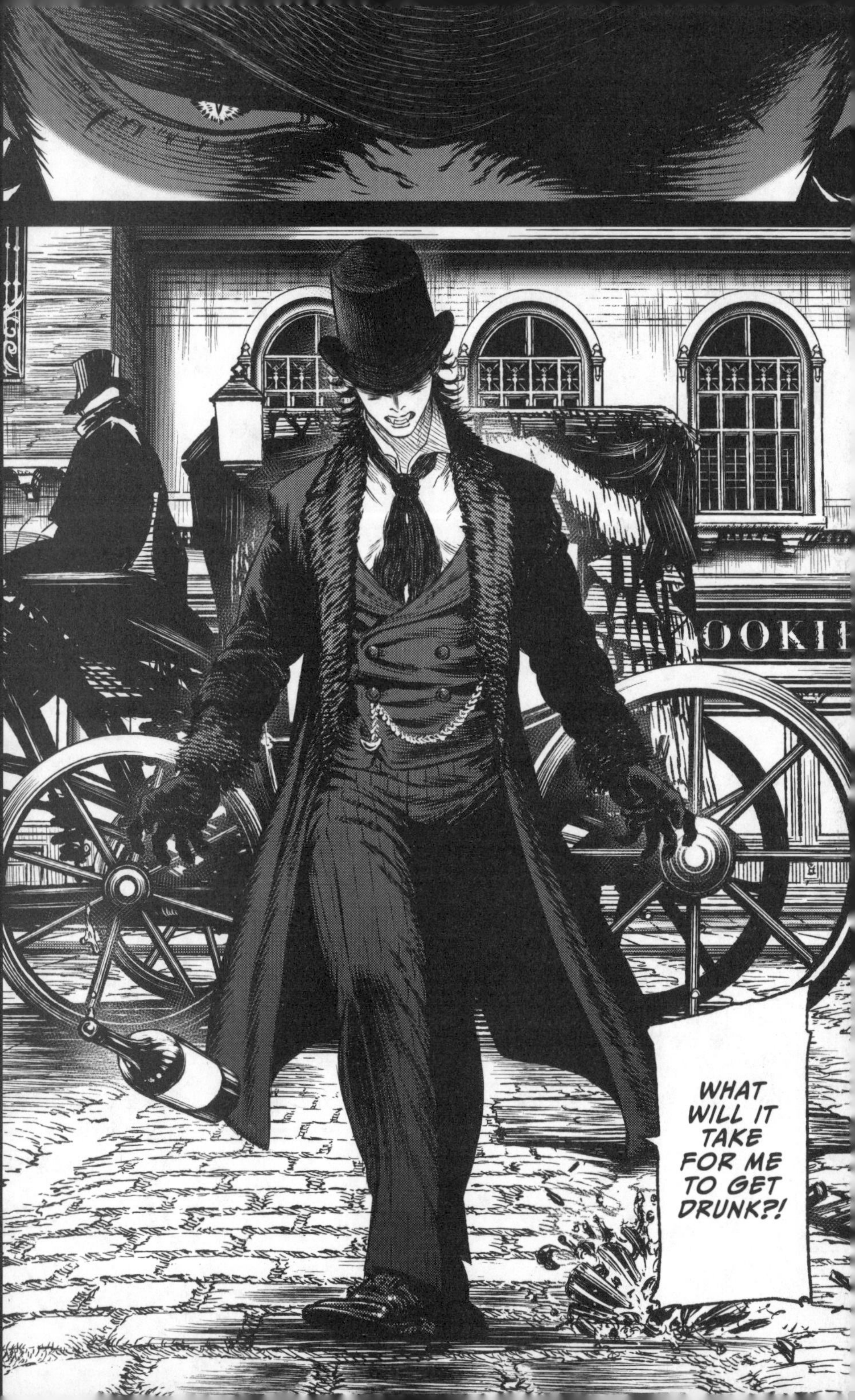
WHAT WILL IT TAKE FOR ME TO GET DRUNK?!

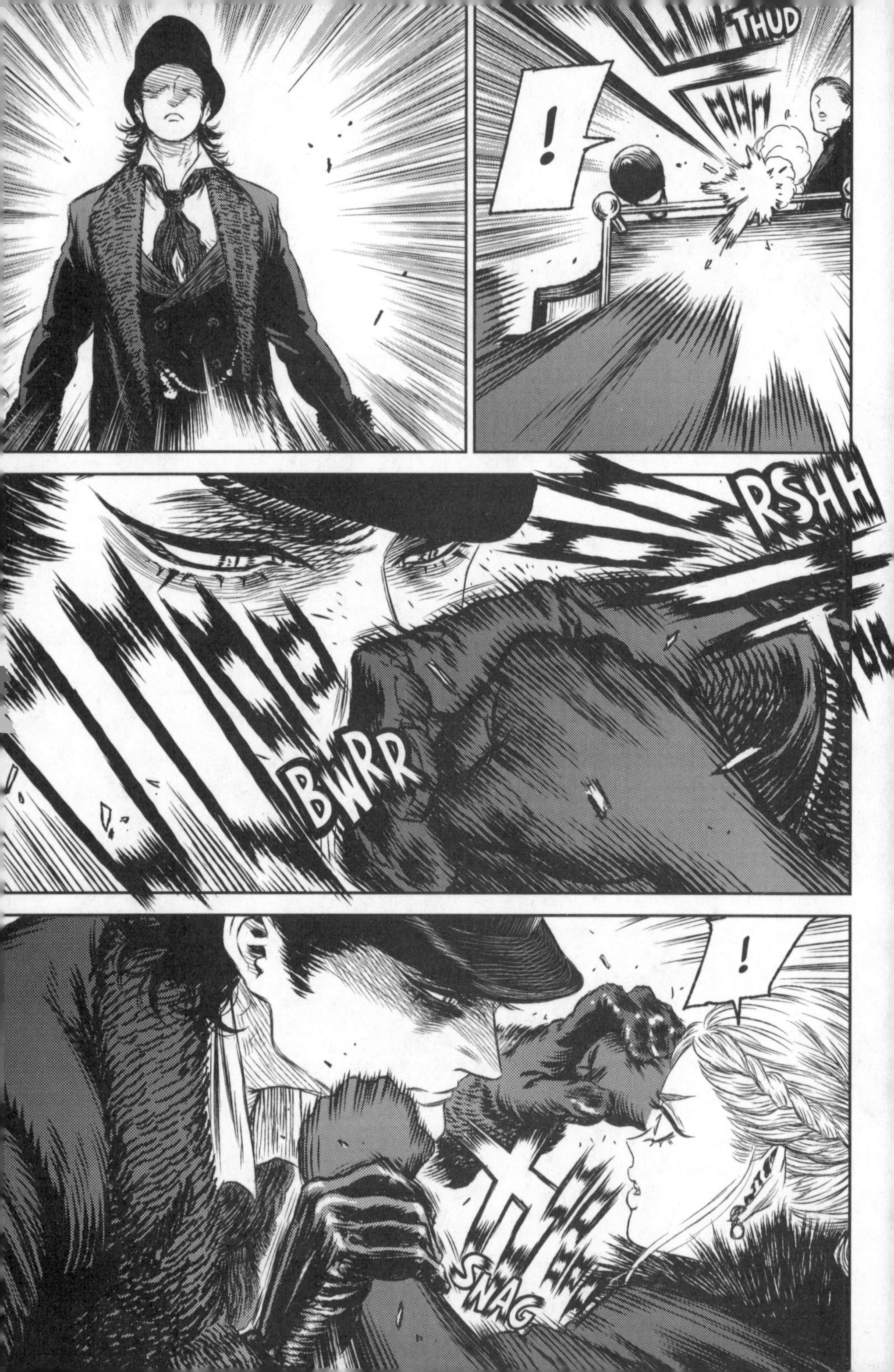
THUD
!
RSHH
BWRR
!
SNAG

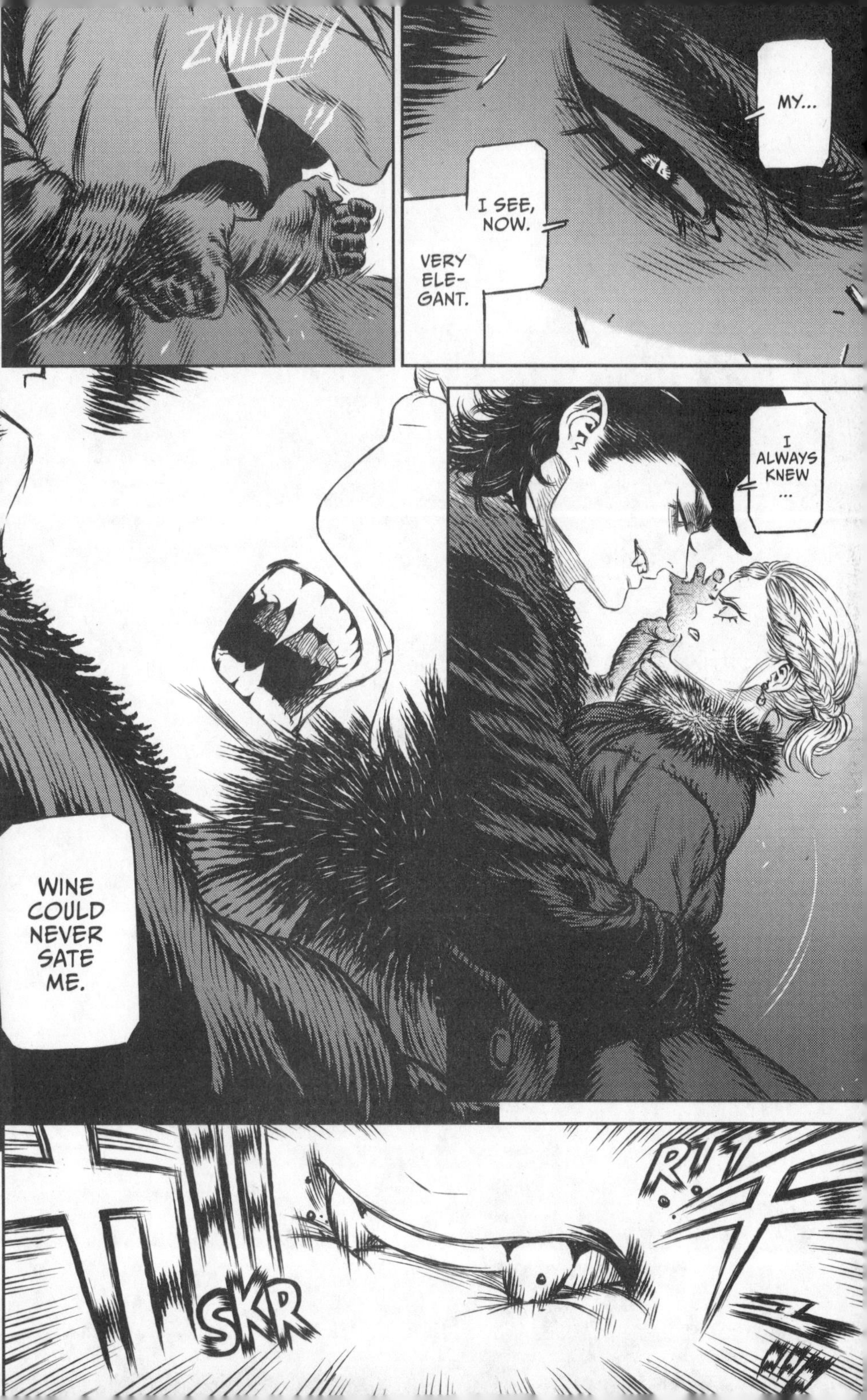
MY...
I SEE, NOW.
VERY ELE-GANT.
ZWIP!!
I ALWAYS KNEW ...
WINE COULD NEVER SATE ME.
RIT
SKR

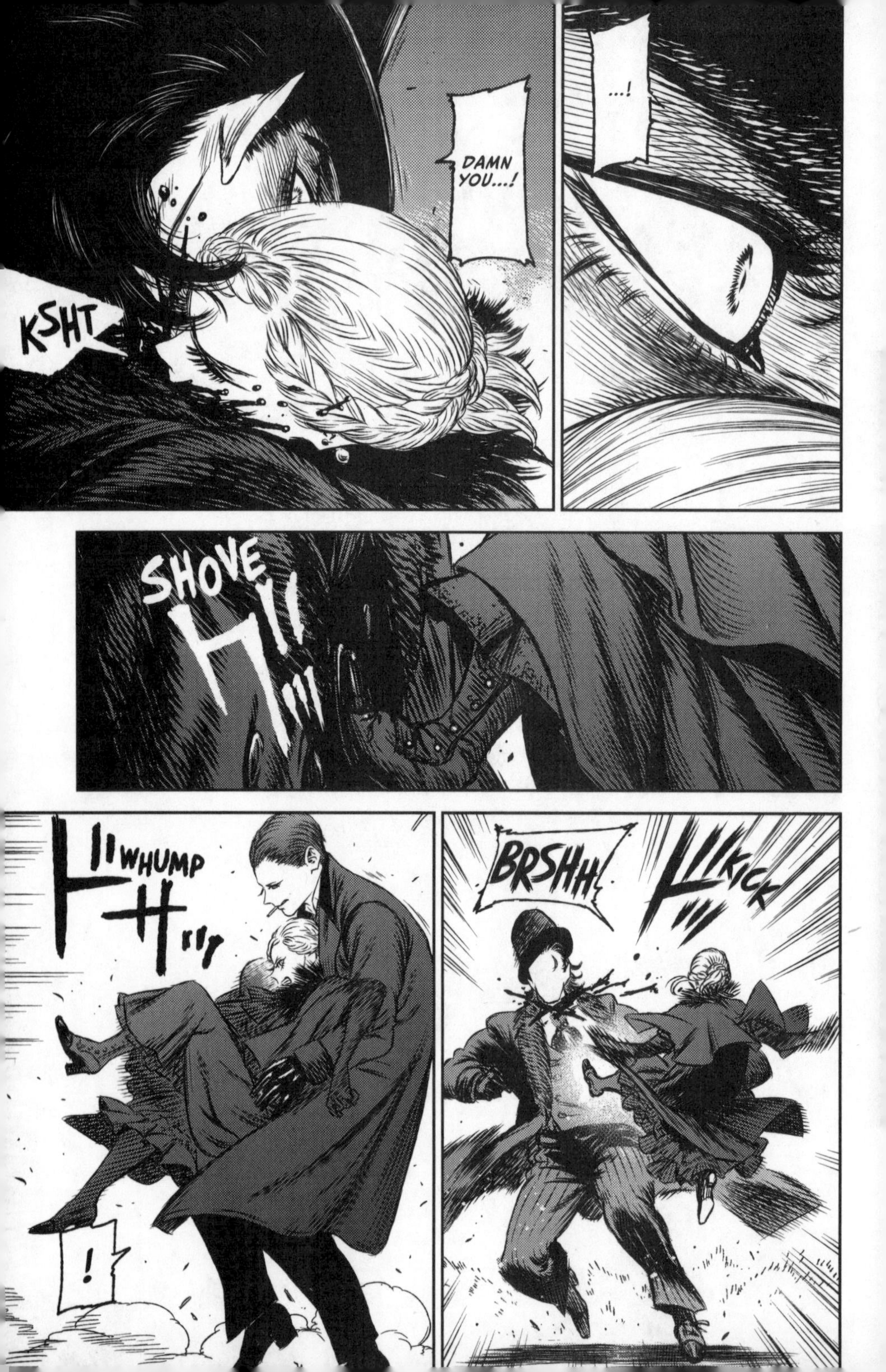
...!
DAMN YOU...!
KSHT
SHOVE
BRSHH
KICK
WHUMP
!

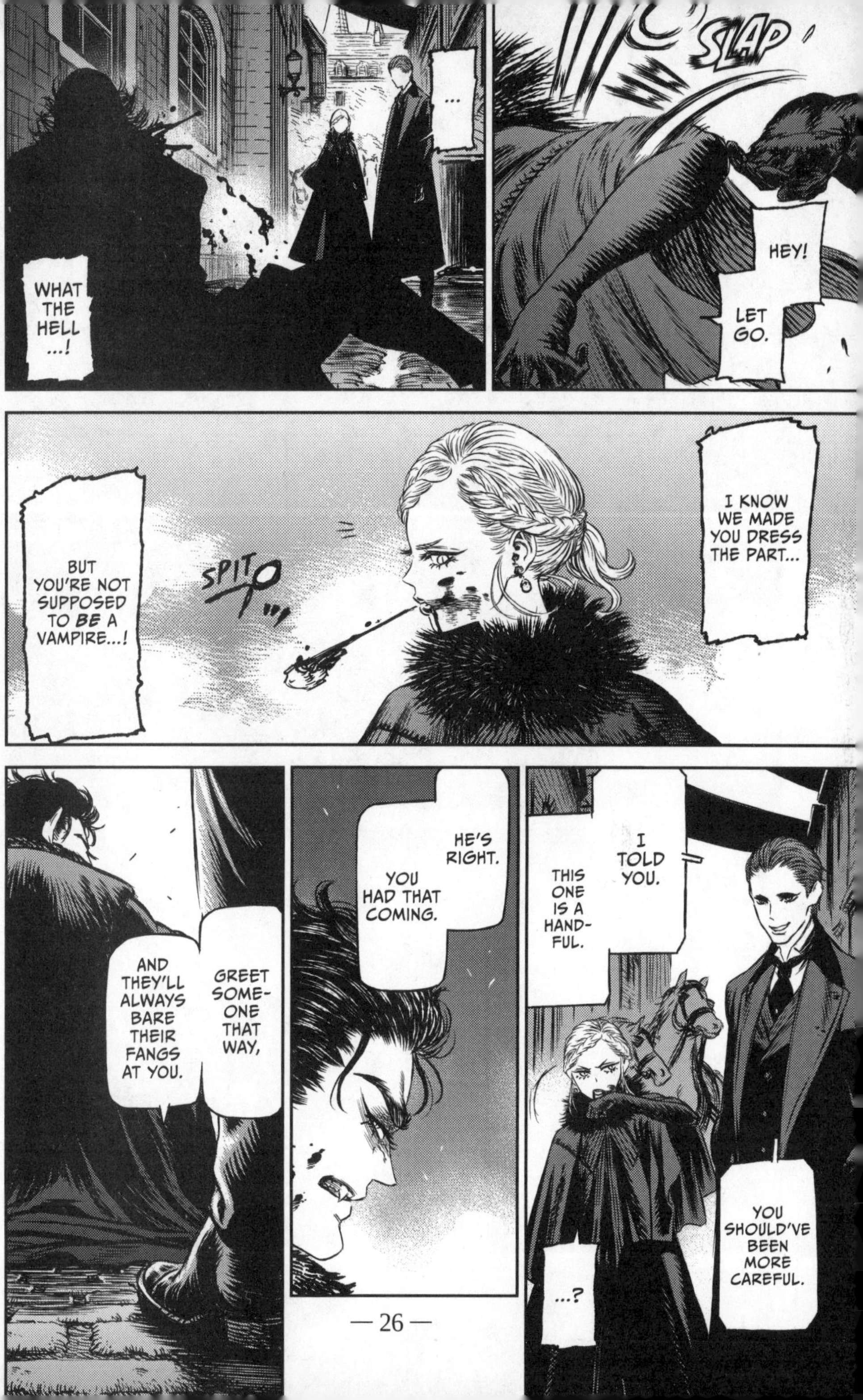
SLAP
HEY!
LET GO.
...
WHAT THE HELL ...!
I KNOW WE MADE YOU DRESS THE PART...
SPIT
BUT YOU'RE NOT SUPPOSED TO *BE* A VAMPIRE...!
I TOLD YOU.
THIS ONE IS A HANDFUL.
YOU SHOULD'VE BEEN MORE CAREFUL.
...?
HE'S RIGHT.
YOU HAD THAT COMING.
GREET SOMEONE THAT WAY,
AND THEY'LL ALWAYS BARE THEIR FANGS AT YOU.

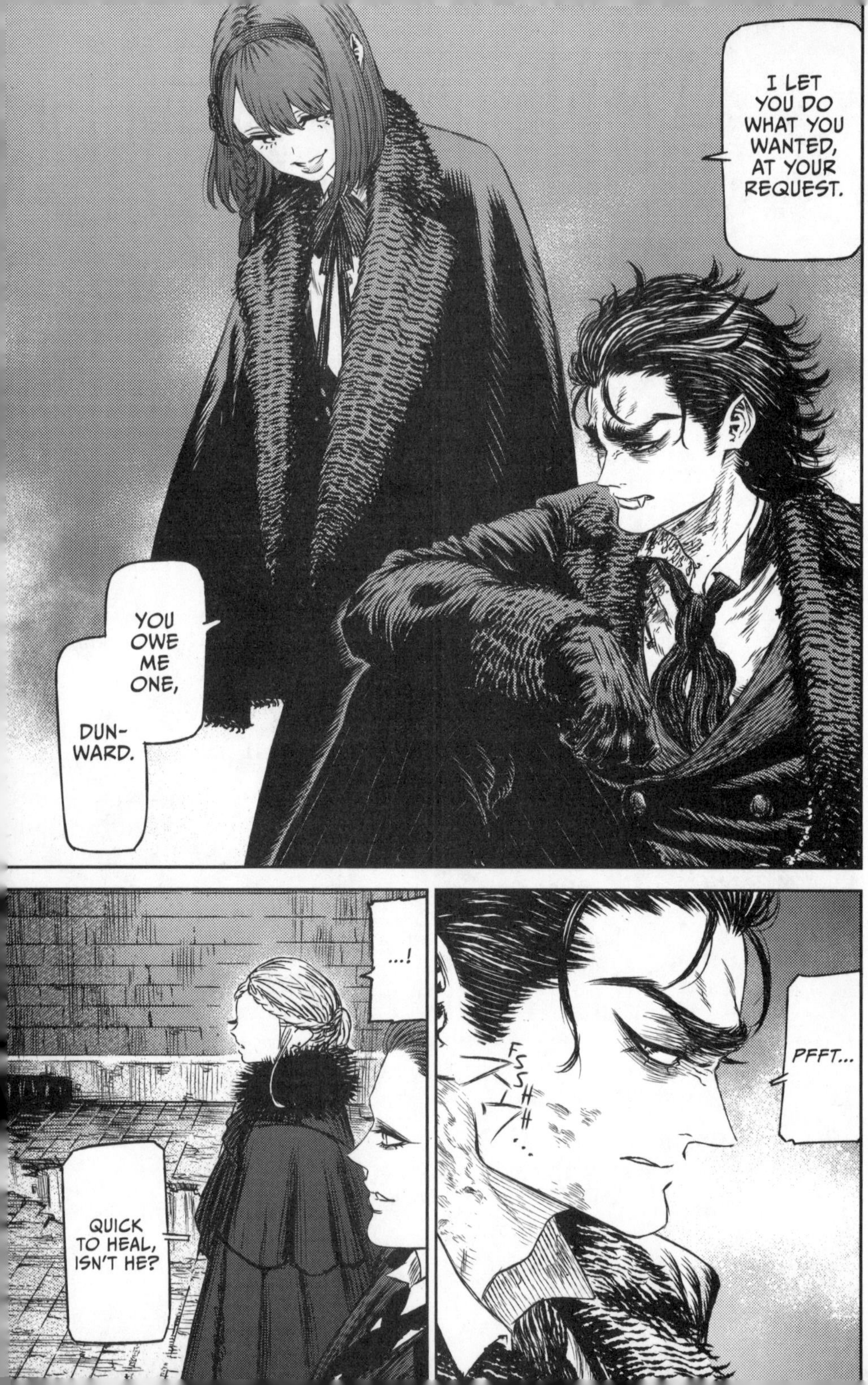
I LET YOU DO WHAT YOU WANTED, AT YOUR REQUEST.
YOU OWE ME ONE,
DUN-WARD.
PFFT...
FSSHH...
...!
QUICK TO HEAL, ISN'T HE?

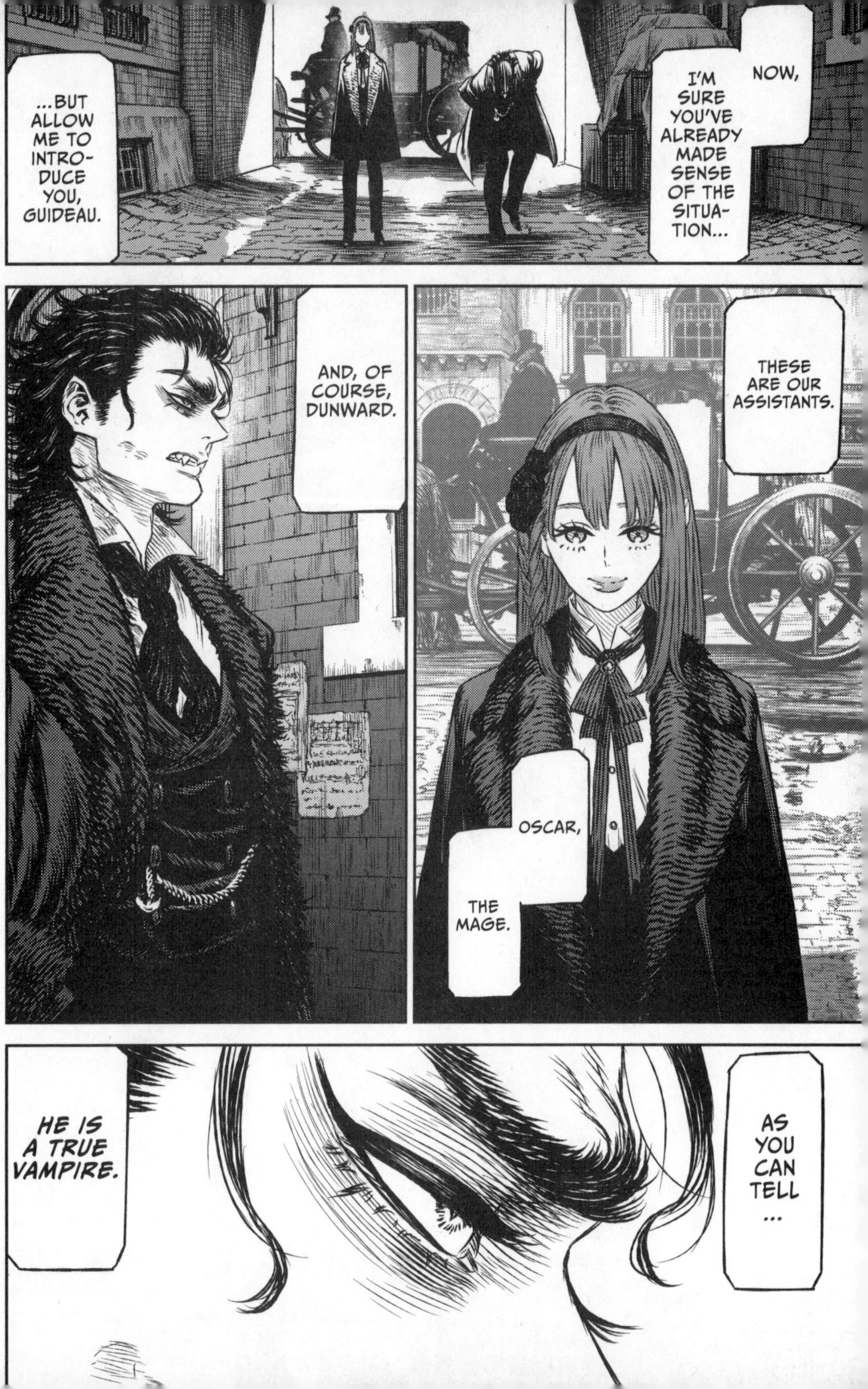
NOW,
I'M SURE YOU'VE ALREADY MADE SENSE OF THE SITUATION...
...BUT ALLOW ME TO INTRODUCE YOU, GUIDEAU.
THESE ARE OUR ASSISTANTS.
OSCAR,
THE MAGE.
AND, OF COURSE, DUNWARD.
AS YOU CAN TELL...
HE IS A TRUE VAMPIRE.

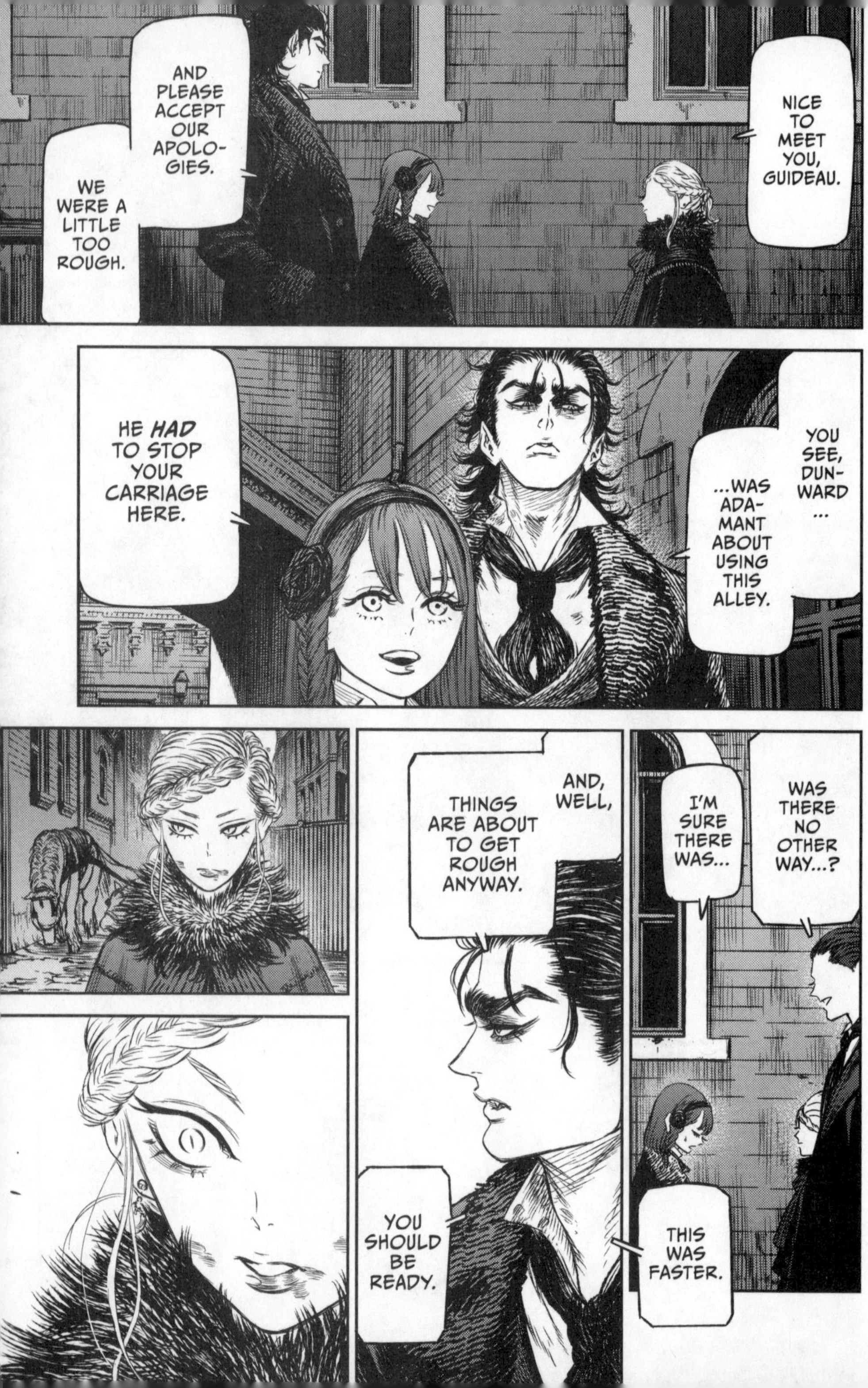
NICE TO MEET YOU, GUIDEAU.
AND PLEASE ACCEPT OUR APOLOGIES.
WE WERE A LITTLE TOO ROUGH.
YOU SEE, DUNWARD...
...WAS ADAMANT ABOUT USING THIS ALLEY.
HE *HAD* TO STOP YOUR CARRIAGE HERE.
WAS THERE NO OTHER WAY...?
I'M SURE THERE WAS...
THIS WAS FASTER.
AND, WELL,
THINGS ARE ABOUT TO GET ROUGH ANYWAY.
YOU SHOULD BE READY.

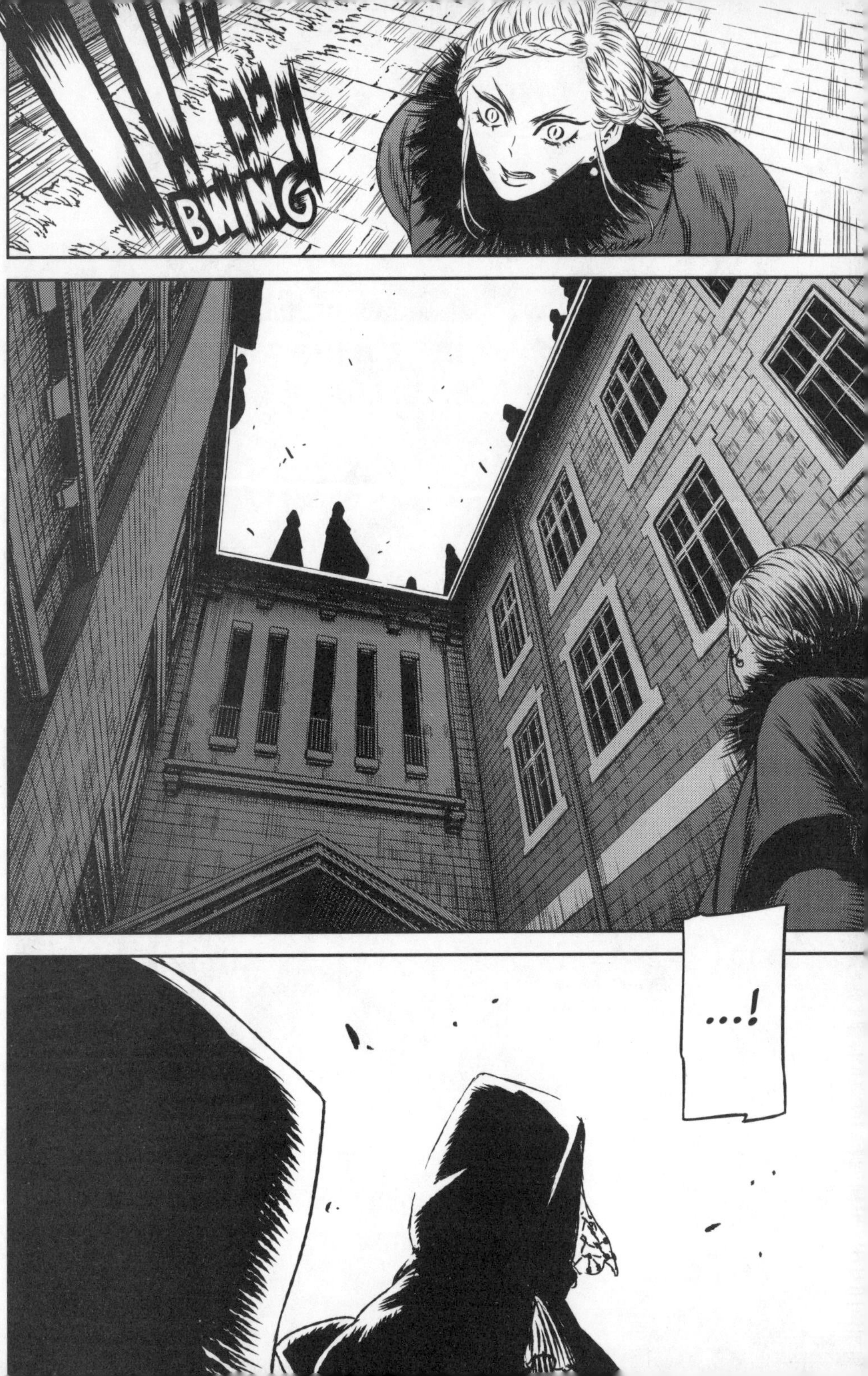
BWING
...!

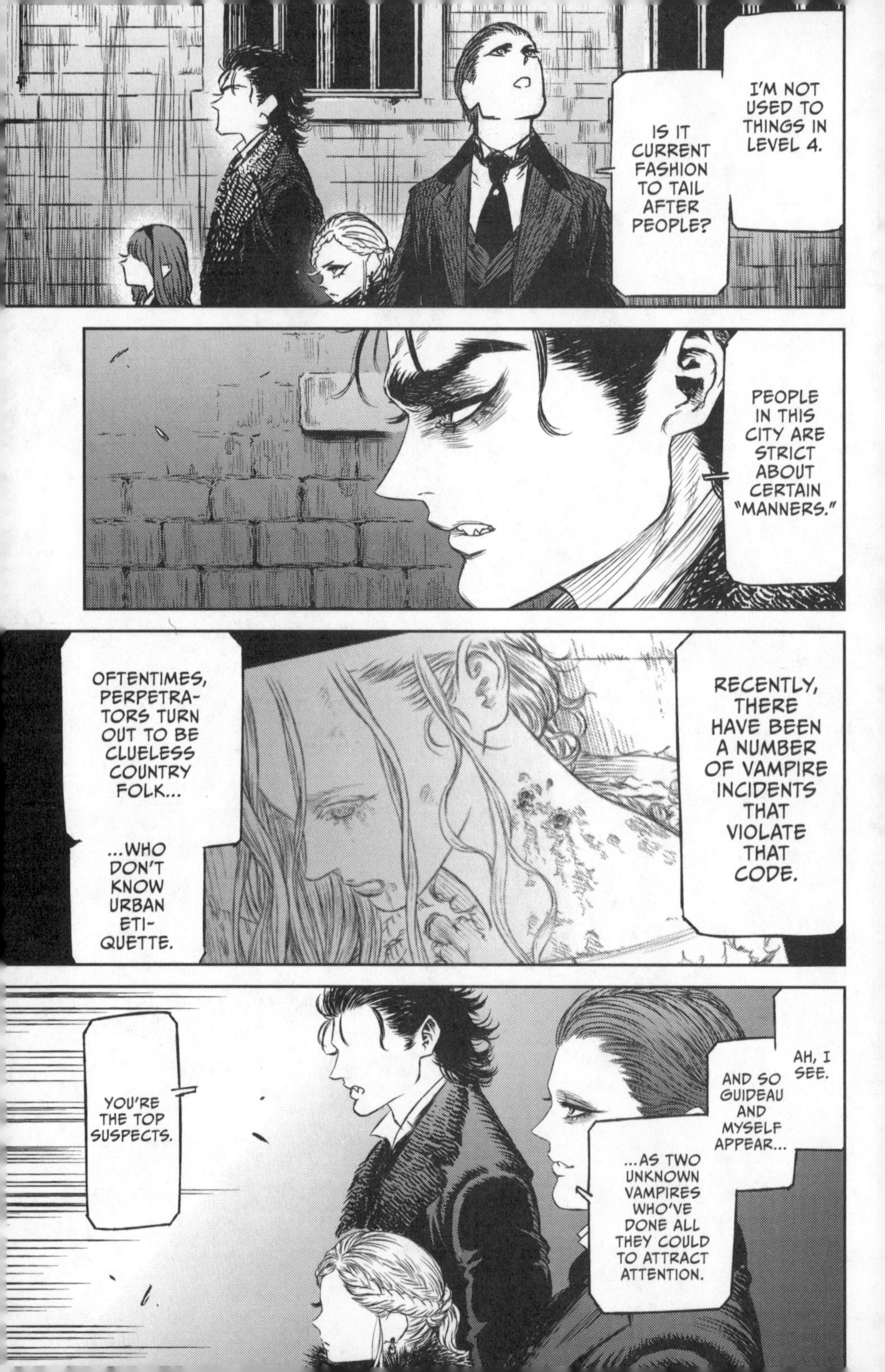
I'M NOT USED TO THINGS IN LEVEL 4.
IS IT CURRENT FASHION TO TAIL AFTER PEOPLE?
PEOPLE IN THIS CITY ARE STRICT ABOUT CERTAIN "MANNERS."
RECENTLY, THERE HAVE BEEN A NUMBER OF VAMPIRE INCIDENTS THAT VIOLATE THAT CODE.
OFTENTIMES, PERPETRATORS TURN OUT TO BE CLUELESS COUNTRY FOLK...
...WHO DON'T KNOW URBAN ETIQUETTE.
AH, I SEE.
AND SO GUIDEAU AND MYSELF APPEAR...
...AS TWO UNKNOWN VAMPIRES WHO'VE DONE ALL THEY COULD TO ATTRACT ATTENTION.
YOU'RE THE TOP SUSPECTS.

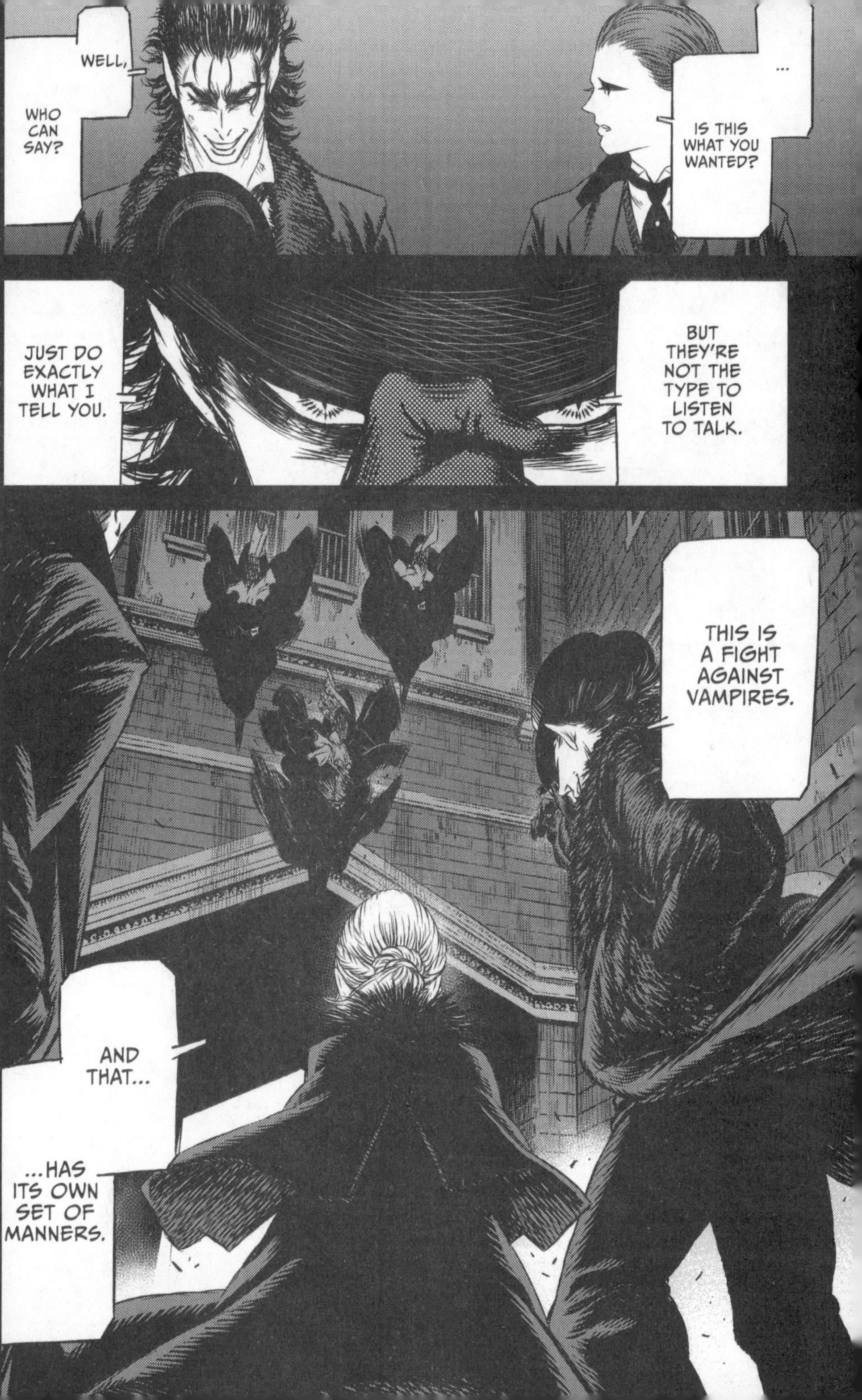
...
IS THIS WHAT YOU WANTED?
WELL,
WHO CAN SAY?
BUT THEY'RE NOT THE TYPE TO LISTEN TO TALK.
JUST DO EXACTLY WHAT I TELL YOU.
THIS IS A FIGHT AGAINST VAMPIRES.
AND THAT...
...HAS ITS OWN SET OF MANNERS.

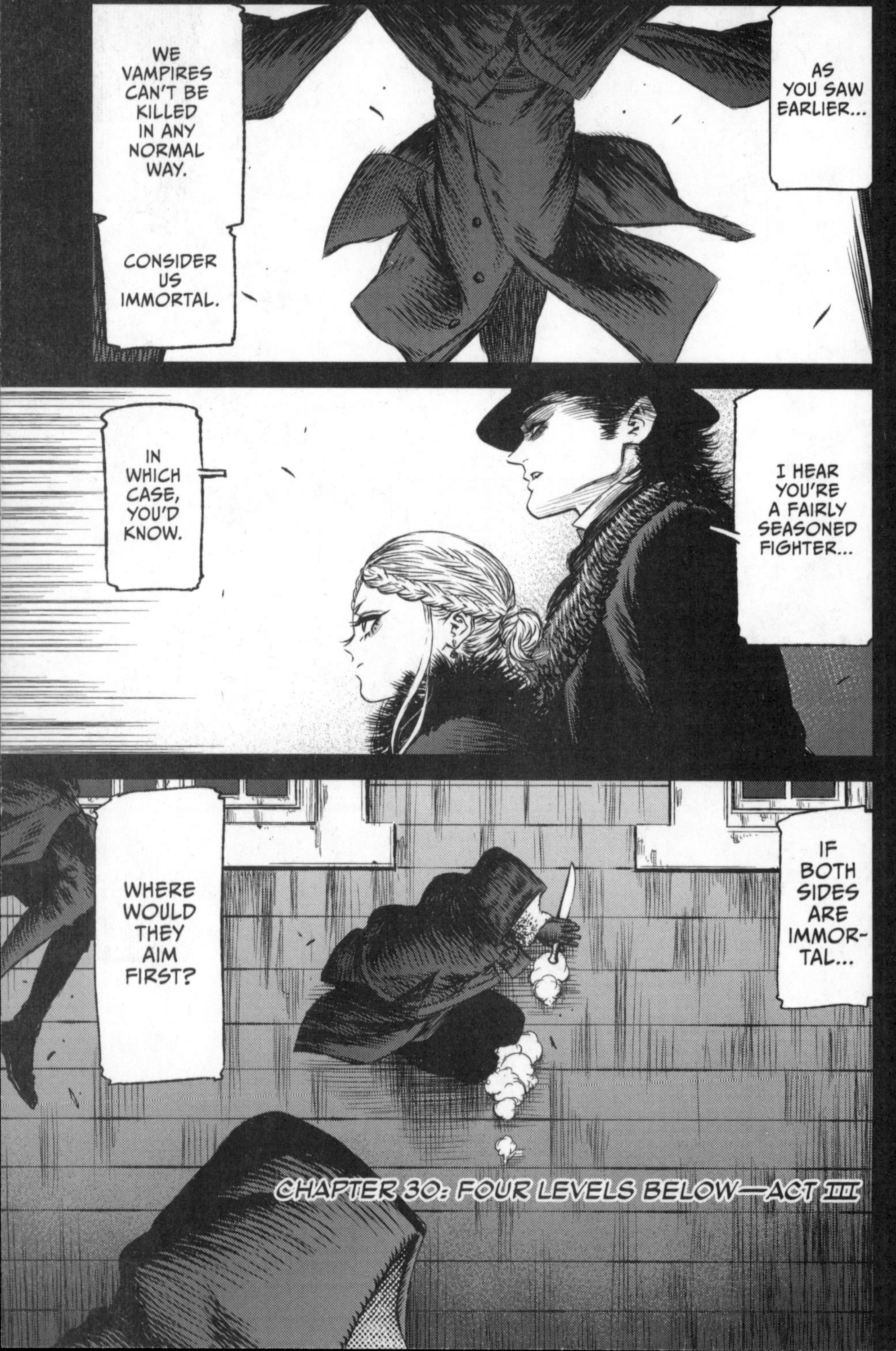
AS YOU SAW EARLIER...
WE VAMPIRES CAN'T BE KILLED IN ANY NORMAL WAY.
CONSIDER US IMMORTAL.
I HEAR YOU'RE A FAIRLY SEASONED FIGHTER...
IN WHICH CASE, YOU'D KNOW.
IF BOTH SIDES ARE IMMORTAL...
WHERE WOULD THEY AIM FIRST?
CHAPTER 30: FOUR LEVELS BELOW—ACT III

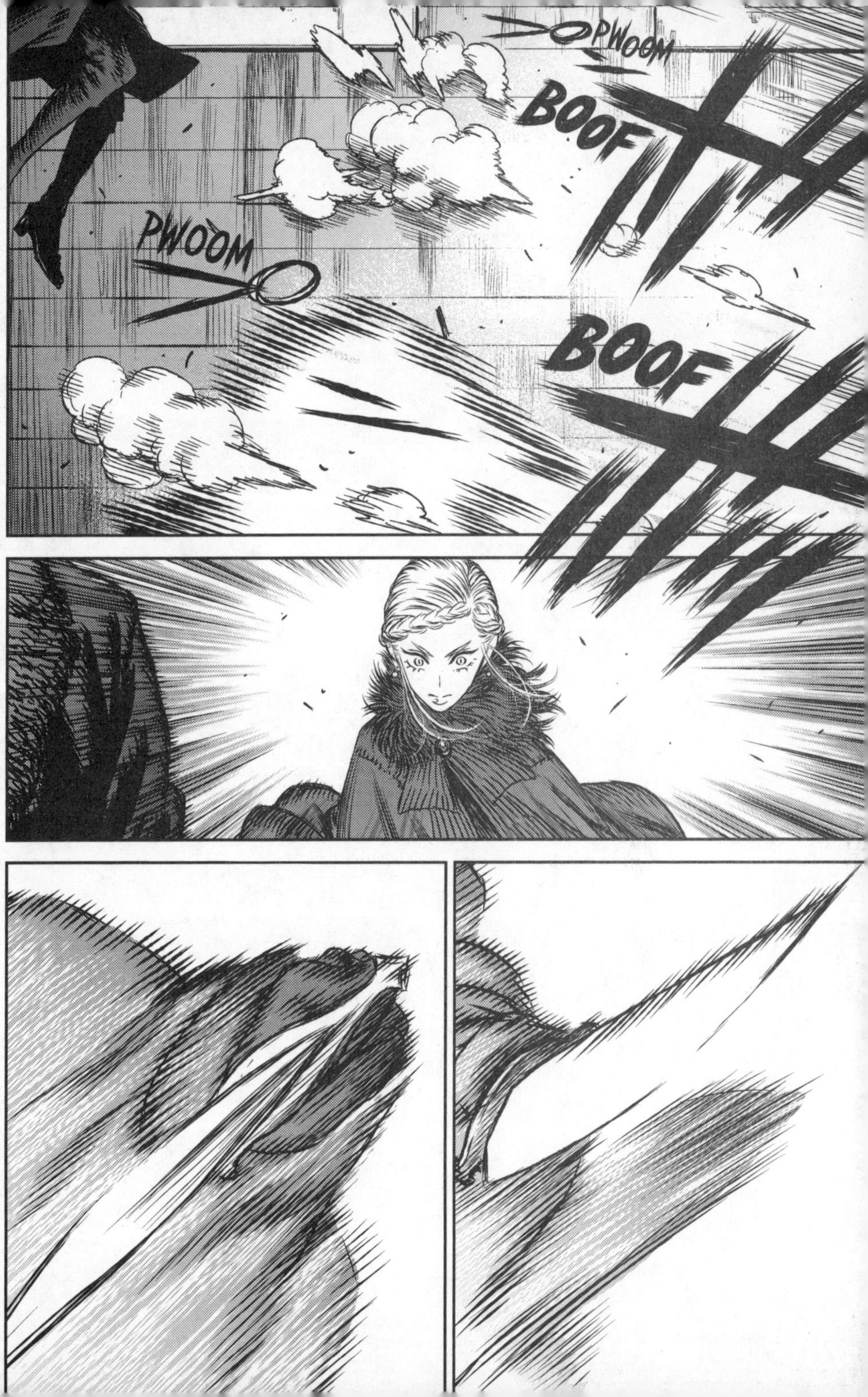
PWOOM
BOOF
BOOF
PWOOM

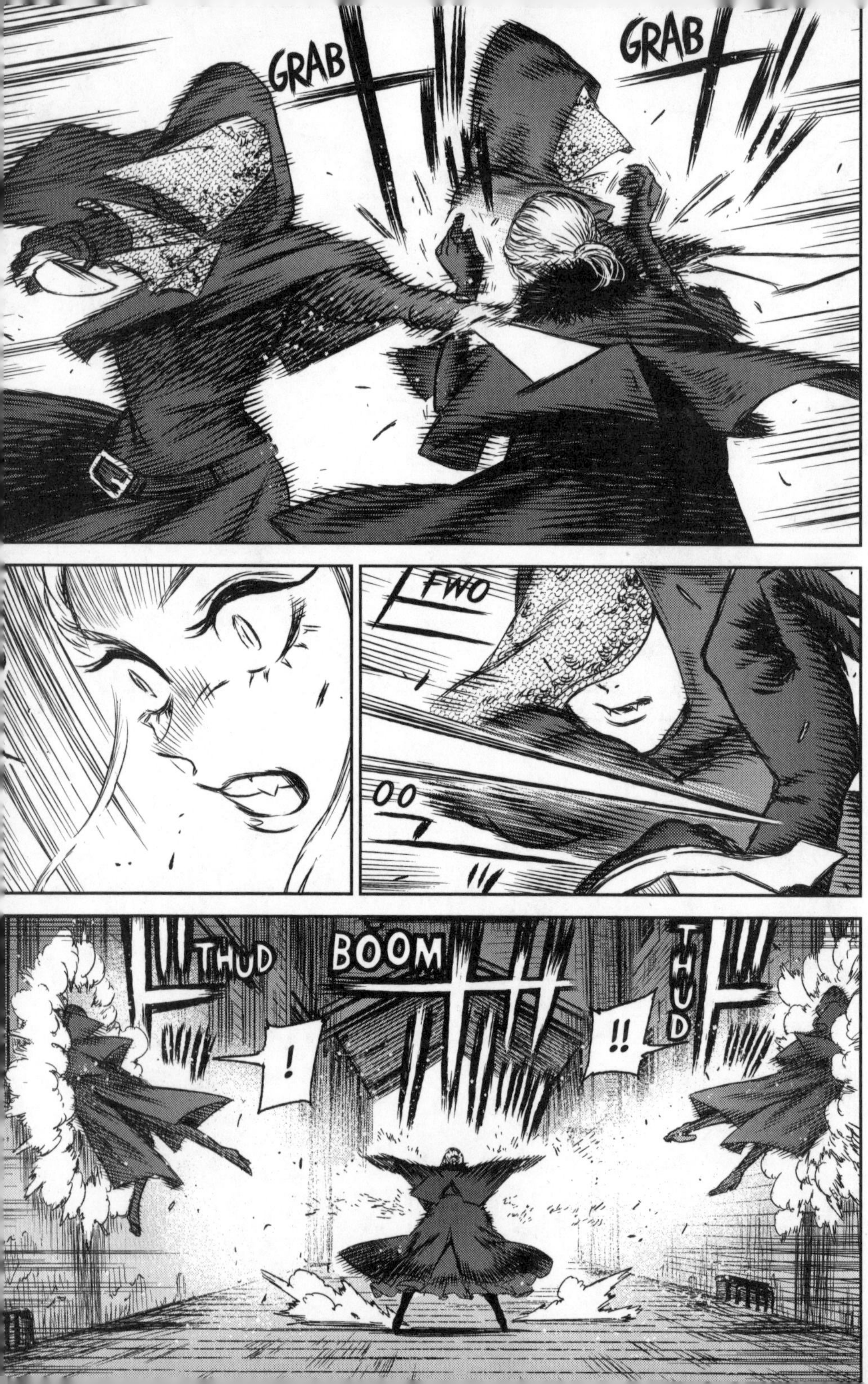
GRAB
GRAB
FWO
OO
THUD
!!
BOOM
!
THUD

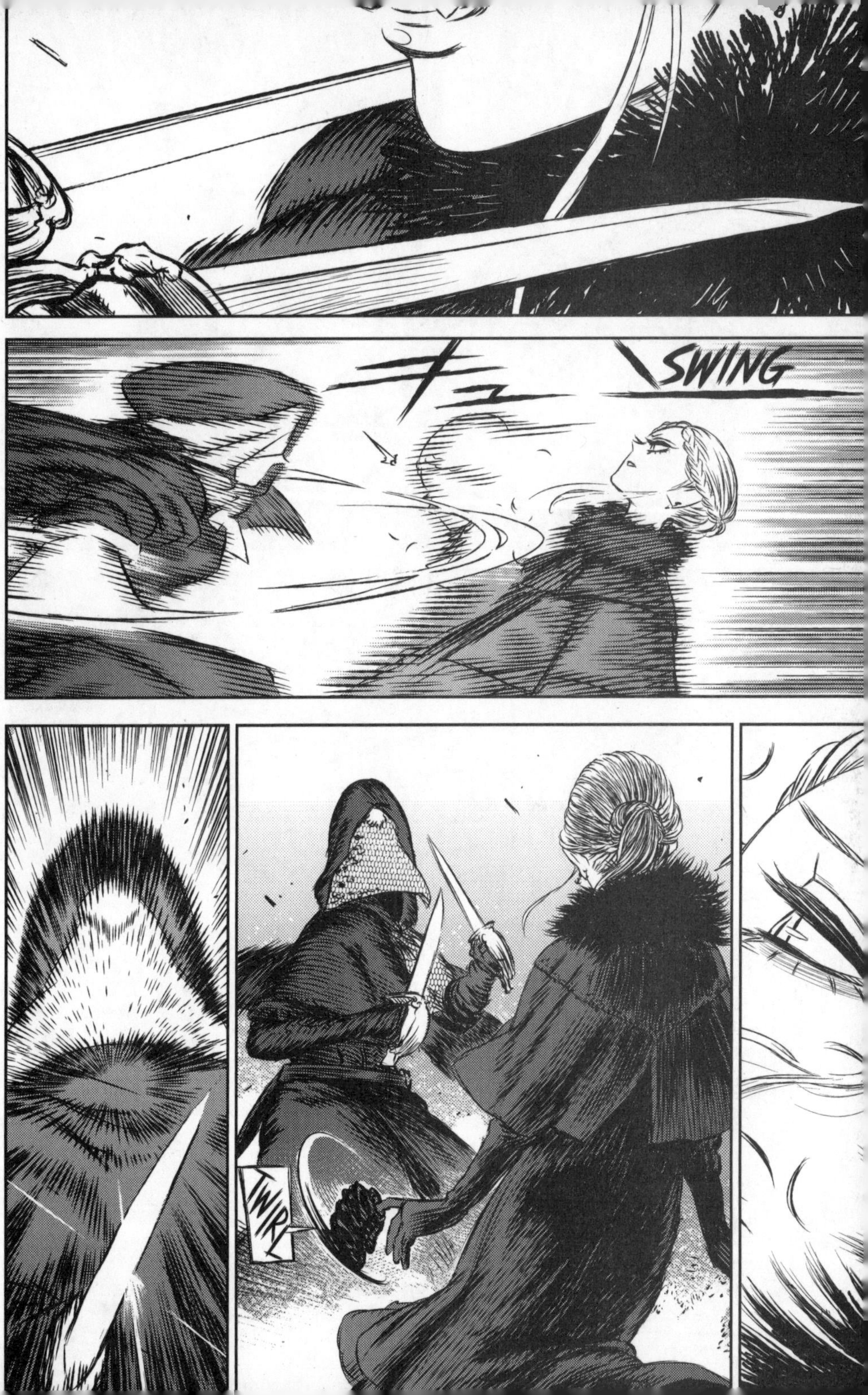
キュ
SWING
TWIRL

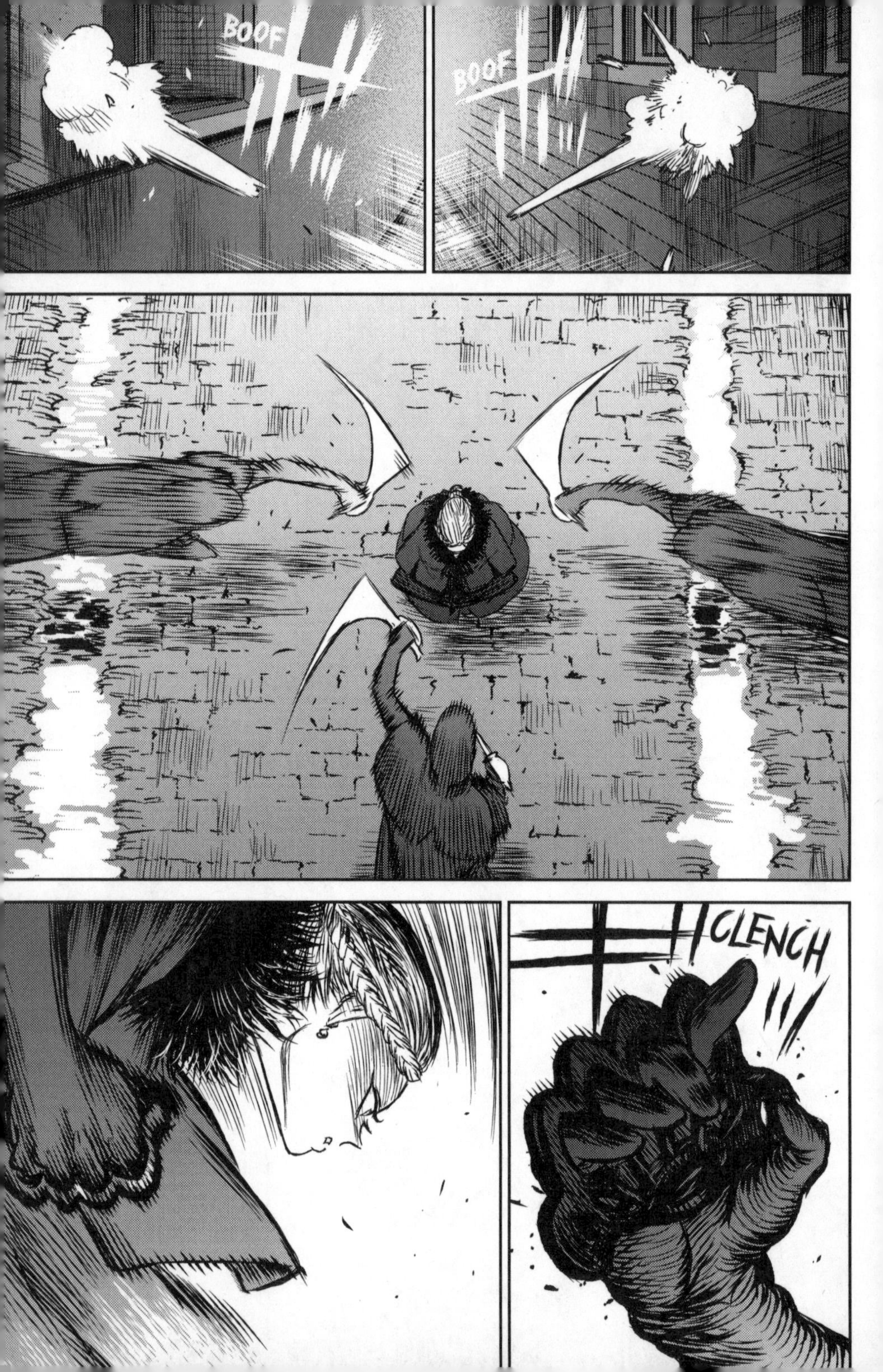
BOOF
BOOF
CLENCH

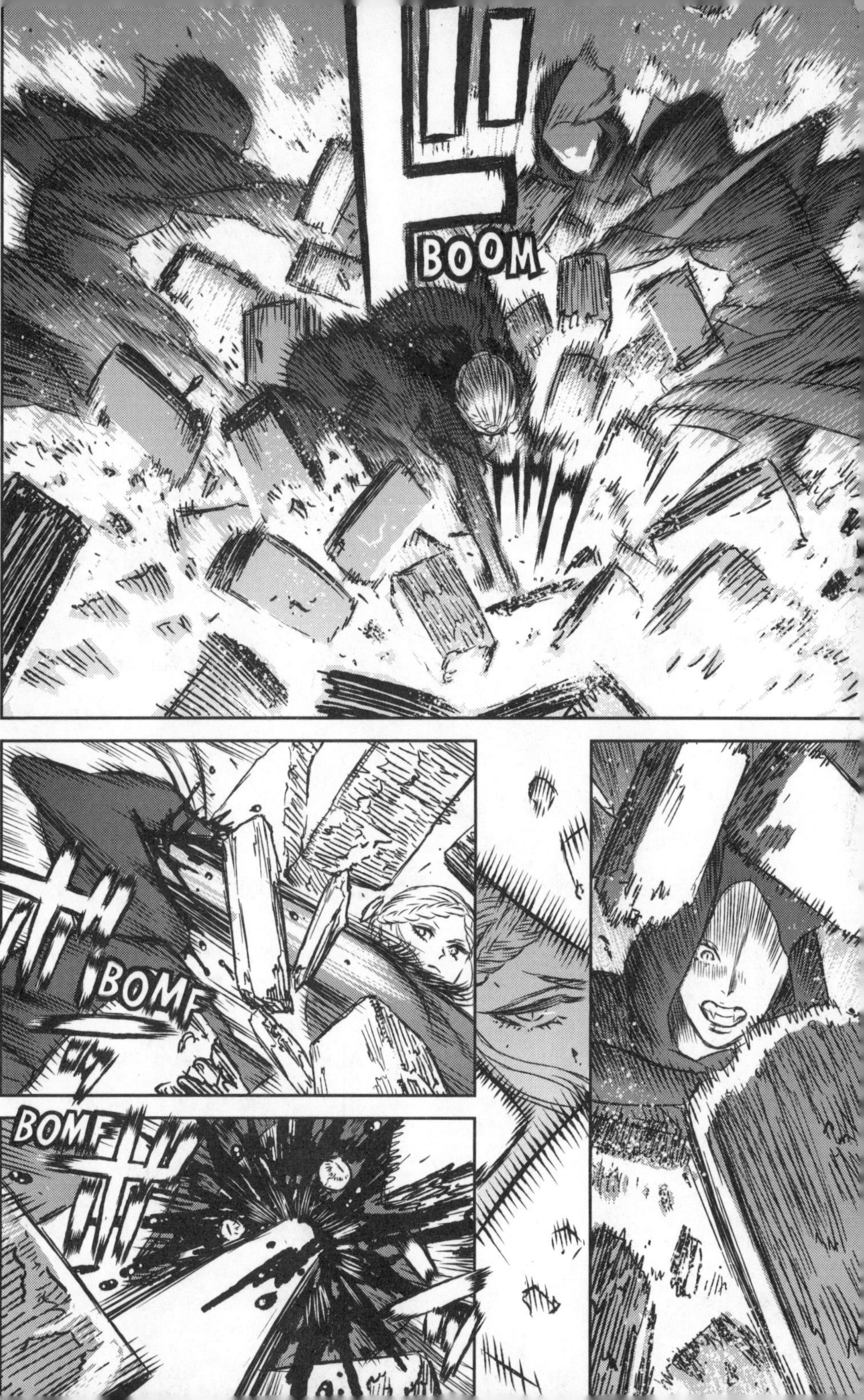
BOOM
BOMF
BOMF

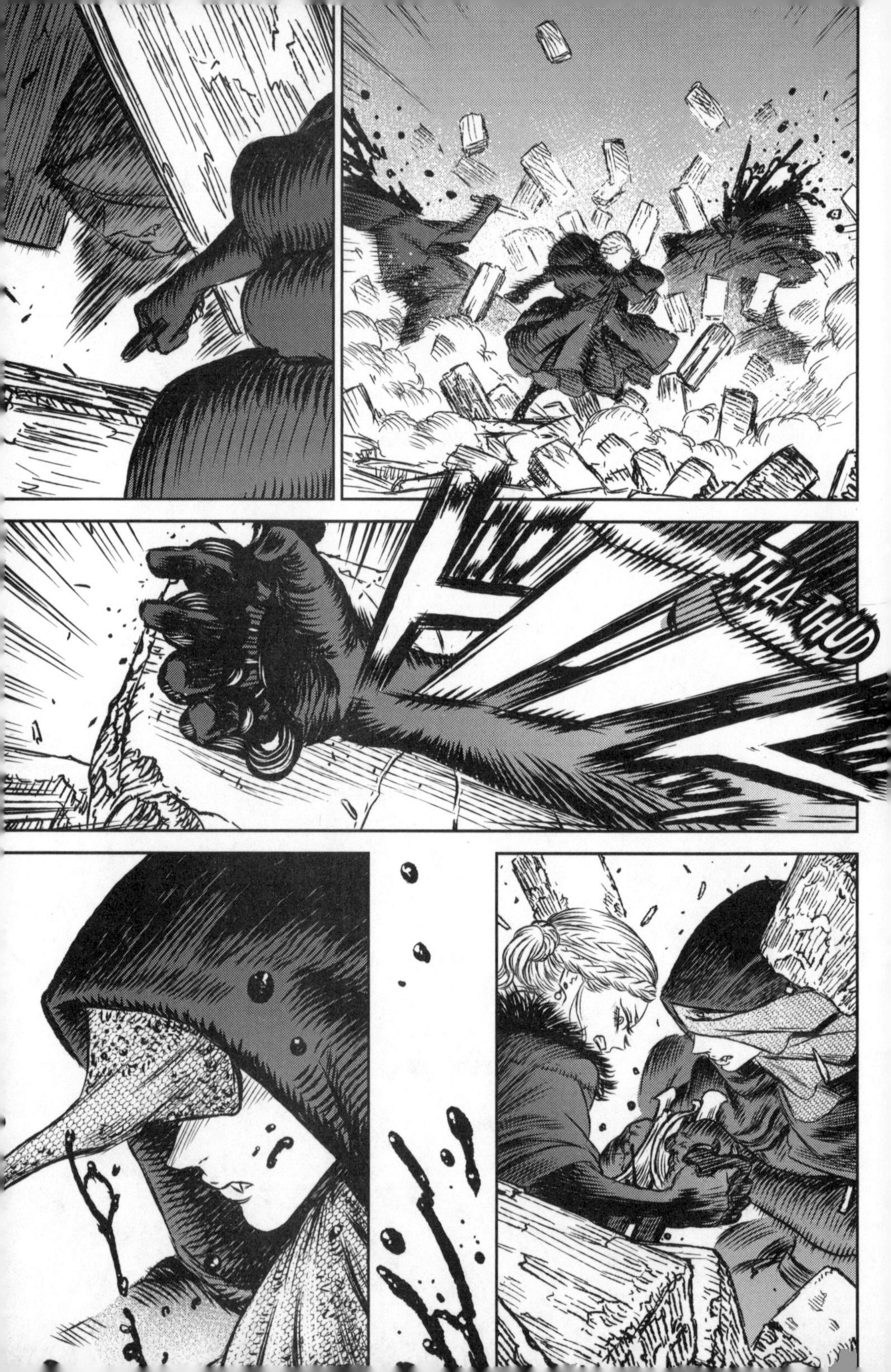
THA-THUD

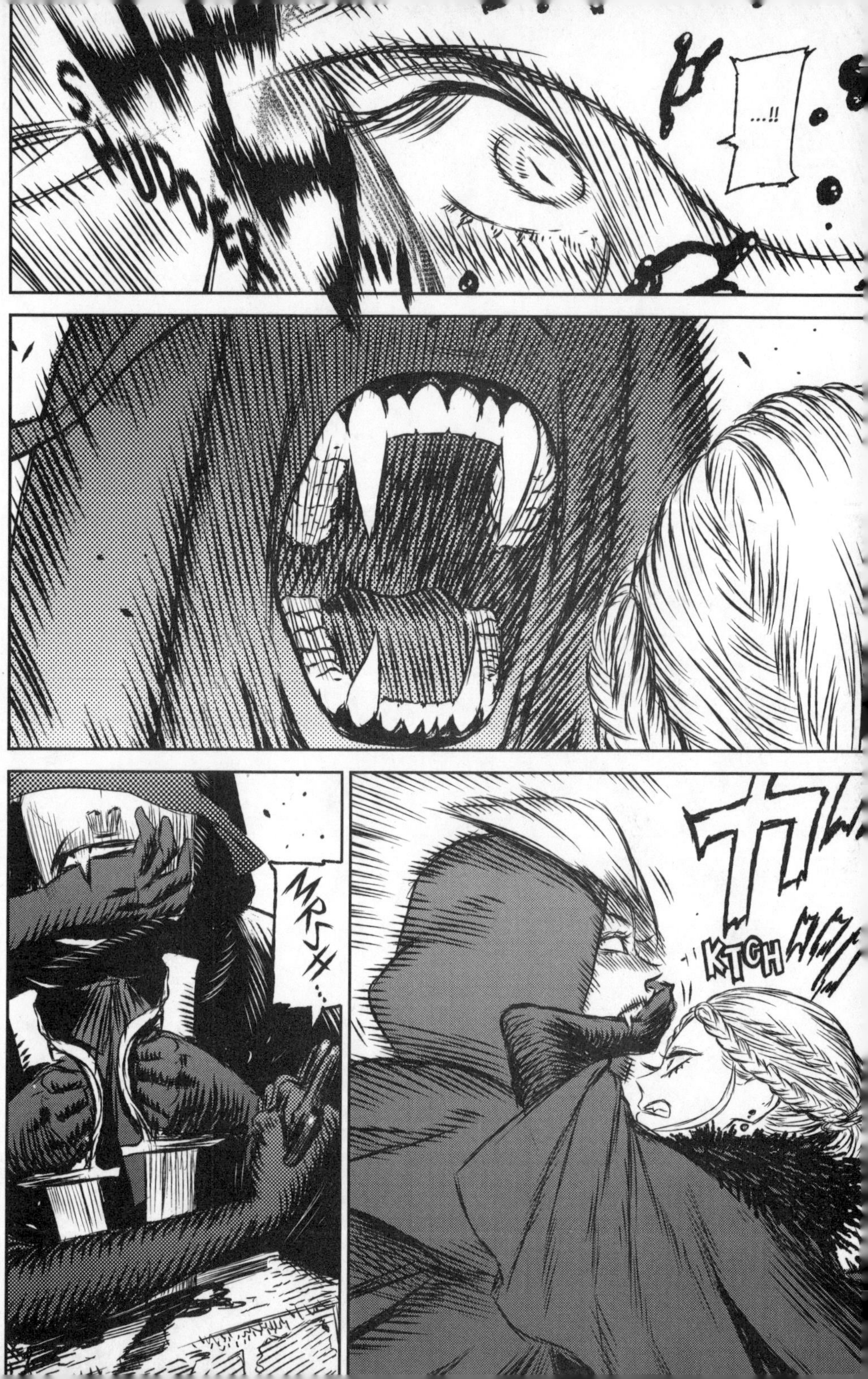
...!!
SHUDDER
KTCH
MRSH...

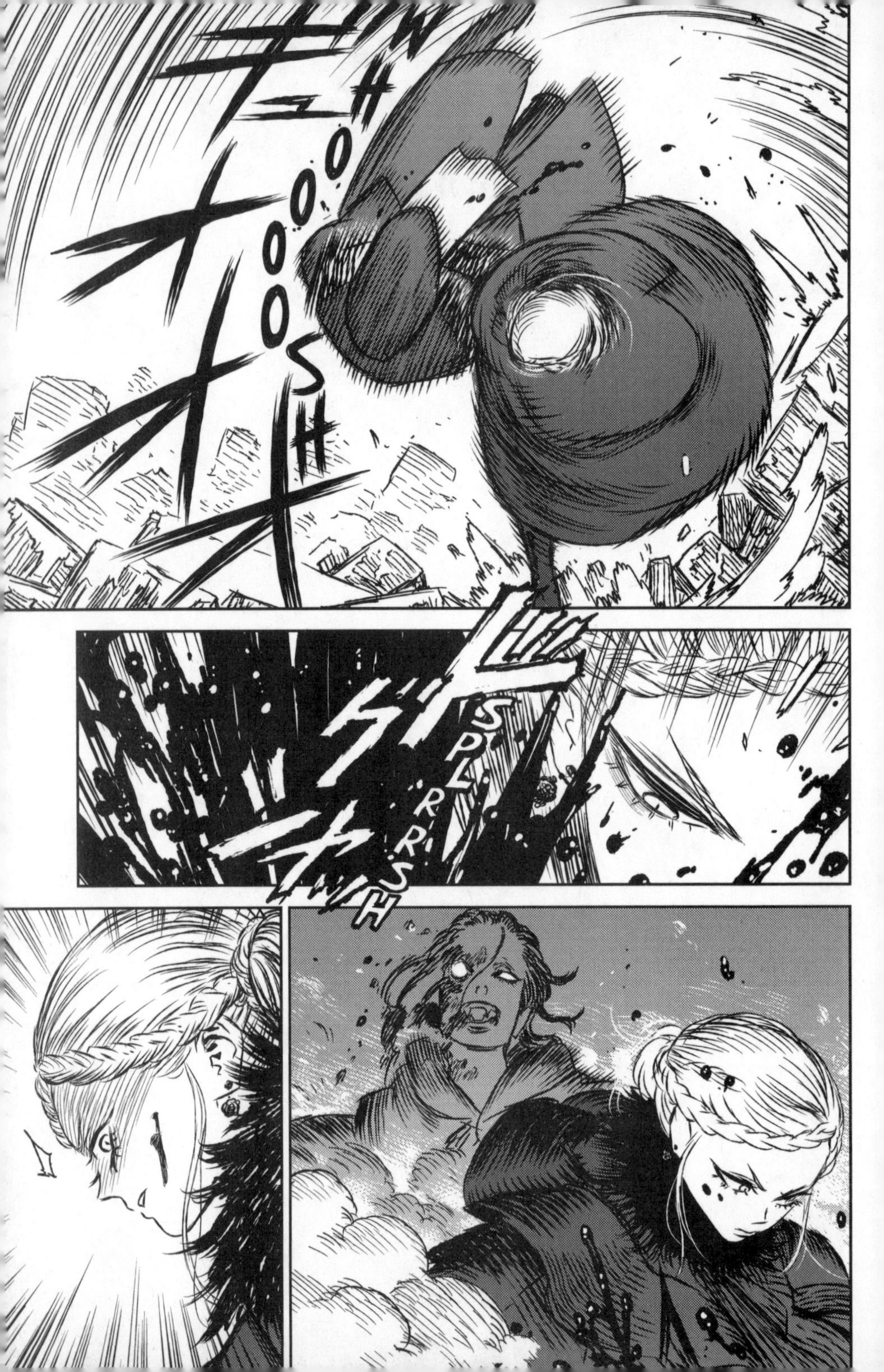
WHOOOOSH
SPLRRRSH

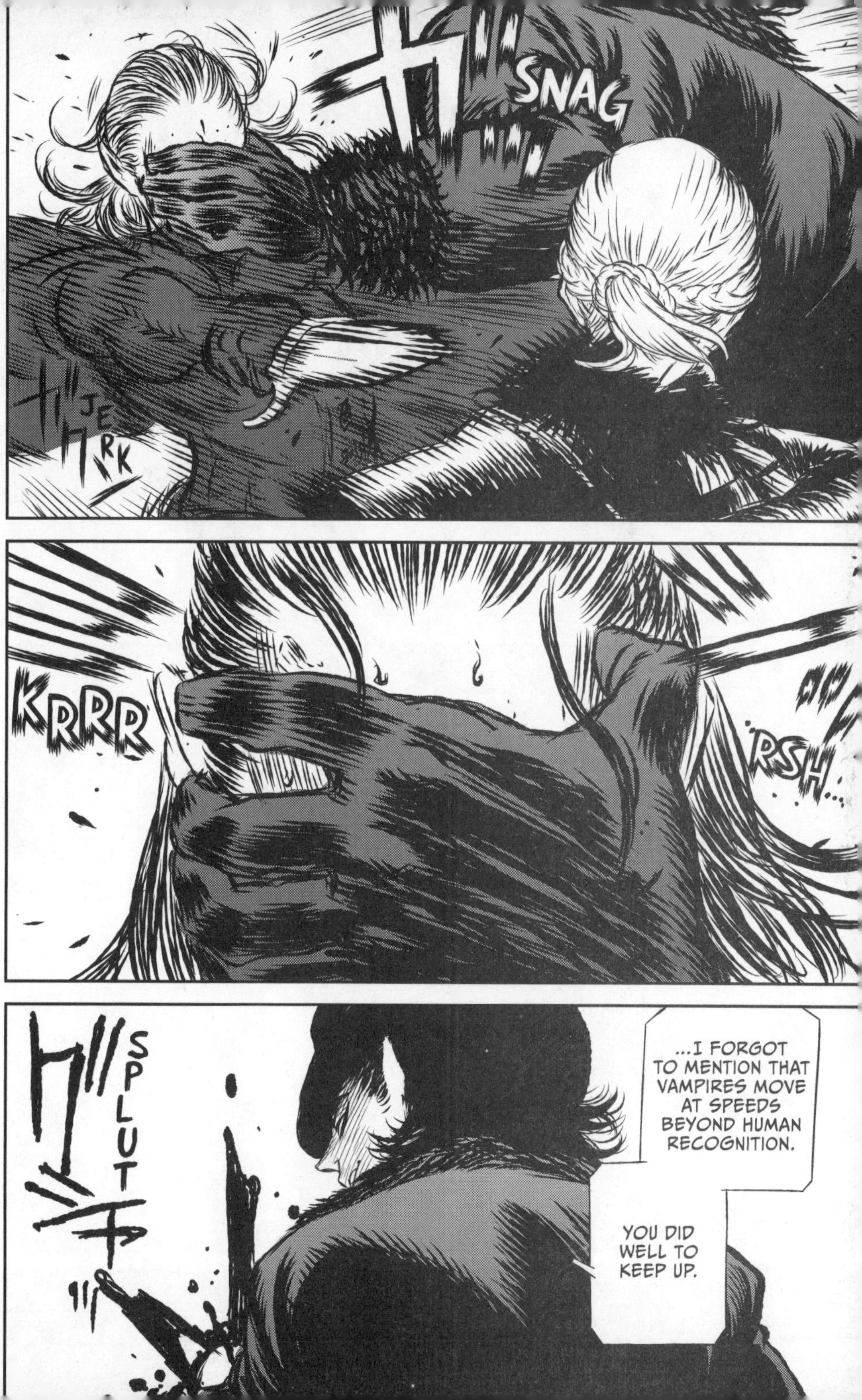
SNAG
JERK
RSH...
KRRR
...I FORGOT TO MENTION THAT VAMPIRES MOVE AT SPEEDS BEYOND HUMAN RECOGNITION.
YOU DID WELL TO KEEP UP.
SPLUT

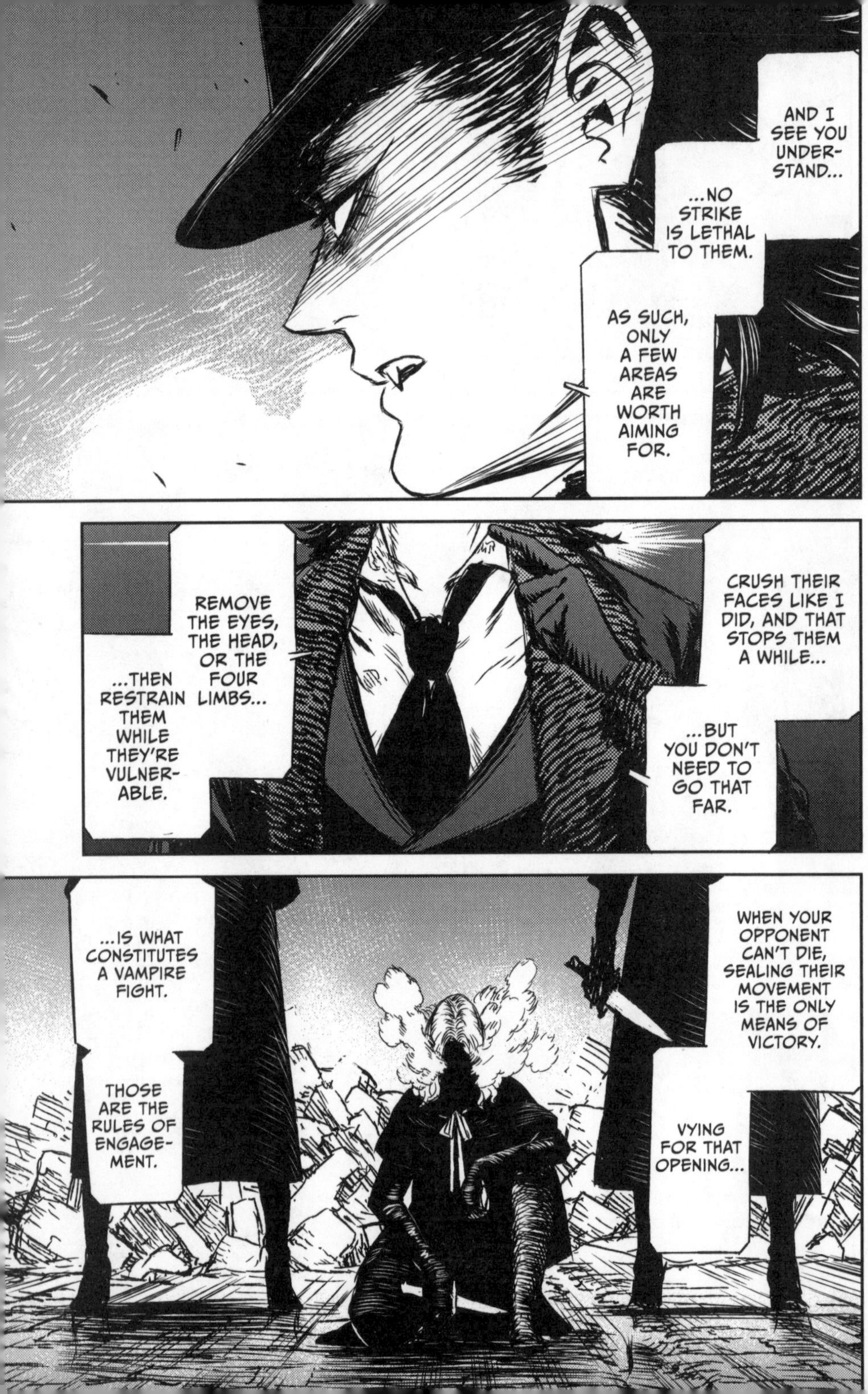
AND I SEE YOU UNDER-STAND...
...NO STRIKE IS LETHAL TO THEM.
AS SUCH, ONLY A FEW AREAS ARE WORTH AIMING FOR.
CRUSH THEIR FACES LIKE I DID, AND THAT STOPS THEM A WHILE...
...BUT YOU DON'T NEED TO GO THAT FAR.
REMOVE THE EYES, THE HEAD, OR THE FOUR LIMBS...
...THEN RESTRAIN THEM WHILE THEY'RE VULNER-ABLE.
WHEN YOUR OPPONENT CAN'T DIE, SEALING THEIR MOVEMENT IS THE ONLY MEANS OF VICTORY.
VYING FOR THAT OPENING...
...IS WHAT CONSTITUTES A VAMPIRE FIGHT.
THOSE ARE THE RULES OF ENGAGE-MENT.

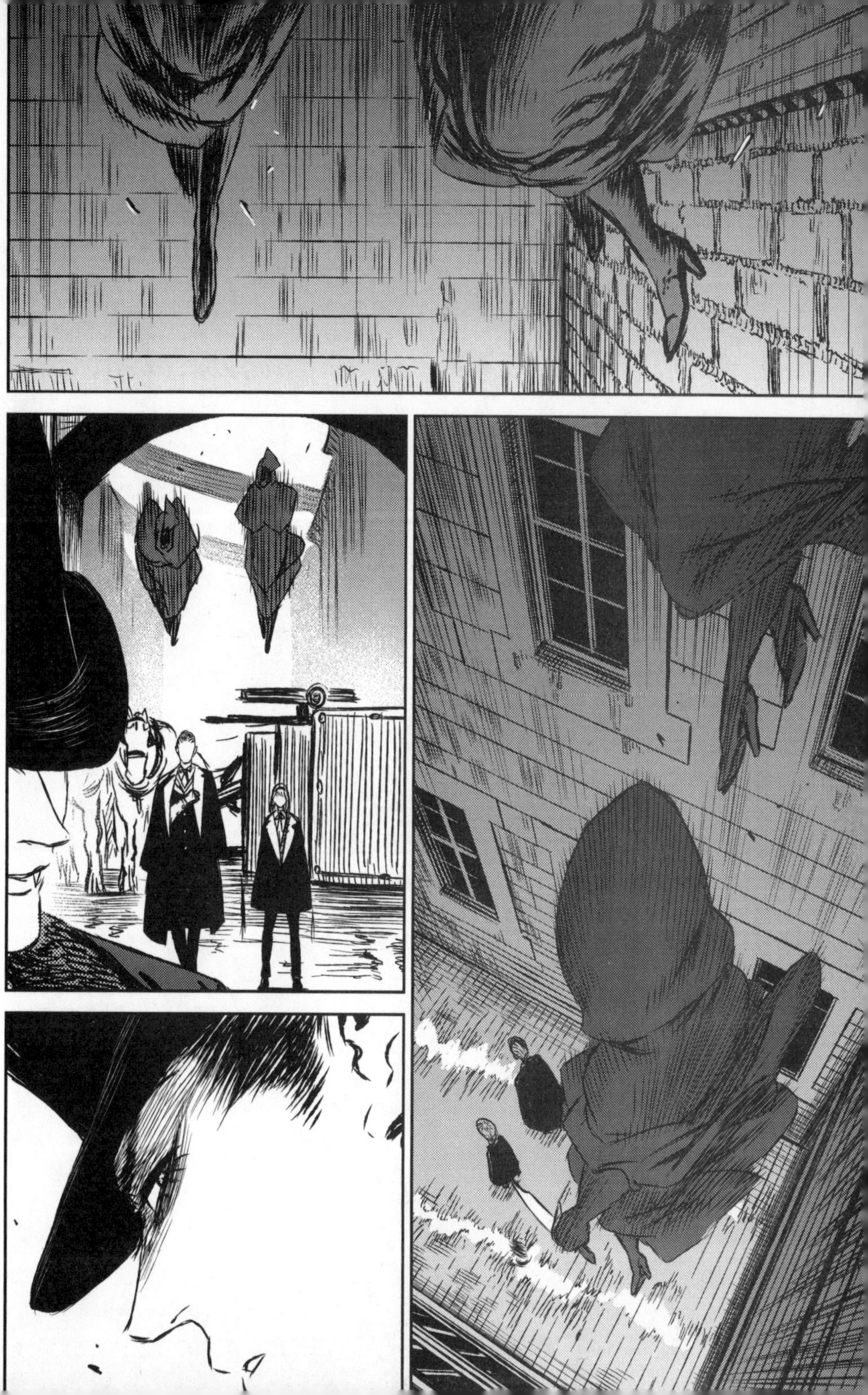

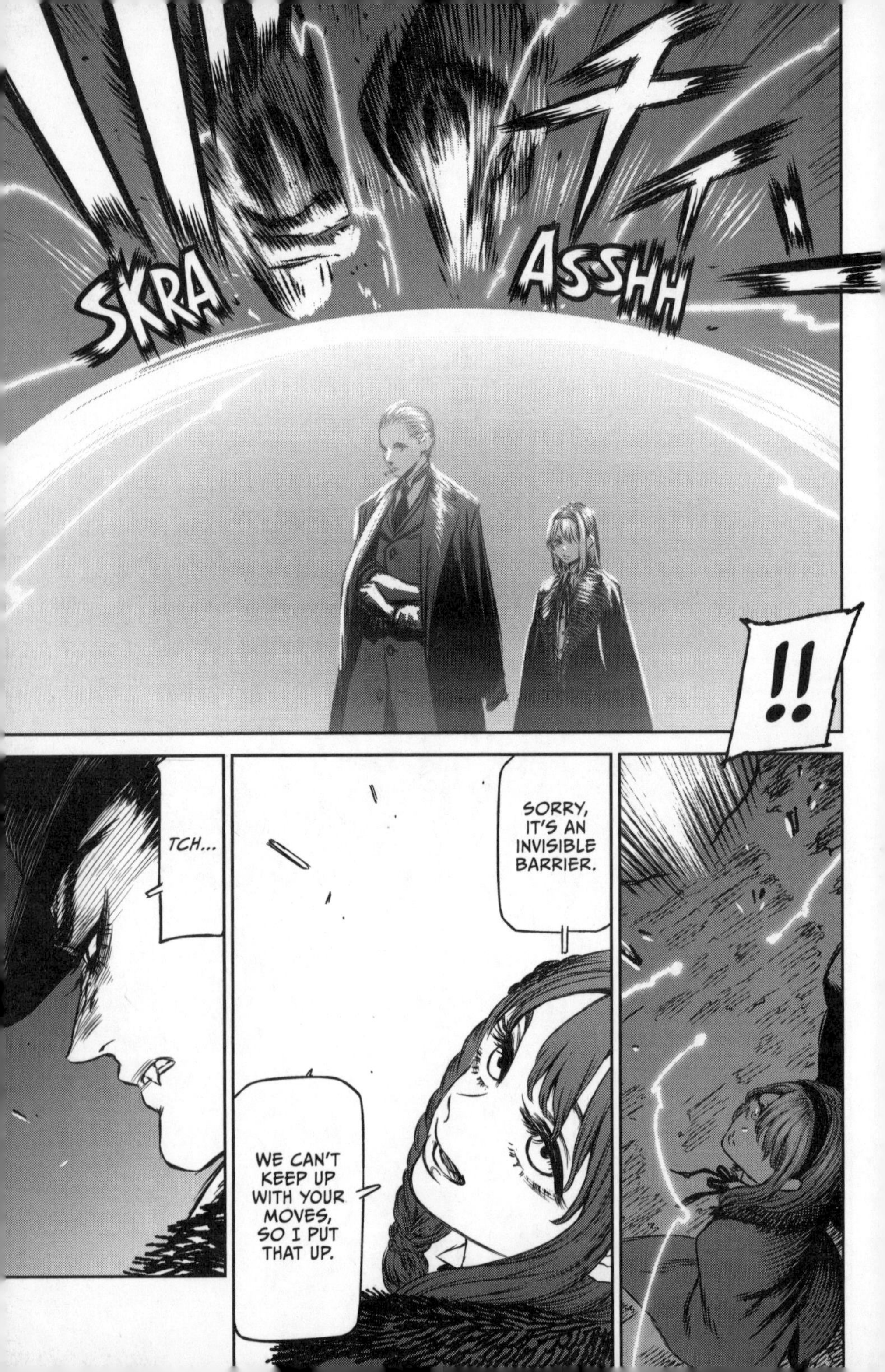
SKRA ASSHH
!!
SORRY, IT'S AN INVISIBLE BARRIER.
WE CAN'T KEEP UP WITH YOUR MOVES, SO I PUT THAT UP.
TCH...

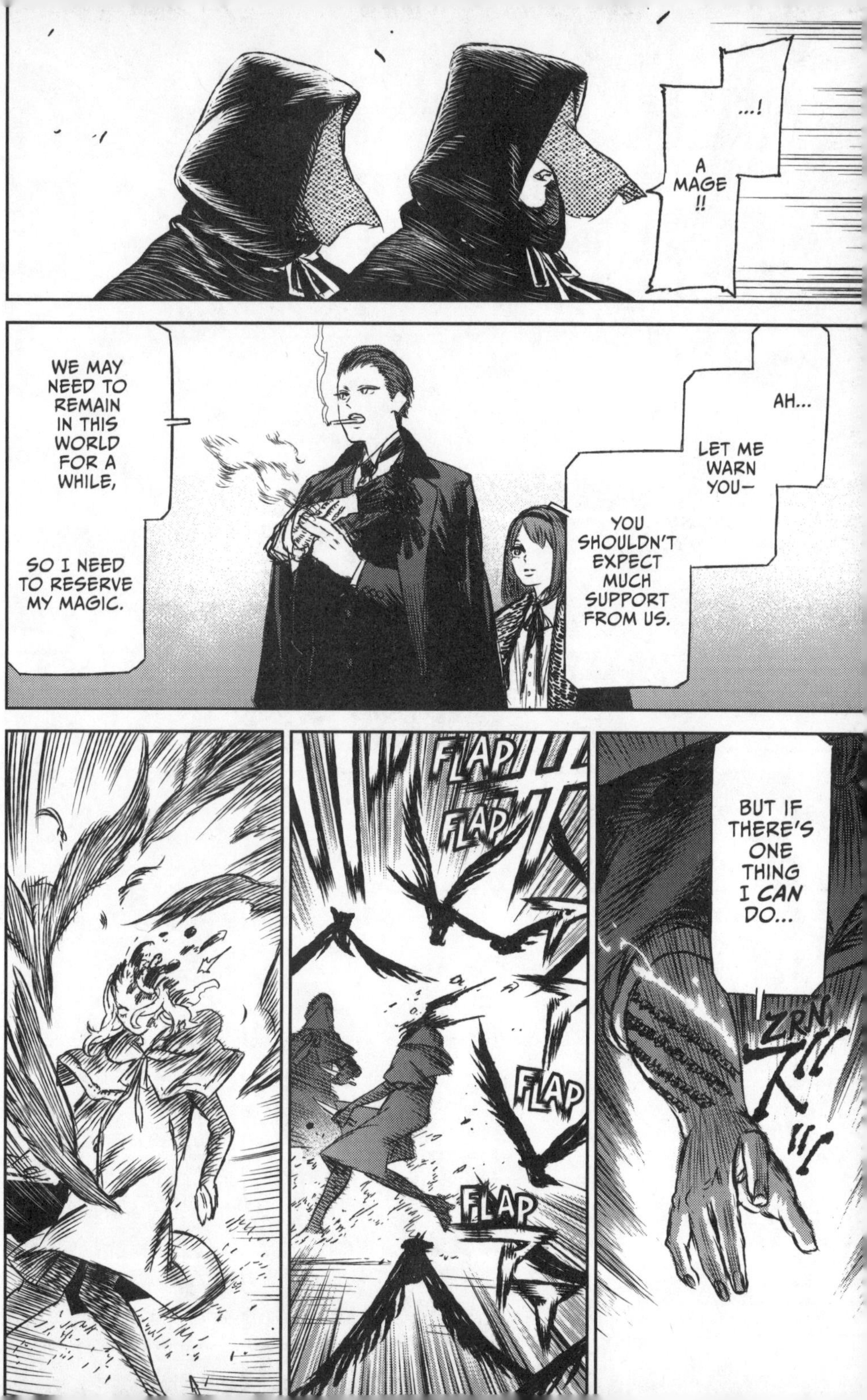
...!
A MAGE !!
AH...
LET ME WARN YOU—
YOU SHOULDN'T EXPECT MUCH SUPPORT FROM US.
WE MAY NEED TO REMAIN IN THIS WORLD FOR A WHILE,
SO I NEED TO RESERVE MY MAGIC.
BUT IF THERE'S ONE THING I *CAN* DO...
ZRNK
FLAP
FLAP
FLAP
FLAP

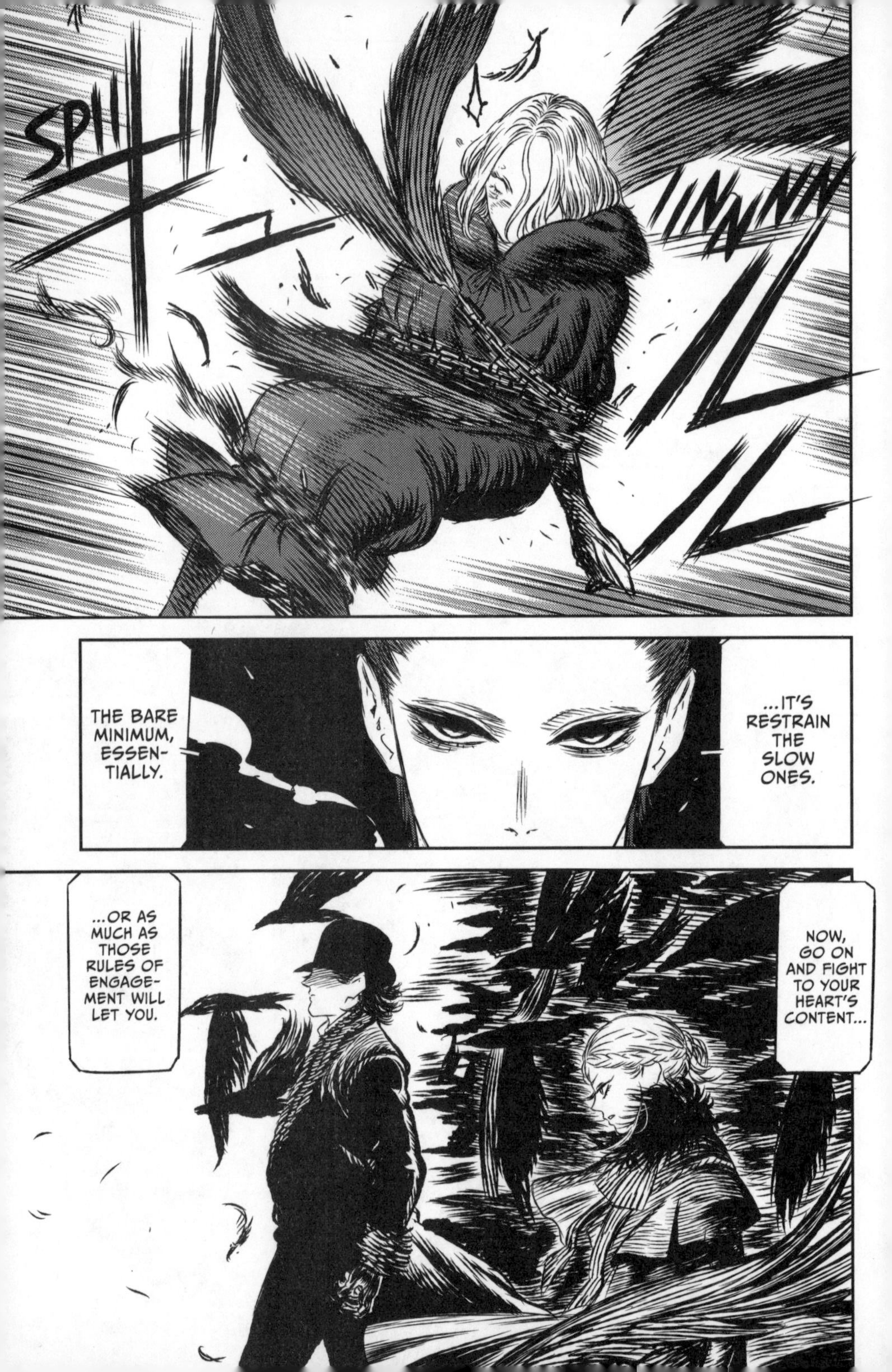
SPIIIINNNNN
...IT'S RESTRAIN THE SLOW ONES.
THE BARE MINIMUM, ESSENTIALLY.
NOW, GO ON AND FIGHT TO YOUR HEART'S CONTENT...
...OR AS MUCH AS THOSE RULES OF ENGAGEMENT WILL LET YOU.

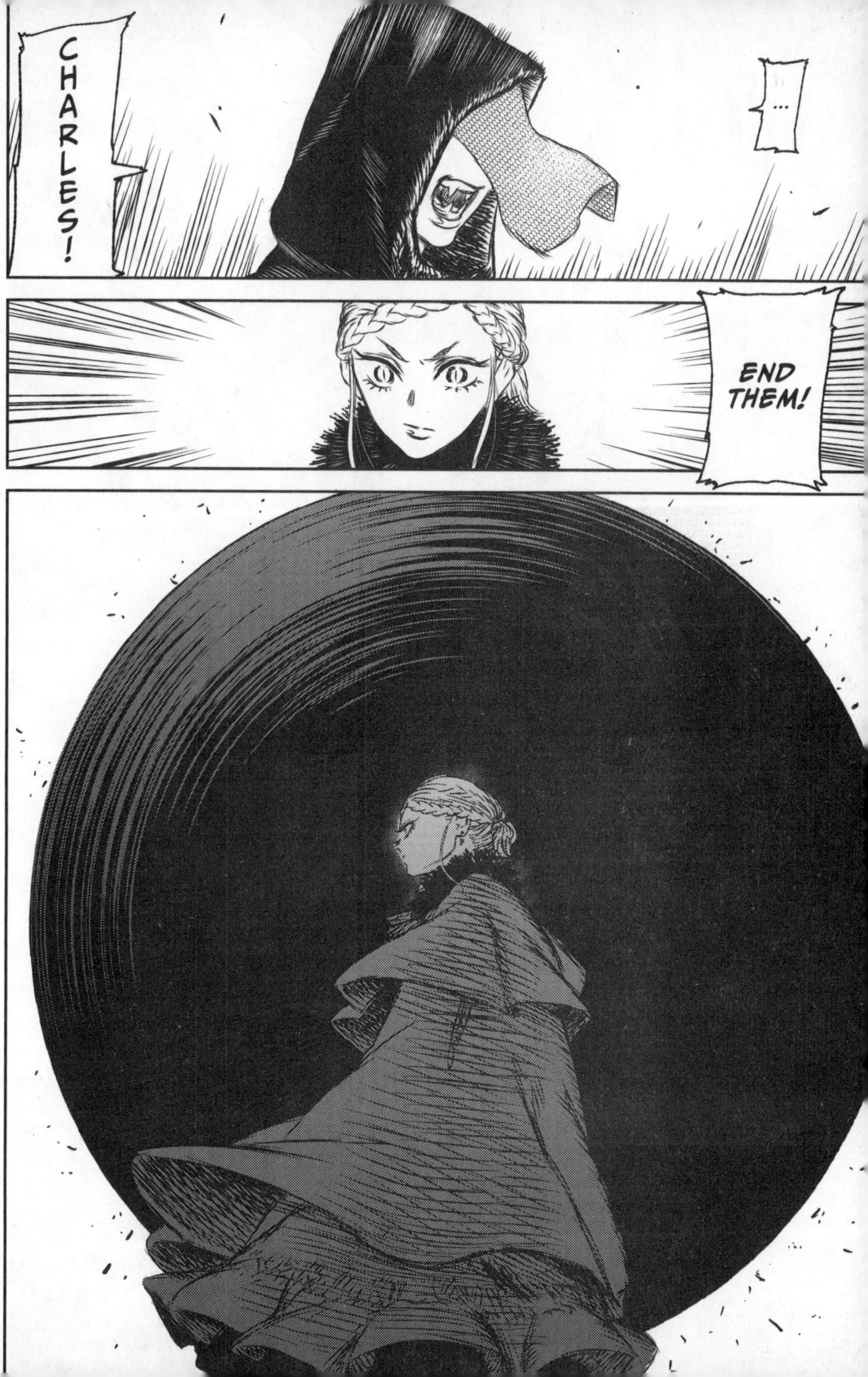
...
CHARLES!
END THEM!

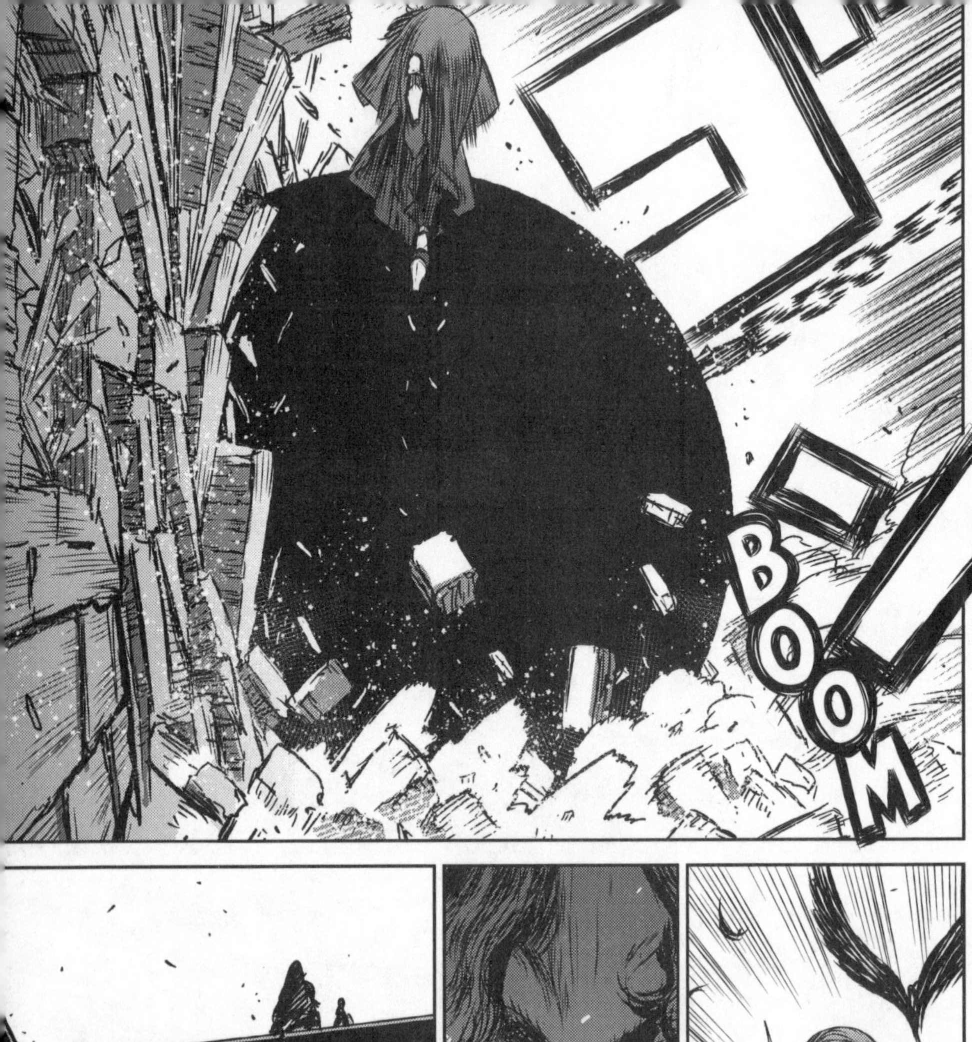
BOOOM
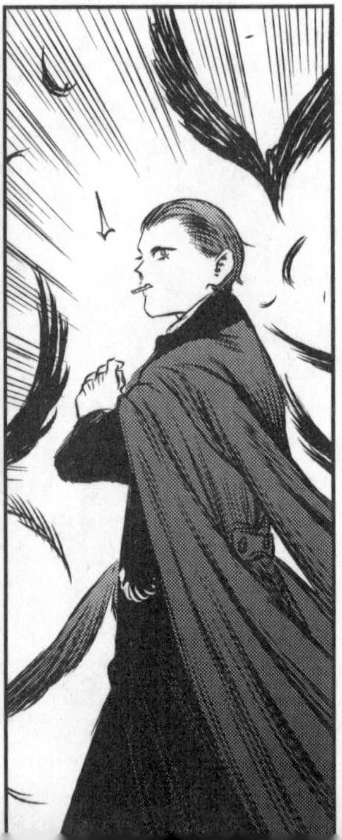
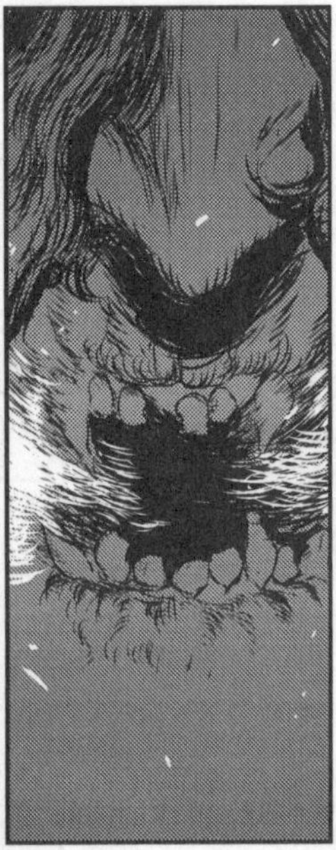
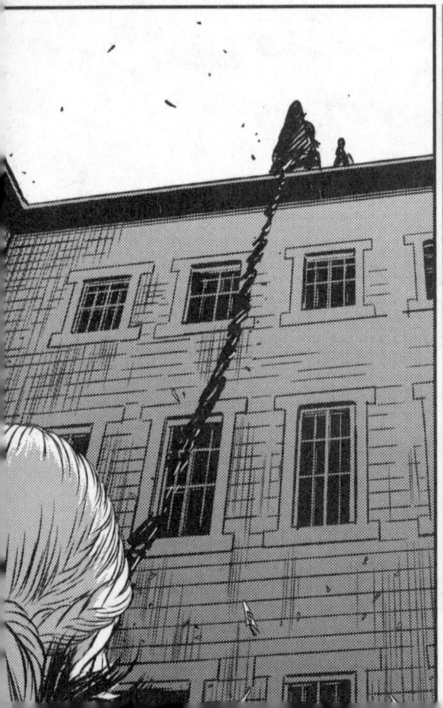

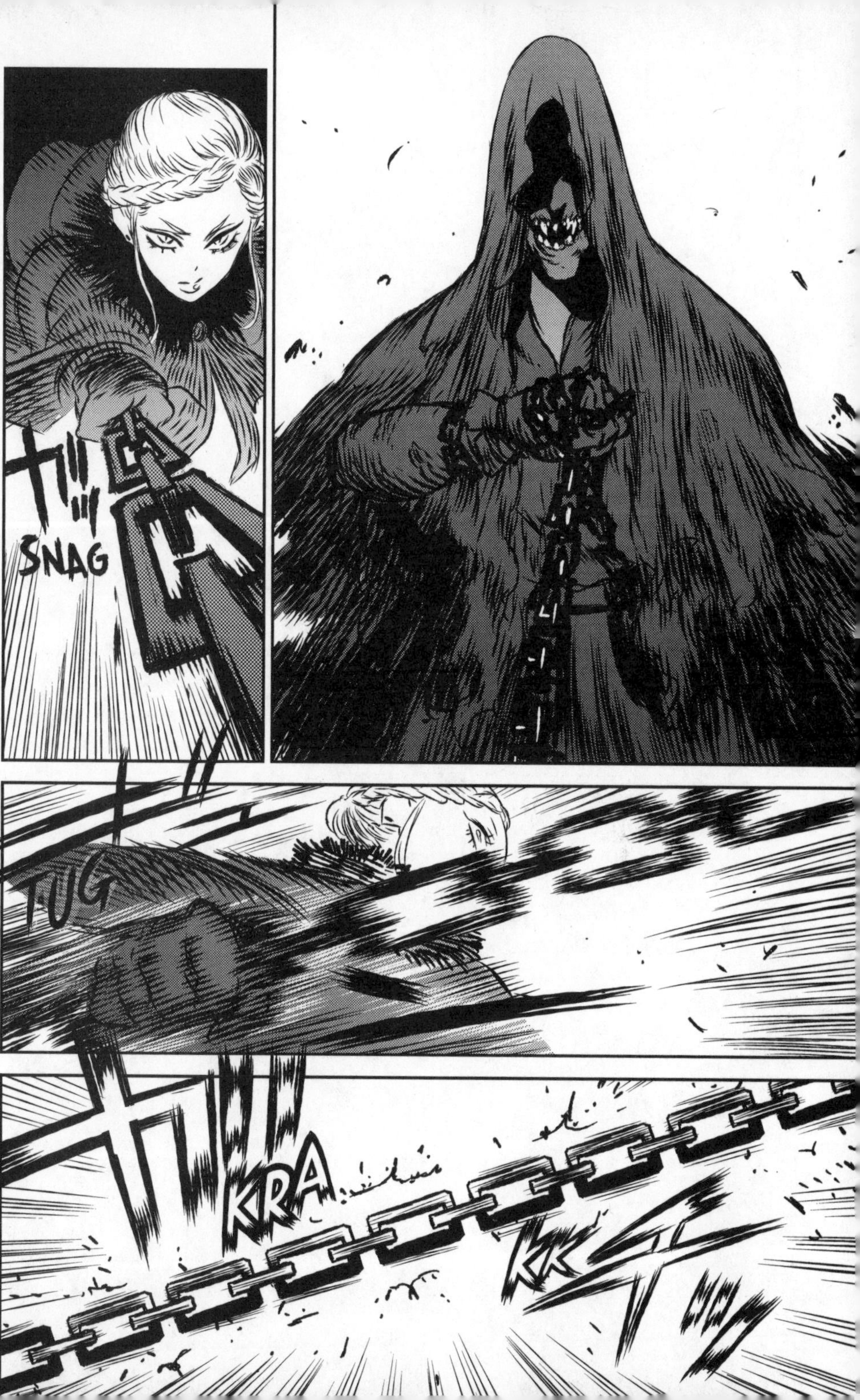
SNAG
TUG
KRA
KK

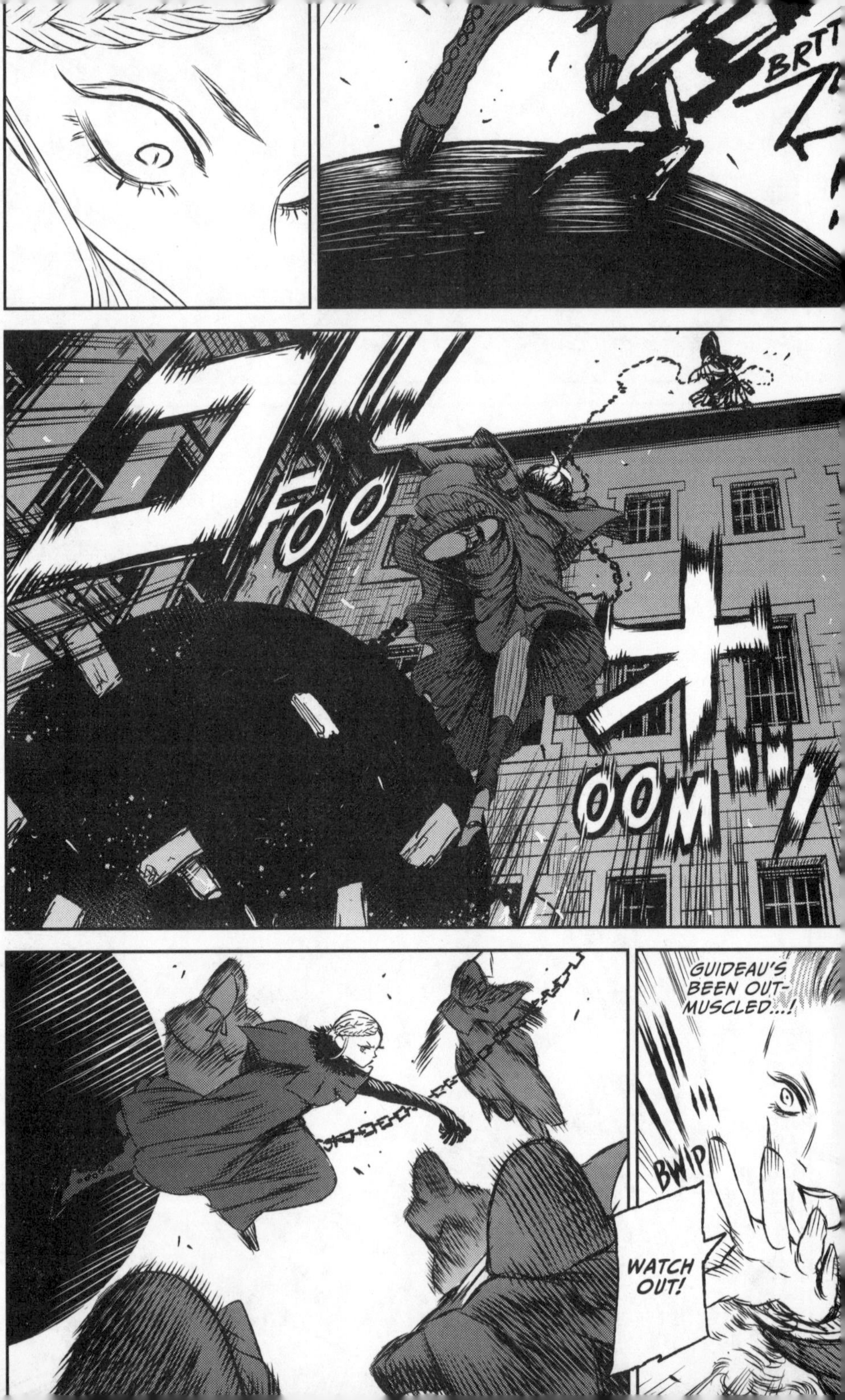
BRTT
FOO
OOM
GUIDEAU'S BEEN OUT-MUSCLED...!
BWIP
WATCH OUT!

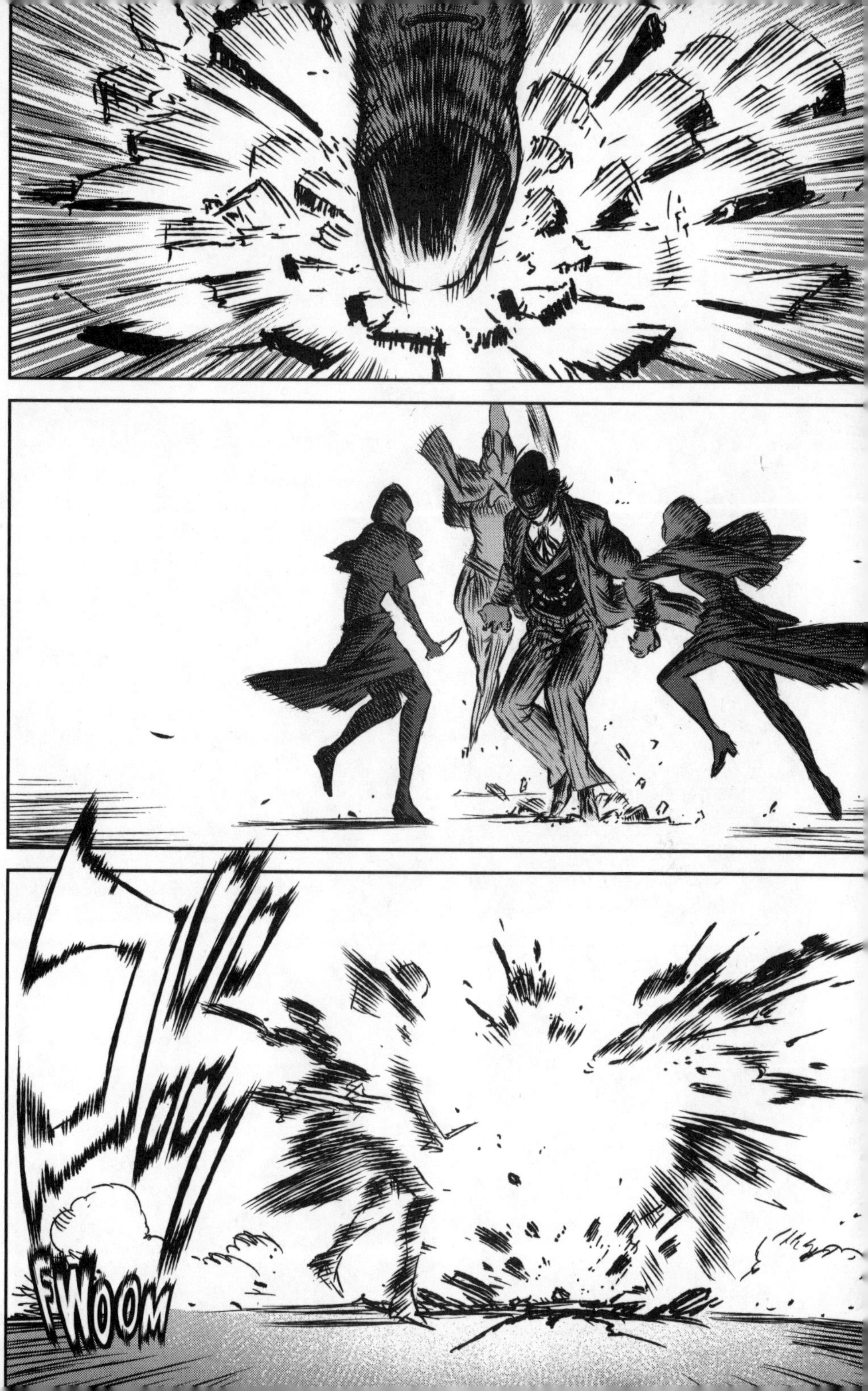
FWOOM

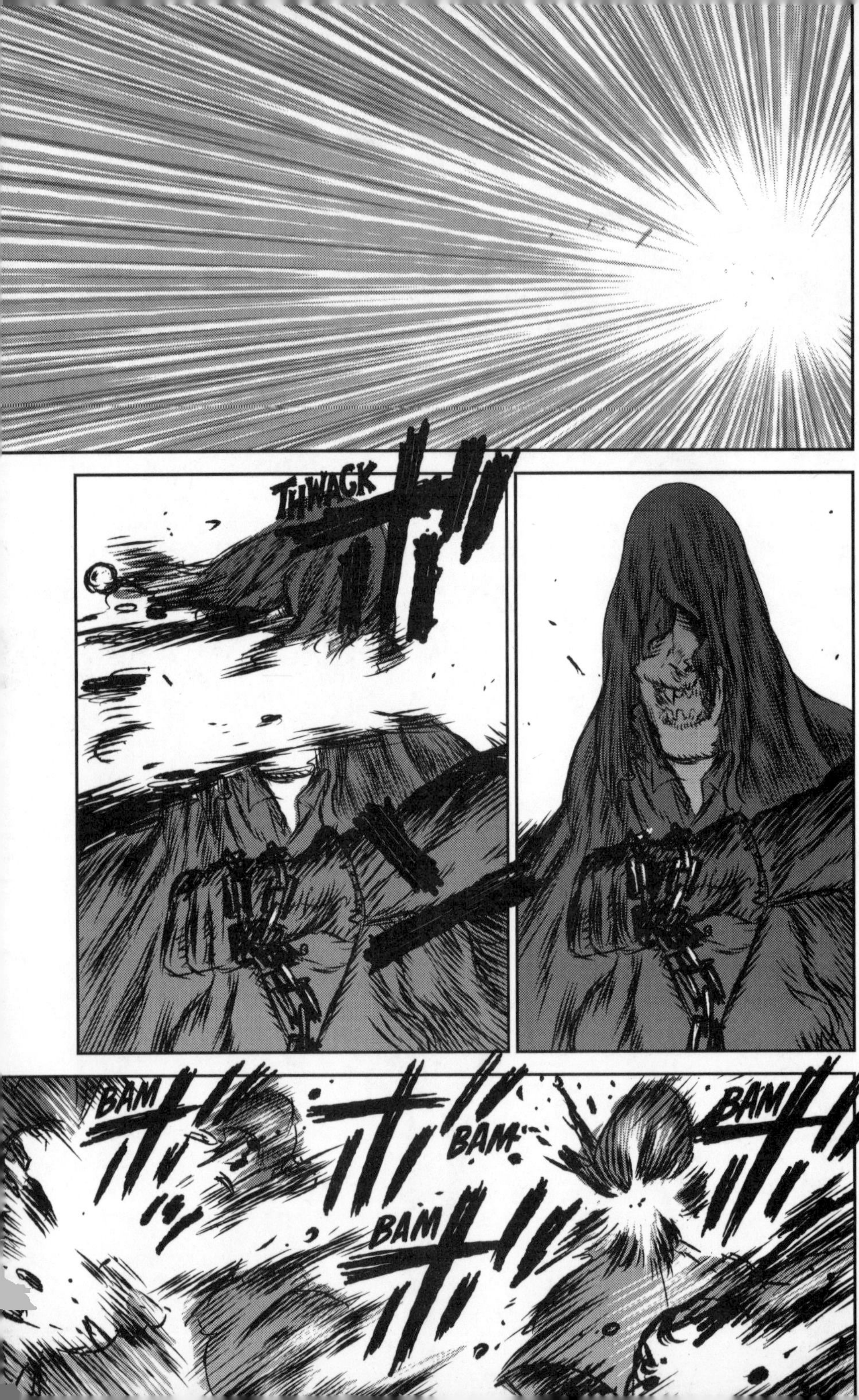
THWACK
BAM
BAM
BAM
BAM

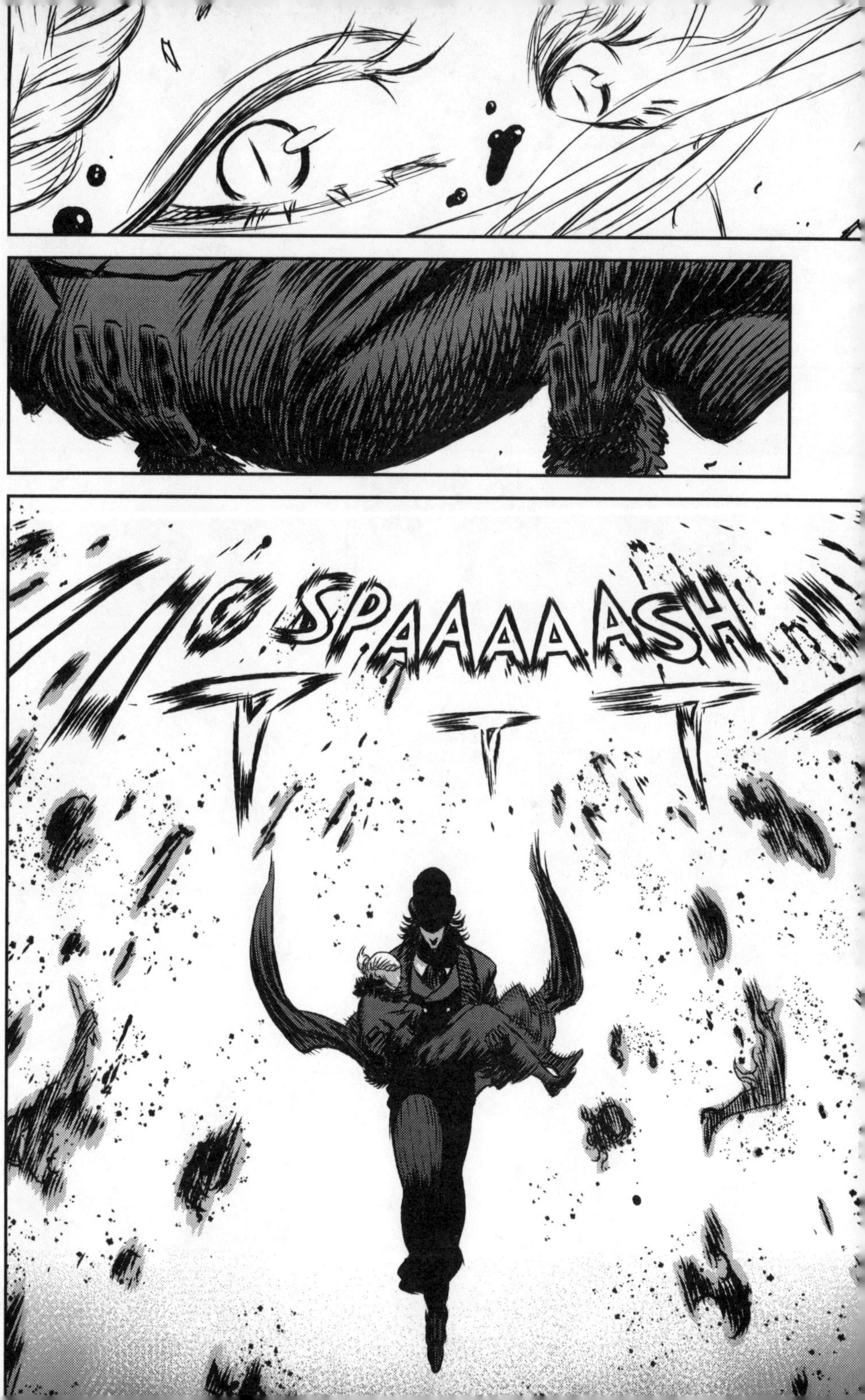
SPAAAASH

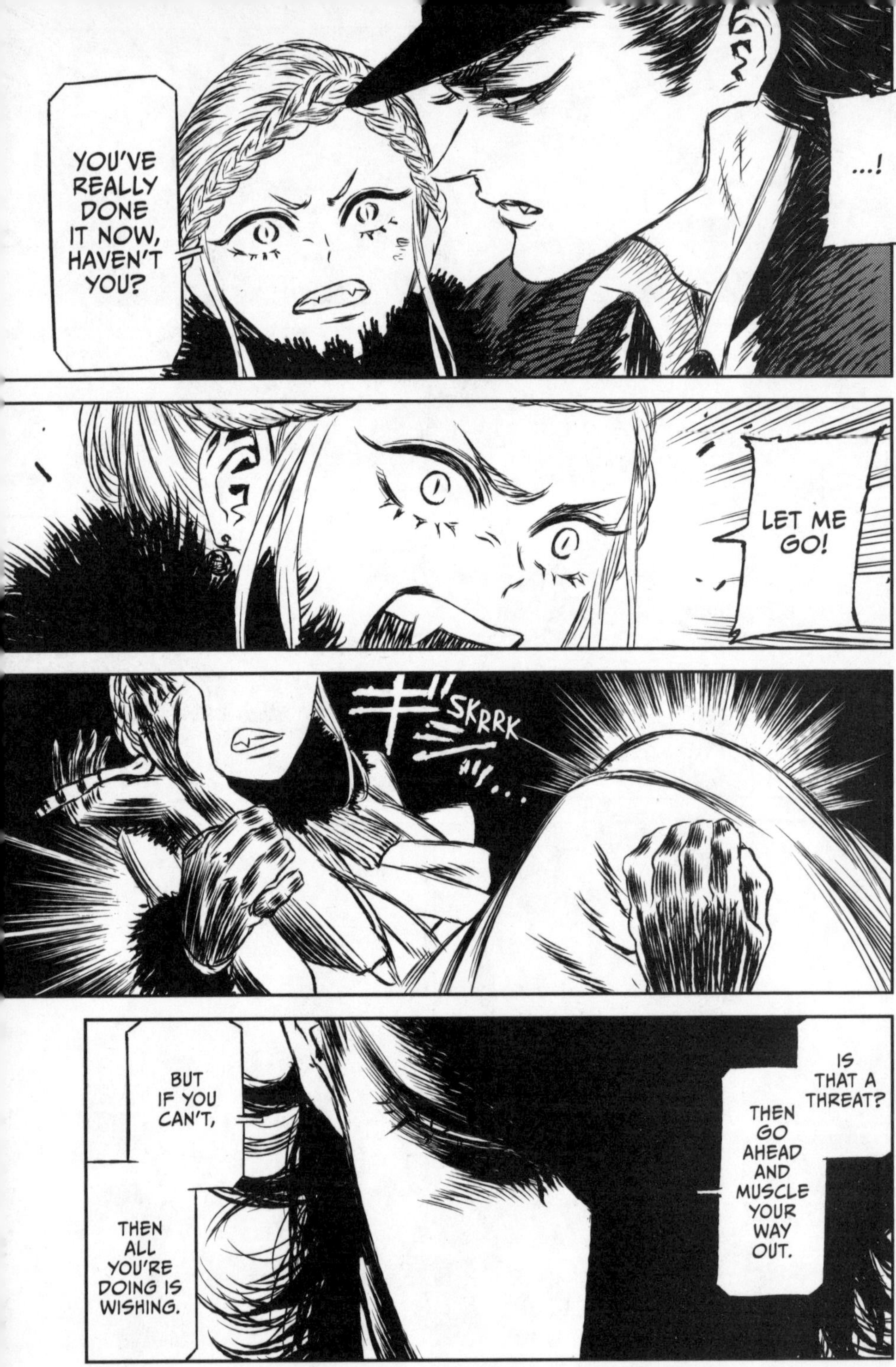
...!
YOU'VE REALLY DONE IT NOW, HAVEN'T YOU?
LET ME GO!
SKRRK
IS THAT A THREAT?
THEN GO AHEAD AND MUSCLE YOUR WAY OUT.
BUT IF YOU CAN'T,
THEN ALL YOU'RE DOING IS WISHING.

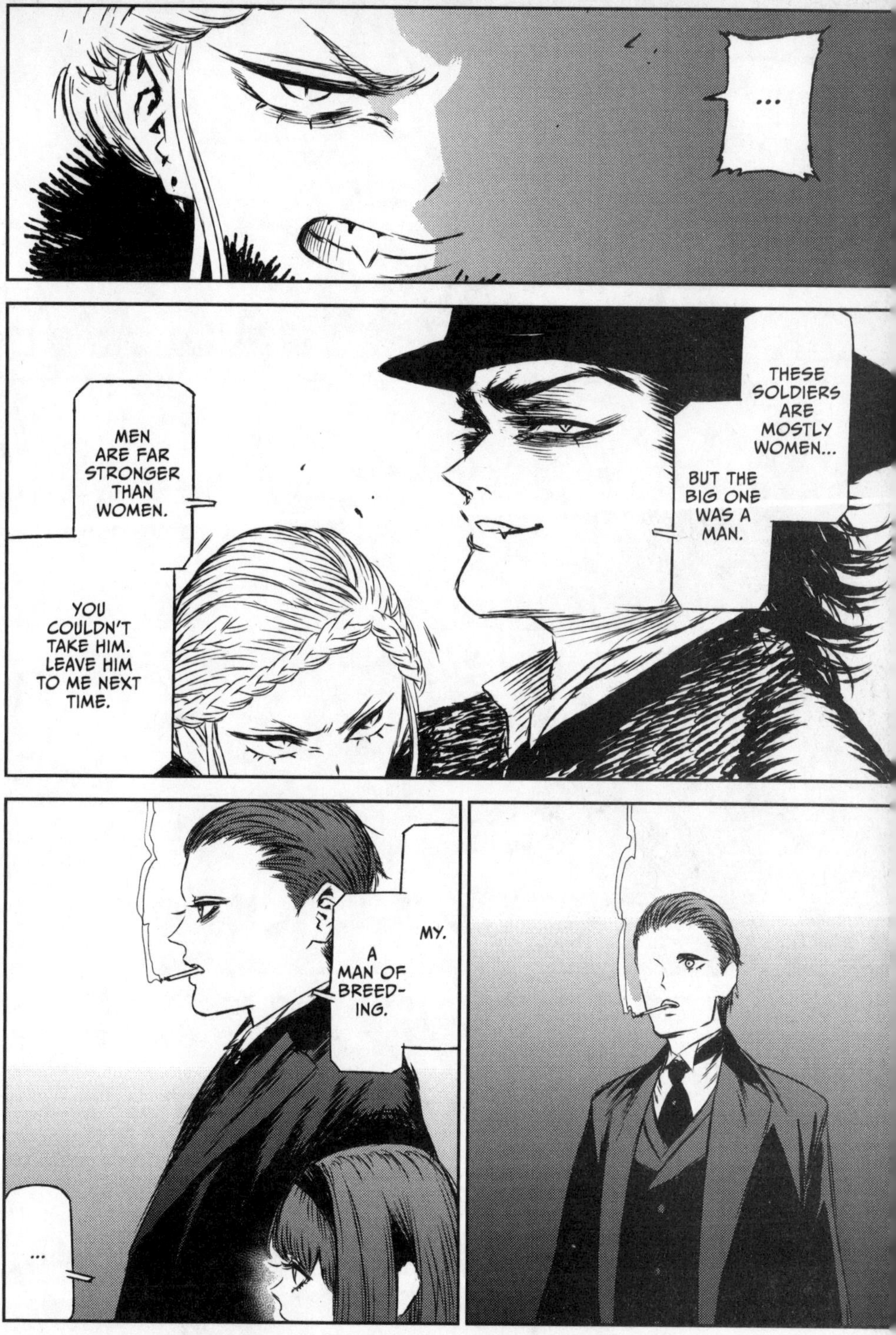
...
THESE SOLDIERS ARE MOSTLY WOMEN... BUT THE BIG ONE WAS A MAN.
MEN ARE FAR STRONGER THAN WOMEN.
YOU COULDN'T TAKE HIM. LEAVE HIM TO ME NEXT TIME.
MY. A MAN OF BREED-ING.
...

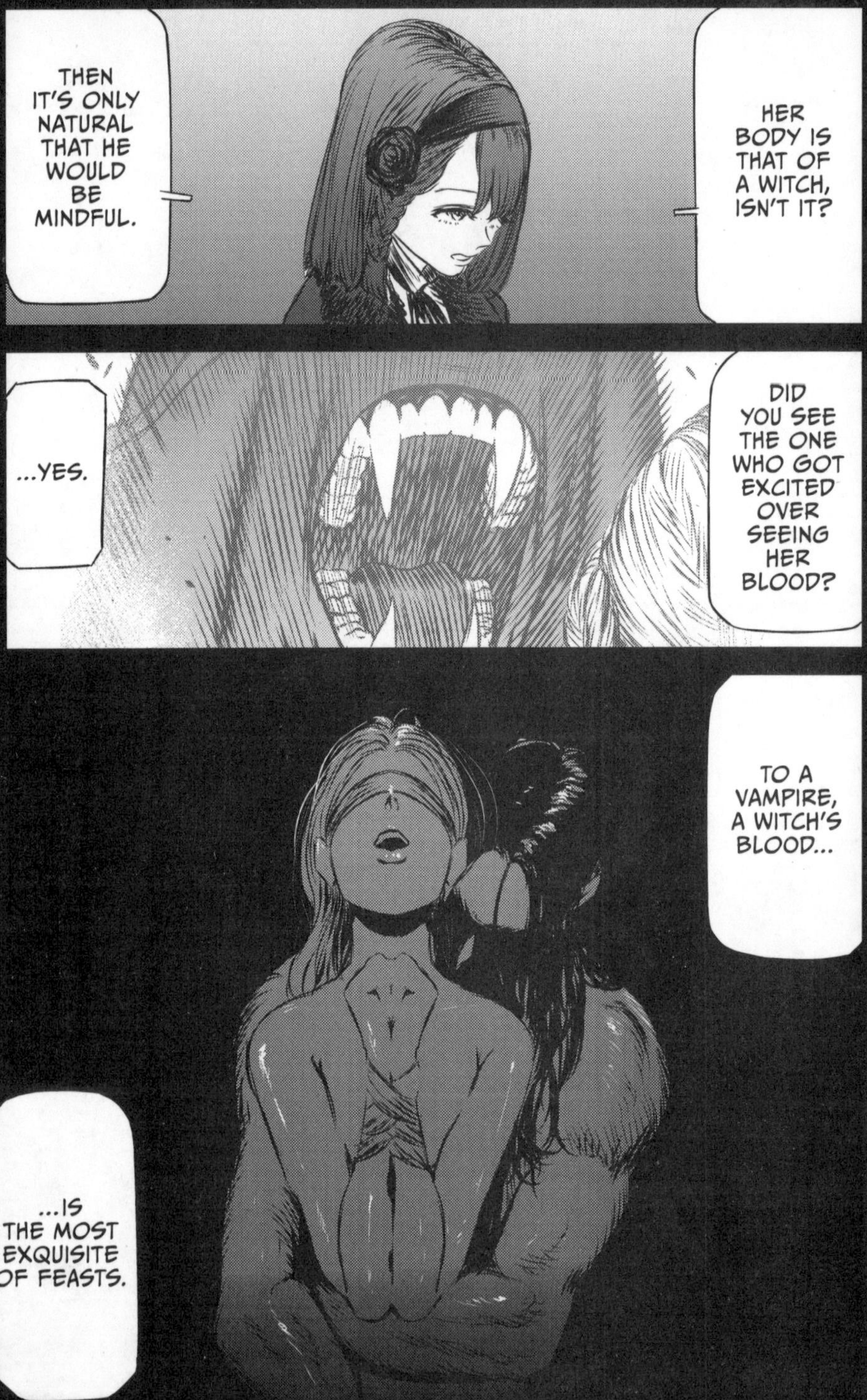
HER BODY IS THAT OF A WITCH, ISN'T IT?
THEN IT'S ONLY NATURAL THAT HE WOULD BE MINDFUL.
DID YOU SEE THE ONE WHO GOT EXCITED OVER SEEING HER BLOOD?
...YES.
TO A VAMPIRE, A WITCH'S BLOOD...
...IS THE MOST EXQUISITE OF FEASTS.

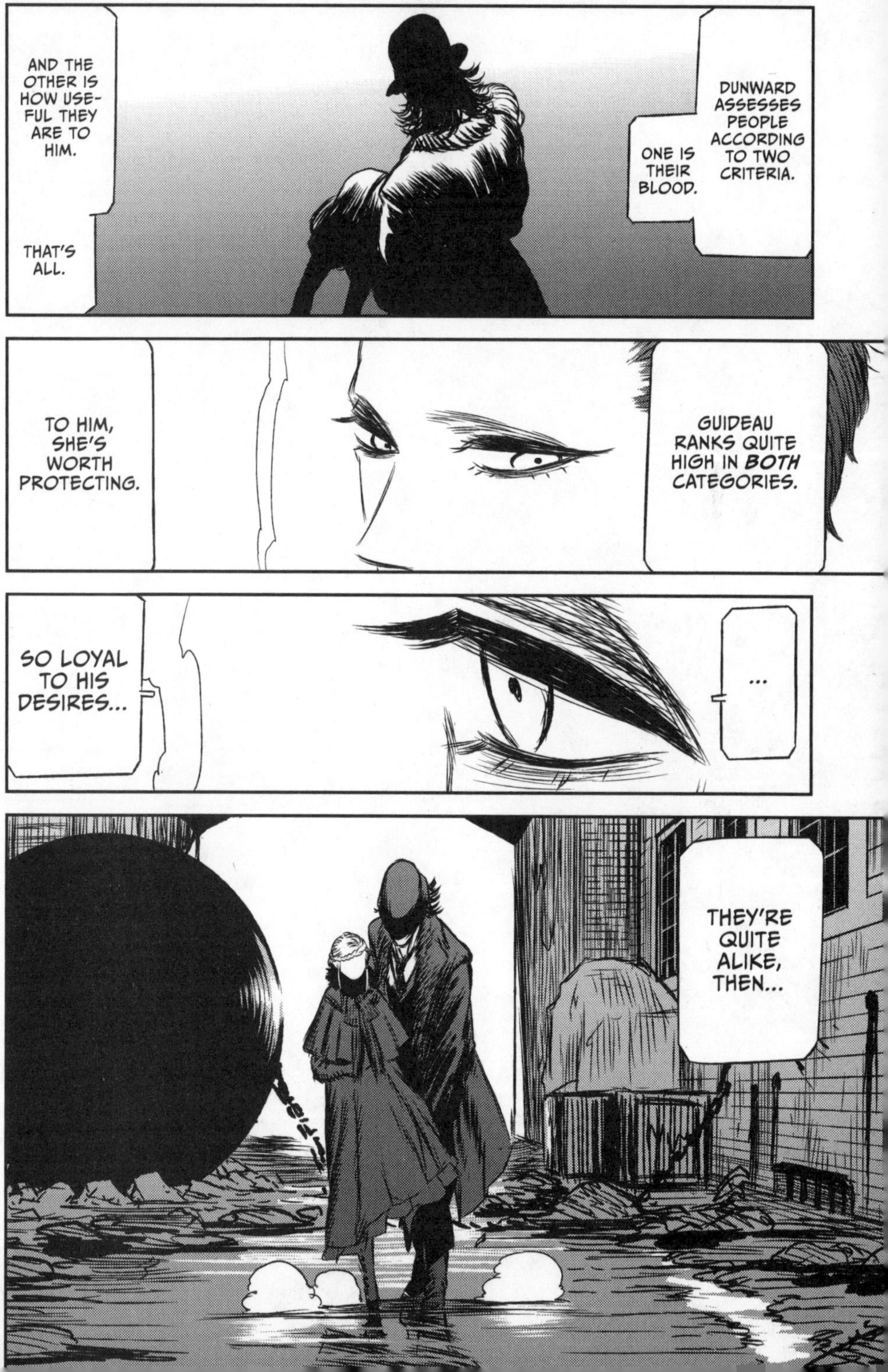
DUNWARD ASSESSES PEOPLE ACCORDING TO TWO CRITERIA.
ONE IS THEIR BLOOD.
AND THE OTHER IS HOW USE-FUL THEY ARE TO HIM.
THAT'S ALL.
GUIDEAU RANKS QUITE HIGH IN *BOTH* CATEGORIES.
TO HIM, SHE'S WORTH PROTECTING.
...
SO LOYAL TO HIS DESIRES...
THEY'RE QUITE ALIKE, THEN...

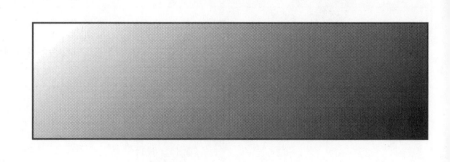

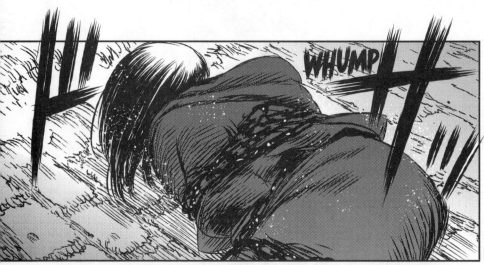

WHUMP

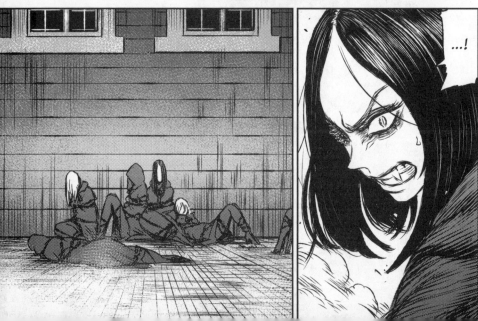

...!

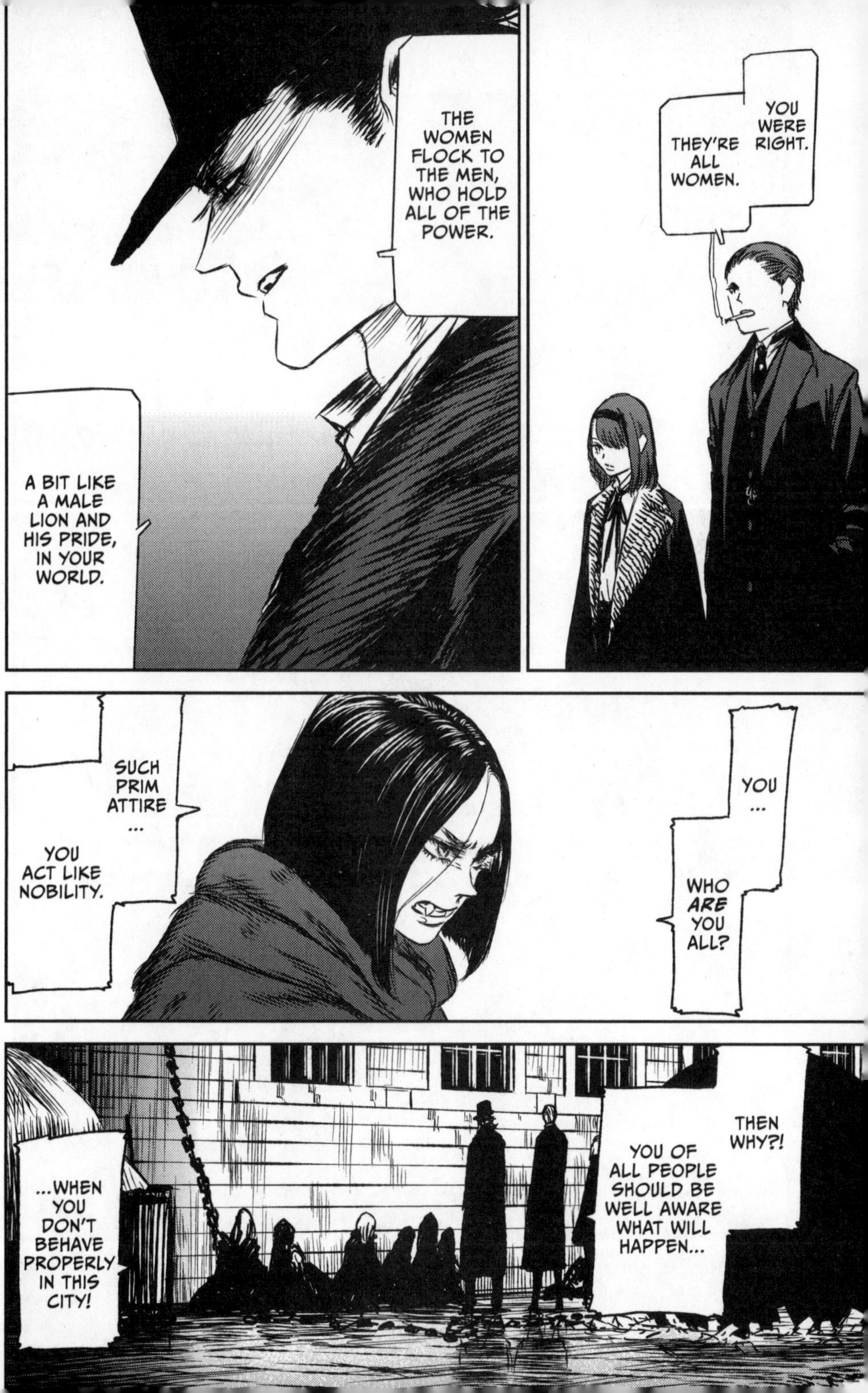
YOU WERE RIGHT.
THEY'RE ALL WOMEN.
THE WOMEN FLOCK TO THE MEN, WHO HOLD ALL OF THE POWER.
A BIT LIKE A MALE LION AND HIS PRIDE, IN YOUR WORLD.
YOU ...
WHO *ARE* YOU ALL?
SUCH PRIM ATTIRE ...
YOU ACT LIKE NOBILITY.
THEN WHY?!
YOU OF ALL PEOPLE SHOULD BE WELL AWARE WHAT WILL HAPPEN...
...WHEN YOU DON'T BEHAVE PROPERLY IN THIS CITY!

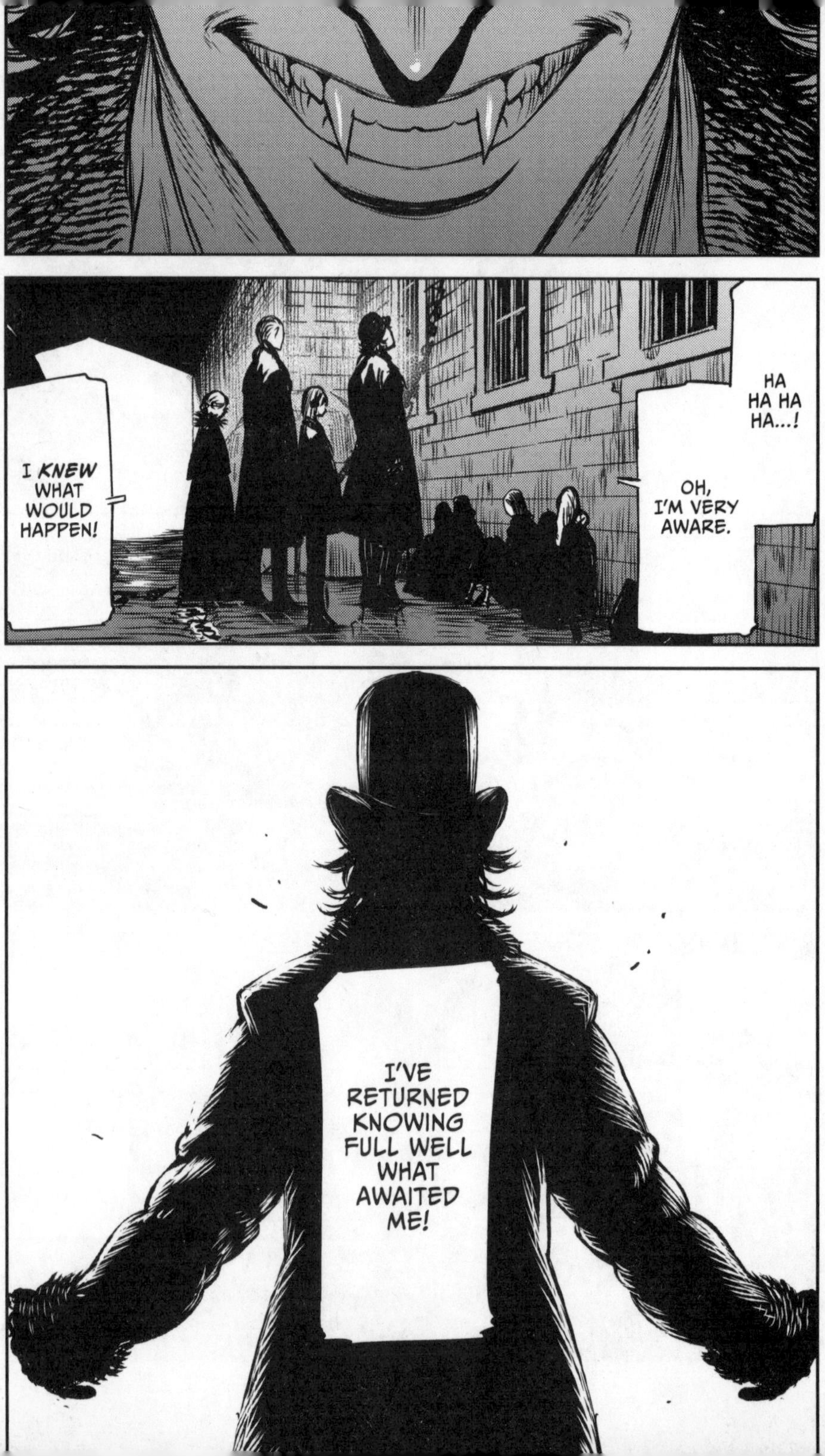
HA HA HA HA...!
OH, I'M VERY AWARE.
I *KNEW* WHAT WOULD HAPPEN!
I'VE RETURNED KNOWING FULL WELL WHAT AWAITED ME!

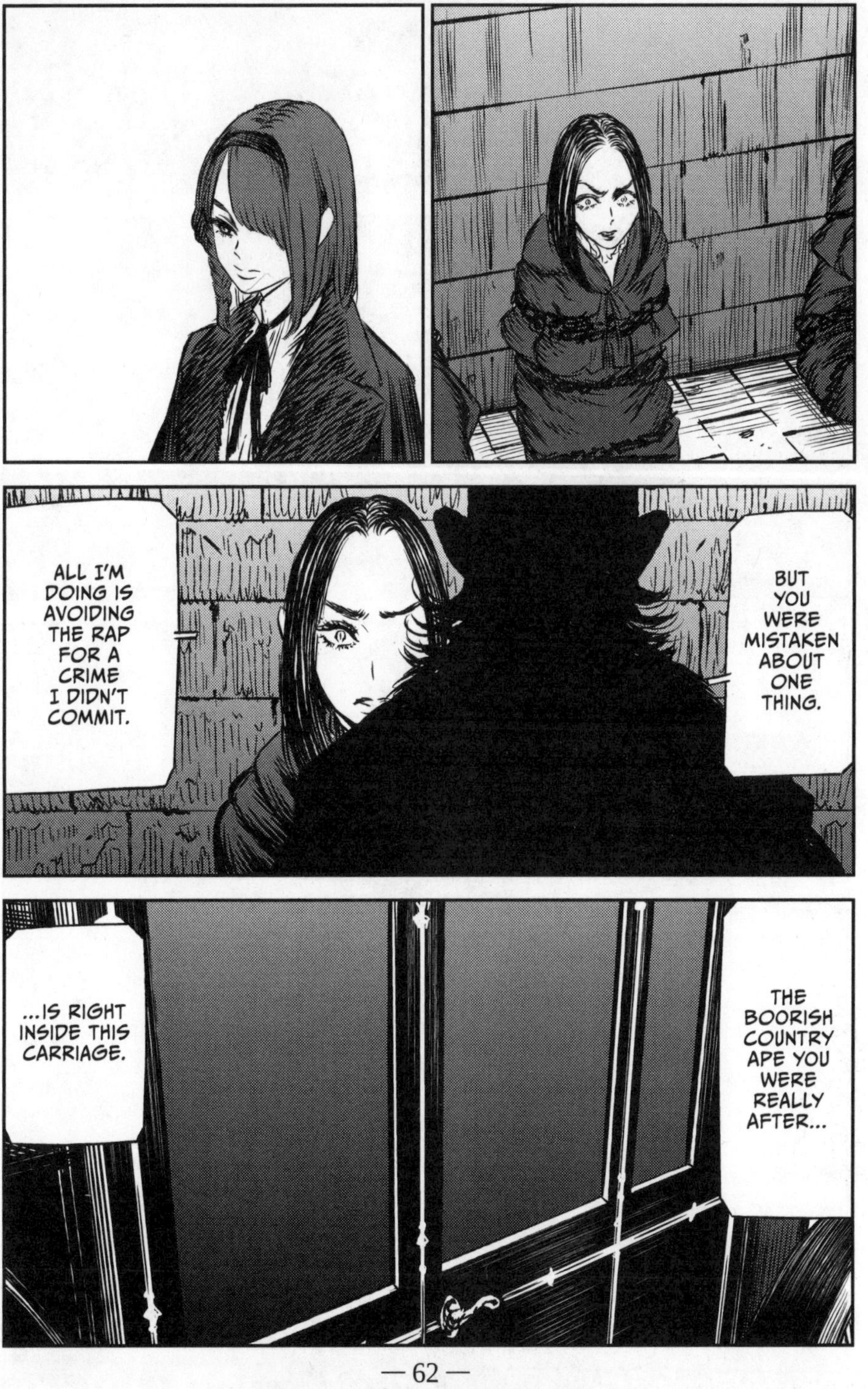
BUT YOU WERE MISTAKEN ABOUT ONE THING.
ALL I'M DOING IS AVOIDING THE RAP FOR A CRIME I DIDN'T COMMIT.
THE BOORISH COUNTRY APE YOU WERE REALLY AFTER...
...IS RIGHT INSIDE THIS CARRIAGE.

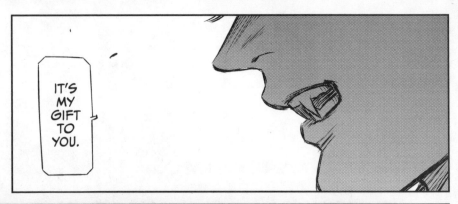

IT'S MY GIFT TO YOU.

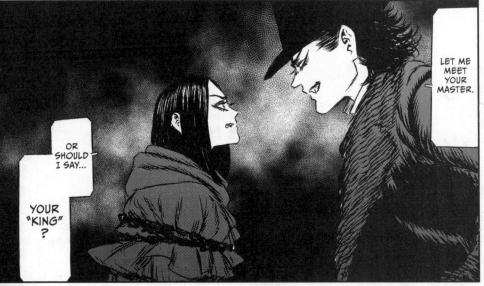

LET ME MEET YOUR MASTER.

OR SHOULD I SAY...

YOUR "KING"?

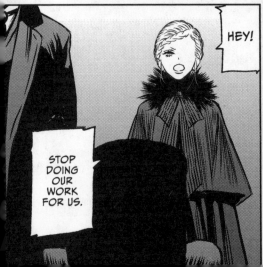

HEY!

STOP DOING OUR WORK FOR US.

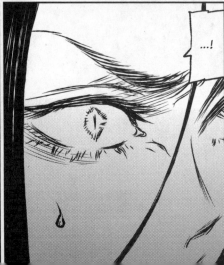

...!

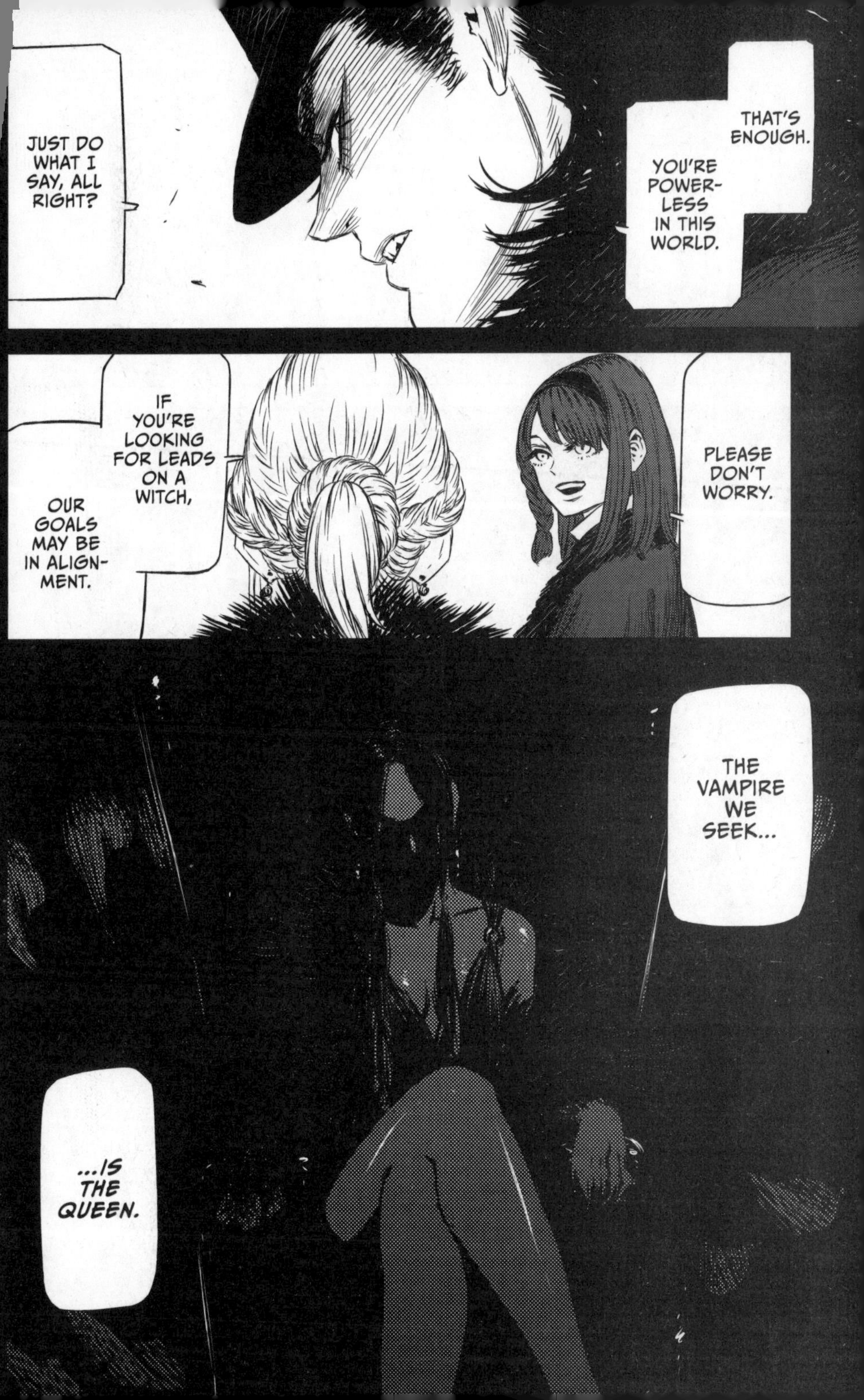
THAT'S ENOUGH.
YOU'RE POWER-LESS IN THIS WORLD.
JUST DO WHAT I SAY, ALL RIGHT?
PLEASE DON'T WORRY.
IF YOU'RE LOOKING FOR LEADS ON A WITCH,
OUR GOALS MAY BE IN ALIGN-MENT.
THE VAMPIRE WE SEEK...
...IS THE QUEEN.

# THE WITCH AND THE BEAST

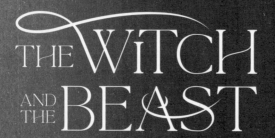

THE WITCH AND THE BEAST

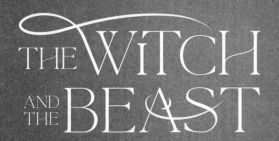

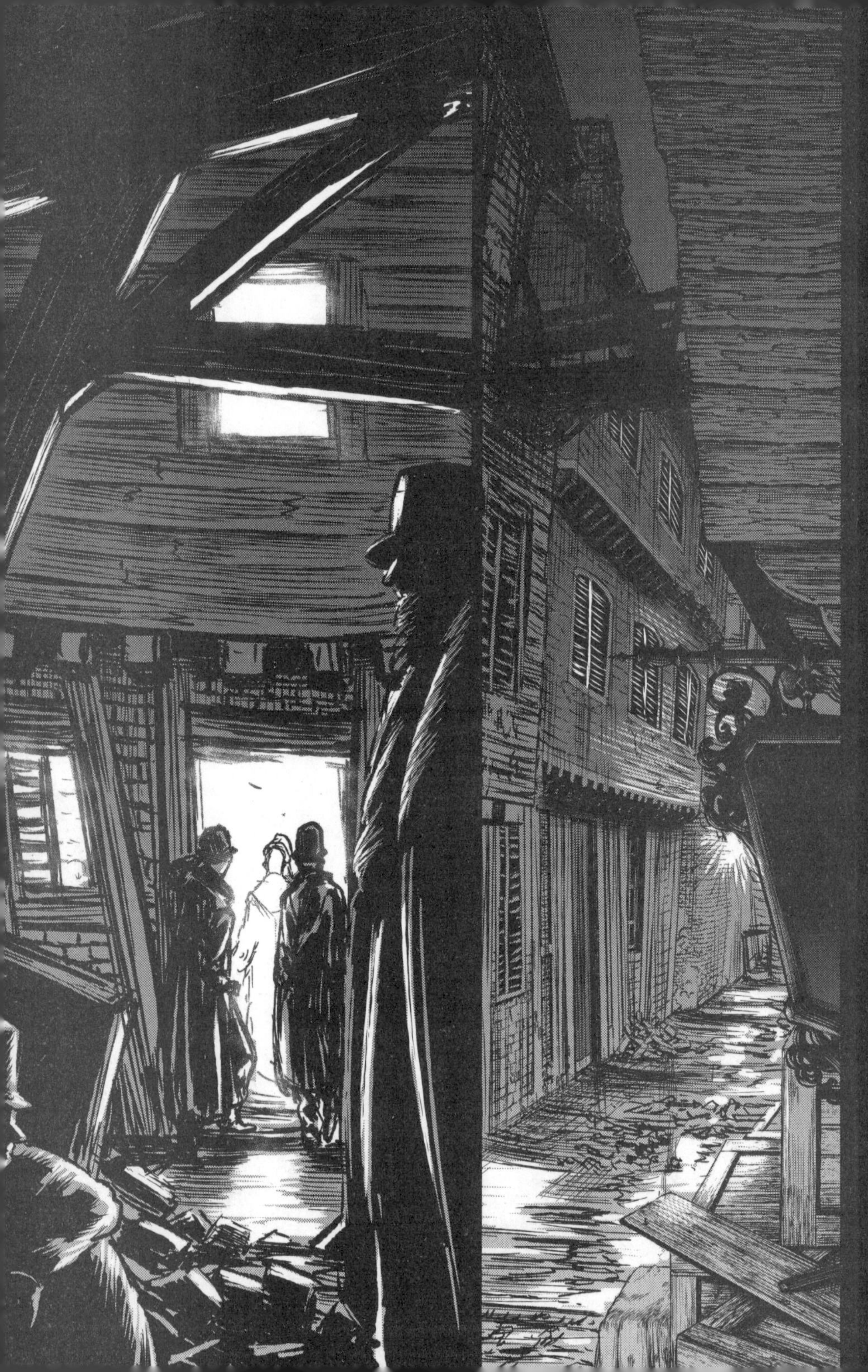

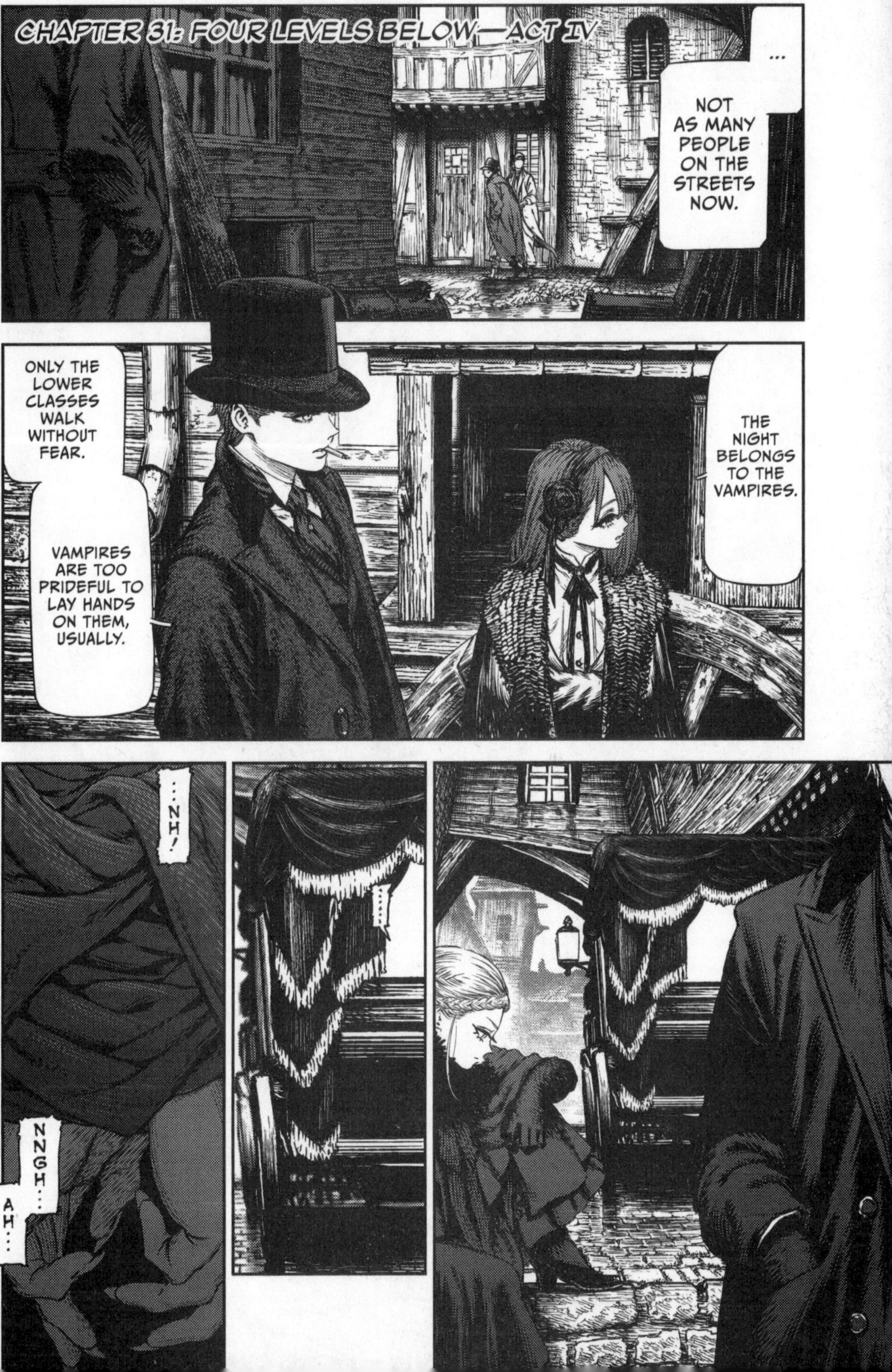
CHAPTER 31: FOUR LEVELS BELOW—ACT IV
...
NOT AS MANY PEOPLE ON THE STREETS NOW.
THE NIGHT BELONGS TO THE VAMPIRES.
ONLY THE LOWER CLASSES WALK WITHOUT FEAR.
VAMPIRES ARE TOO PRIDEFUL TO LAY HANDS ON THEM, USUALLY.
......
...NH!
NNGH...
AH...

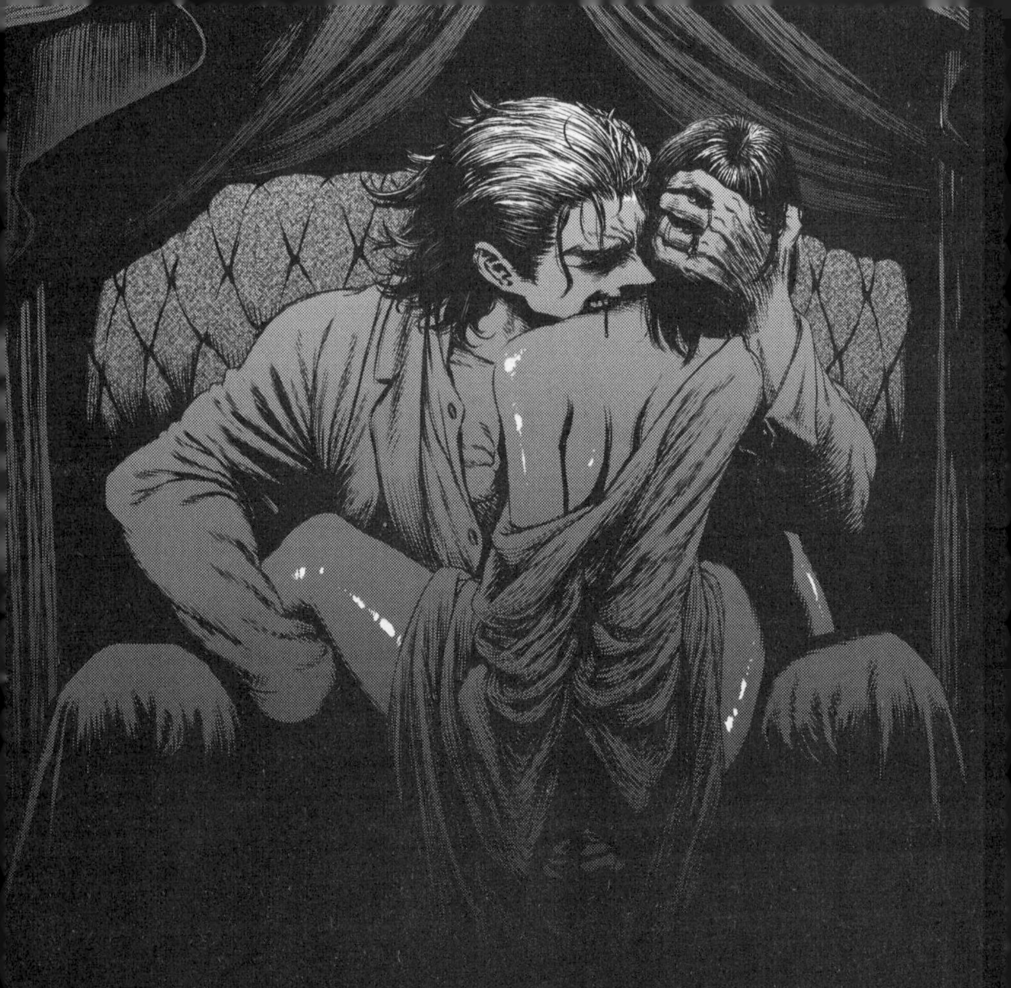

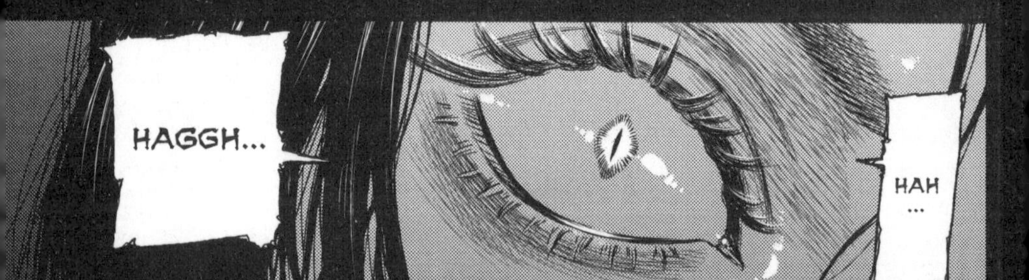
HAH
...
HAGGH...

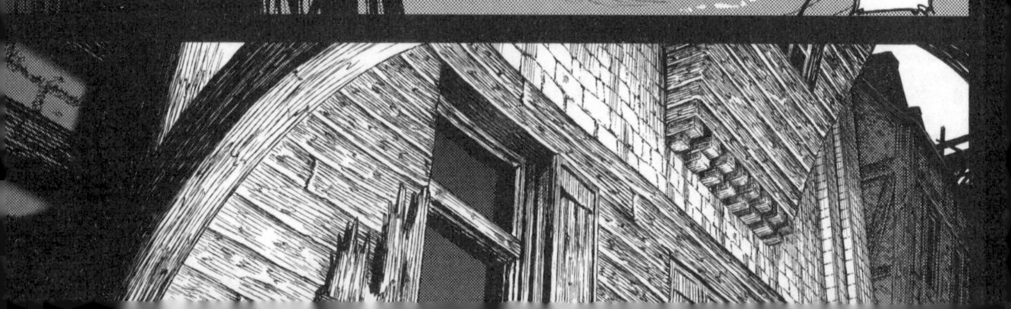

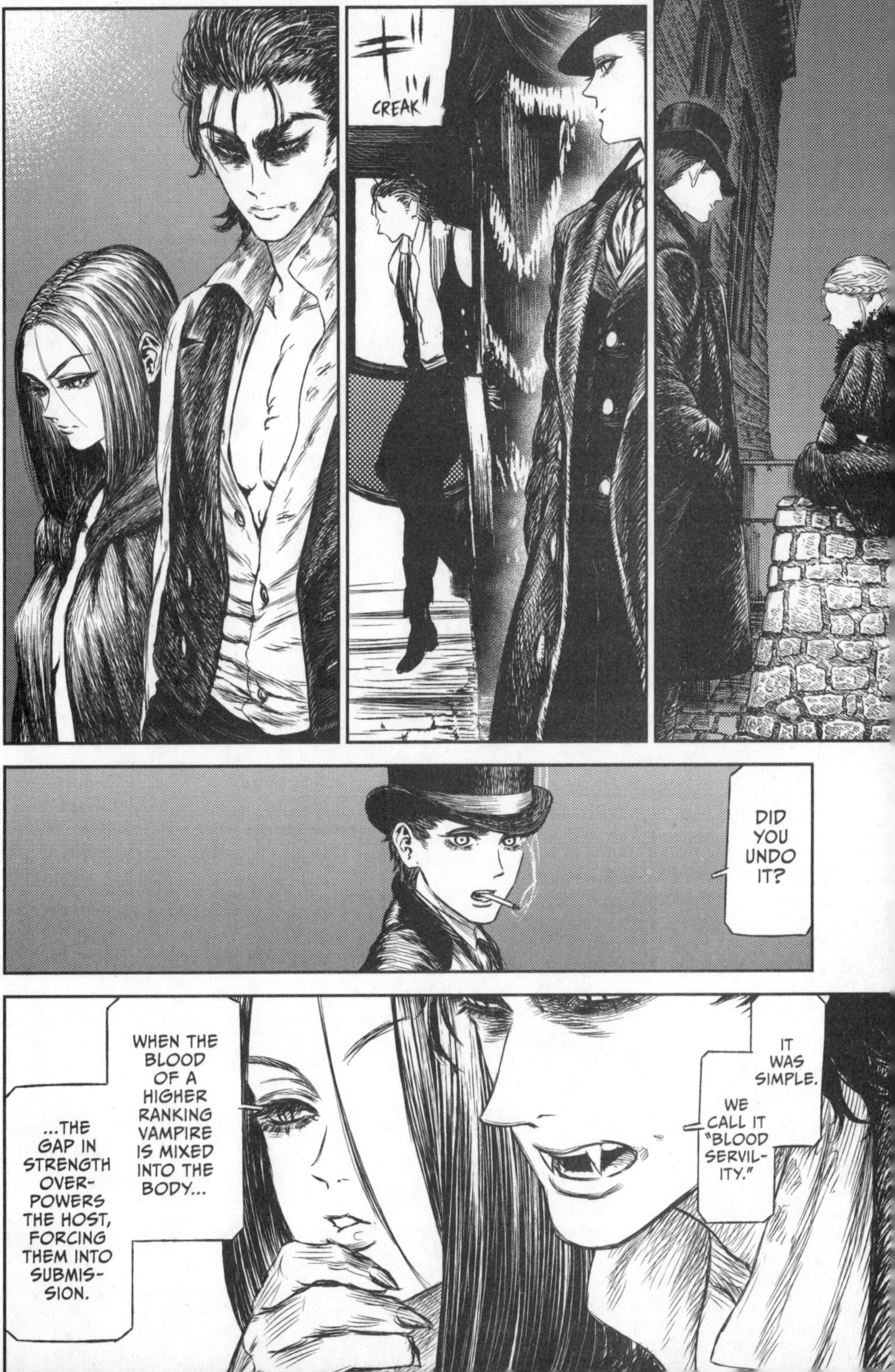
CREAK
DID YOU UNDO IT?
IT WAS SIMPLE.
WE CALL IT "BLOOD SERVILITY."
WHEN THE BLOOD OF A HIGHER RANKING VAMPIRE IS MIXED INTO THE BODY...
...THE GAP IN STRENGTH OVERPOWERS THE HOST, FORCING THEM INTO SUBMISSION.

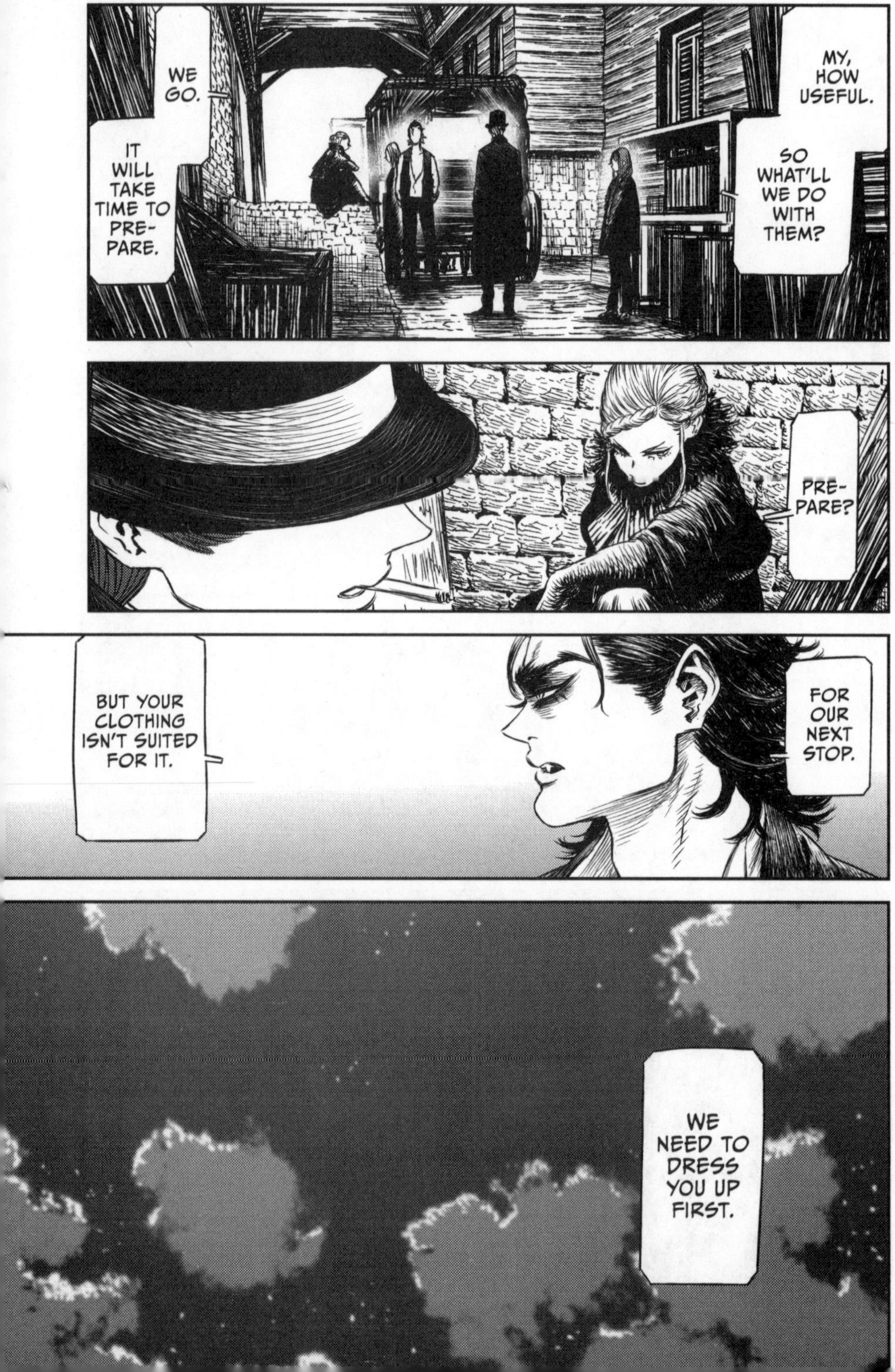
MY, HOW USEFUL.
SO WHAT'LL WE DO WITH THEM?
WE GO.
IT WILL TAKE TIME TO PRE-PARE.
PRE-PARE?
FOR OUR NEXT STOP.
BUT YOUR CLOTHING ISN'T SUITED FOR IT.
WE NEED TO DRESS YOU UP FIRST.

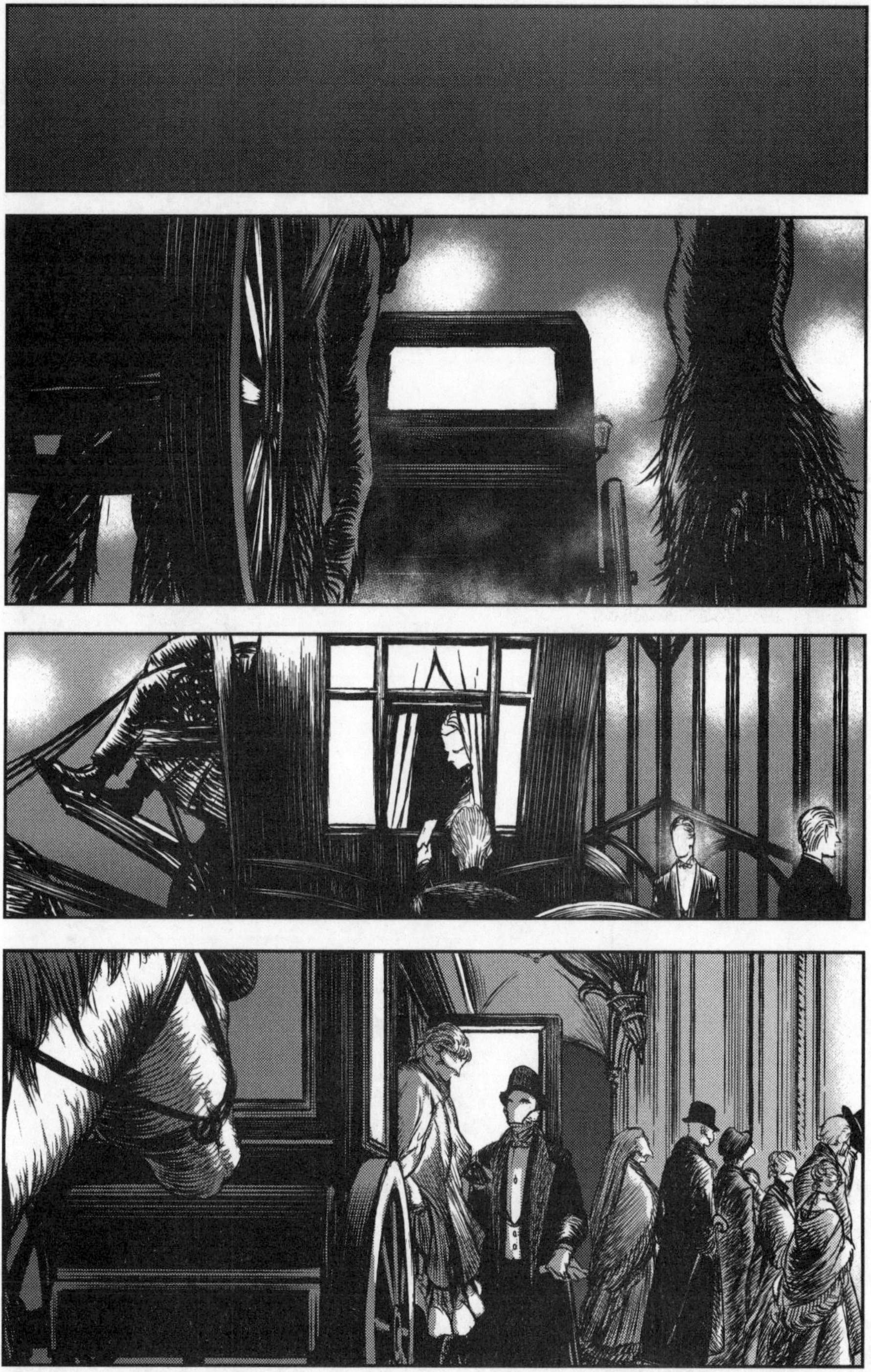

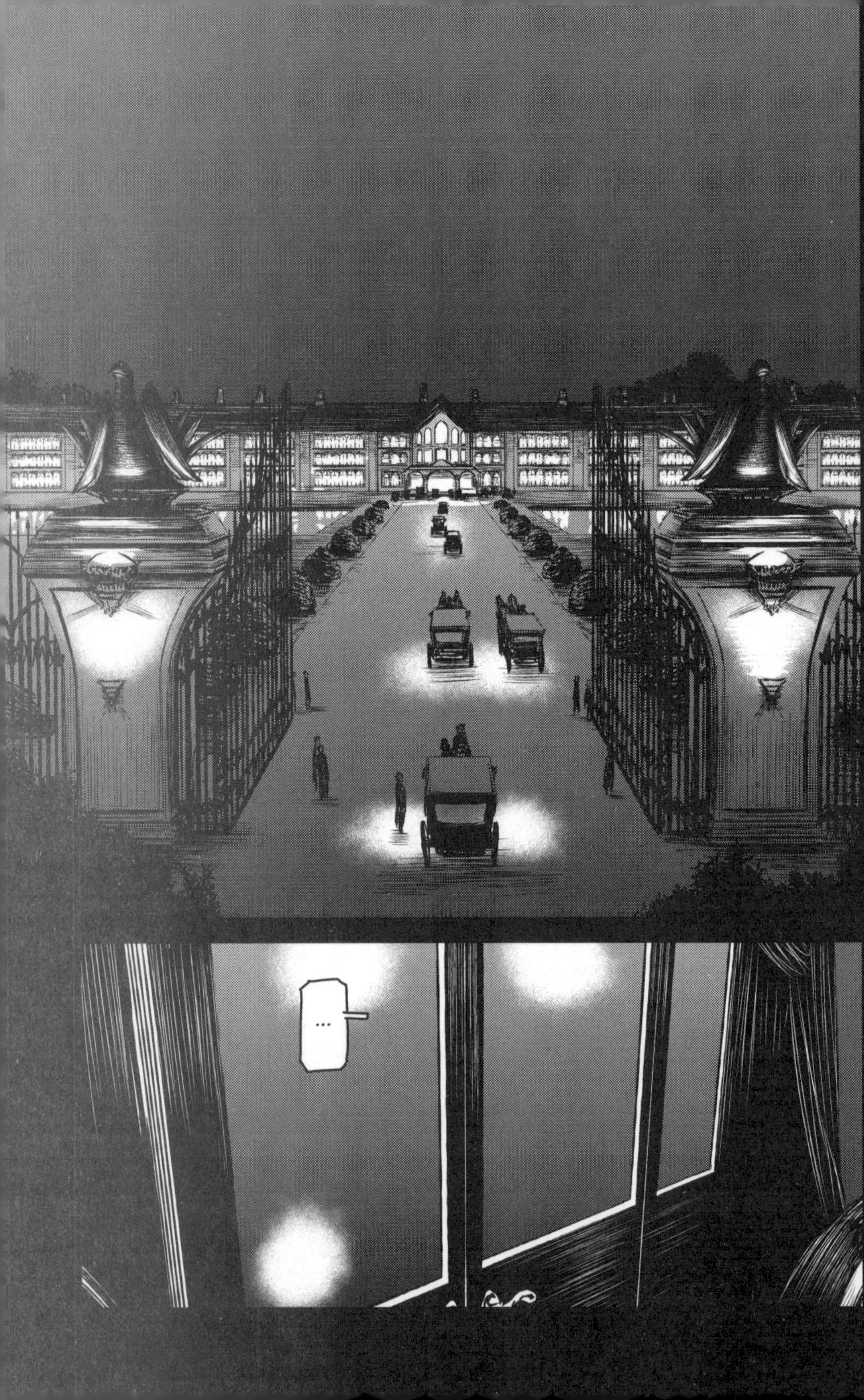
...

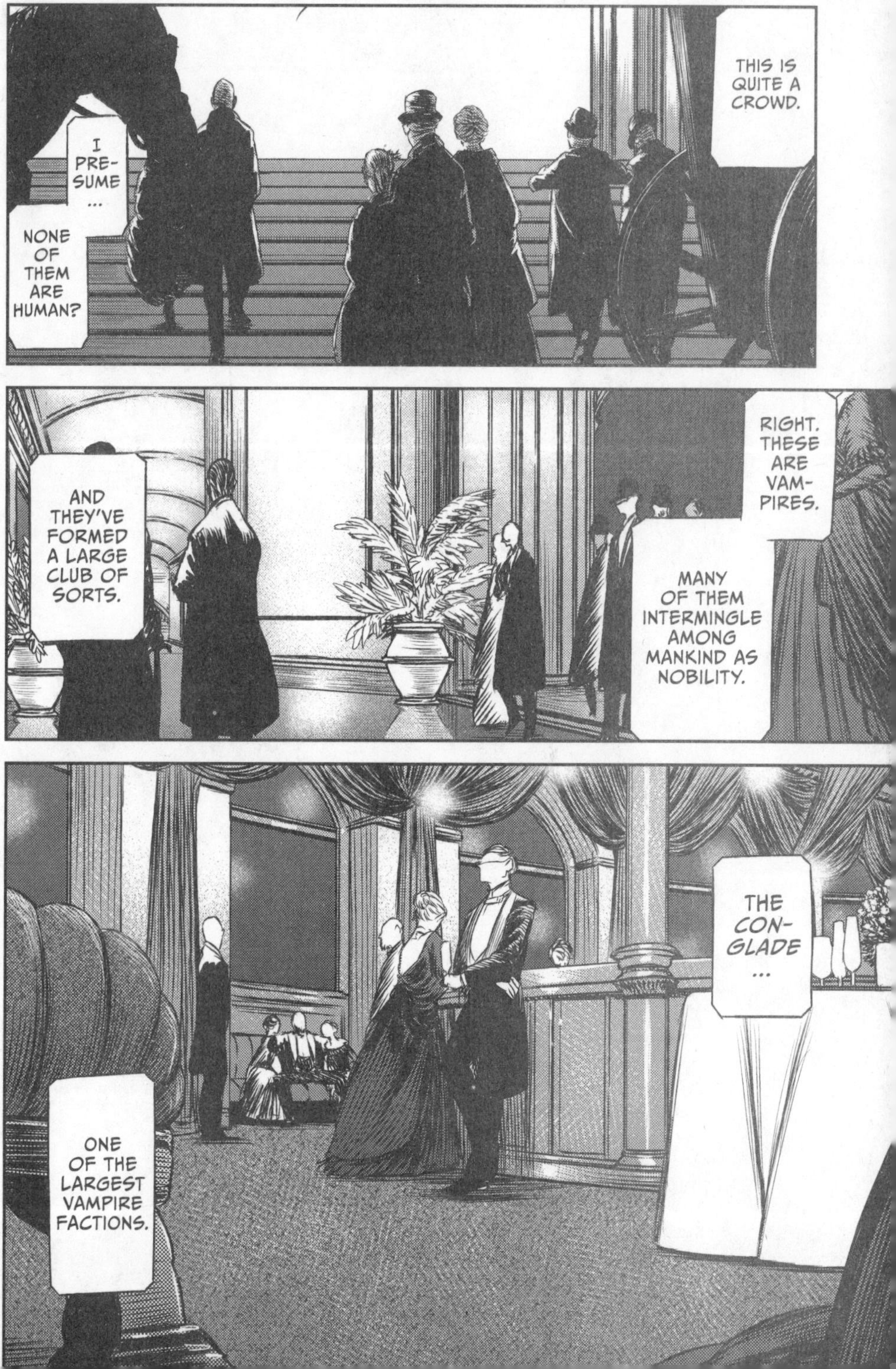
THIS IS QUITE A CROWD.
I PRESUME...
NONE OF THEM ARE HUMAN?
RIGHT. THESE ARE VAMPIRES.
MANY OF THEM INTERMINGLE AMONG MANKIND AS NOBILITY.
AND THEY'VE FORMED A LARGE CLUB OF SORTS.
THE CONGLADE...
ONE OF THE LARGEST VAMPIRE FACTIONS.

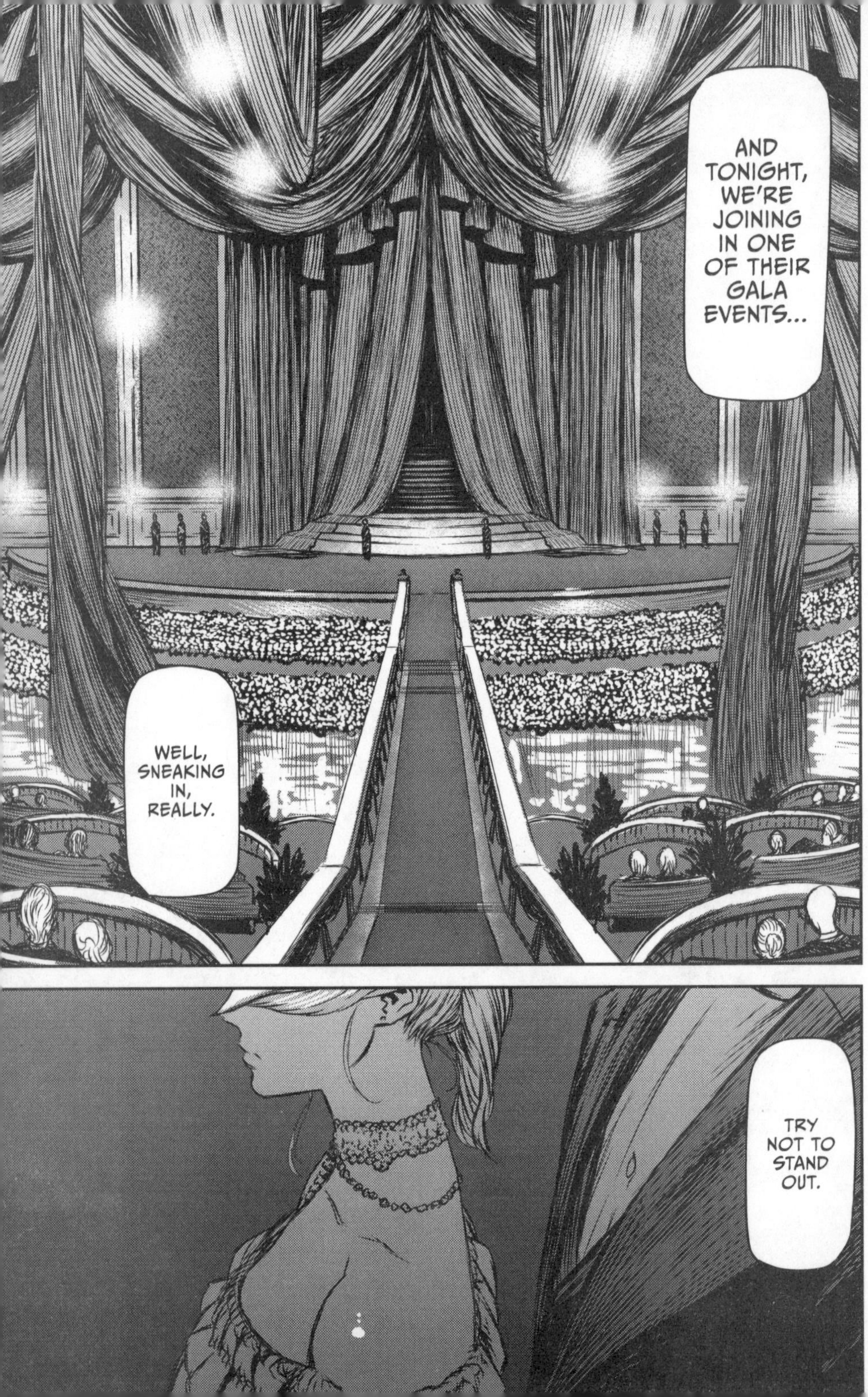
AND TONIGHT, WE'RE JOINING IN ONE OF THEIR GALA EVENTS...
WELL, SNEAKING IN, REALLY.
TRY NOT TO STAND OUT.

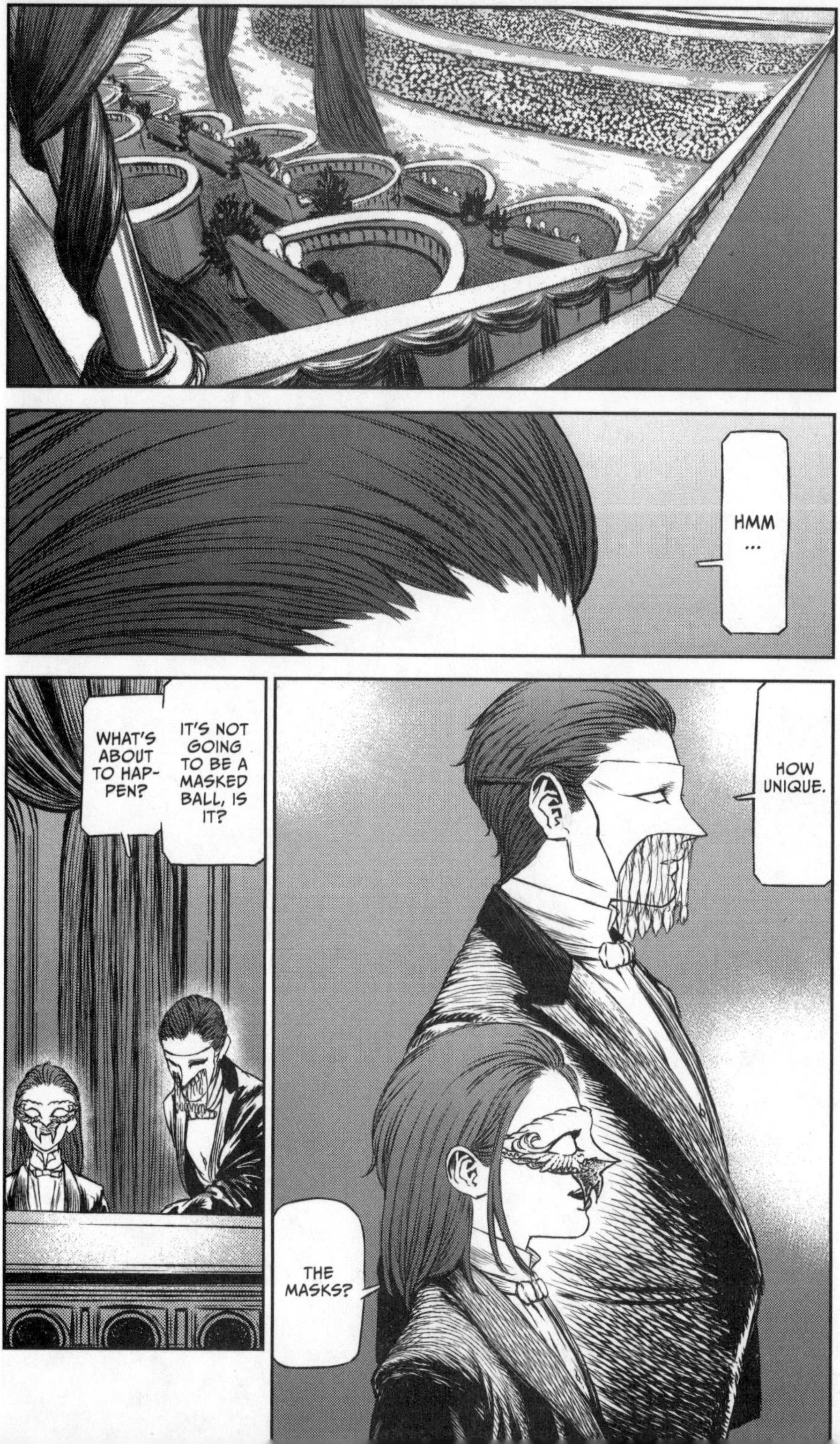
HMM ...
HOW UNIQUE.
THE MASKS?
IT'S NOT GOING TO BE A MASKED BALL, IS IT?
WHAT'S ABOUT TO HAP-PEN?

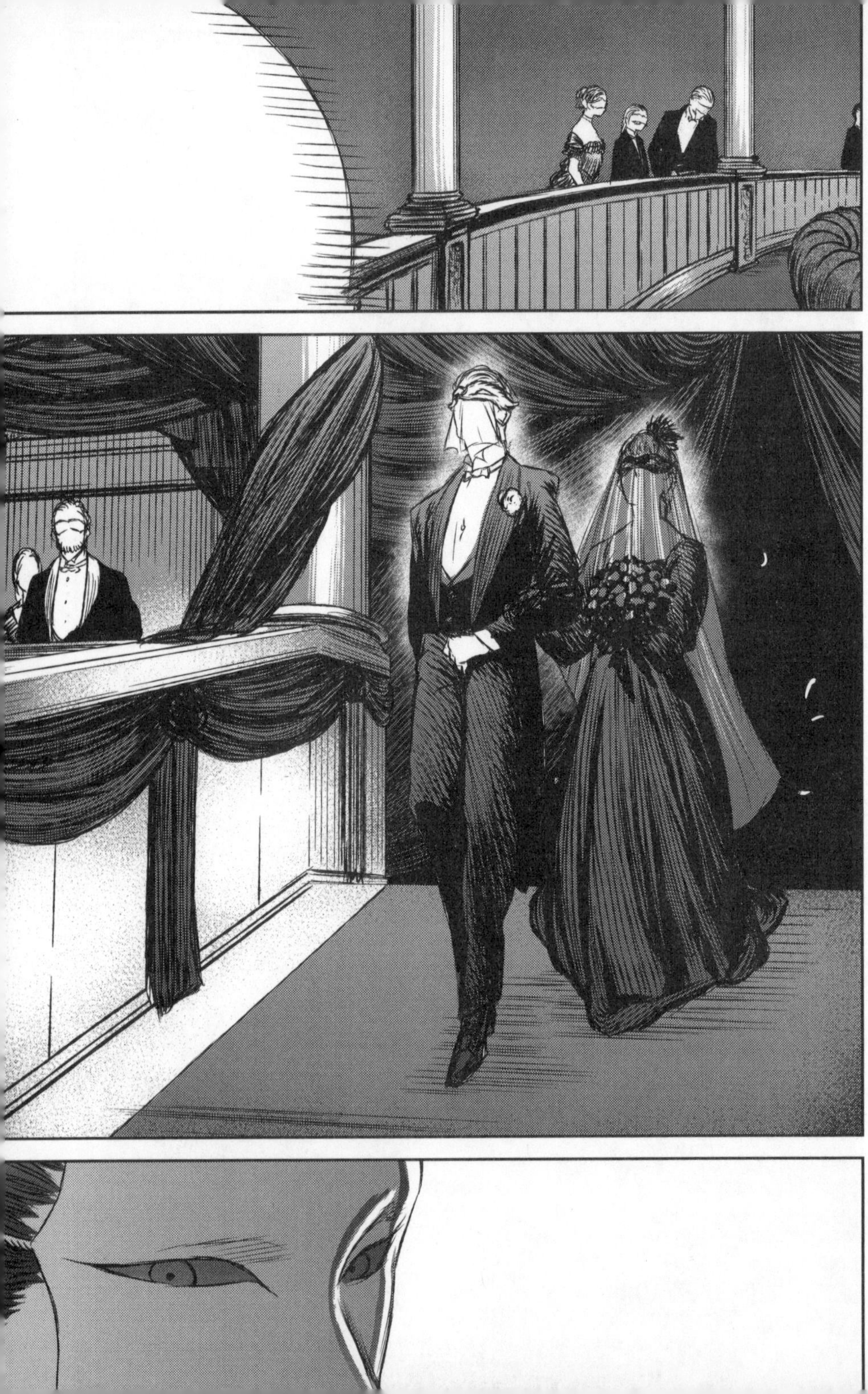

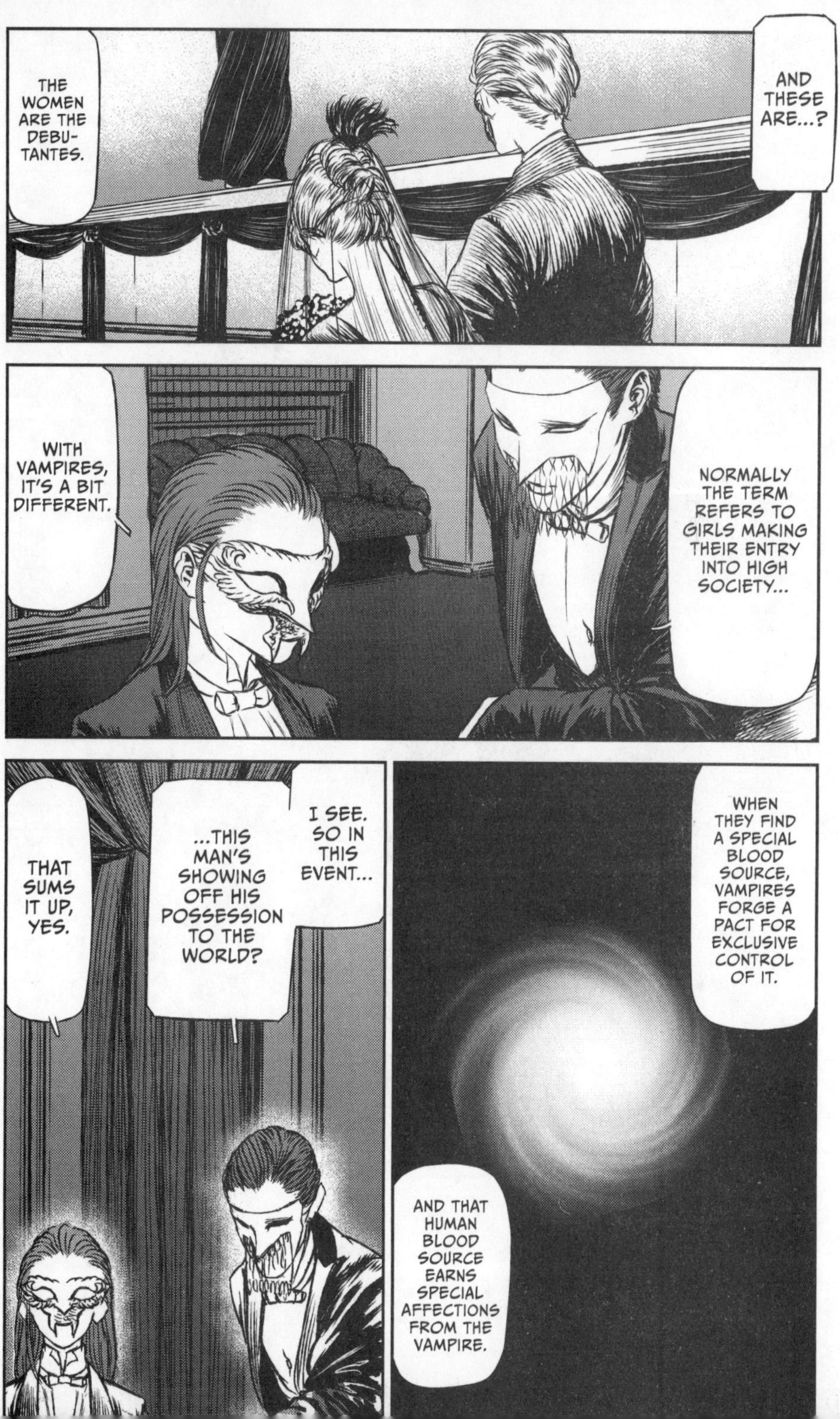
AND THESE ARE...?
THE WOMEN ARE THE DEBU-TANTES.
NORMALLY THE TERM REFERS TO GIRLS MAKING THEIR ENTRY INTO HIGH SOCIETY...
WITH VAMPIRES, IT'S A BIT DIFFERENT.
WHEN THEY FIND A SPECIAL BLOOD SOURCE, VAMPIRES FORGE A PACT FOR EXCLUSIVE CONTROL OF IT.
AND THAT HUMAN BLOOD SOURCE EARNS SPECIAL AFFECTIONS FROM THE VAMPIRE.
I SEE. SO IN THIS EVENT...
...THIS MAN'S SHOWING OFF HIS POSSESSION TO THE WORLD?
THAT SUMS IT UP, YES.

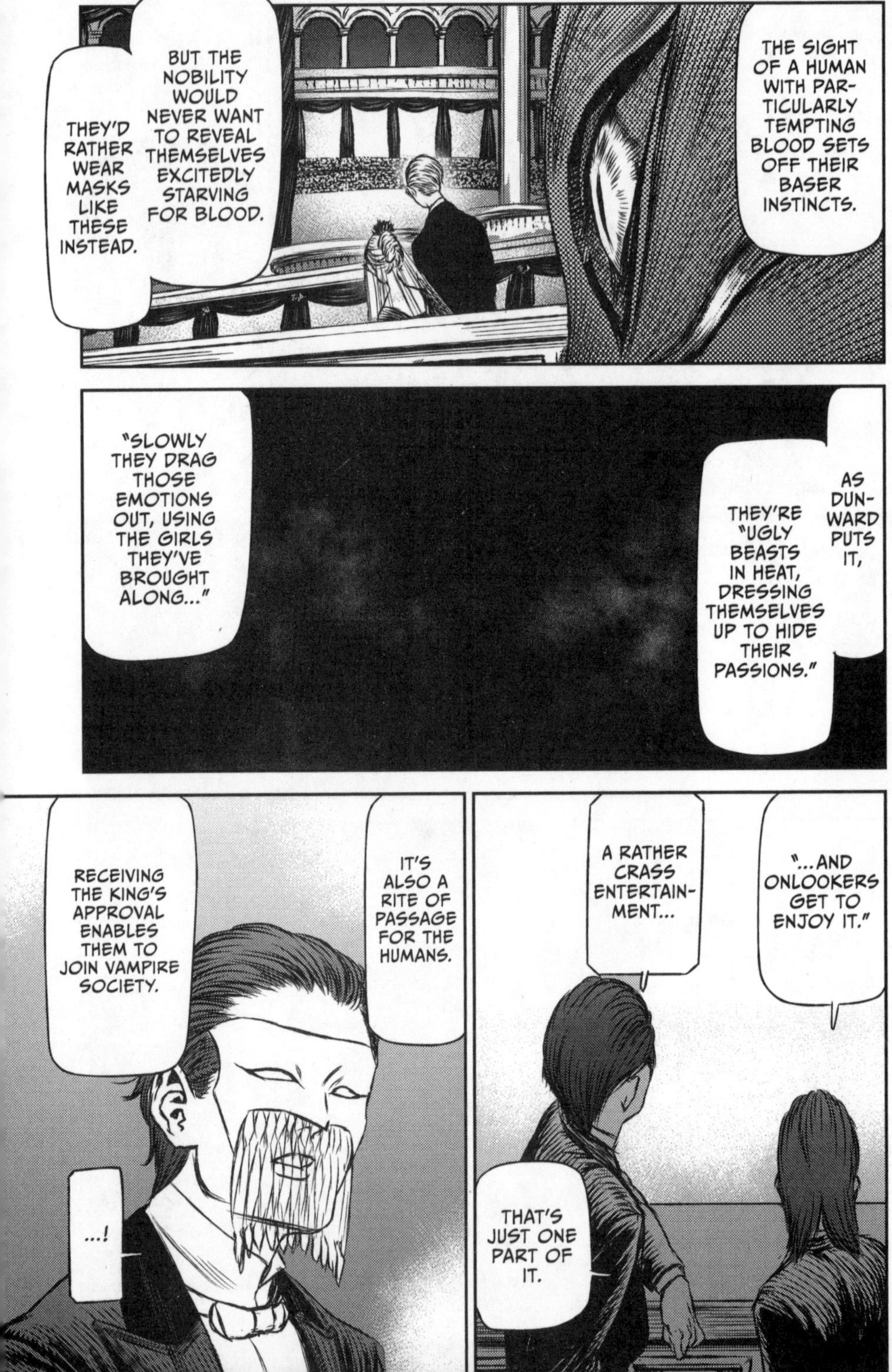
THE SIGHT OF A HUMAN WITH PARTICULARLY TEMPTING BLOOD SETS OFF THEIR BASER INSTINCTS.
BUT THE NOBILITY WOULD NEVER WANT TO REVEAL THEMSELVES EXCITEDLY STARVING FOR BLOOD.
THEY'D RATHER WEAR MASKS LIKE THESE INSTEAD.
AS DUNWARD PUTS IT,
THEY'RE "UGLY BEASTS IN HEAT, DRESSING THEMSELVES UP TO HIDE THEIR PASSIONS."
"SLOWLY THEY DRAG THOSE EMOTIONS OUT, USING THE GIRLS THEY'VE BROUGHT ALONG..."
"...AND ONLOOKERS GET TO ENJOY IT."
A RATHER CRASS ENTERTAINMENT...
THAT'S JUST ONE PART OF IT.
IT'S ALSO A RITE OF PASSAGE FOR THE HUMANS.
RECEIVING THE KING'S APPROVAL ENABLES THEM TO JOIN VAMPIRE SOCIETY.
...!

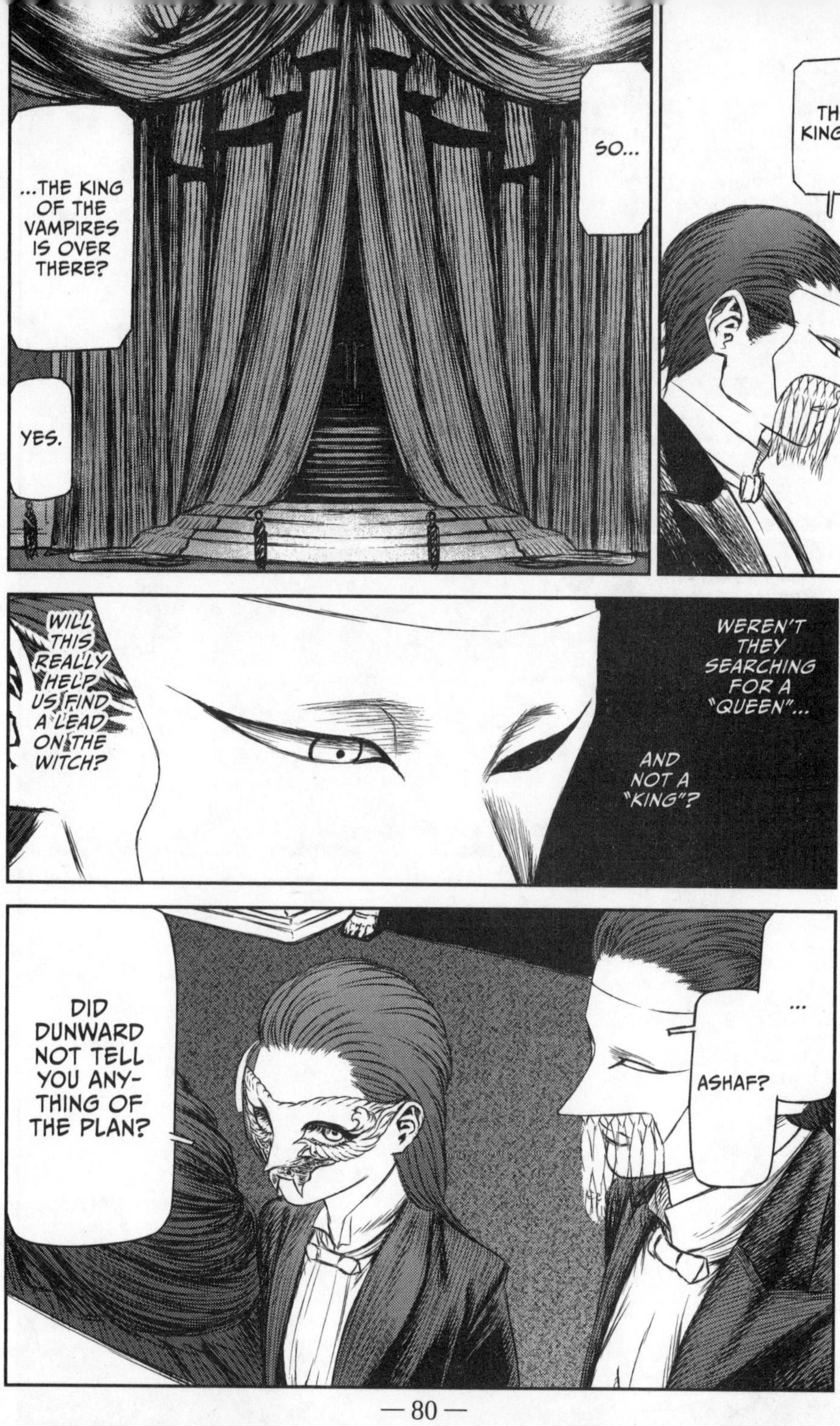
THE KING...!
SO...
...THE KING OF THE VAMPIRES IS OVER THERE?
YES.
WEREN'T THEY SEARCHING FOR A "QUEEN"...
AND NOT A "KING"?
WILL THIS REALLY HELP US FIND A LEAD ON THE WITCH?
... ASHAF?
DID DUNWARD NOT TELL YOU ANY-THING OF THE PLAN?

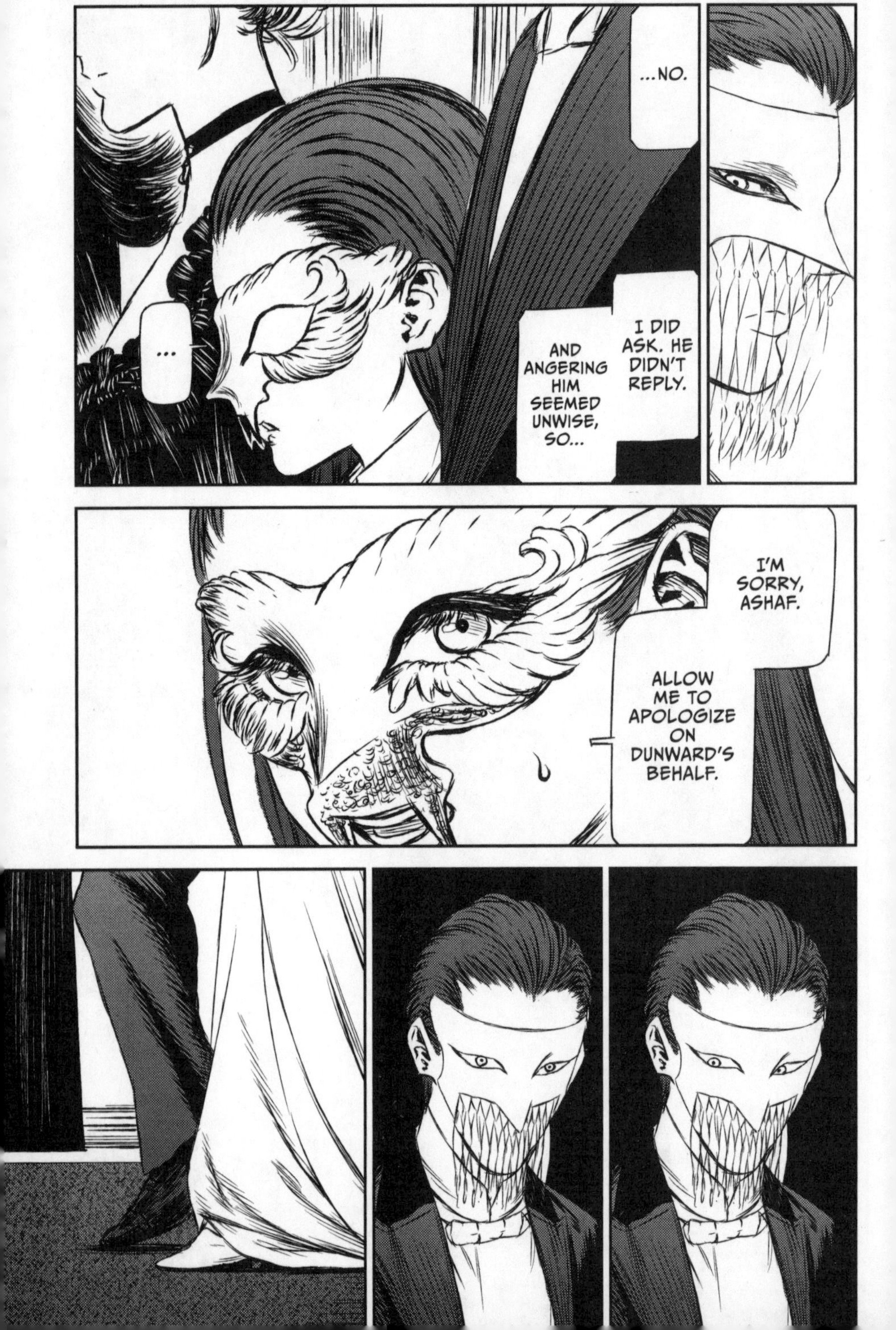
...NO.
I DID ASK. HE DIDN'T REPLY.
AND ANGERING HIM SEEMED UNWISE, SO...
...
I'M SORRY, ASHAF.
ALLOW ME TO APOLOGIZE ON DUNWARD'S BEHALF.

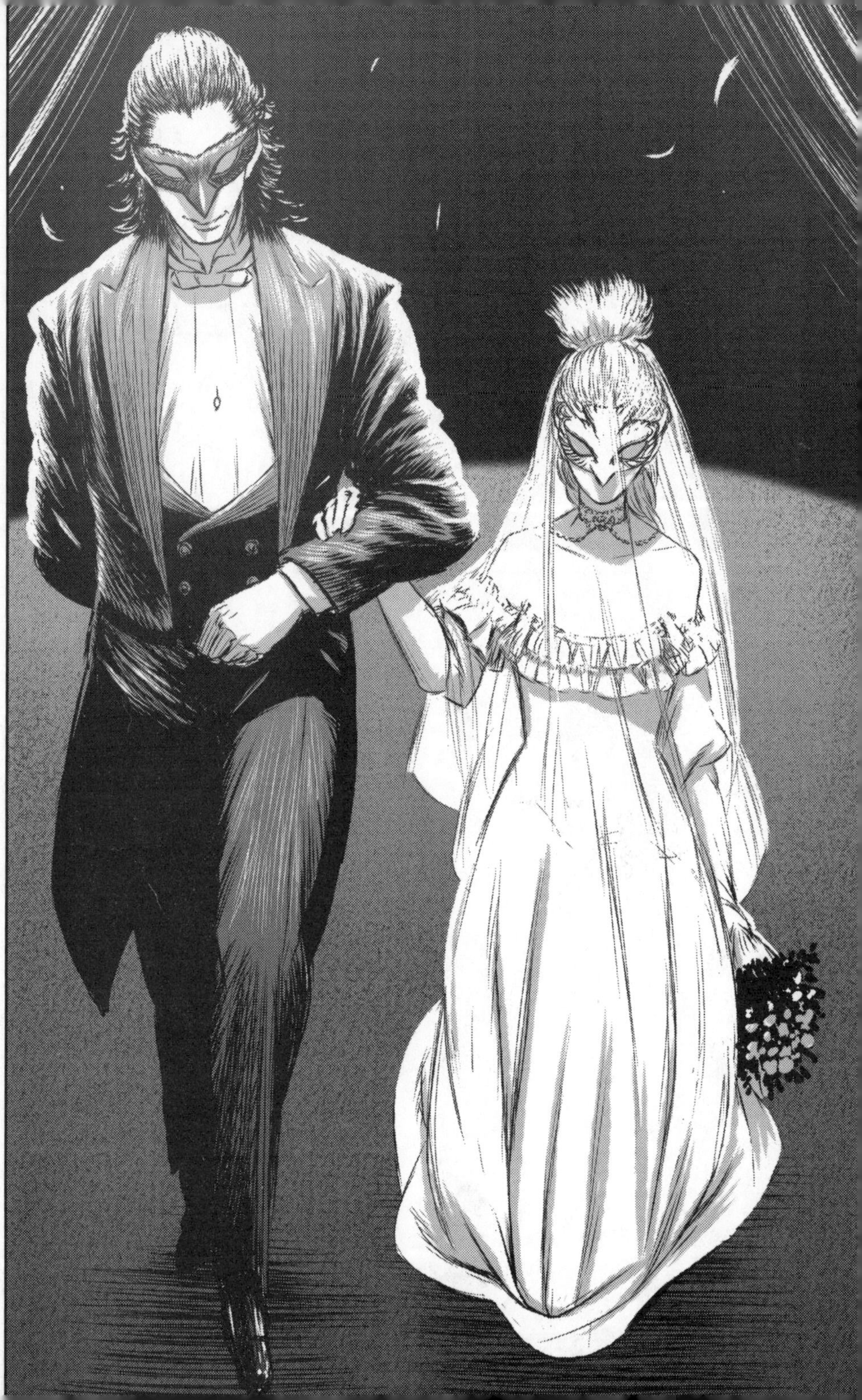

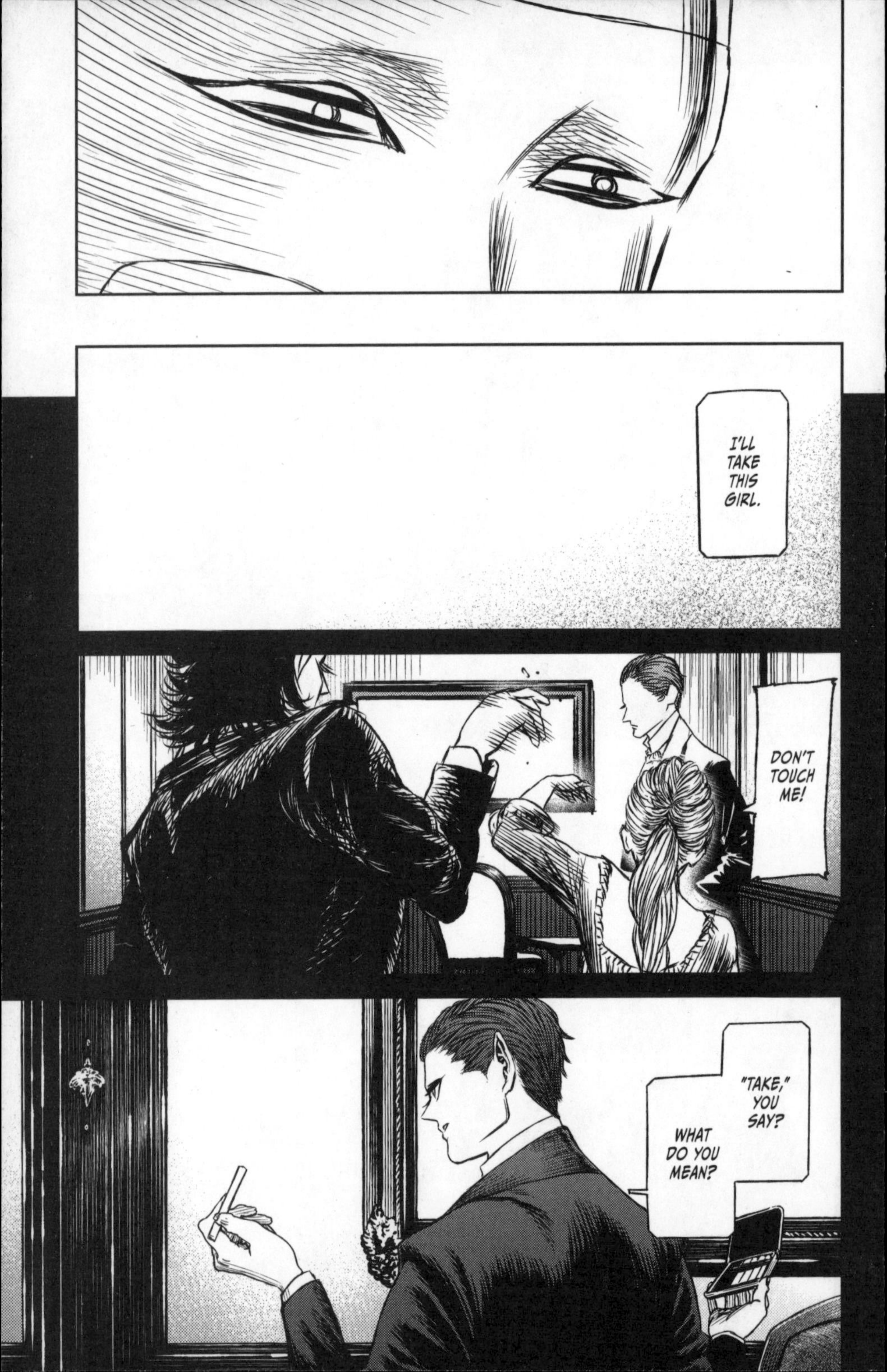
I'LL TAKE THIS GIRL.
DON'T TOUCH ME!
"TAKE," YOU SAY?
WHAT DO YOU MEAN?

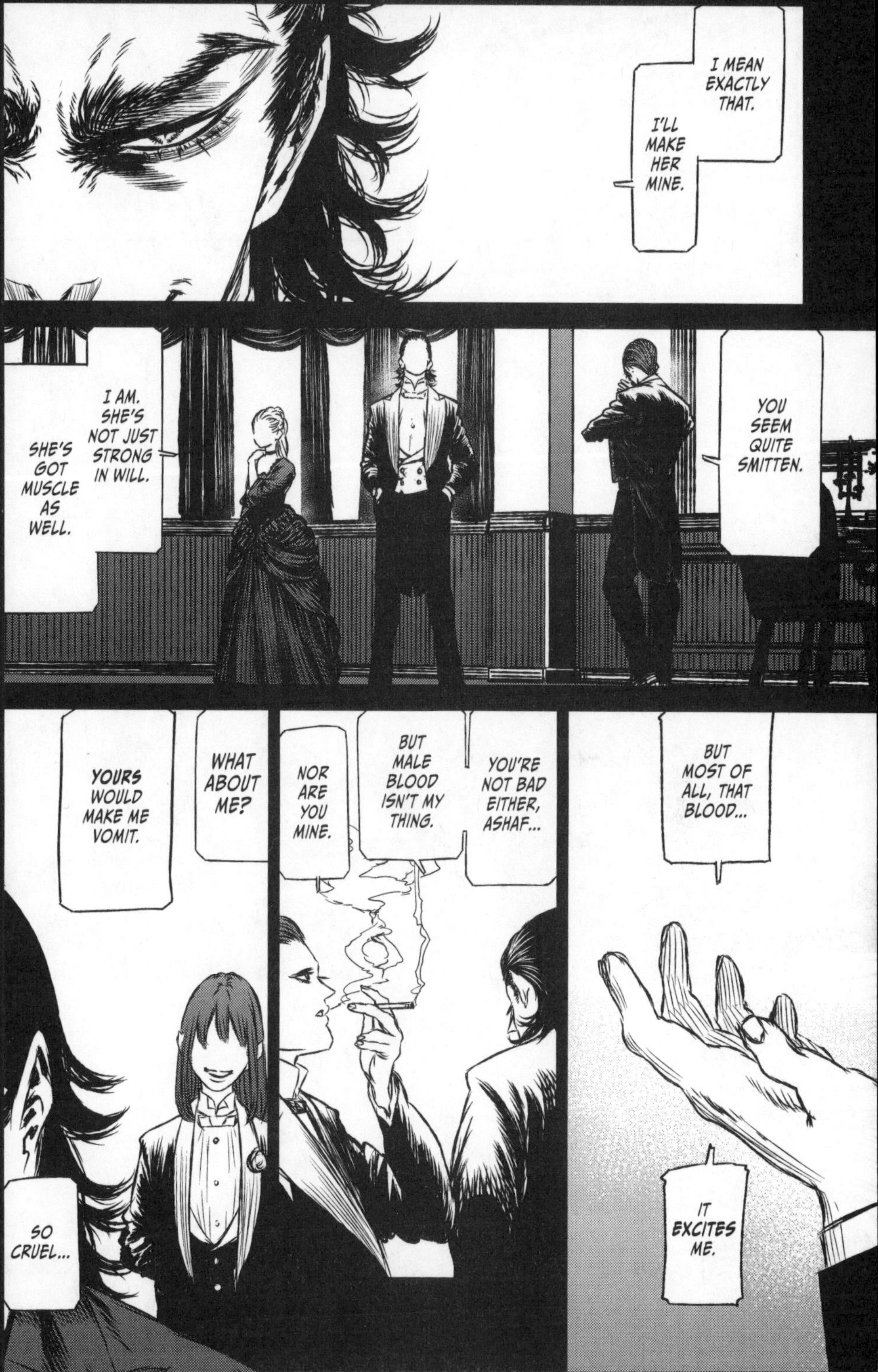
I MEAN EXACTLY THAT.
I'LL MAKE HER MINE.
YOU SEEM QUITE SMITTEN.
I AM. SHE'S NOT JUST STRONG IN WILL.
SHE'S GOT MUSCLE AS WELL.
BUT MOST OF ALL, THAT BLOOD...
IT EXCITES ME.
YOU'RE NOT BAD EITHER, ASHAF...
BUT MALE BLOOD ISN'T MY THING.
NOR ARE YOU MINE.
WHAT ABOUT ME?
YOURS WOULD MAKE ME VOMIT.
SO CRUEL...

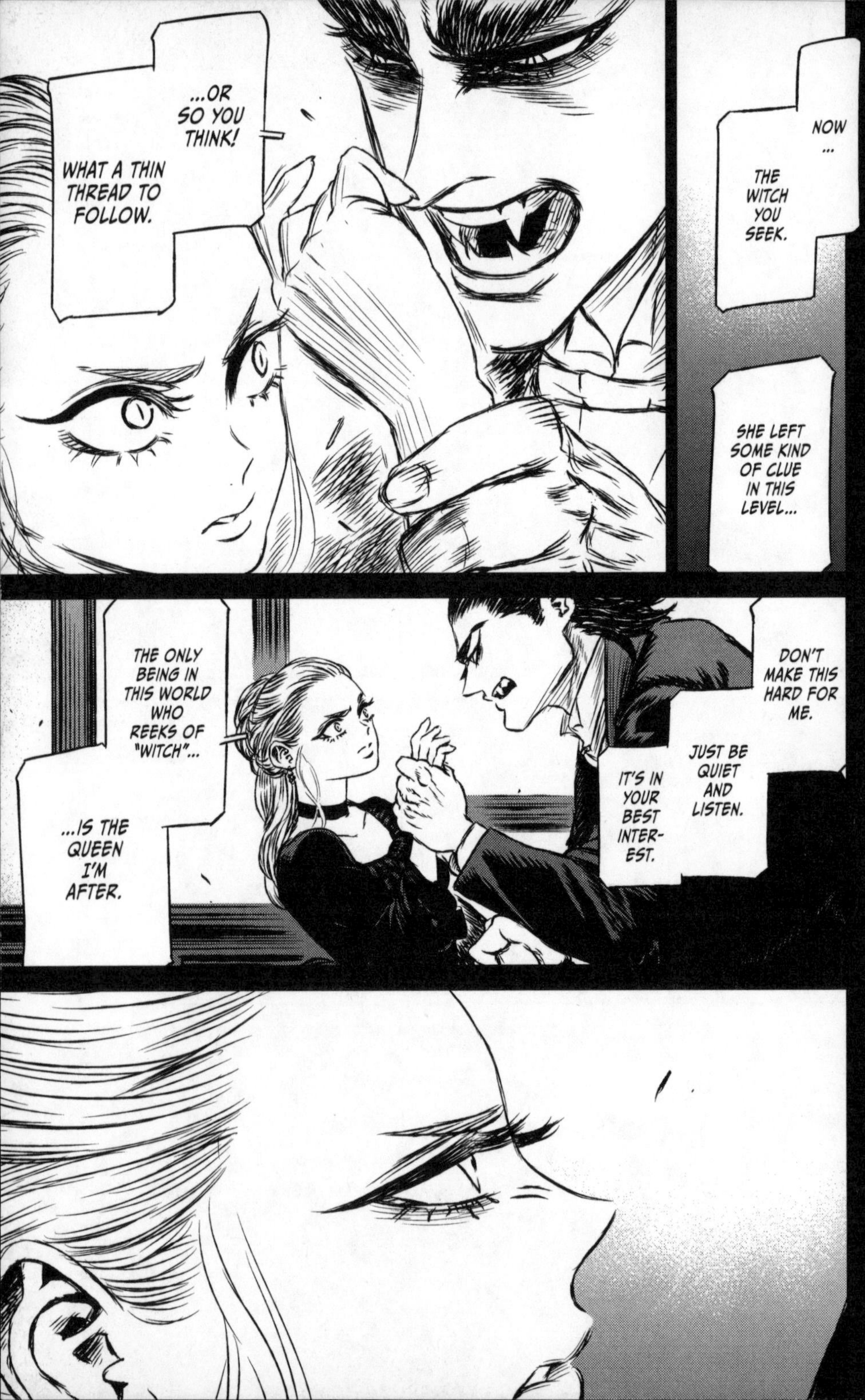
NOW ... THE WITCH YOU SEEK.
SHE LEFT SOME KIND OF CLUE IN THIS LEVEL...
...OR SO YOU THINK!
WHAT A THIN THREAD TO FOLLOW.
DON'T MAKE THIS HARD FOR ME.
JUST BE QUIET AND LISTEN.
IT'S IN YOUR BEST INTER-EST.
THE ONLY BEING IN THIS WORLD WHO REEKS OF "WITCH"...
...IS THE QUEEN I'M AFTER.

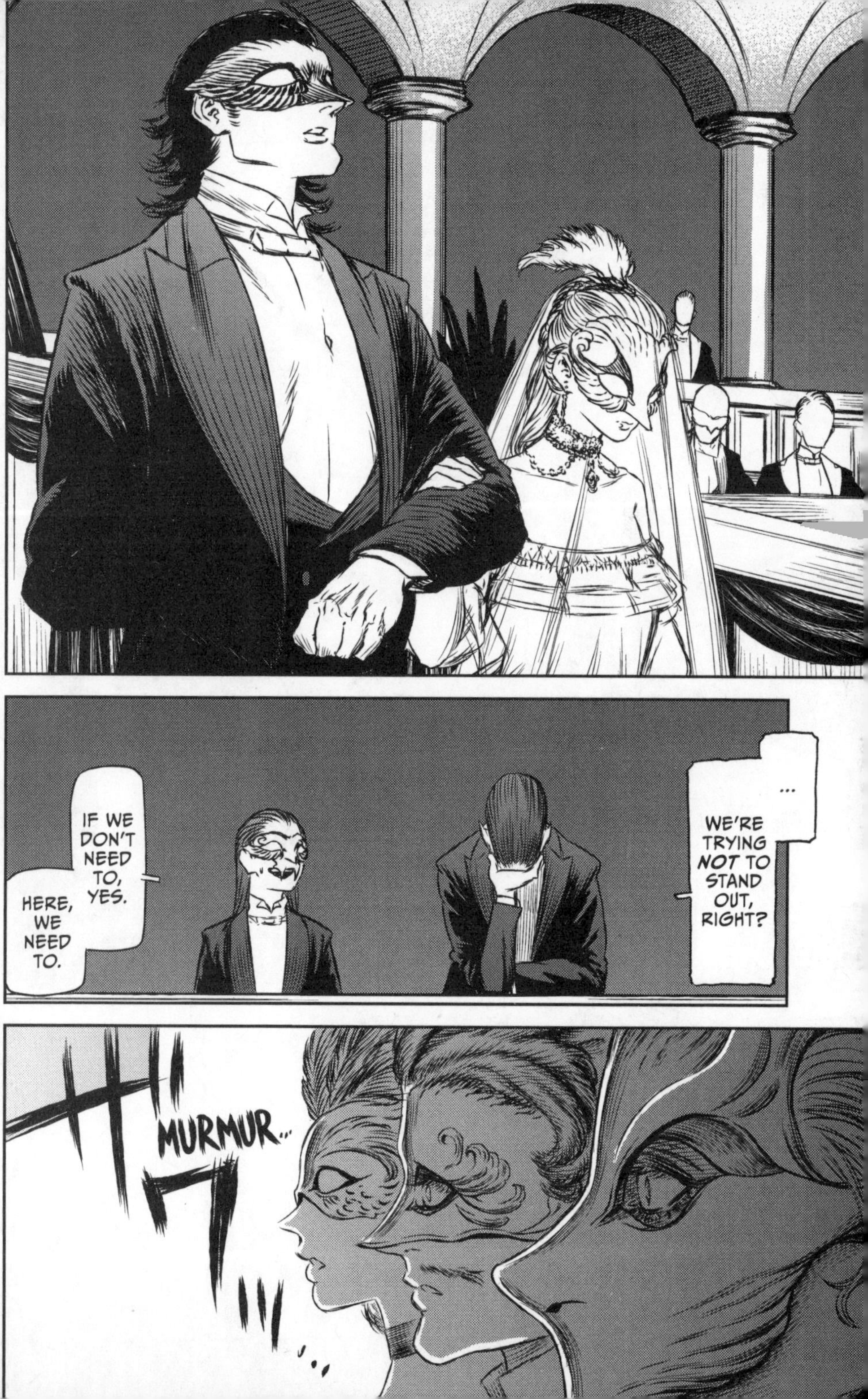
...
WE'RE TRYING *NOT* TO STAND OUT, RIGHT?
IF WE DON'T NEED TO, YES.
HERE, WE NEED TO.
MURMUR...

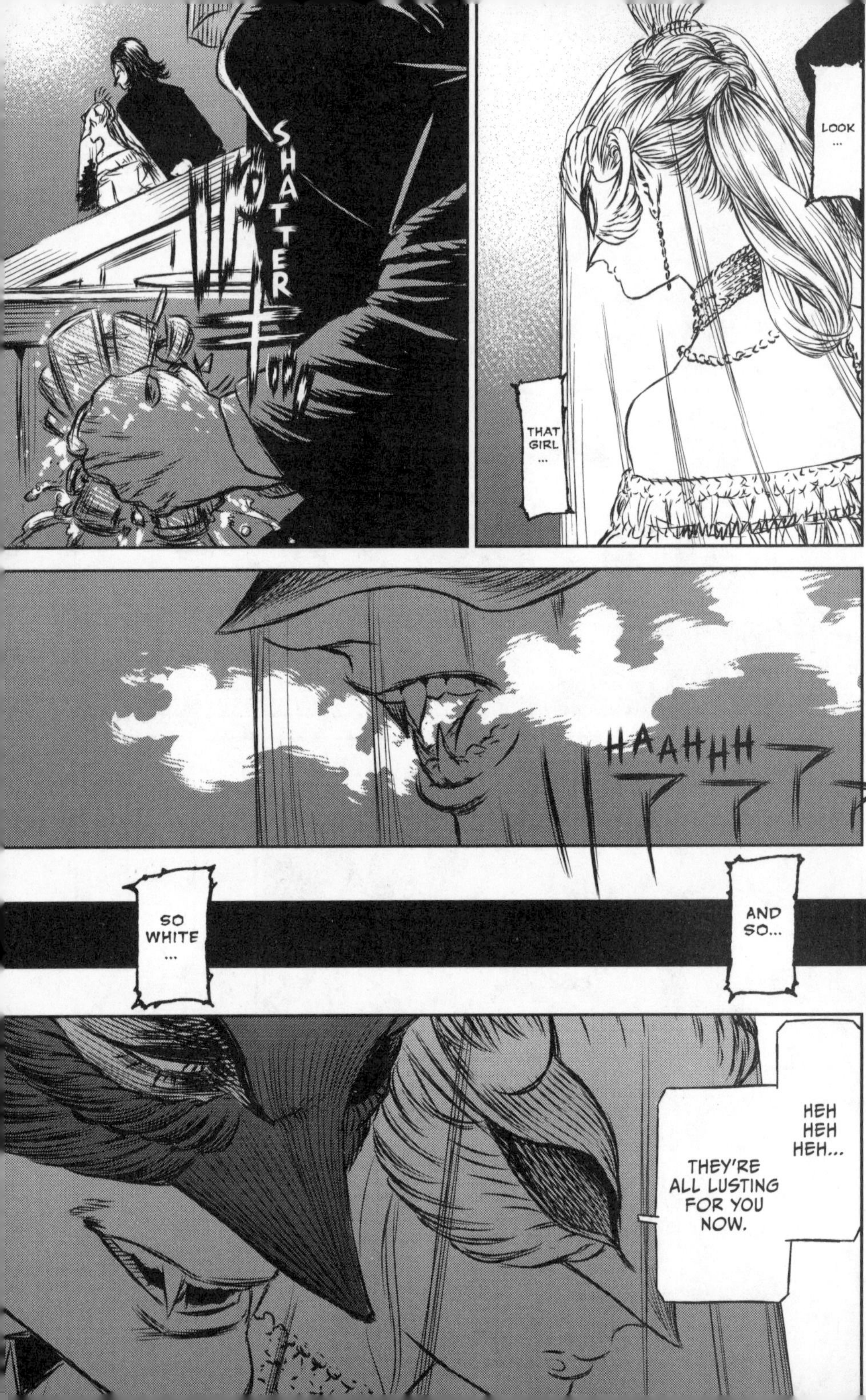
LOOK ...
THAT GIRL ...
SHATTER
HAAHHH
AND SO...
SO WHITE ...
HEH HEH HEH...
THEY'RE ALL LUSTING FOR YOU NOW.

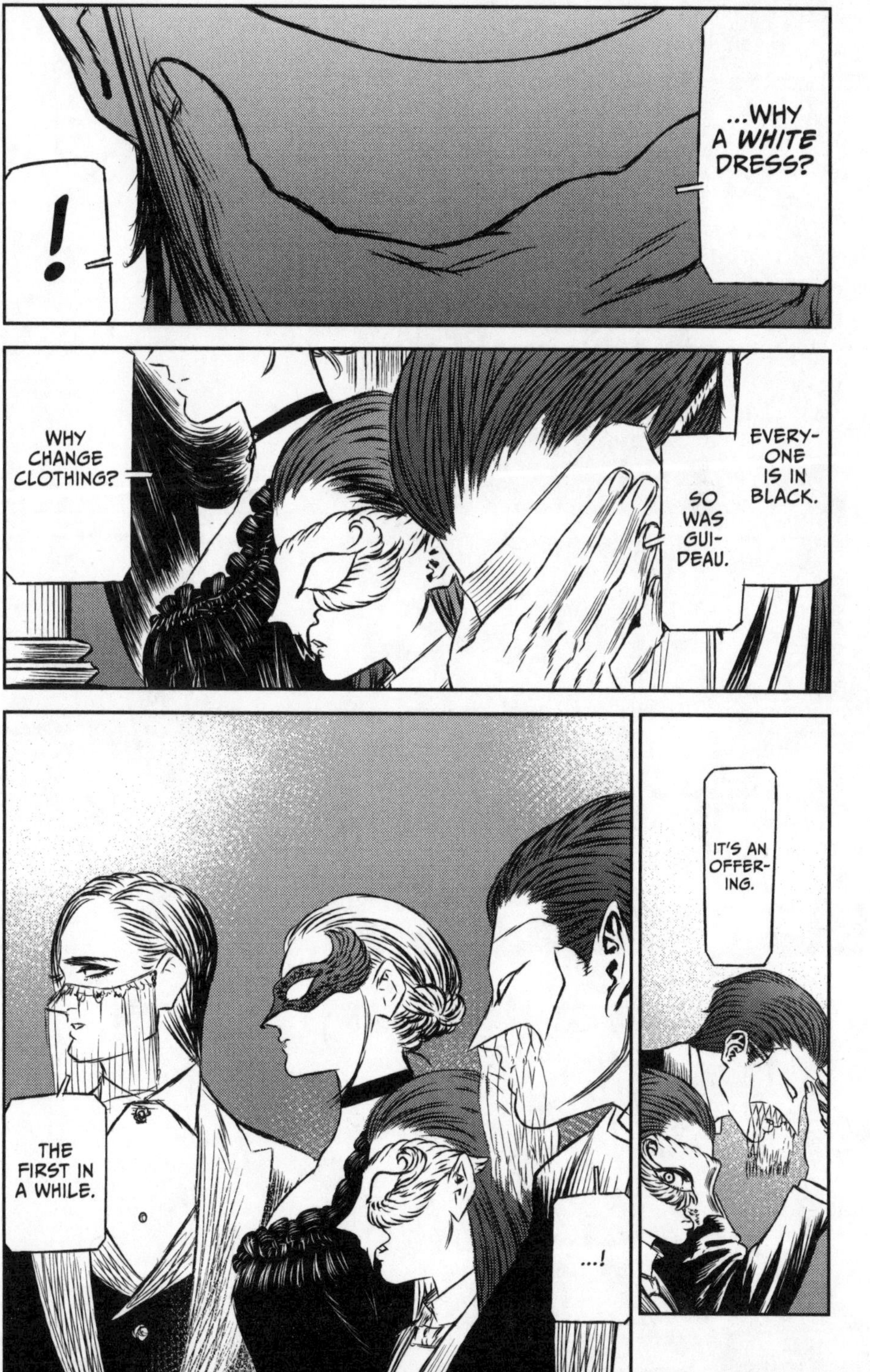
...WHY A WHITE DRESS?
!
EVERY-ONE IS IN BLACK.
SO WAS GUI-DEAU.
WHY CHANGE CLOTHING?
IT'S AN OFFER-ING.
THE FIRST IN A WHILE.
...!

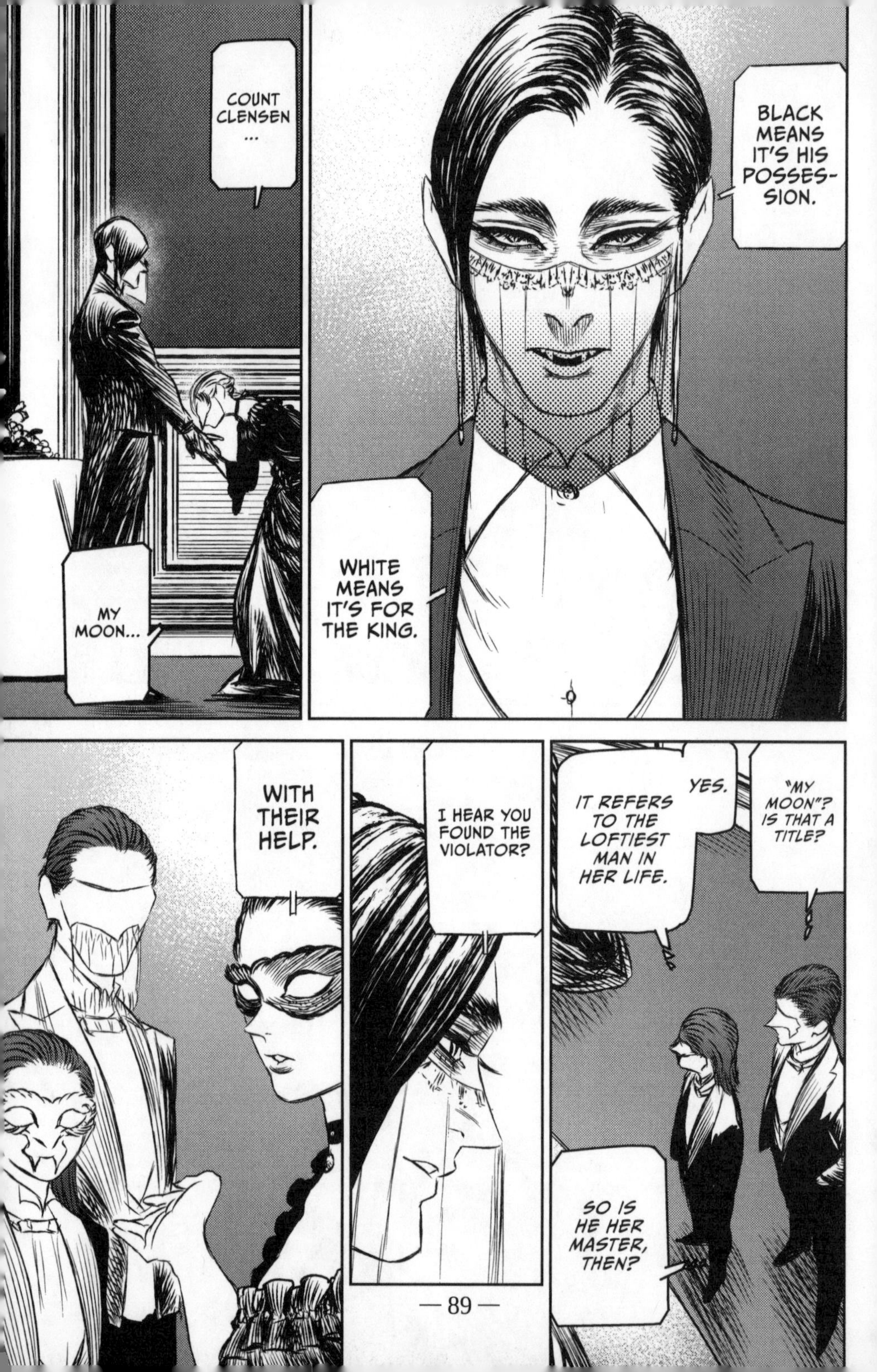
BLACK MEANS IT'S HIS POSSES-SION.
WHITE MEANS IT'S FOR THE KING.
COUNT CLENSEN ...
MY MOON...
"MY MOON"? IS THAT A TITLE?
YES. IT REFERS TO THE LOFTIEST MAN IN HER LIFE.
SO IS HE HER MASTER, THEN?
I HEAR YOU FOUND THE VIOLATOR?
WITH THEIR HELP.

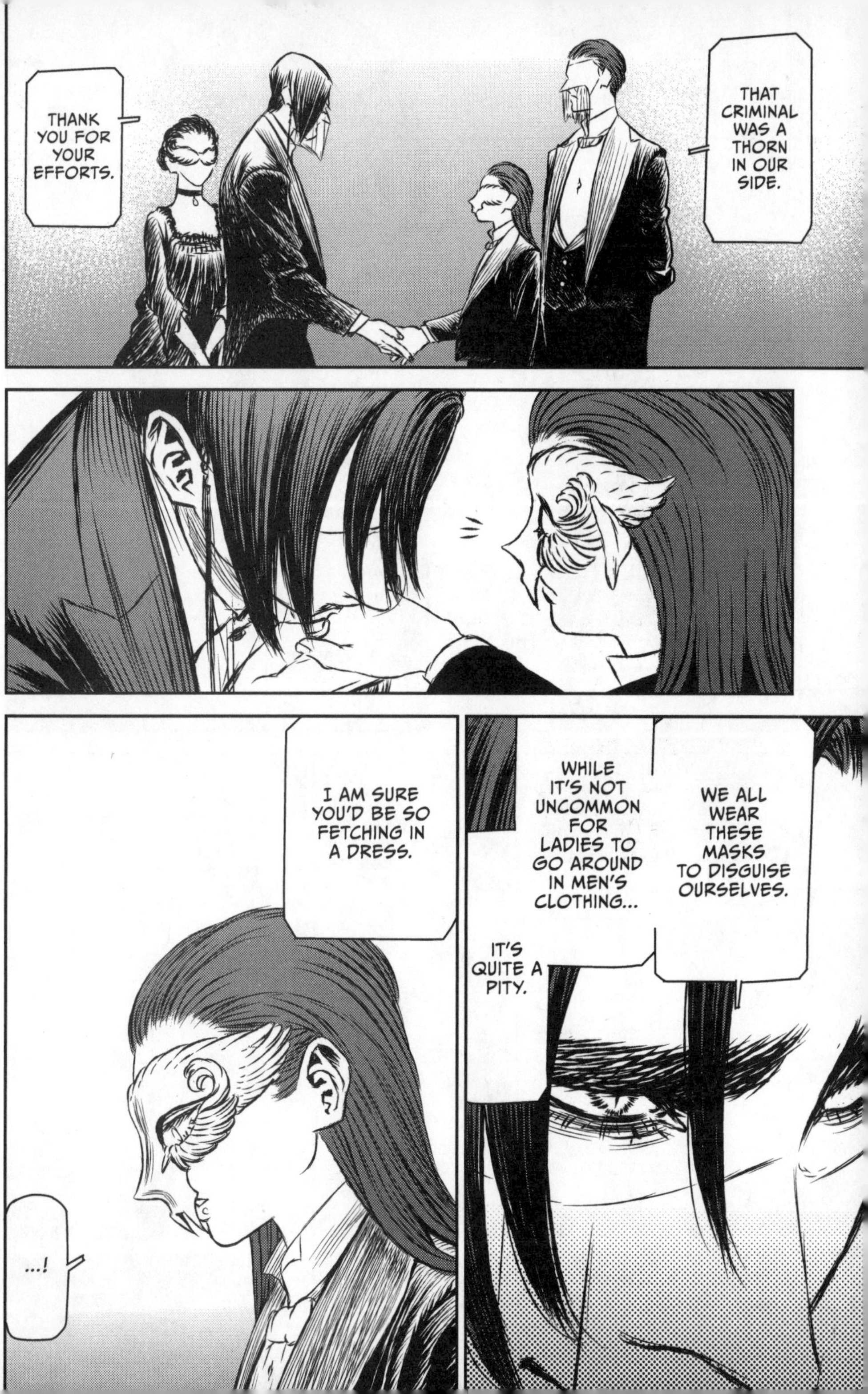
THAT CRIMINAL WAS A THORN IN OUR SIDE.
THANK YOU FOR YOUR EFFORTS.
WE ALL WEAR THESE MASKS TO DISGUISE OURSELVES.
WHILE IT'S NOT UNCOMMON FOR LADIES TO GO AROUND IN MEN'S CLOTHING...
IT'S QUITE A PITY.
I AM SURE YOU'D BE SO FETCHING IN A DRESS.
...!

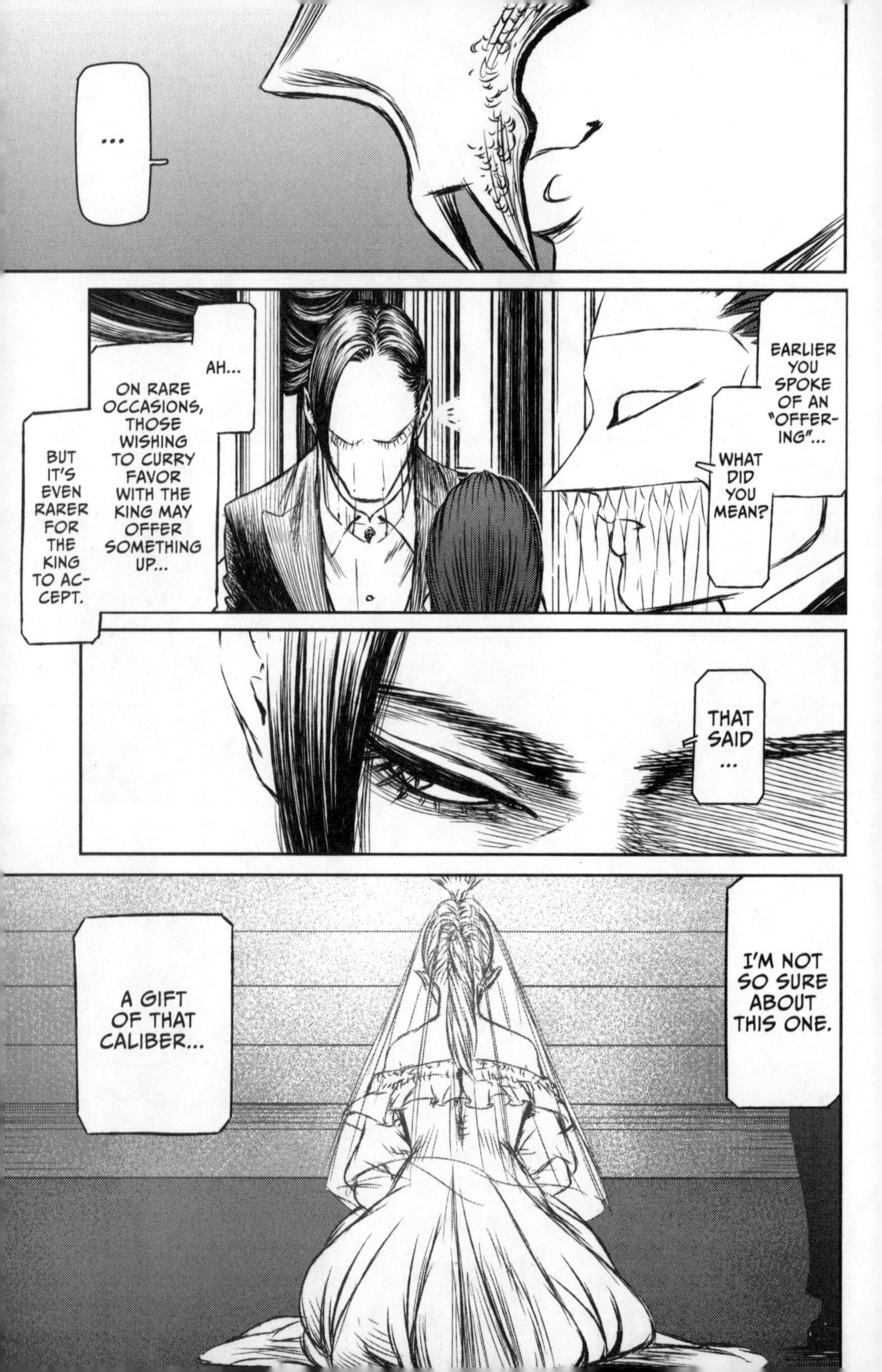
...
EARLIER YOU SPOKE OF AN "OFFERING"...
WHAT DID YOU MEAN?
AH...
ON RARE OCCASIONS, THOSE WISHING TO CURRY FAVOR WITH THE KING MAY OFFER SOMETHING UP...
BUT IT'S EVEN RARER FOR THE KING TO ACCEPT.
THAT SAID...
I'M NOT SO SURE ABOUT THIS ONE.
A GIFT OF THAT CALIBER...

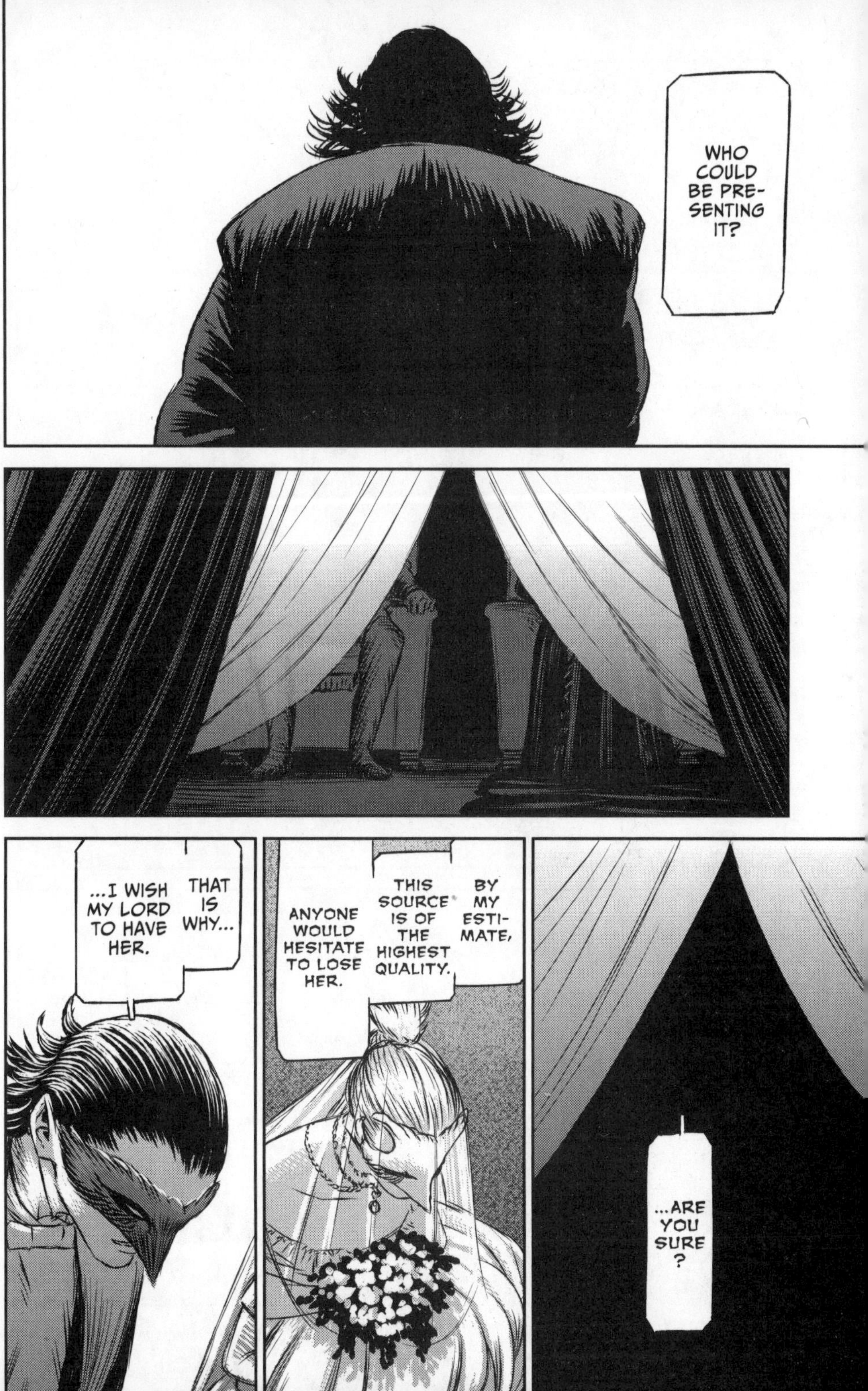
WHO COULD BE PRE-SENTING IT?
...ARE YOU SURE?
BY MY ESTI-MATE,
THIS SOURCE IS OF THE HIGHEST QUALITY.
ANYONE WOULD HESITATE TO LOSE HER.
THAT IS WHY...
...I WISH MY LORD TO HAVE HER.

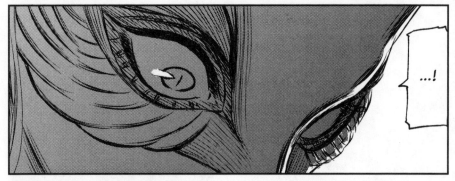

...!

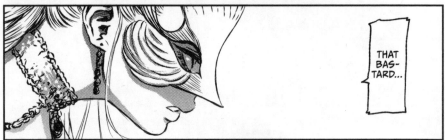

THAT BAS- TARD...

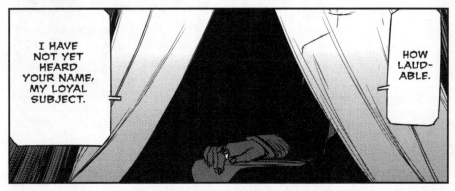

I HAVE NOT YET HEARD YOUR NAME, MY LOYAL SUBJECT.

HOW LAUD- ABLE.

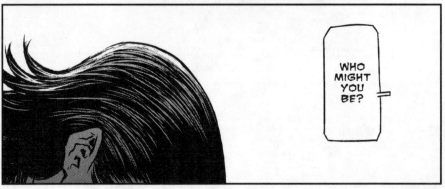

WHO MIGHT YOU BE?

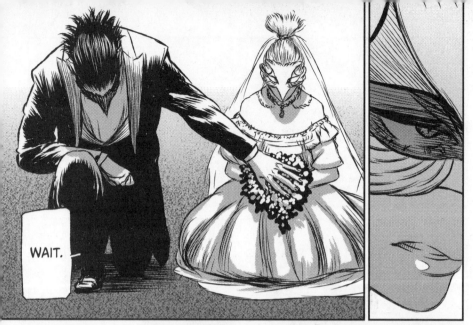

WAIT.

...?!

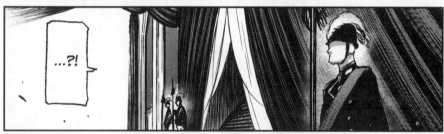

YOU WANT THE QUEEN.

NOT THE KING.

HUH?!

I TOLD YOU...

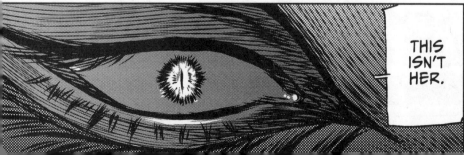

THIS ISN'T HER.

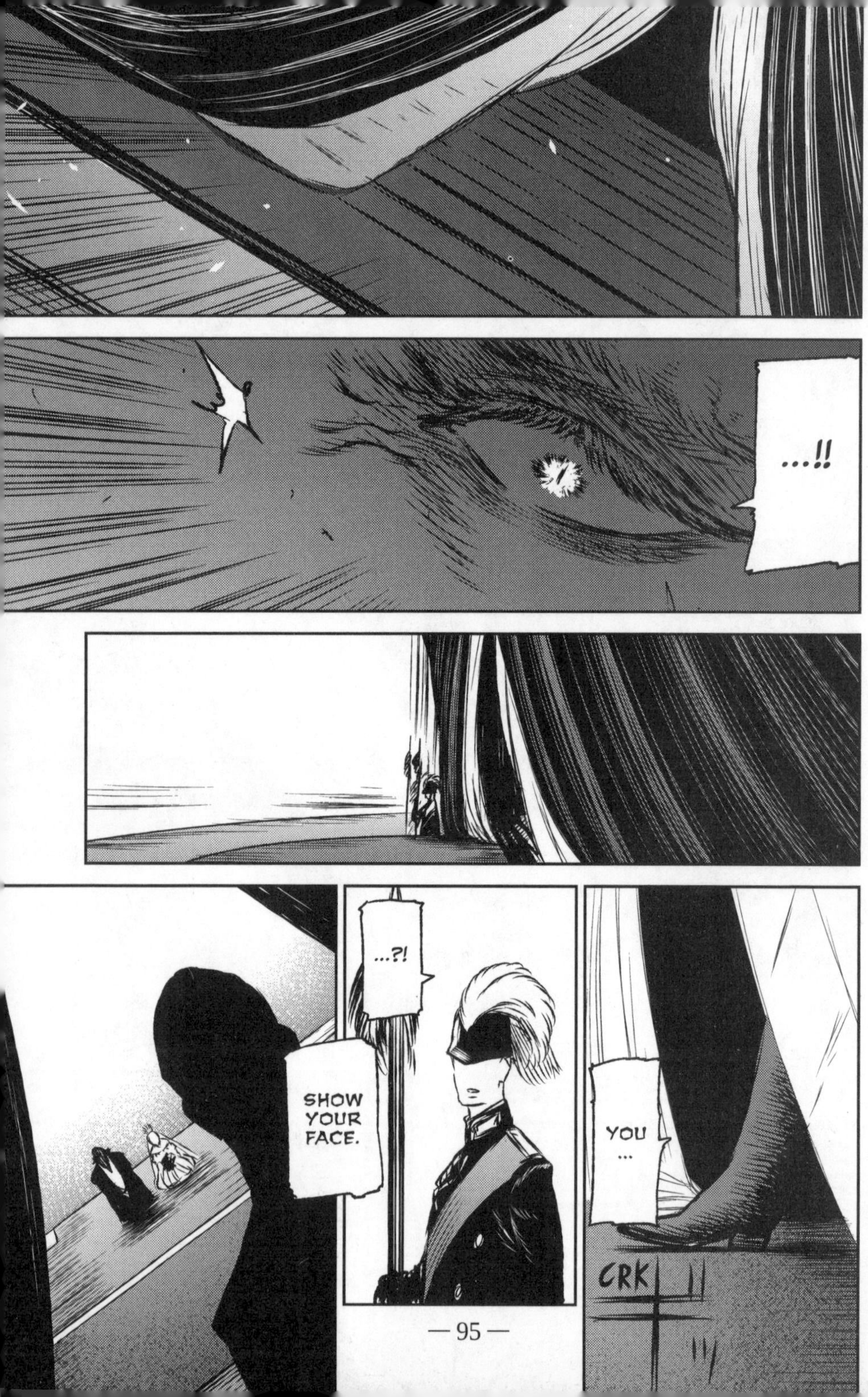
...!!
YOU ...
CRK
...?!
SHOW YOUR FACE.

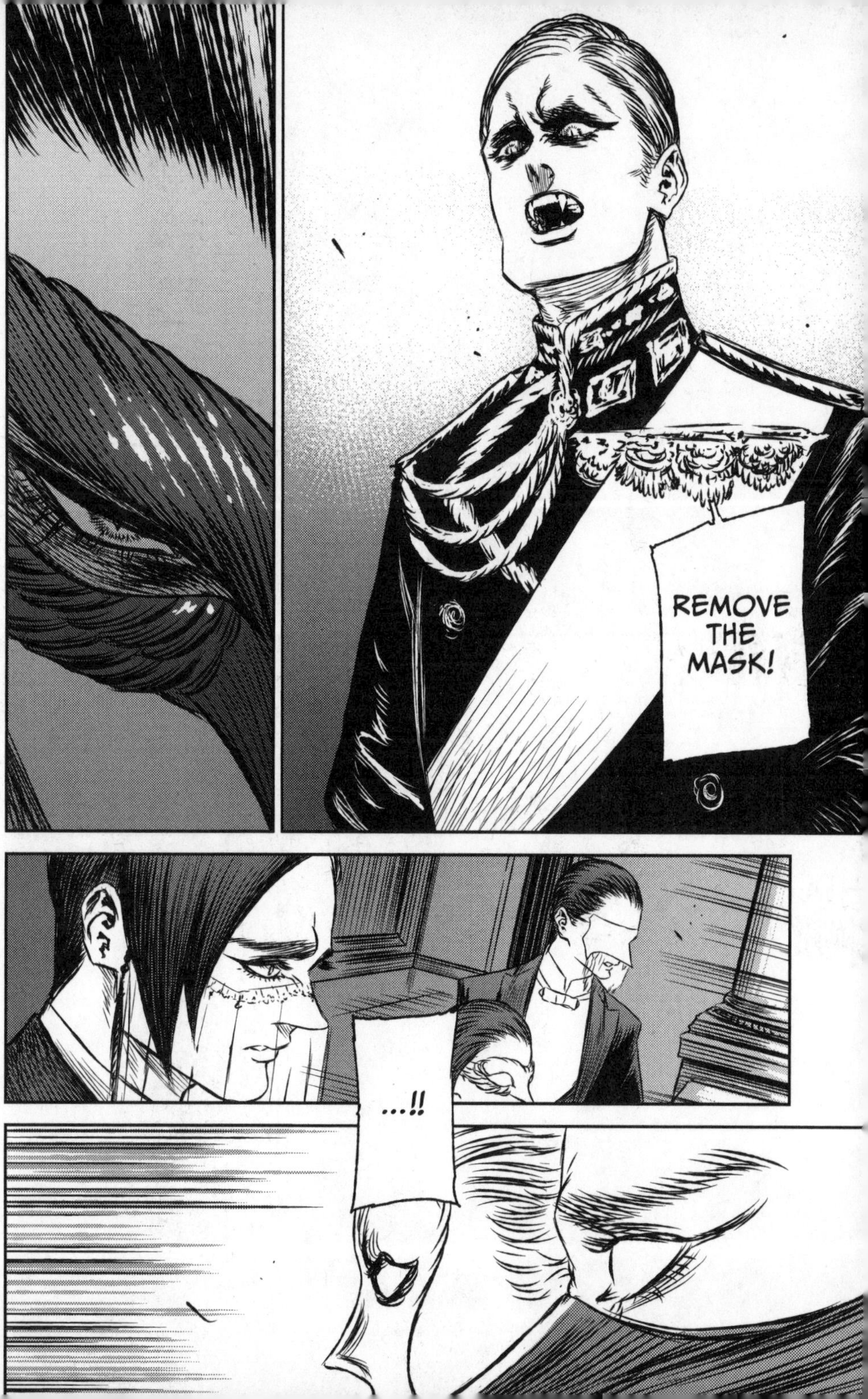
REMOVE THE MASK!
...!!

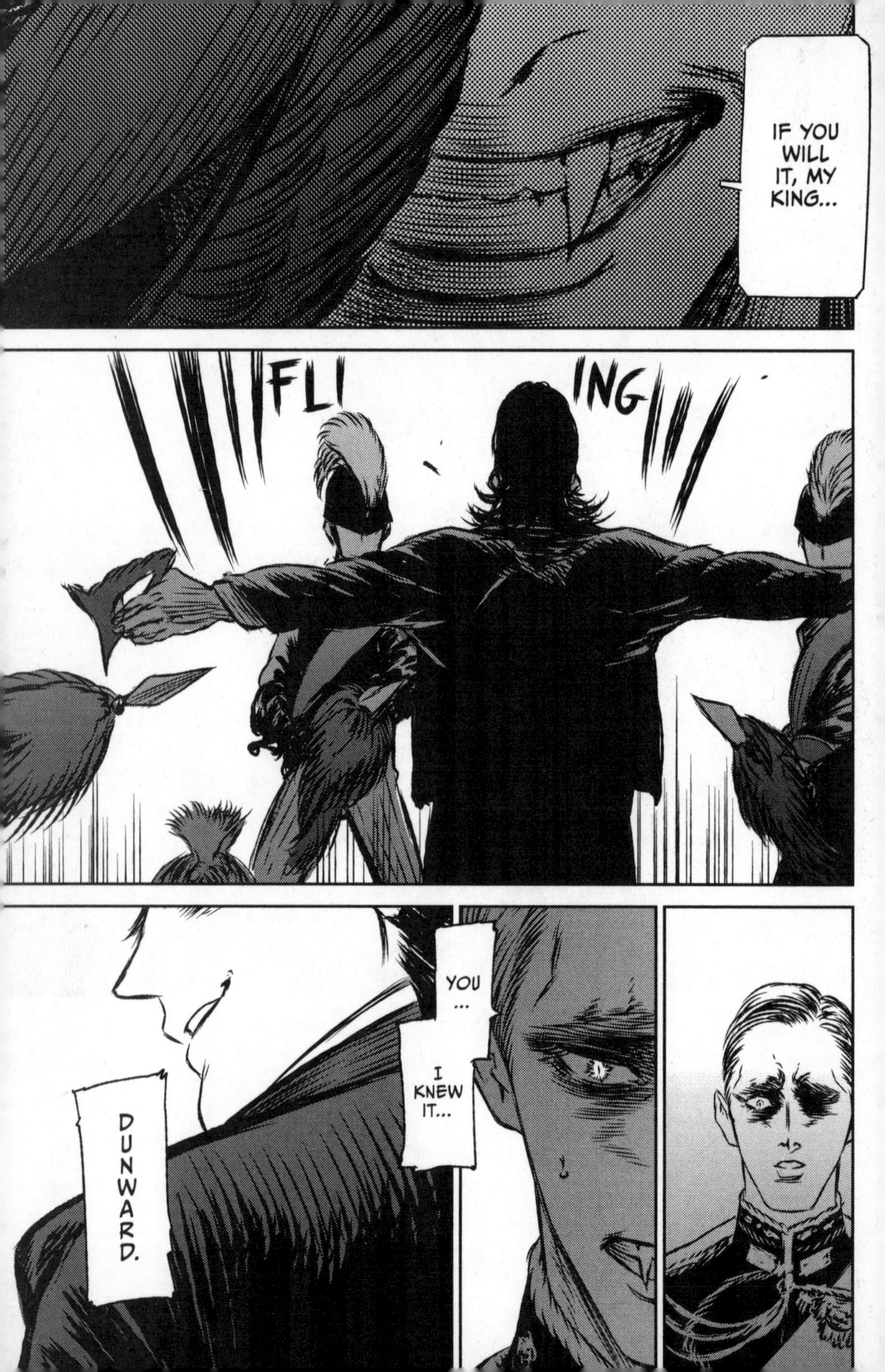
IF YOU WILL IT, MY KING...
FLIING
YOU ...
I KNEW IT...
DUNWARD.

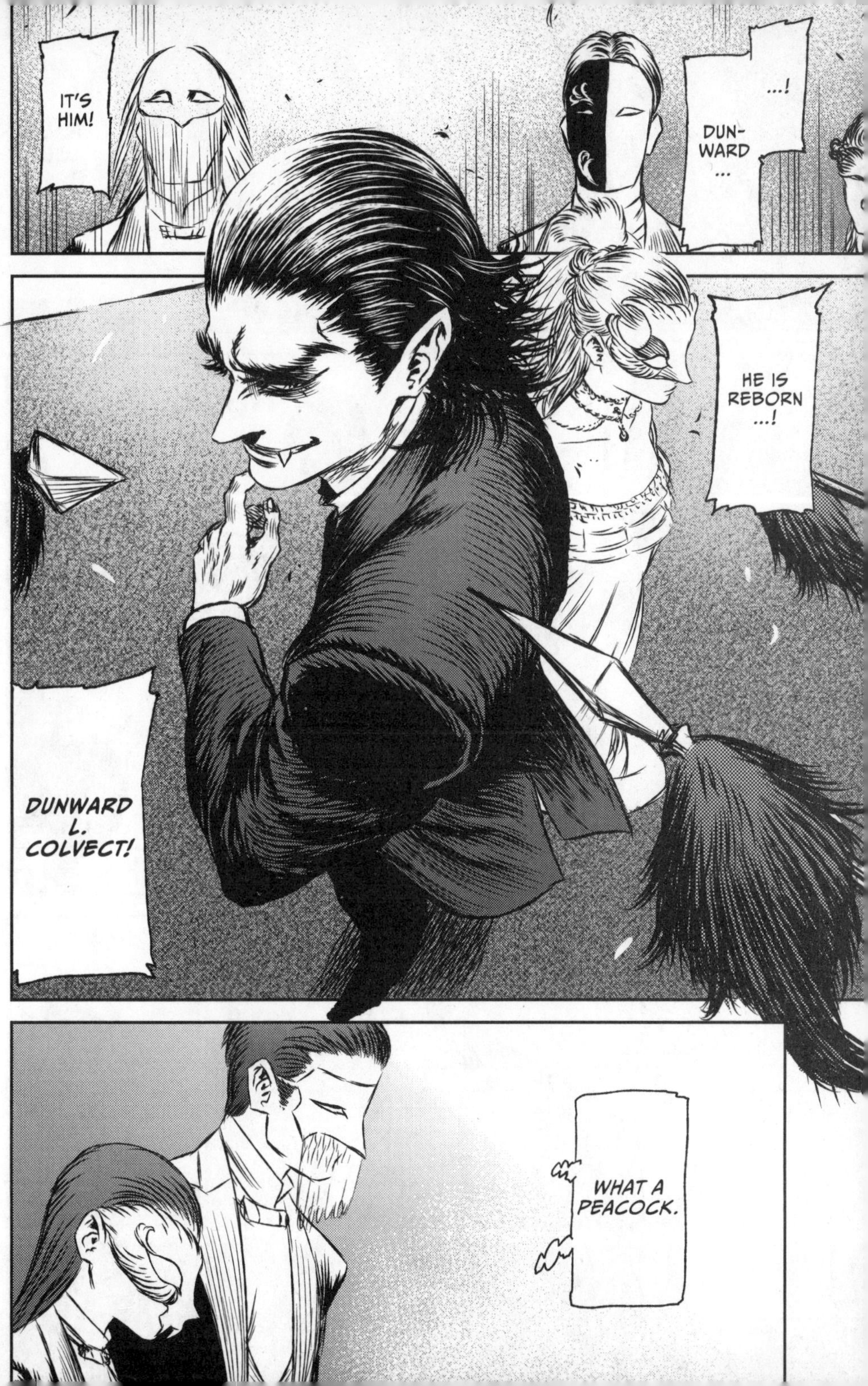
...!
DUNWARD...
IT'S HIM!
HE IS REBORN...!
DUNWARD L. COLVECT!
WHAT A PEACOCK.

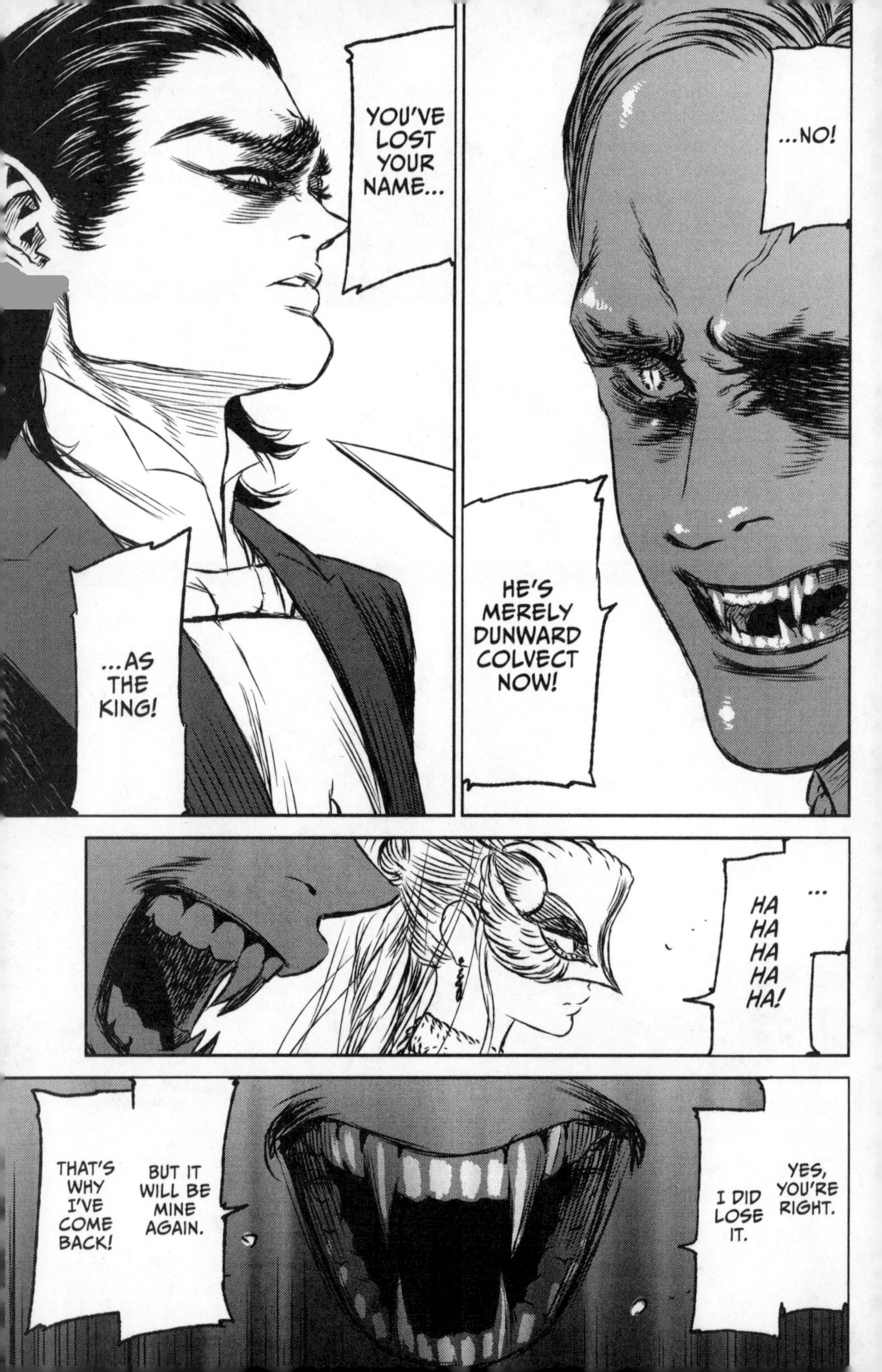
...NO!
HE'S MERELY DUNWARD COLVECT NOW!
YOU'VE LOST YOUR NAME...
...AS THE KING!
... HA HA HA HA HA!
YES, YOU'RE RIGHT.
I DID LOSE IT.
BUT IT WILL BE MINE AGAIN.
THAT'S WHY I'VE COME BACK!

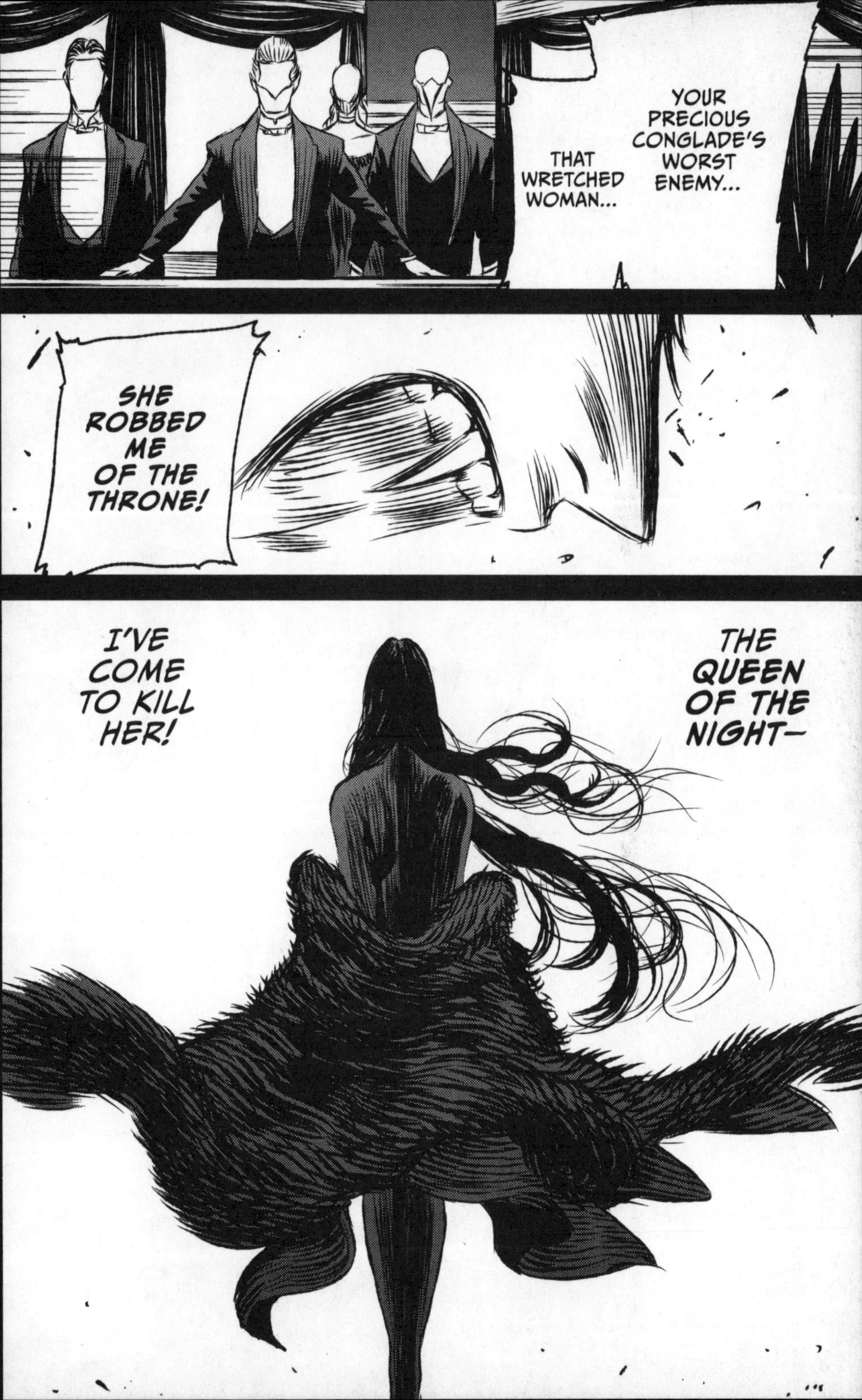
YOUR PRECIOUS CONGLADE'S WORST ENEMY...
THAT WRETCHED WOMAN...
SHE ROBBED ME OF THE THRONE!
THE QUEEN OF THE NIGHT—
I'VE COME TO KILL HER!

# THE WITCH AND THE BEAST

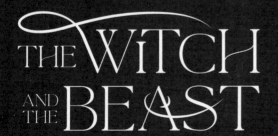

# THE WITCH AND THE BEAST

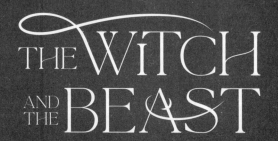

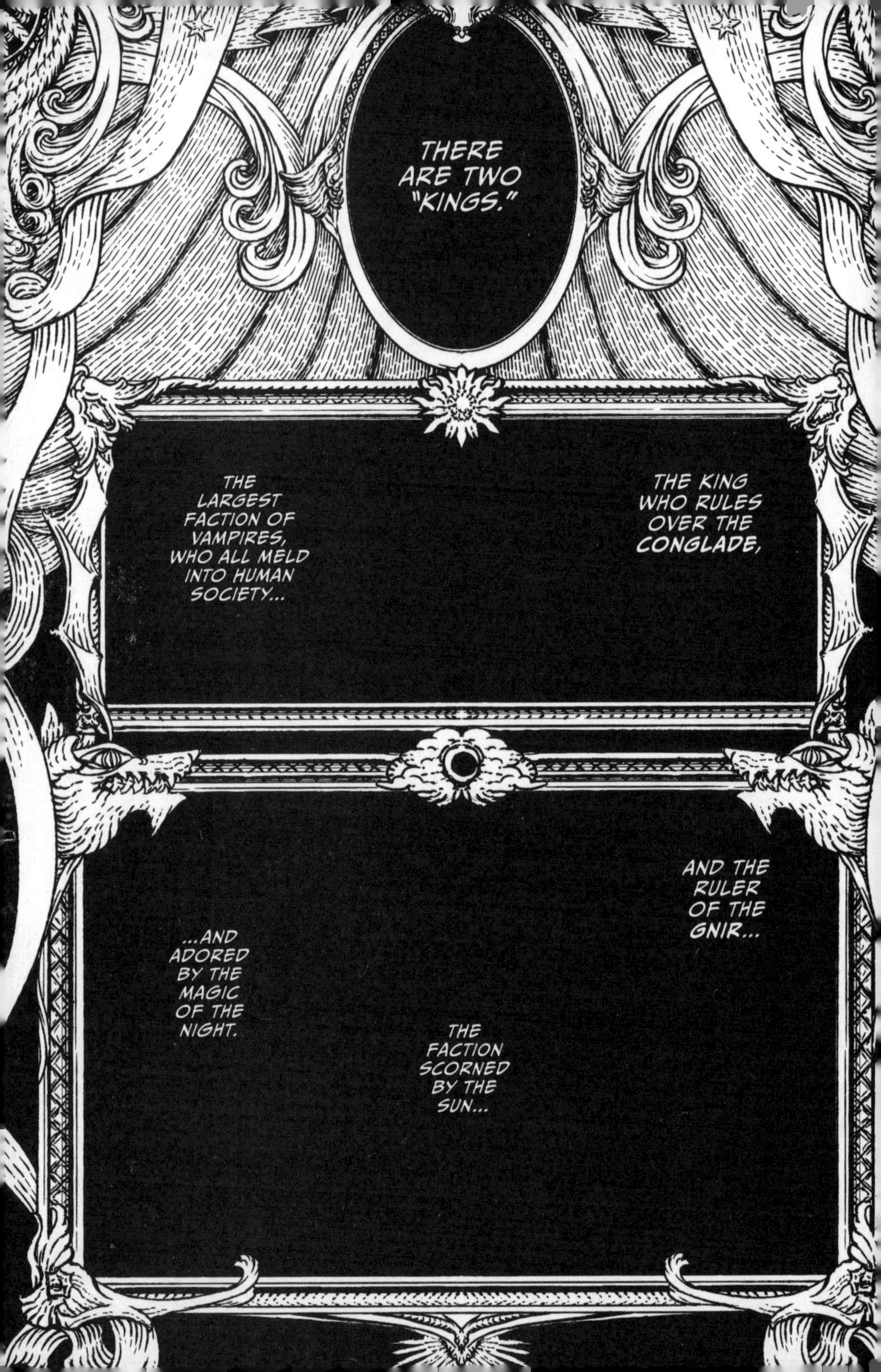
THERE ARE TWO "KINGS."
THE KING WHO RULES OVER THE CONGLADE,
THE LARGEST FACTION OF VAMPIRES, WHO ALL MELD INTO HUMAN SOCIETY...
AND THE RULER OF THE GNIR...
THE FACTION SCORNED BY THE SUN...
...AND ADORED BY THE MAGIC OF THE NIGHT.

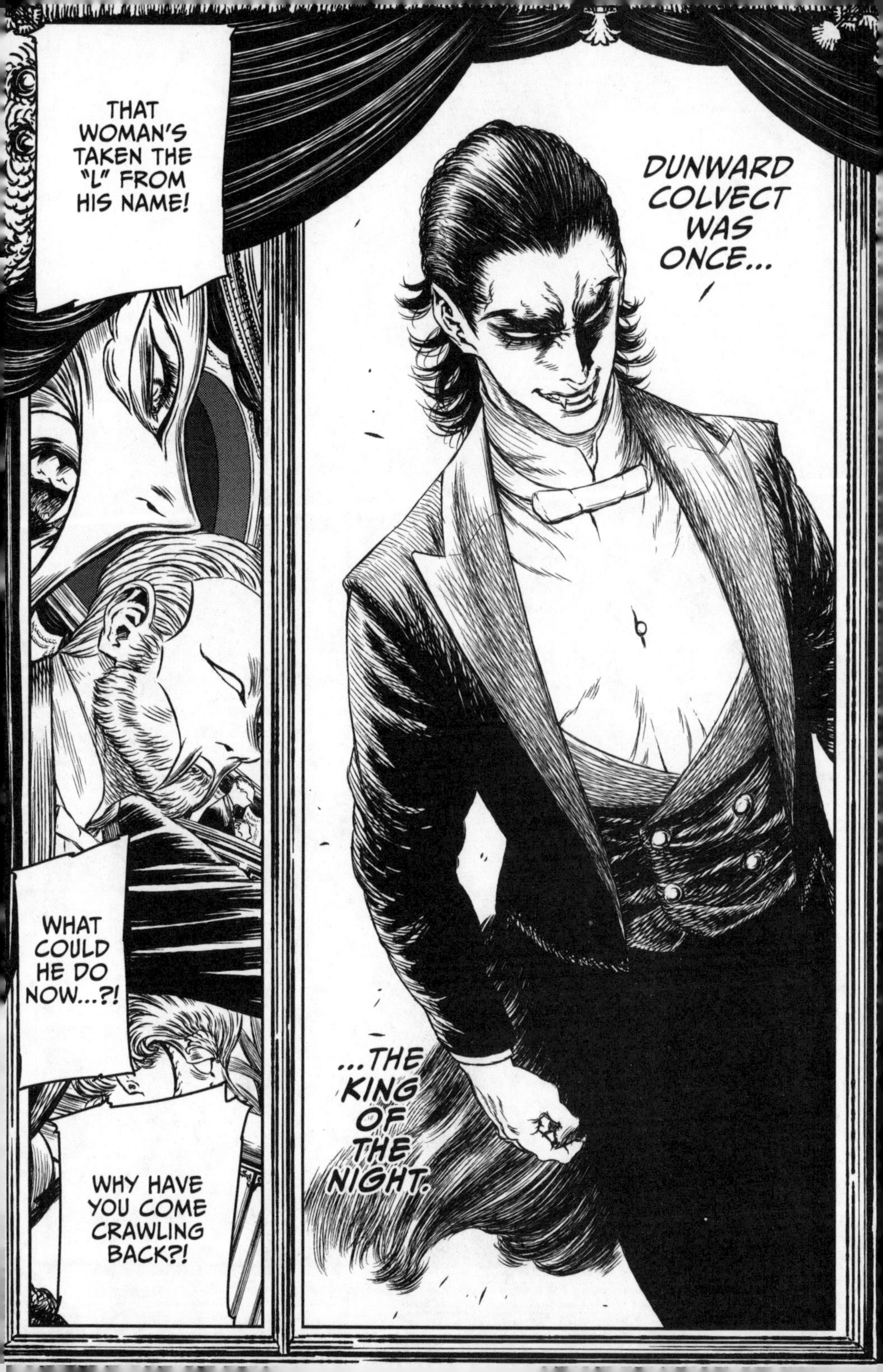
DUNWARD COLVECT WAS ONCE...
...THE KING OF THE NIGHT.
THAT WOMAN'S TAKEN THE "L" FROM HIS NAME!
WHAT COULD HE DO NOW...?!
WHY HAVE YOU COME CRAWLING BACK?!

# CHAPTER 32: FOUR LEVELS BELOW—ACT V

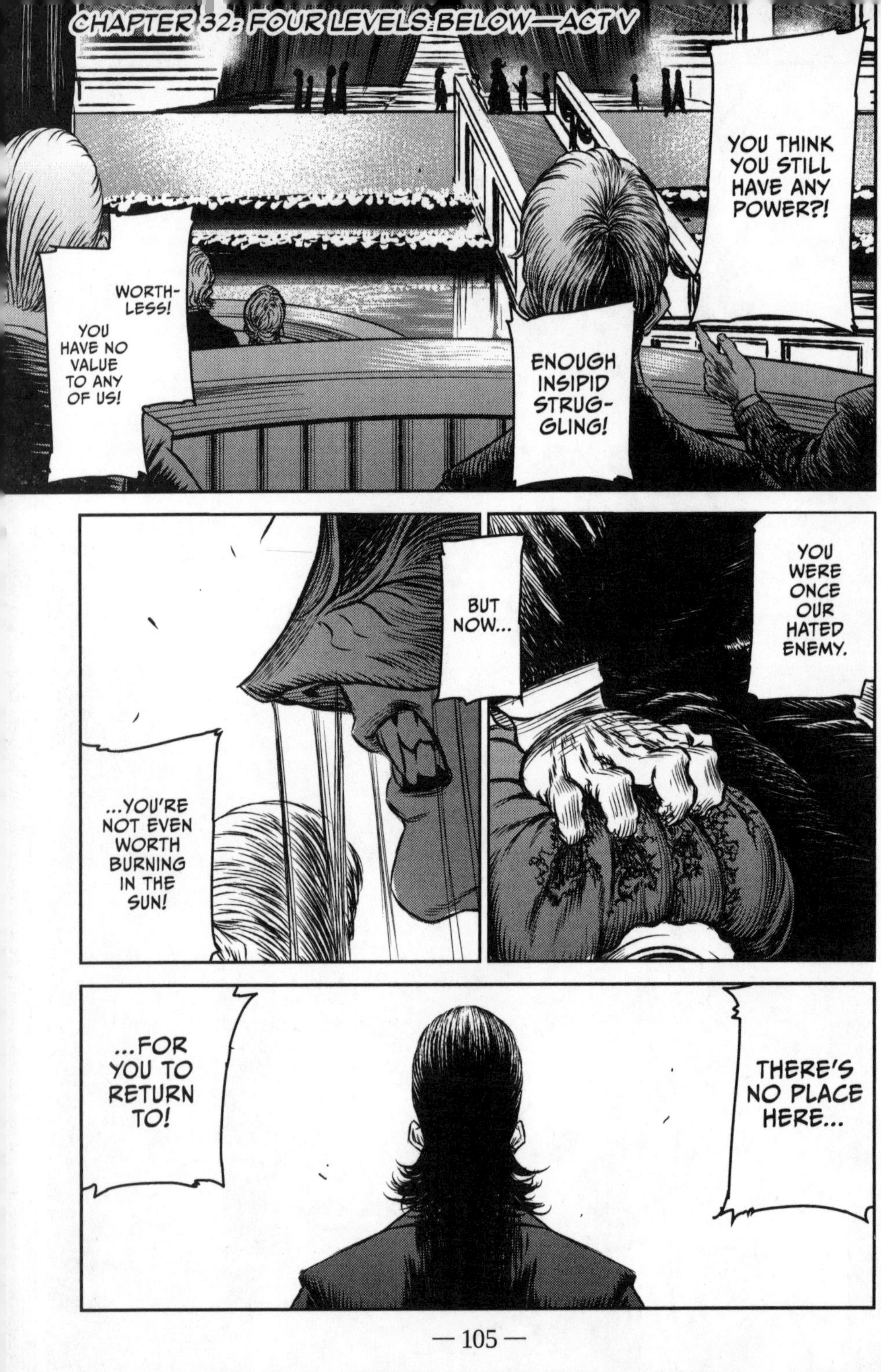
YOU THINK YOU STILL HAVE ANY POWER?!
ENOUGH INSIPID STRUG-GLING!
WORTH-LESS!
YOU HAVE NO VALUE TO ANY OF US!
YOU WERE ONCE OUR HATED ENEMY.
BUT NOW...
...YOU'RE NOT EVEN WORTH BURNING IN THE SUN!
THERE'S NO PLACE HERE...
...FOR YOU TO RETURN TO!

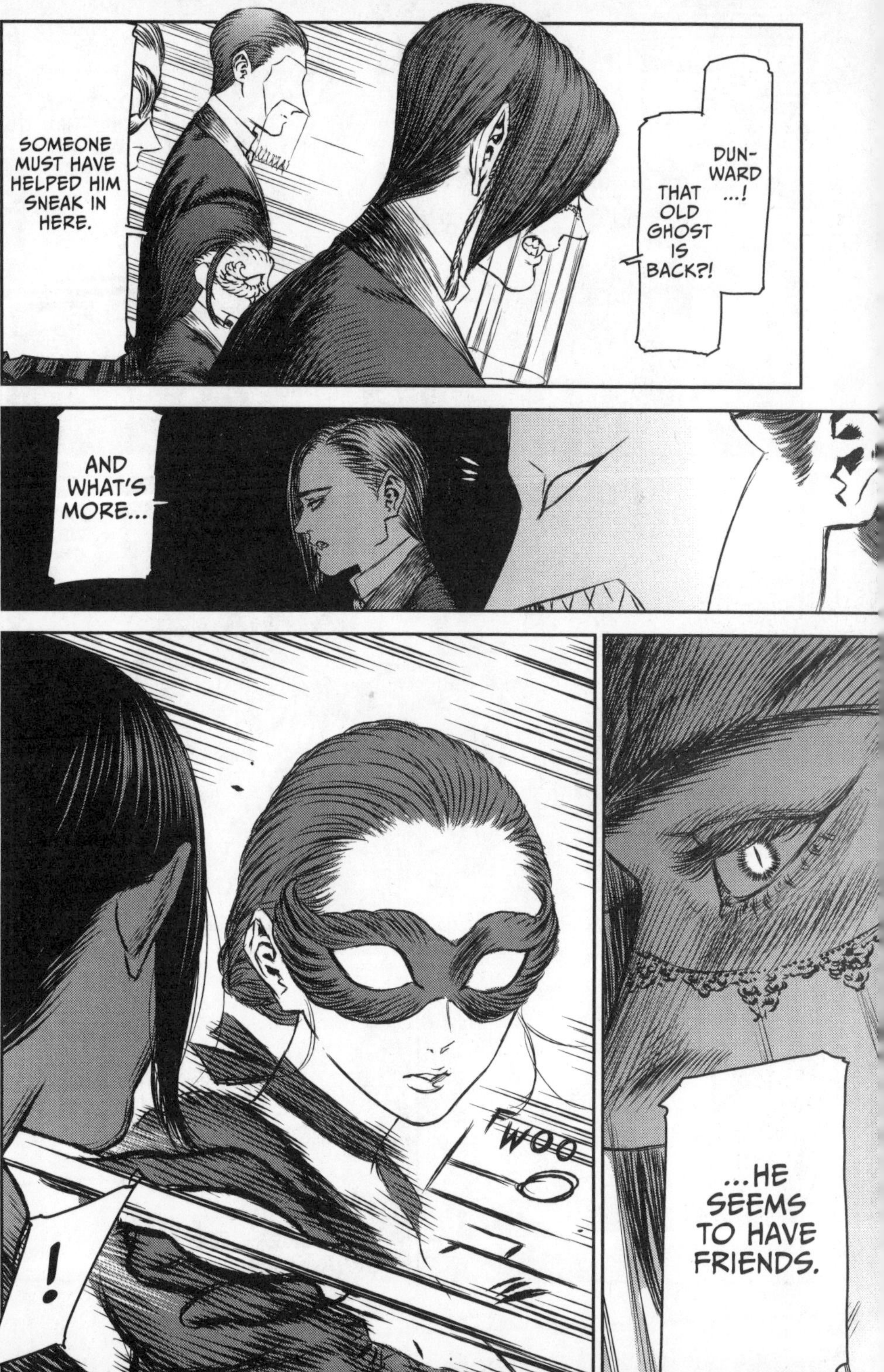
DUNWARD...! THAT OLD GHOST IS BACK?!
SOMEONE MUST HAVE HELPED HIM SNEAK IN HERE.
AND WHAT'S MORE...
...HE SEEMS TO HAVE FRIENDS.
FWOO
!

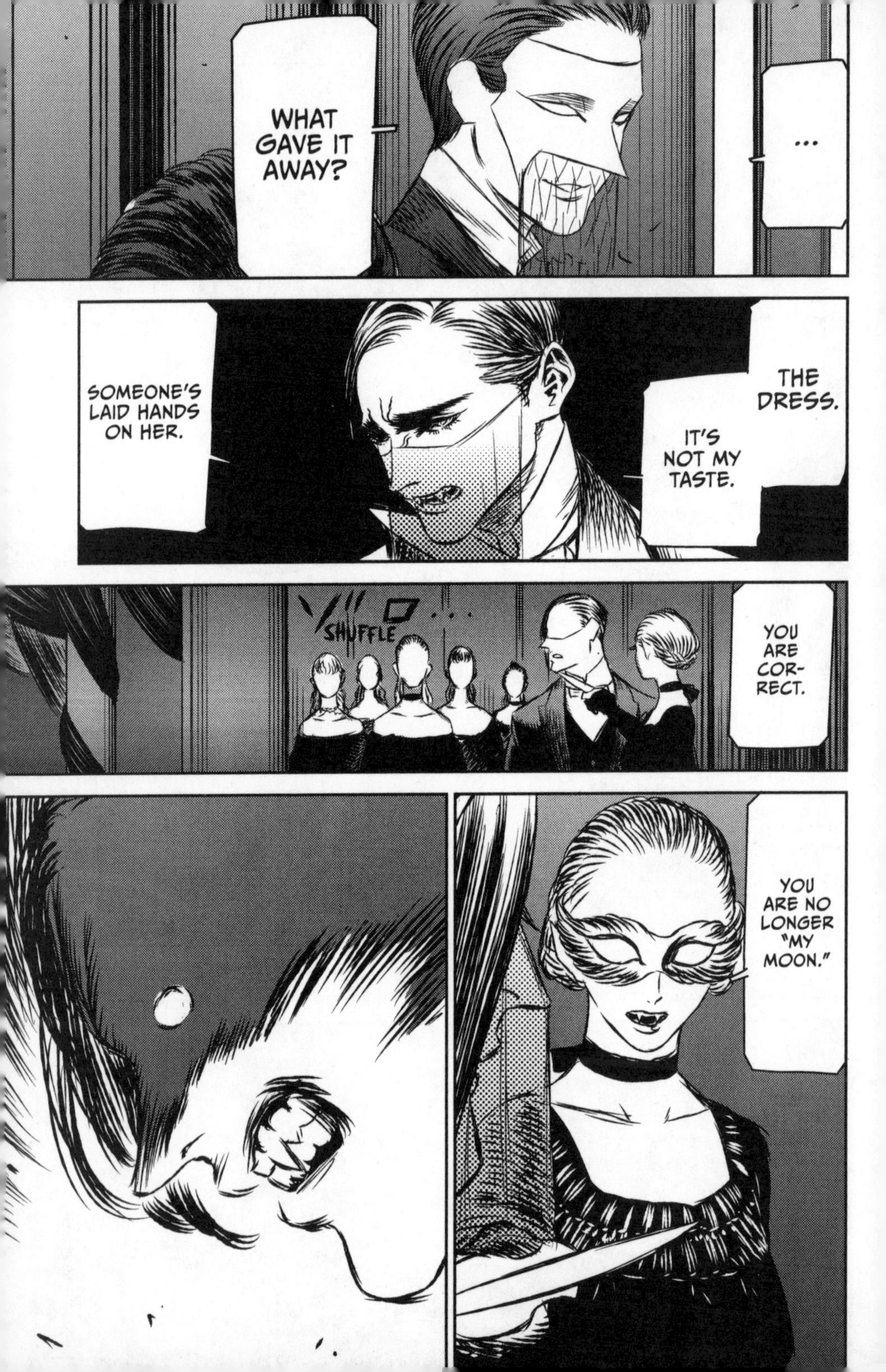
...
WHAT GAVE IT AWAY?
THE DRESS.
IT'S NOT MY TASTE.
SOMEONE'S LAID HANDS ON HER.
YOU ARE COR-RECT.
SHUFFLE
YOU ARE NO LONGER "MY MOON."

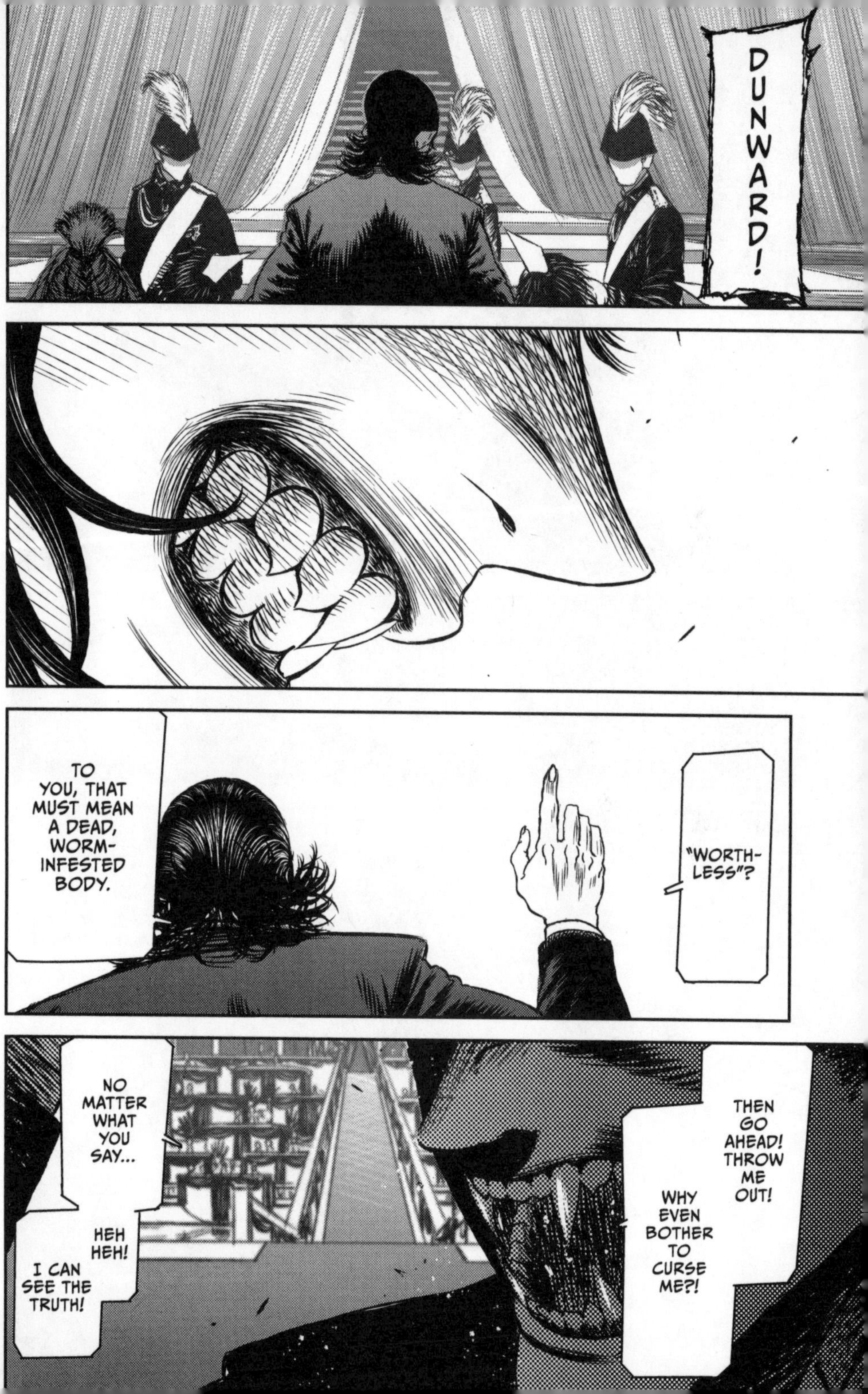
DUNWARD!
"WORTH-LESS"?
TO YOU, THAT MUST MEAN A DEAD, WORM-INFESTED BODY.
THEN GO AHEAD! THROW ME OUT!
WHY EVEN BOTHER TO CURSE ME?!
NO MATTER WHAT YOU SAY...
HEH HEH! I CAN SEE THE TRUTH!

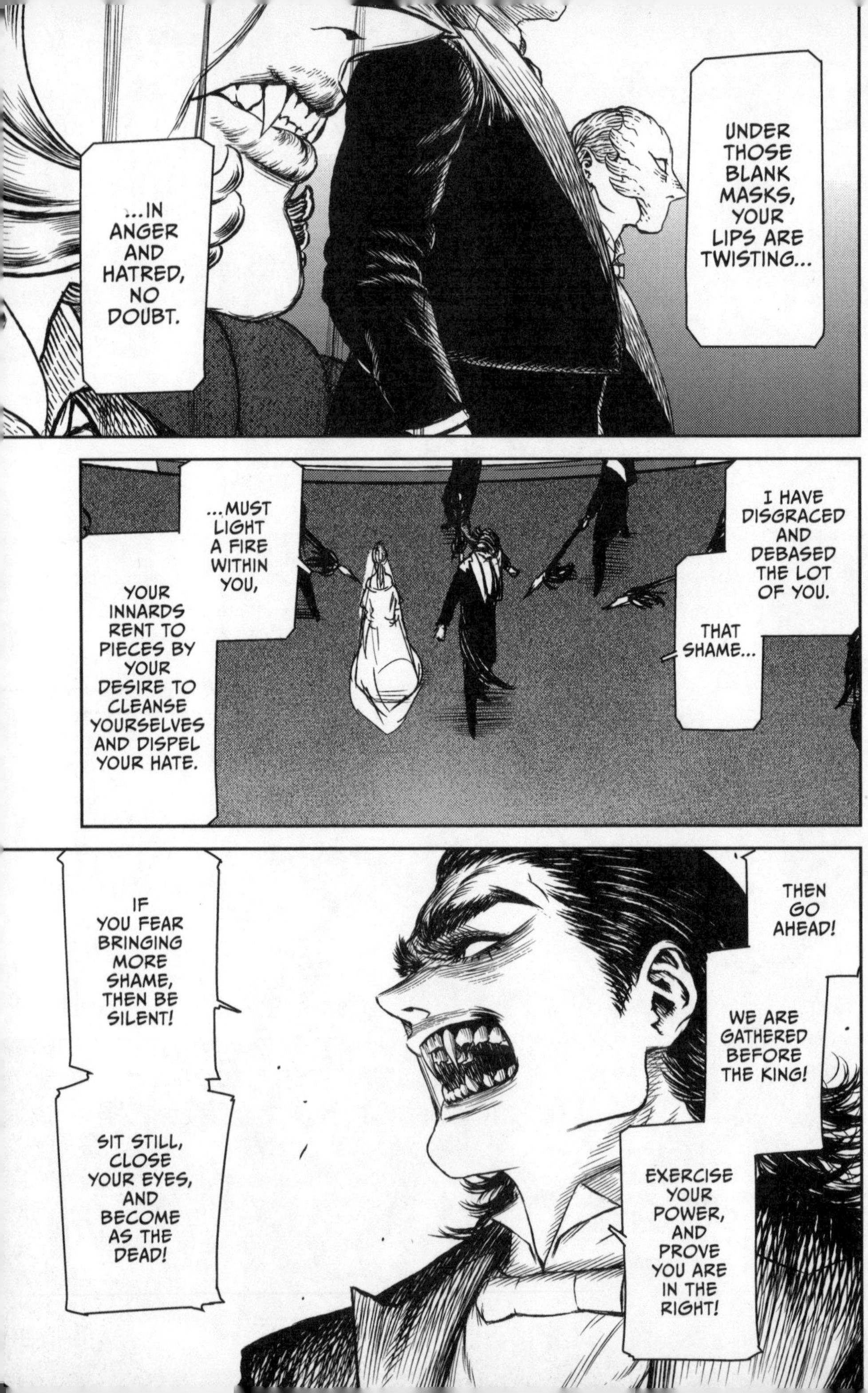
UNDER THOSE BLANK MASKS, YOUR LIPS ARE TWISTING...
...IN ANGER AND HATRED, NO DOUBT.
I HAVE DISGRACED AND DEBASED THE LOT OF YOU.
THAT SHAME...
...MUST LIGHT A FIRE WITHIN YOU,
YOUR INNARDS RENT TO PIECES BY YOUR DESIRE TO CLEANSE YOURSELVES AND DISPEL YOUR HATE.
THEN GO AHEAD!
WE ARE GATHERED BEFORE THE KING!
EXERCISE YOUR POWER, AND PROVE YOU ARE IN THE RIGHT!
IF YOU FEAR BRINGING MORE SHAME, THEN BE SILENT!
SIT STILL, CLOSE YOUR EYES, AND BECOME AS THE DEAD!

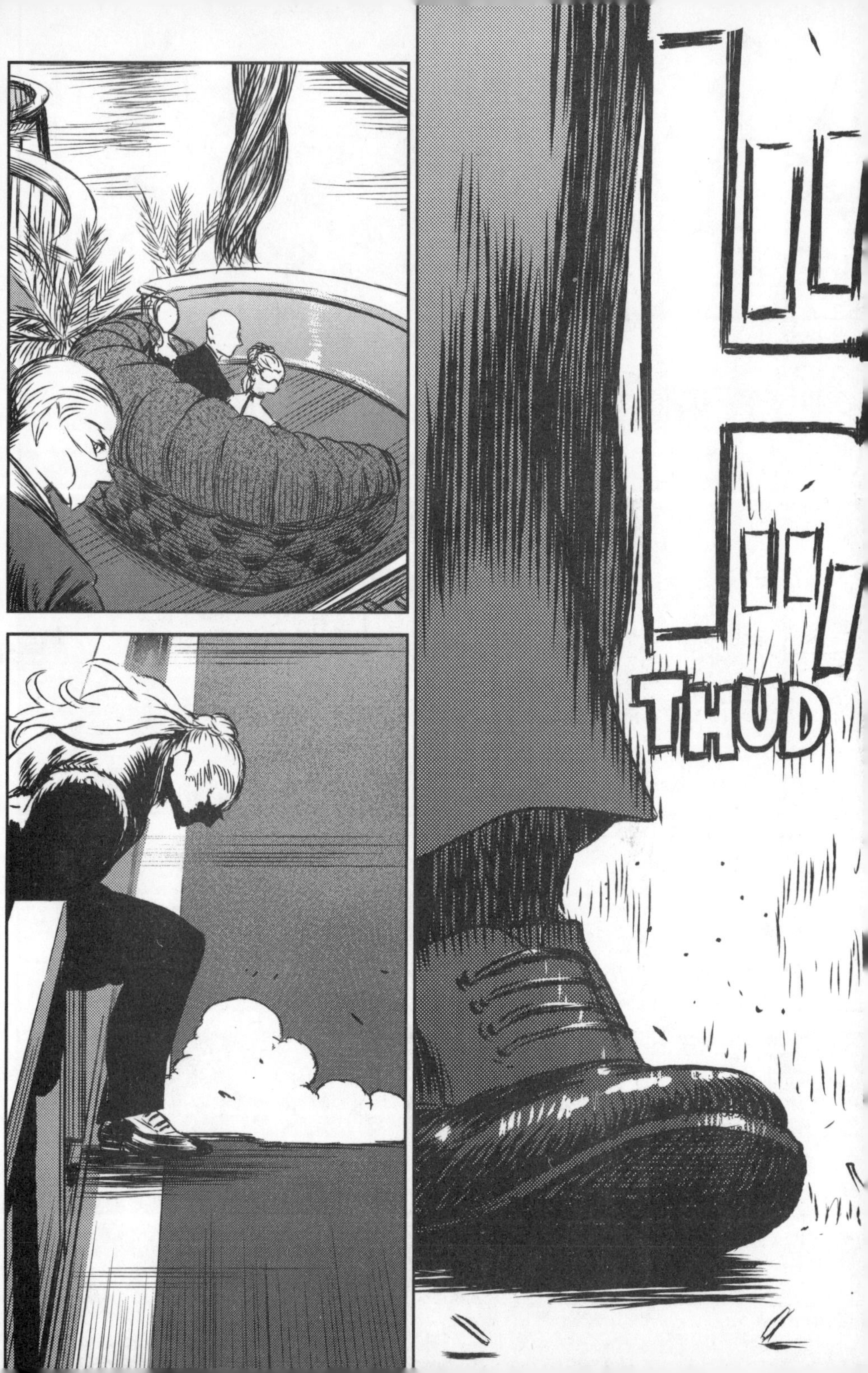
THUD

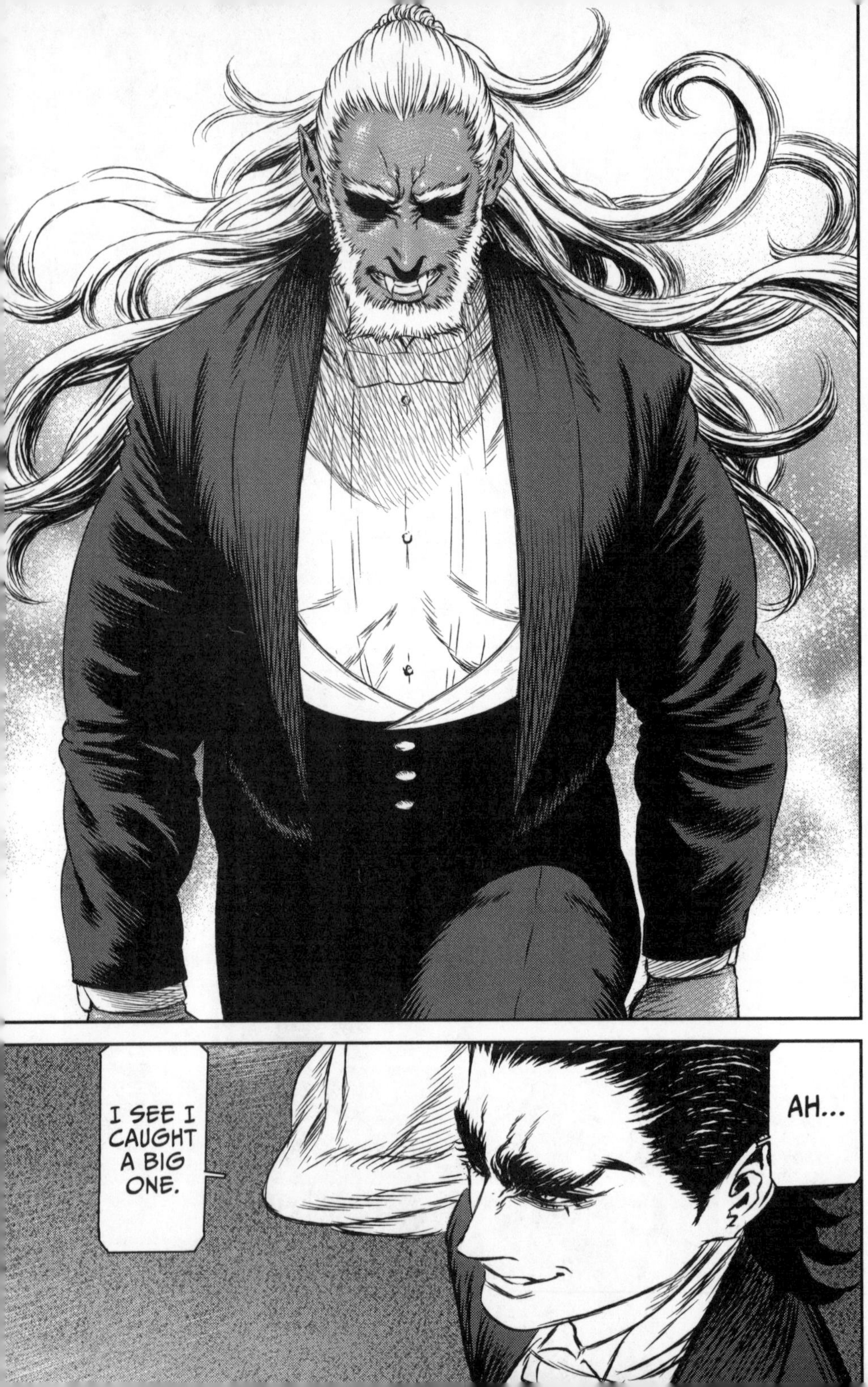
AH...
I SEE I CAUGHT A BIG ONE.

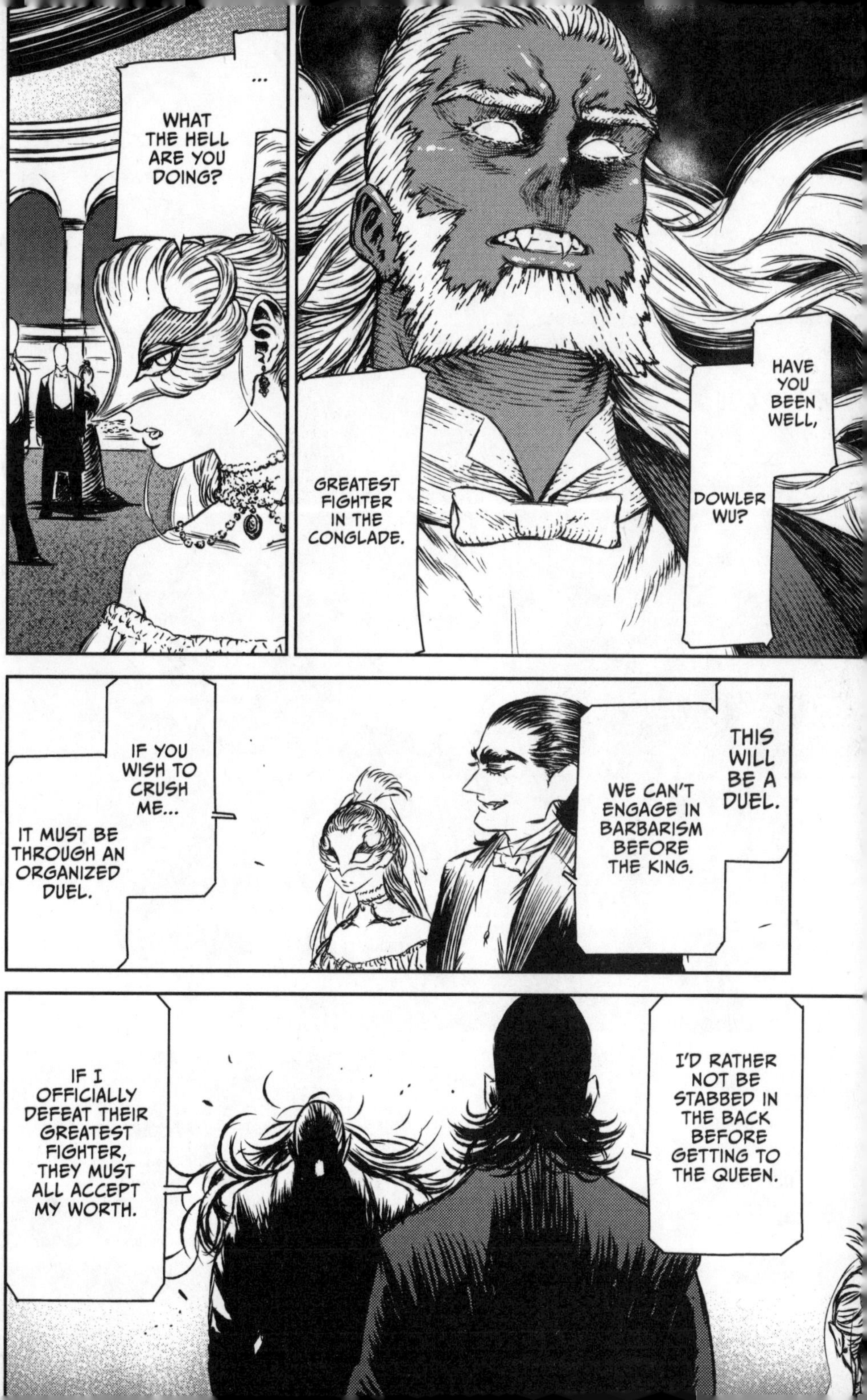
HAVE YOU BEEN WELL,
DOWLER WU?
GREATEST FIGHTER IN THE CONGLADE.
...
WHAT THE HELL ARE YOU DOING?
THIS WILL BE A DUEL.
WE CAN'T ENGAGE IN BARBARISM BEFORE THE KING.
IF YOU WISH TO CRUSH ME...
IT MUST BE THROUGH AN ORGANIZED DUEL.
I'D RATHER NOT BE STABBED IN THE BACK BEFORE GETTING TO THE QUEEN.
IF I OFFICIALLY DEFEAT THEIR GREATEST FIGHTER, THEY MUST ALL ACCEPT MY WORTH.

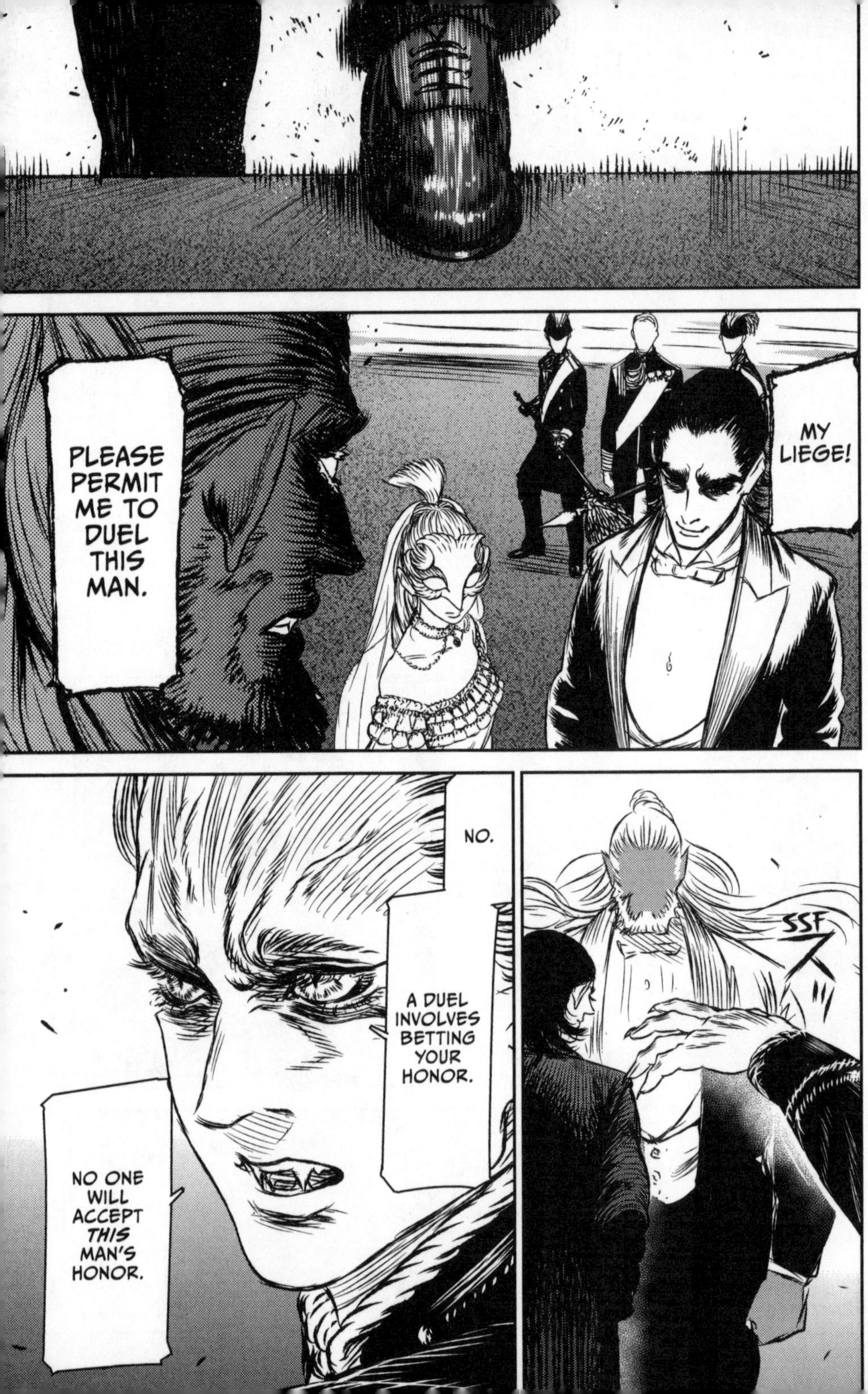
MY LIEGE!
PLEASE PERMIT ME TO DUEL THIS MAN.
SSF
NO.
A DUEL INVOLVES BETTING YOUR HONOR.
NO ONE WILL ACCEPT *THIS* MAN'S HONOR.

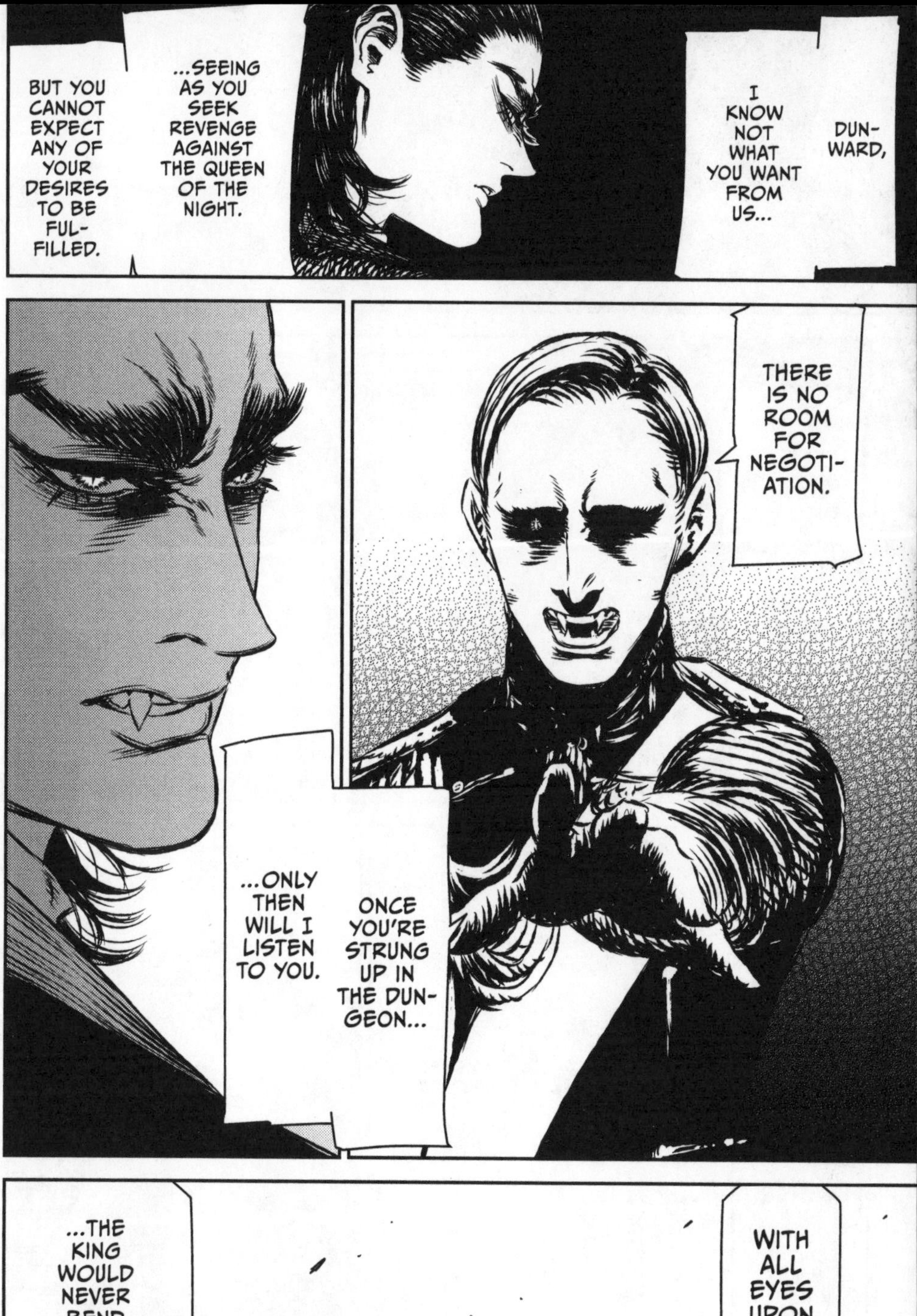
DUNWARD,
I KNOW NOT WHAT YOU WANT FROM US...
...SEEING AS YOU SEEK REVENGE AGAINST THE QUEEN OF THE NIGHT.
BUT YOU CANNOT EXPECT ANY OF YOUR DESIRES TO BE FULFILLED.
THERE IS NO ROOM FOR NEGOTIATION.
ONCE YOU'RE STRUNG UP IN THE DUNGEON...
...ONLY THEN WILL I LISTEN TO YOU.
WITH ALL EYES UPON HIM...
...THE KING WOULD NEVER BEND AGAINST THE GNIR.

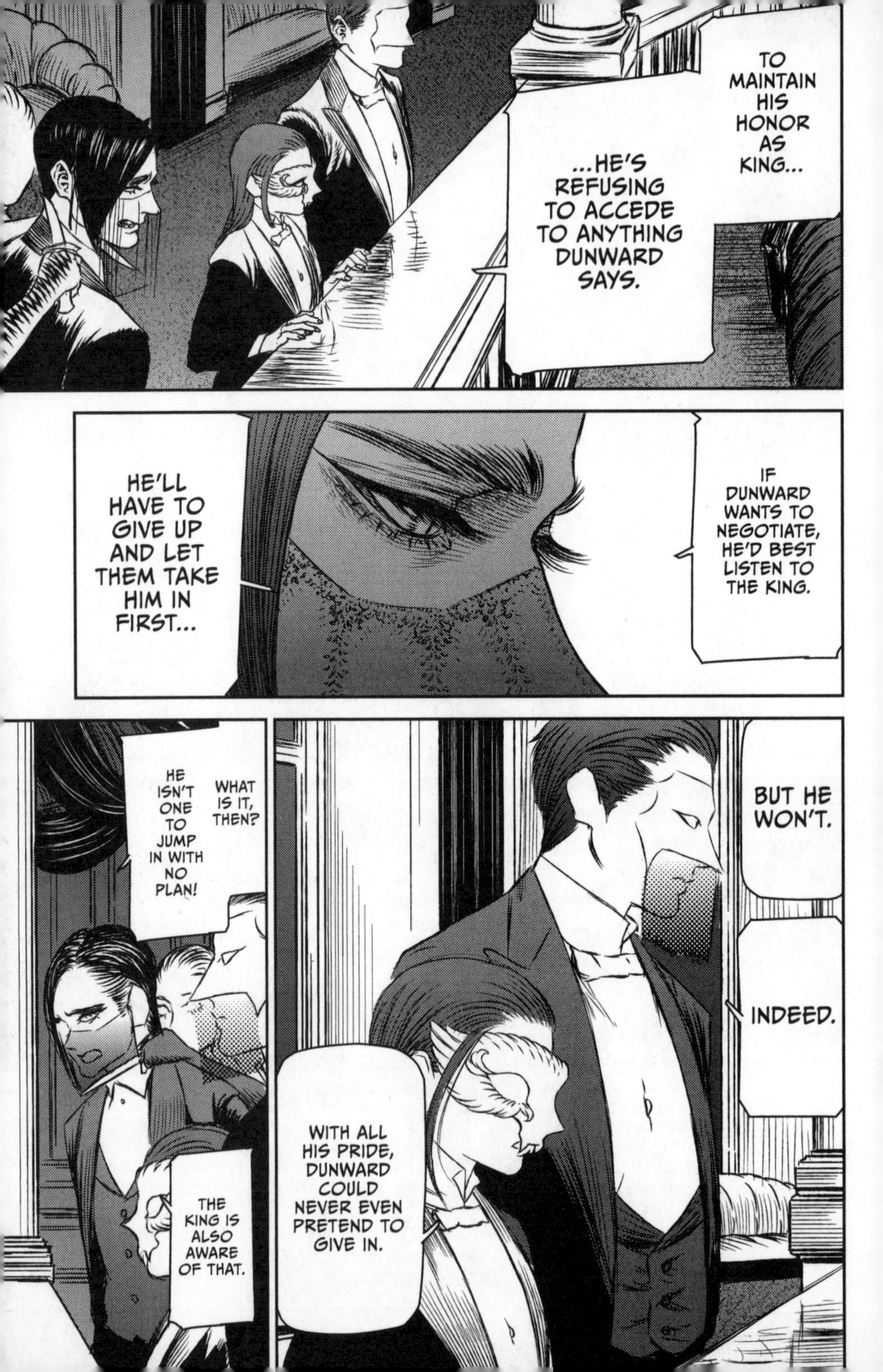
TO MAINTAIN HIS HONOR AS KING...
...HE'S REFUSING TO ACCEDE TO ANYTHING DUNWARD SAYS.
IF DUNWARD WANTS TO NEGOTIATE, HE'D BEST LISTEN TO THE KING.
HE'LL HAVE TO GIVE UP AND LET THEM TAKE HIM IN FIRST...
BUT HE WON'T.
INDEED.
WITH ALL HIS PRIDE, DUNWARD COULD NEVER EVEN PRETEND TO GIVE IN.
WHAT IS IT, THEN?
HE ISN'T ONE TO JUMP IN WITH NO PLAN!
THE KING IS ALSO AWARE OF THAT.

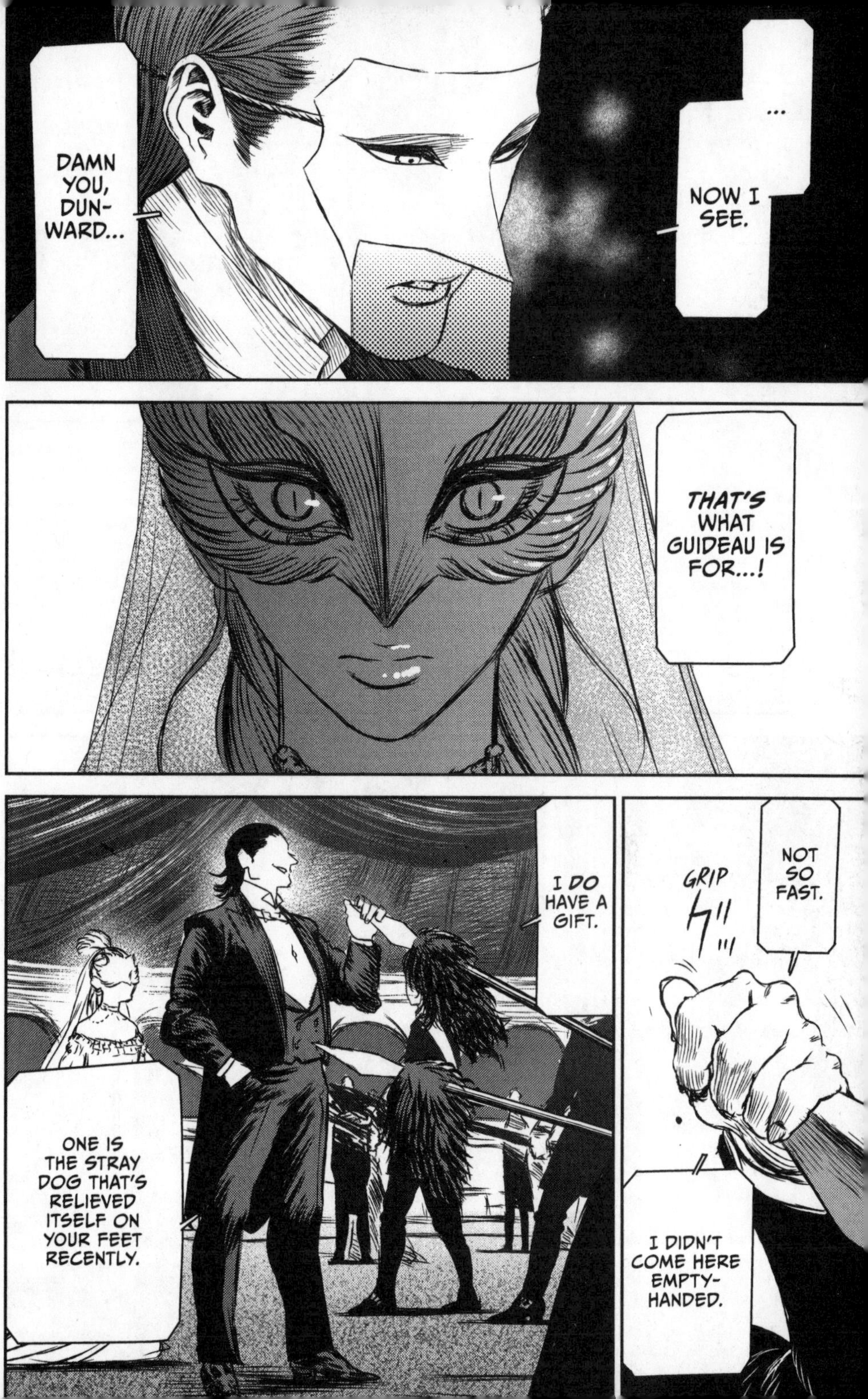
...
NOW I SEE.
DAMN YOU, DUNWARD...
*THAT'S* WHAT GUIDEAU IS FOR...!
NOT SO FAST.
GRIP
I DIDN'T COME HERE EMPTY-HANDED.
I *DO* HAVE A GIFT.
ONE IS THE STRAY DOG THAT'S RELIEVED ITSELF ON YOUR FEET RECENTLY.

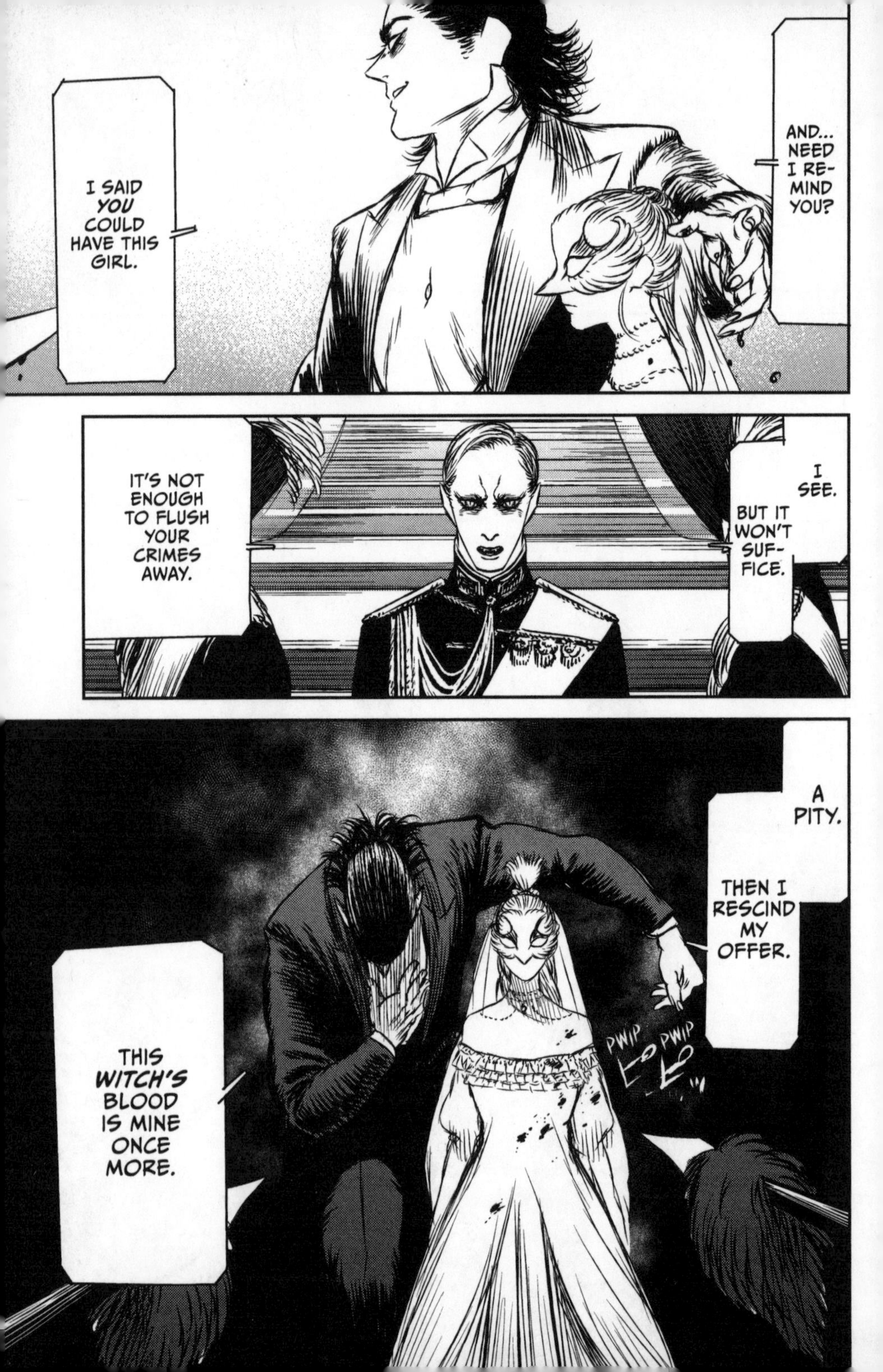
AND... NEED I REMIND YOU?
I SAID *YOU* COULD HAVE THIS GIRL.
I SEE.
BUT IT WON'T SUFFICE.
IT'S NOT ENOUGH TO FLUSH YOUR CRIMES AWAY.
A PITY.
THEN I RESCIND MY OFFER.
PWIP PWIP
THIS *WITCH'S* BLOOD IS MINE ONCE MORE.

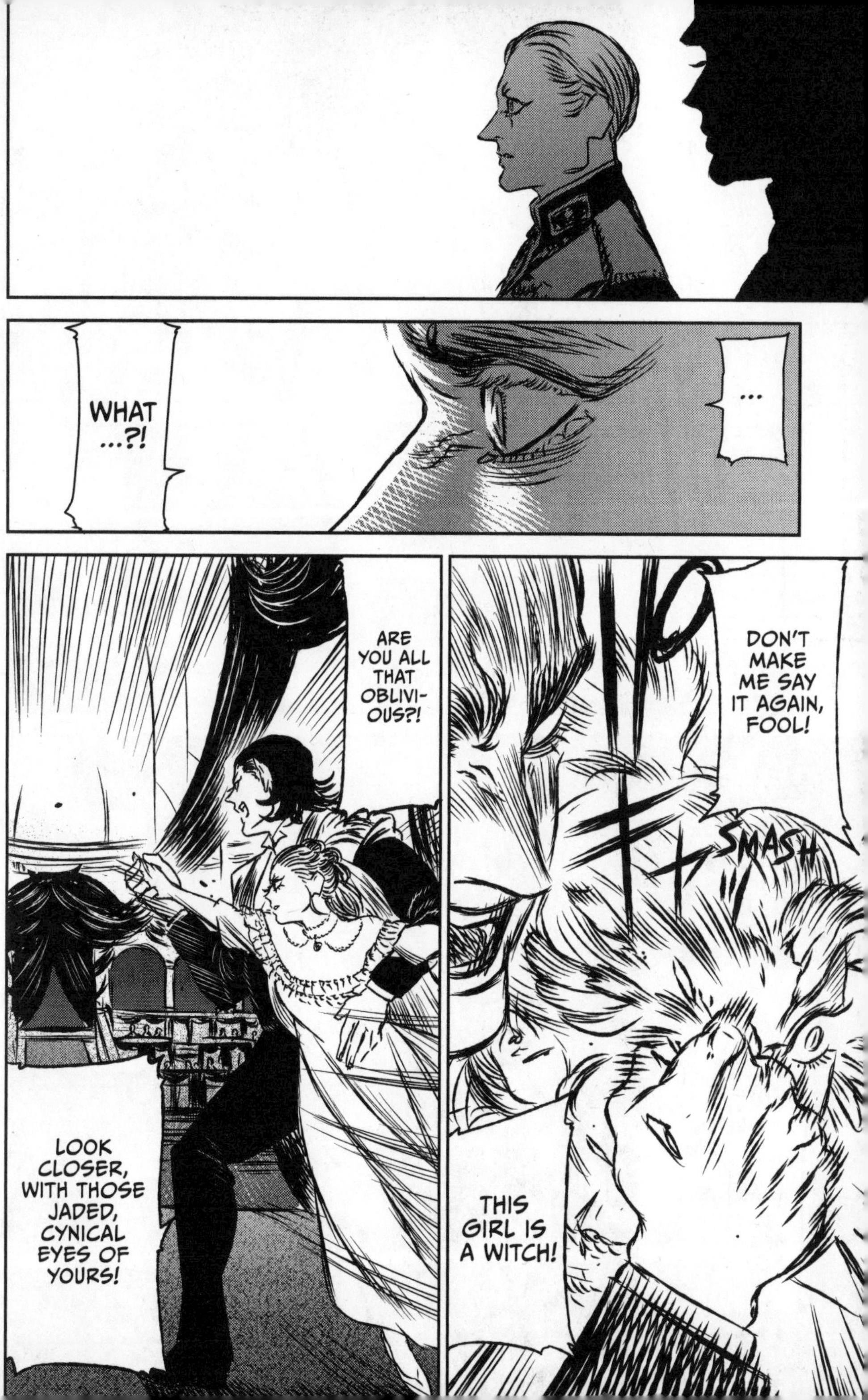
...
WHAT ...?!
DON'T MAKE ME SAY IT AGAIN, FOOL!
SMASH
THIS GIRL IS A WITCH!
ARE YOU ALL THAT OBLIVIOUS?!
LOOK CLOSER, WITH THOSE JADED, CYNICAL EYES OF YOURS!

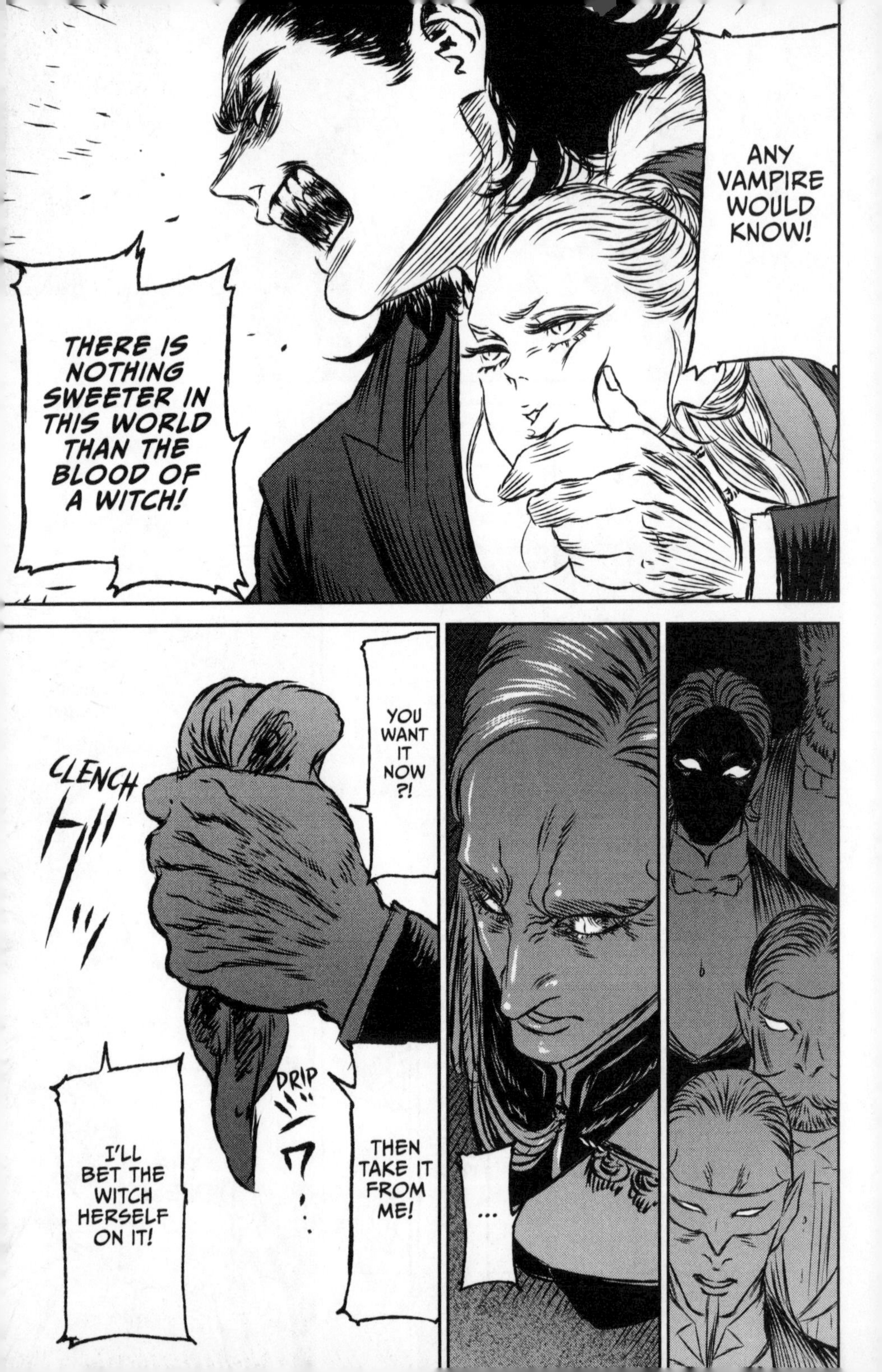
ANY VAMPIRE WOULD KNOW!
THERE IS NOTHING SWEETER IN THIS WORLD THAN THE BLOOD OF A WITCH!
...
YOU WANT IT NOW?!
CLENCH
THEN TAKE IT FROM ME!
DRIP
I'LL BET THE WITCH HERSELF ON IT!

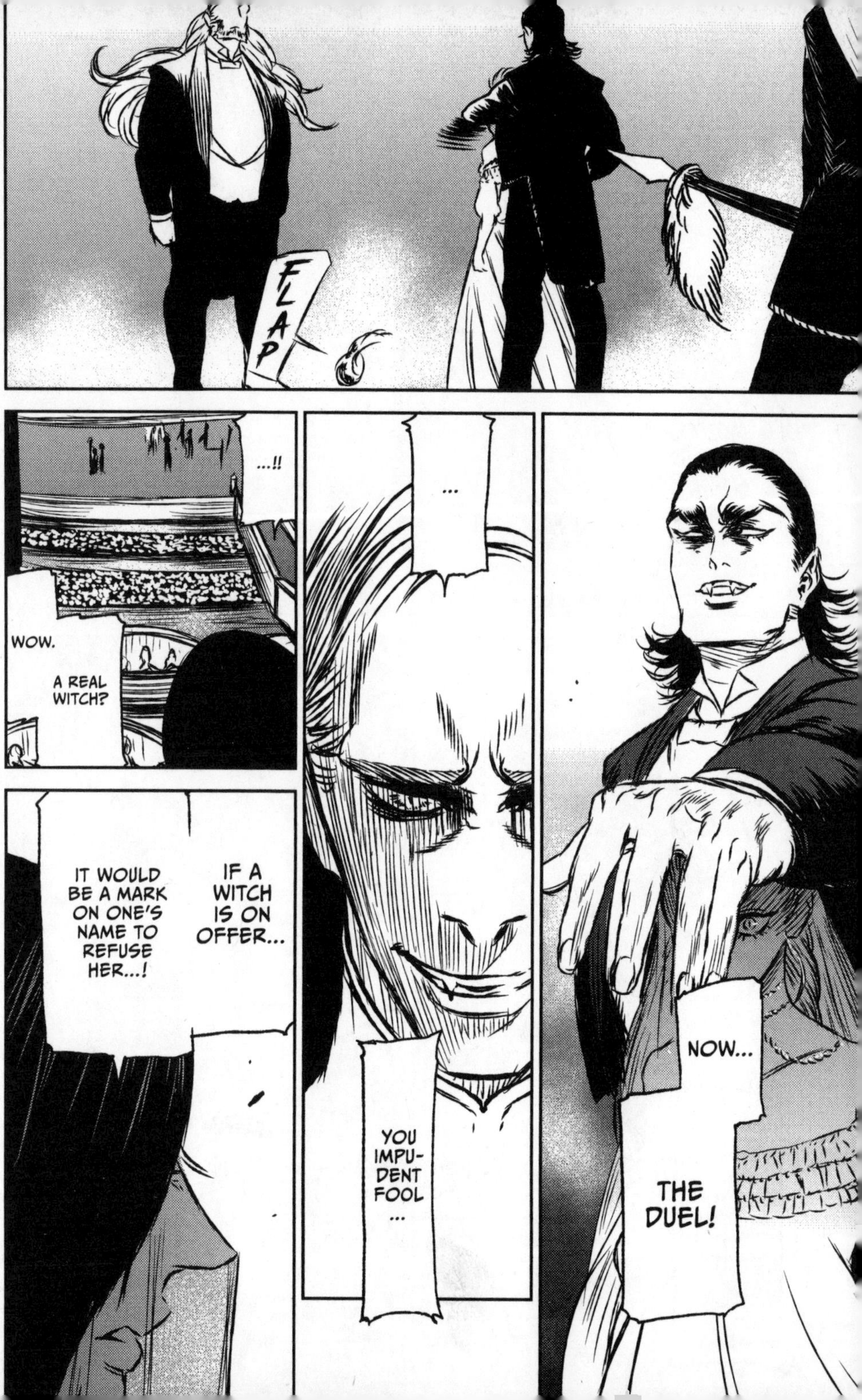
FLAP
NOW...
THE DUEL!
...
YOU IMPUDENT FOOL...
...!!
WOW.
A REAL WITCH?
IF A WITCH IS ON OFFER...
IT WOULD BE A MARK ON ONE'S NAME TO REFUSE HER...!

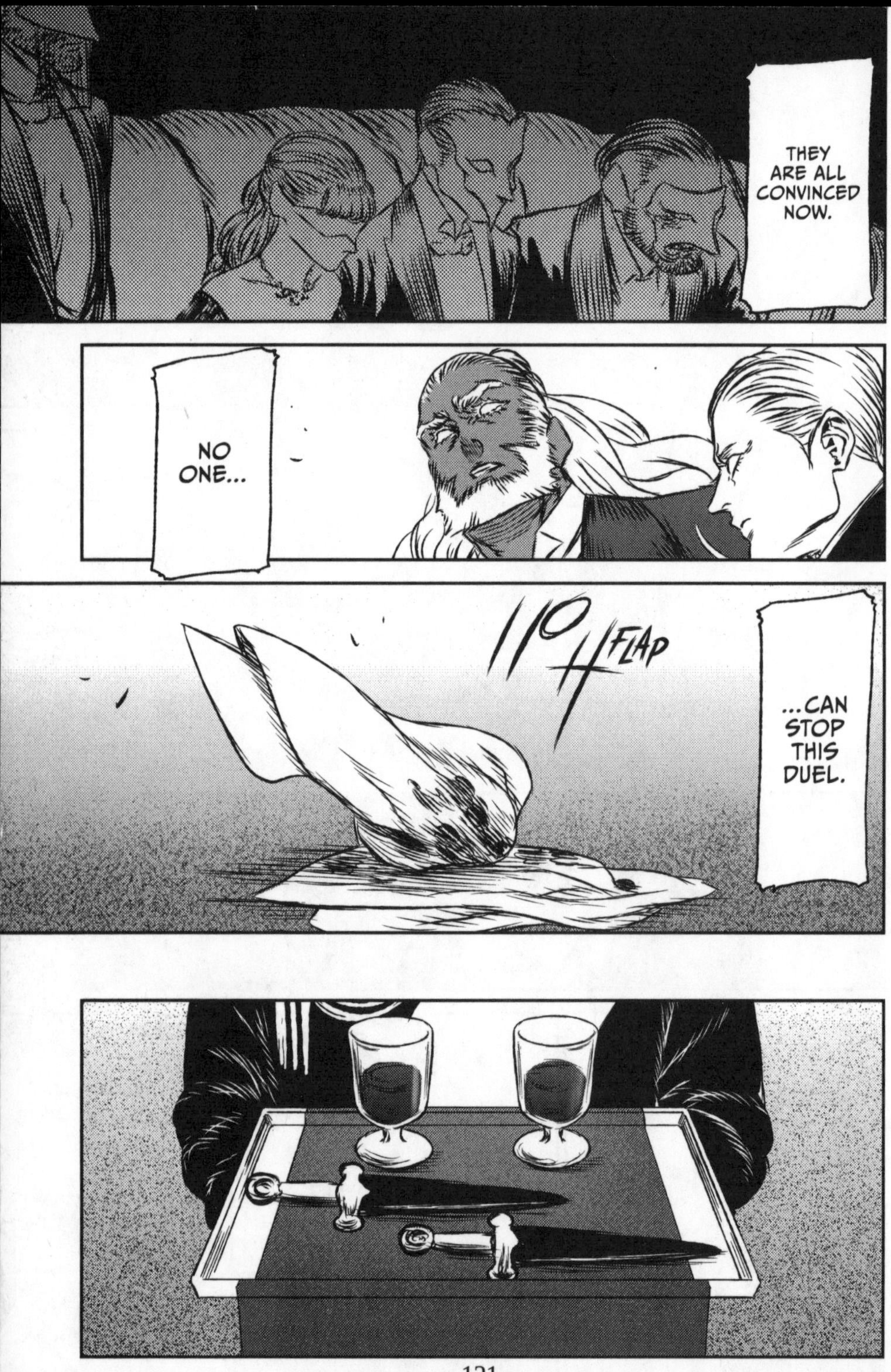
THEY ARE ALL CONVINCED NOW.
NO ONE...
...CAN STOP THIS DUEL.
FLAP

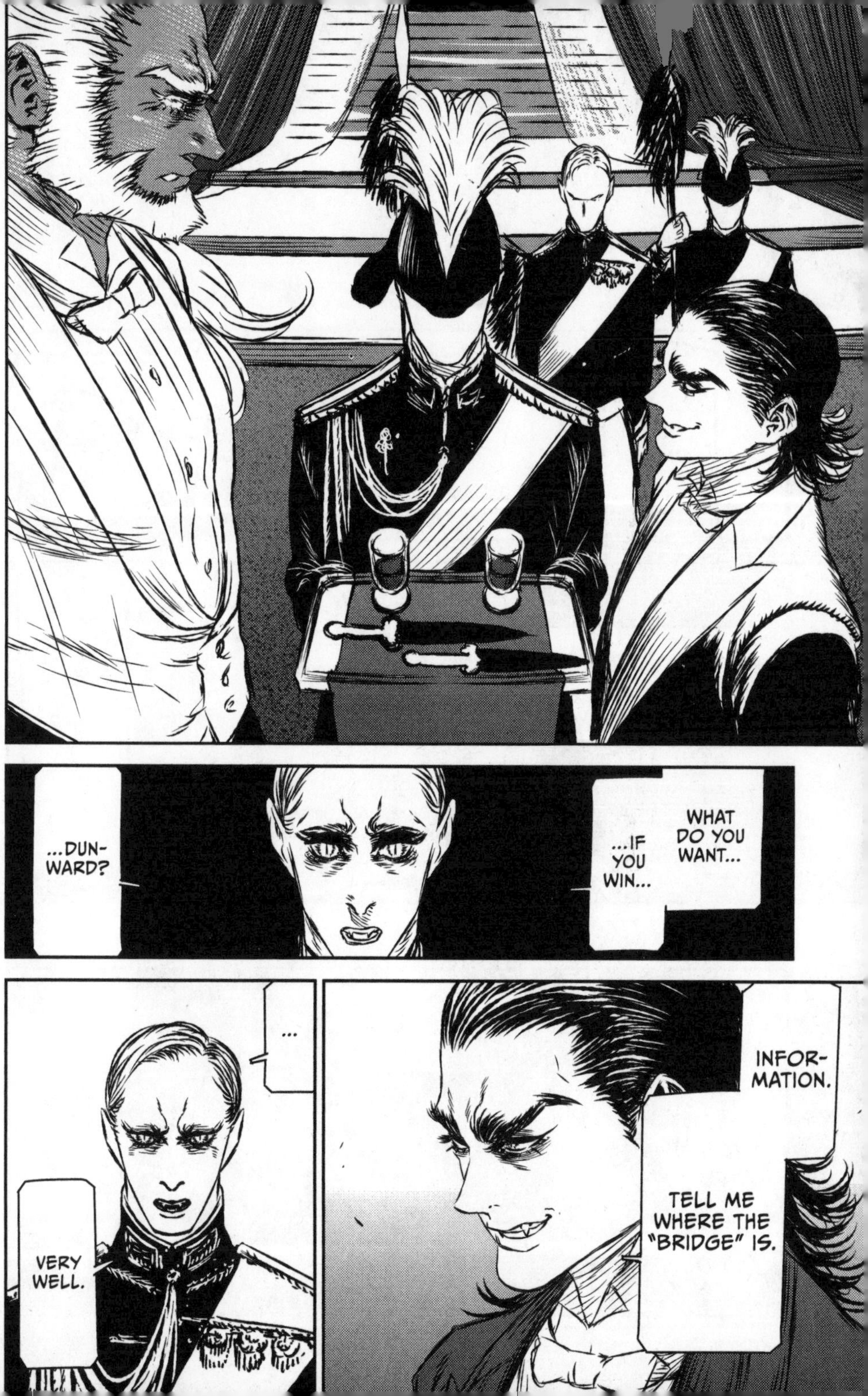
WHAT DO YOU WANT...
...IF YOU WIN...
...DUNWARD?
INFORMATION.
TELL ME WHERE THE "BRIDGE" IS.
...
VERY WELL.

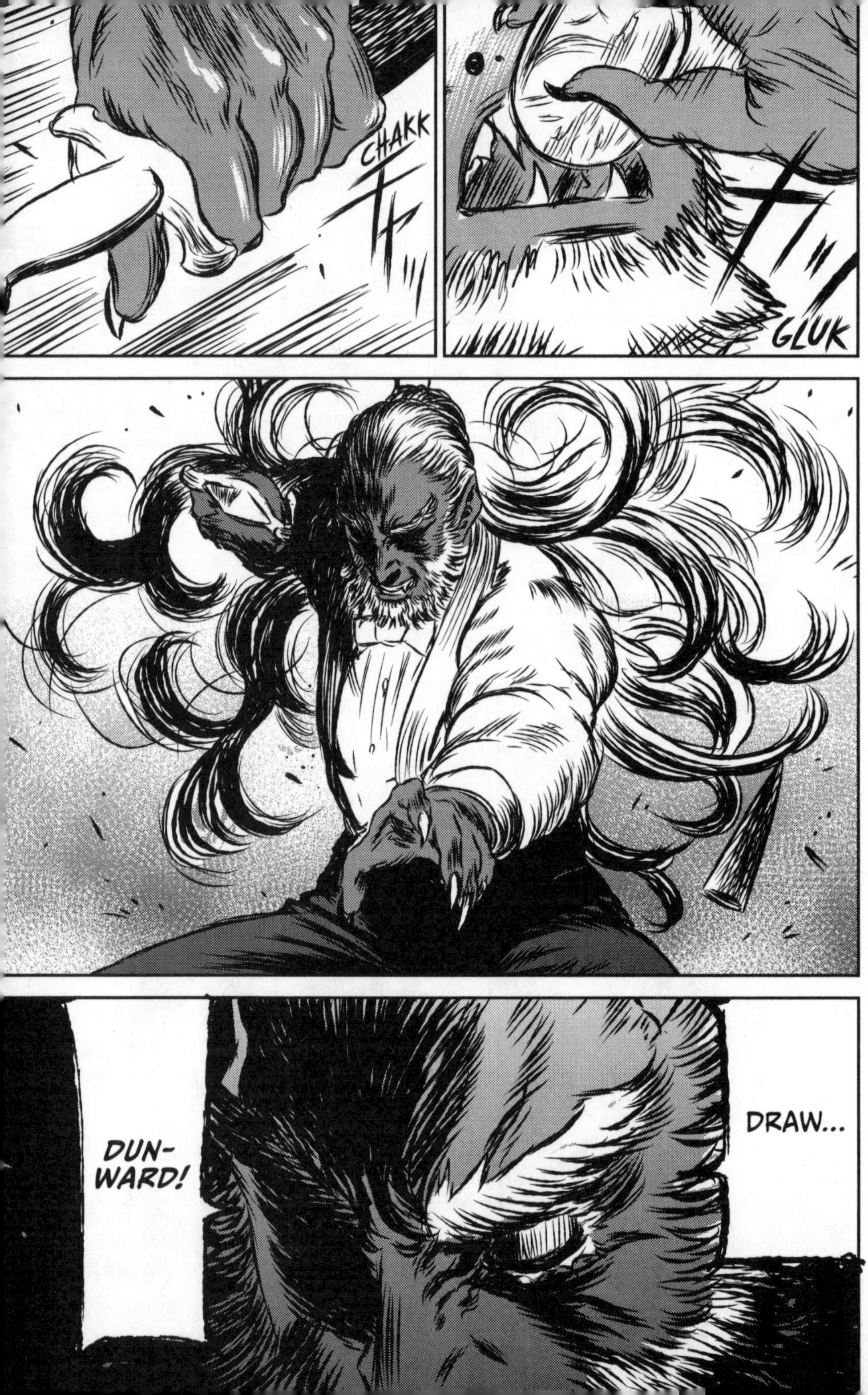
GLUK
CHAKK
DRAW...
DUN-
WARD!

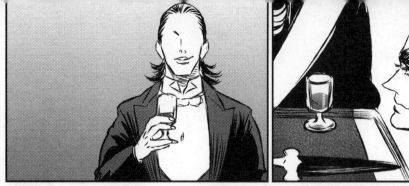

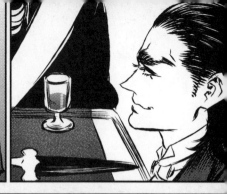

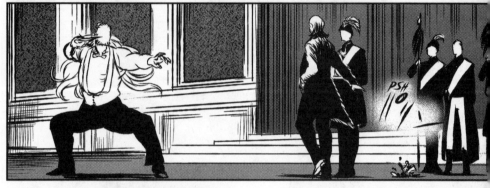

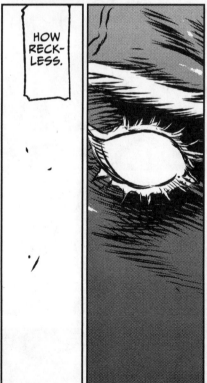

HOW RECK-LESS.

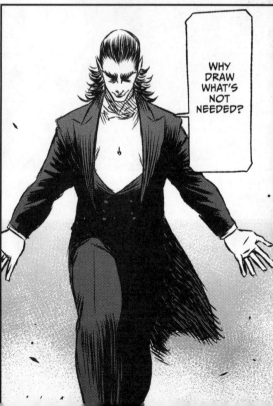

WHY DRAW WHAT'S NOT NEEDED?

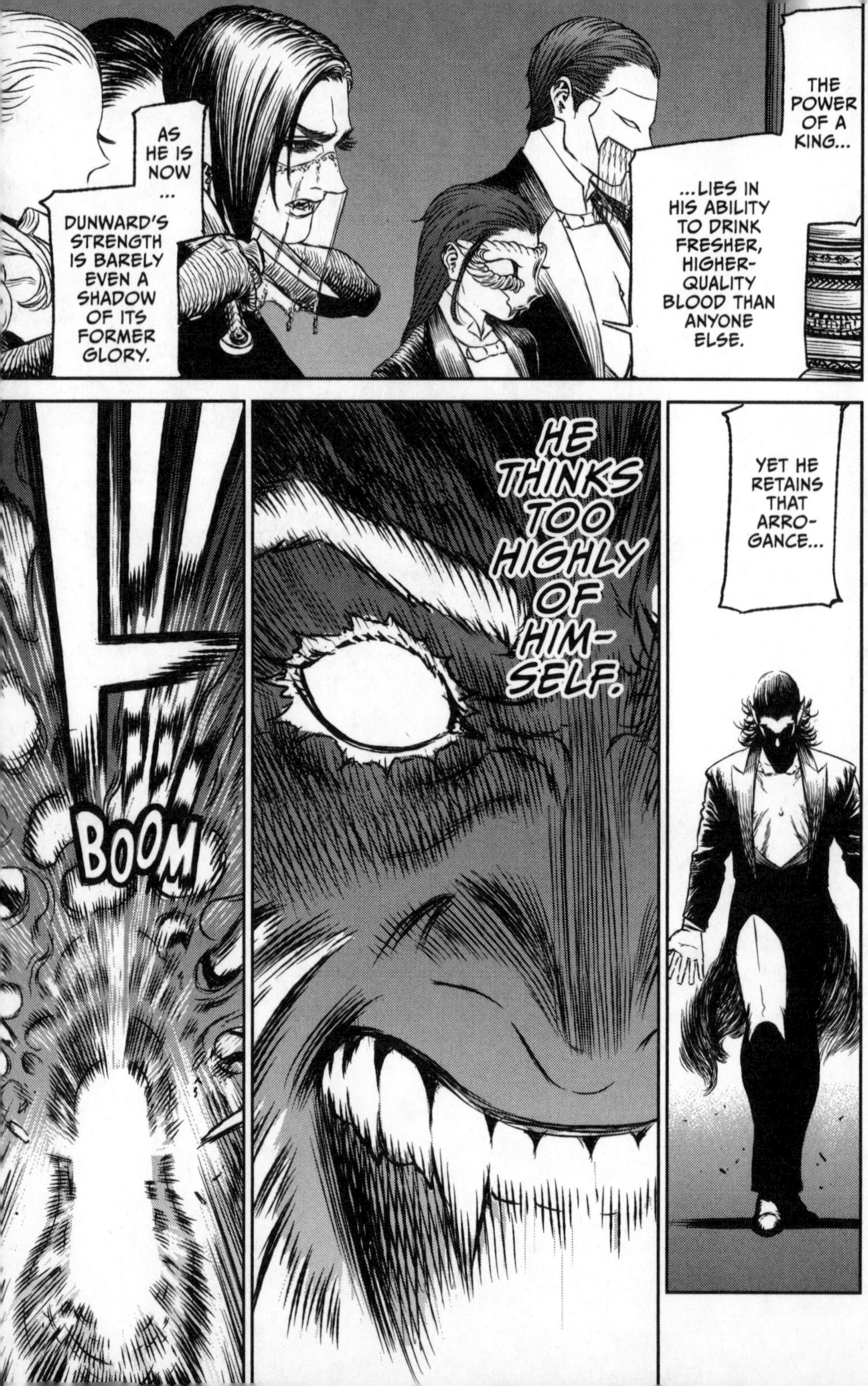
THE POWER OF A KING...
...LIES IN HIS ABILITY TO DRINK FRESHER, HIGHER-QUALITY BLOOD THAN ANYONE ELSE.
AS HE IS NOW...
DUNWARD'S STRENGTH IS BARELY EVEN A SHADOW OF ITS FORMER GLORY.
YET HE RETAINS THAT ARRO-GANCE...
HE THINKS TOO HIGHLY OF HIM-SELF.
BOOM

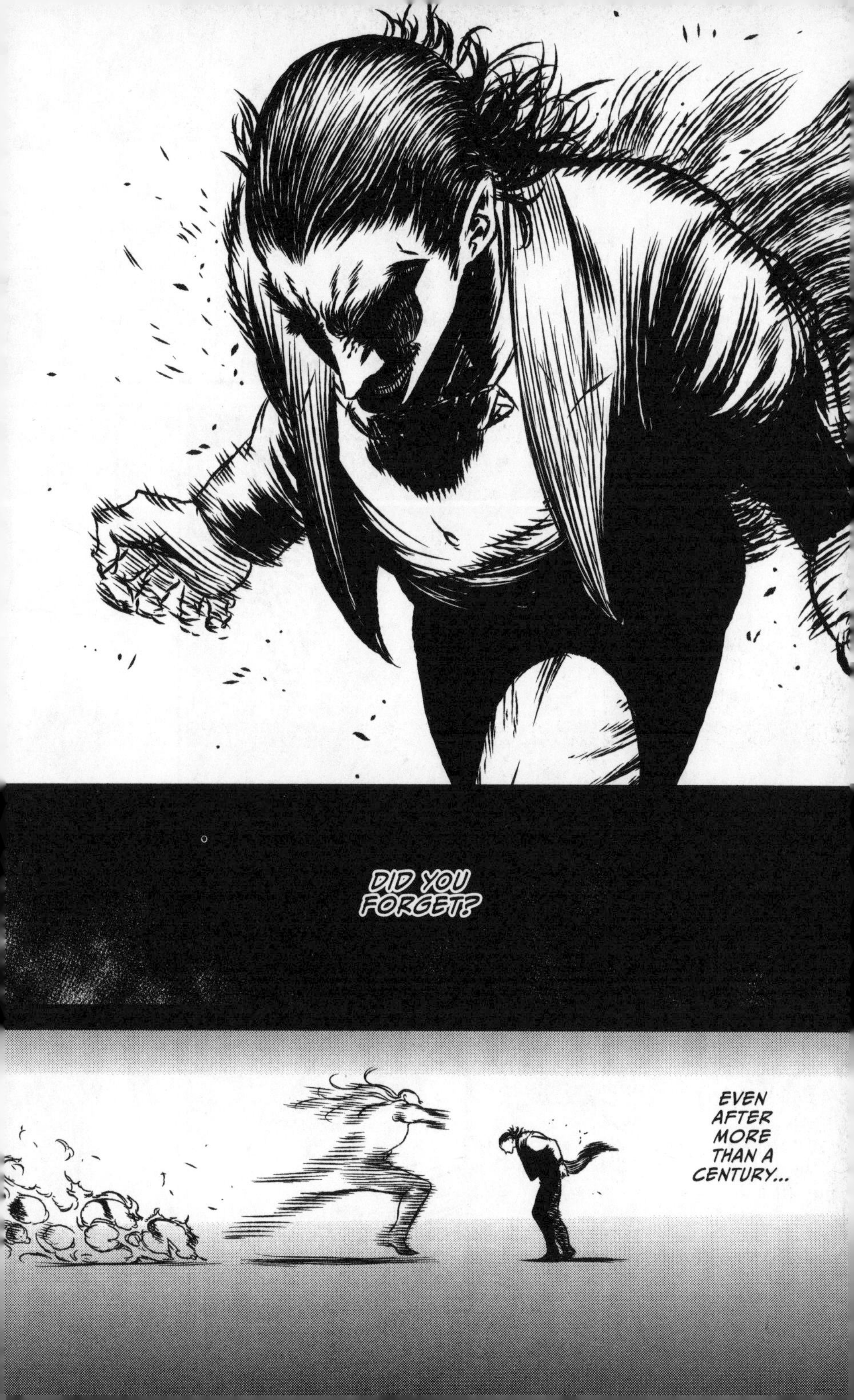
DID YOU FORGET?
EVEN AFTER MORE THAN A CENTURY...

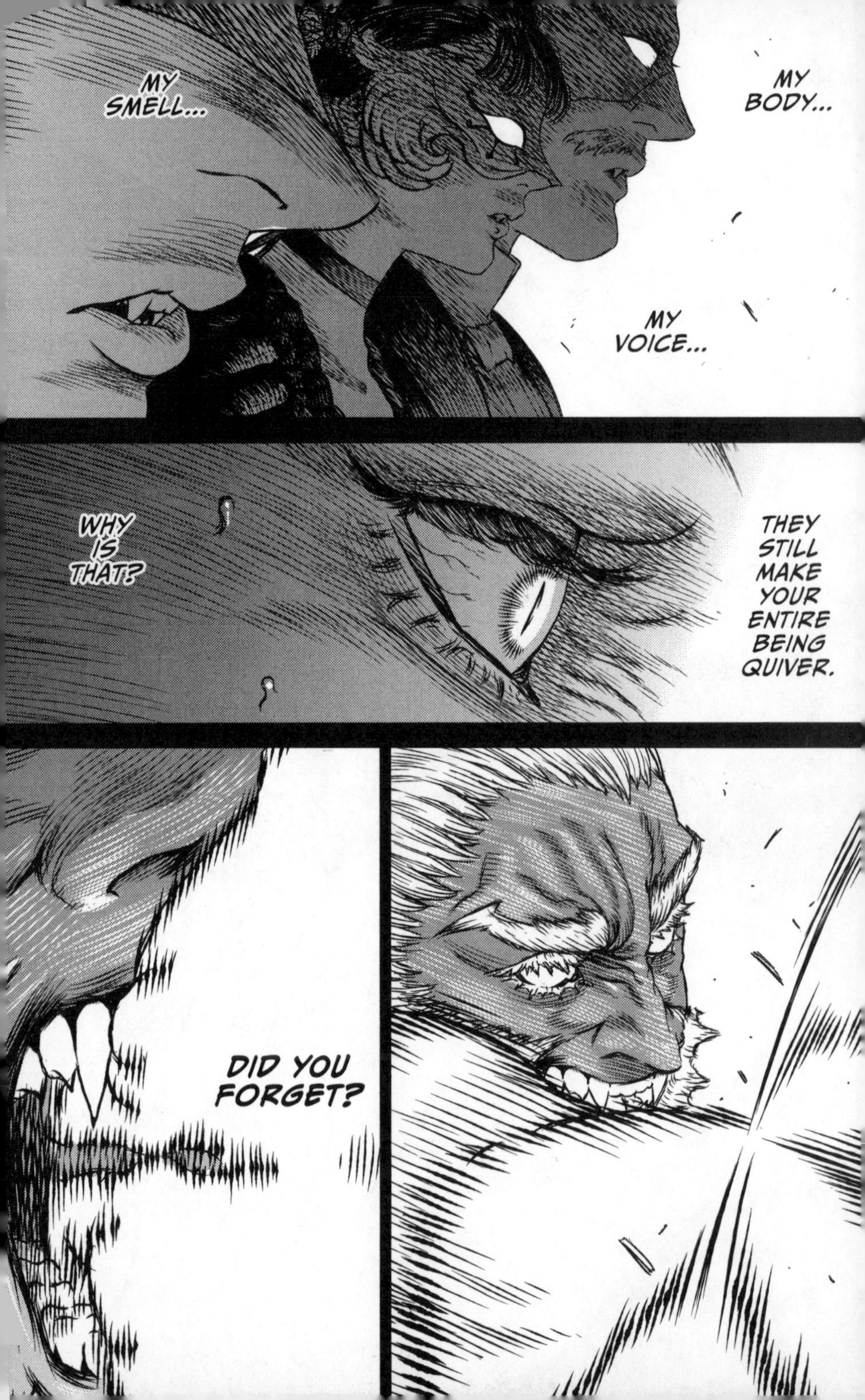
MY BODY...
MY VOICE...
MY SMELL...
THEY STILL MAKE YOUR ENTIRE BEING QUIVER.
WHY IS THAT?
DID YOU FORGET?

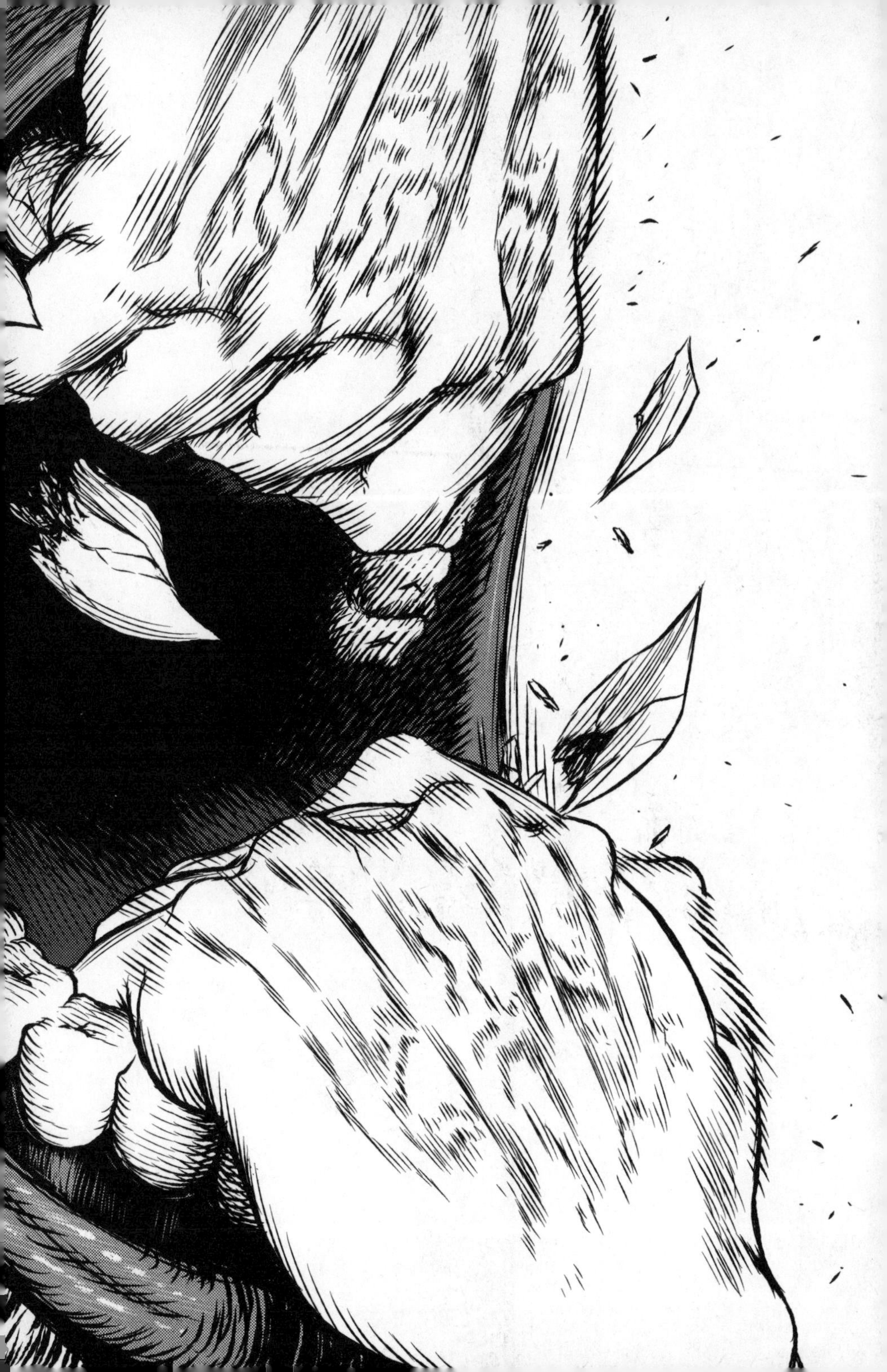

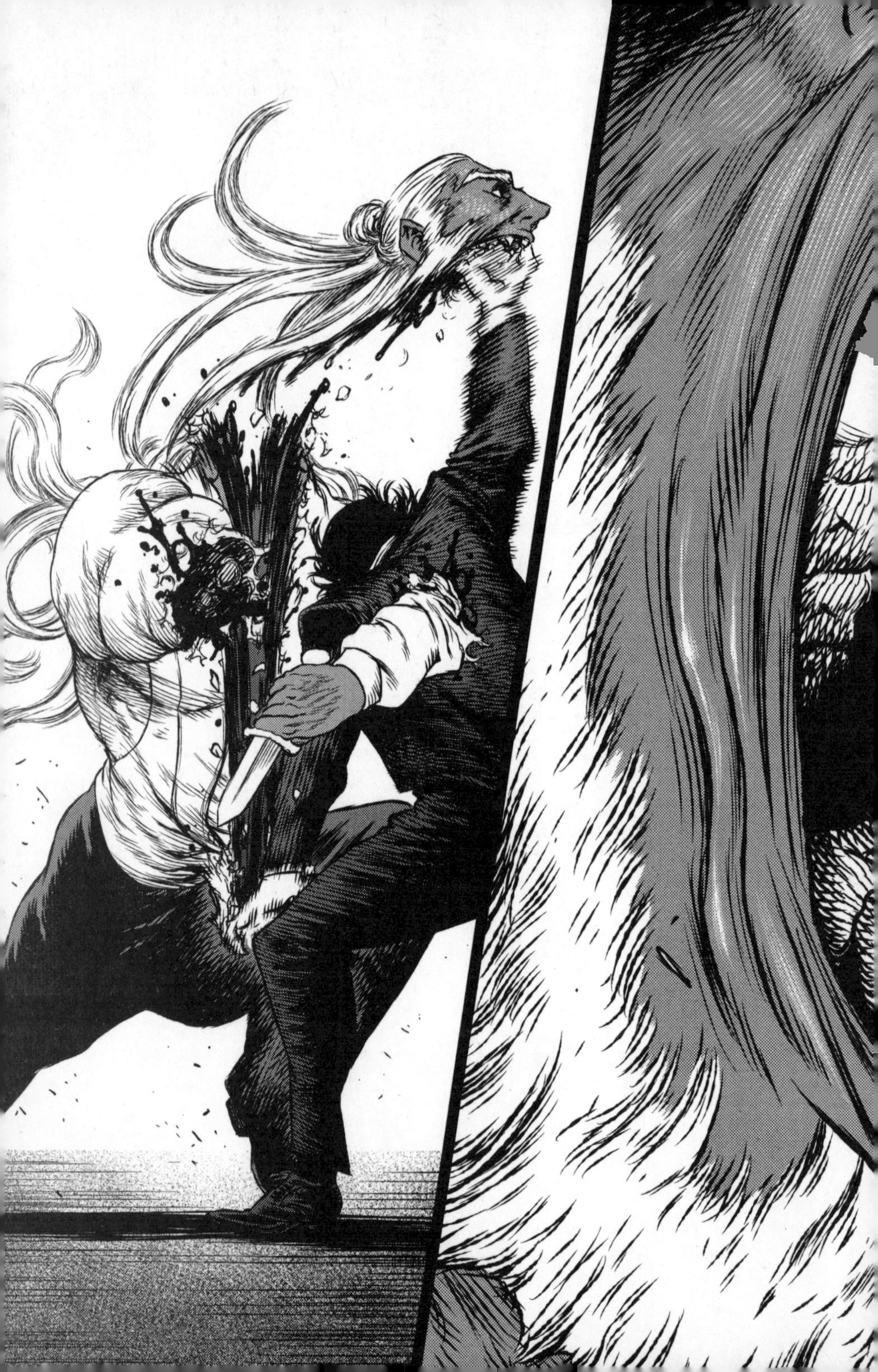

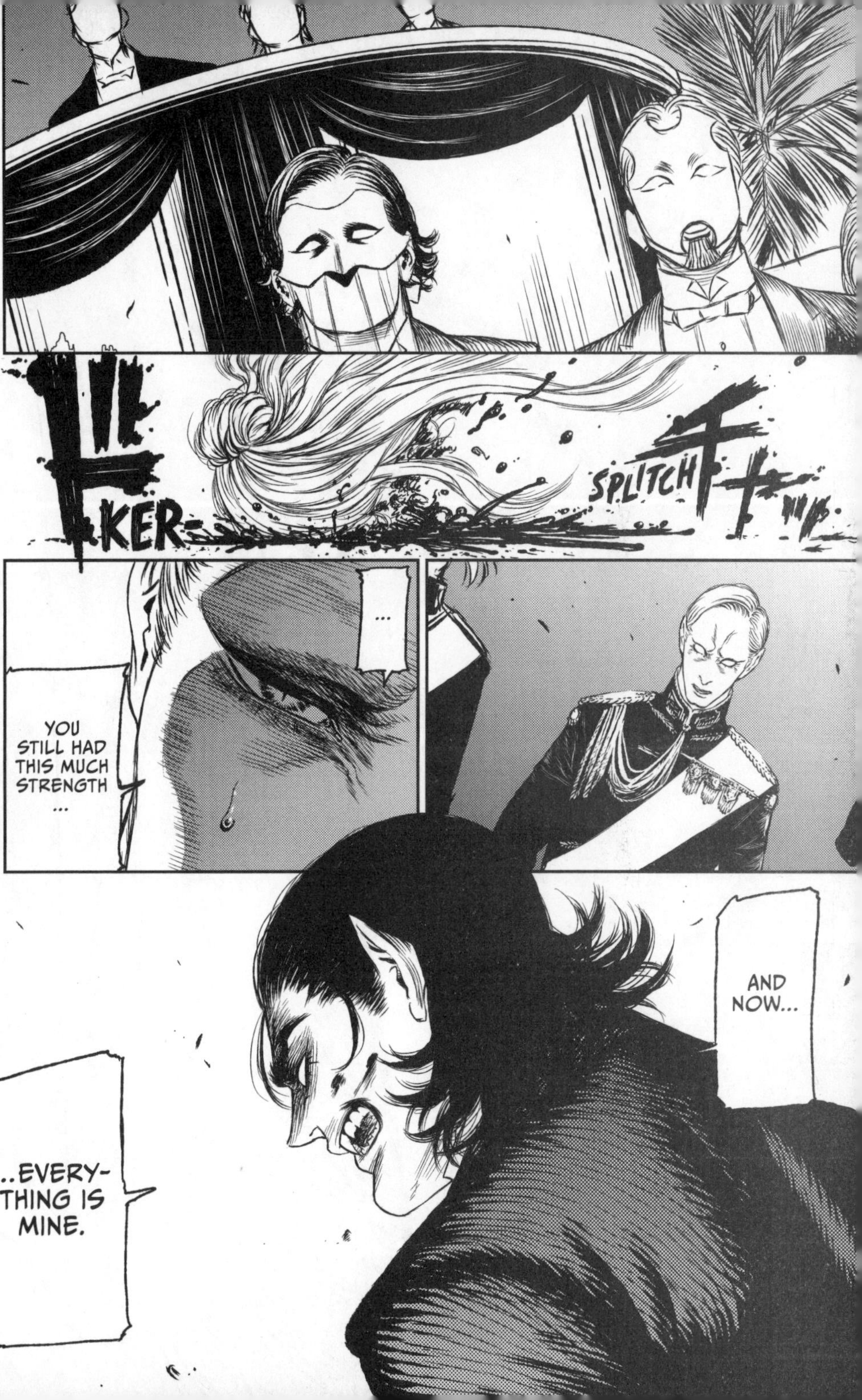
SPLITCH
KER-
...
YOU STILL HAD THIS MUCH STRENGTH ...
AND NOW...
...EVERY-THING IS MINE.

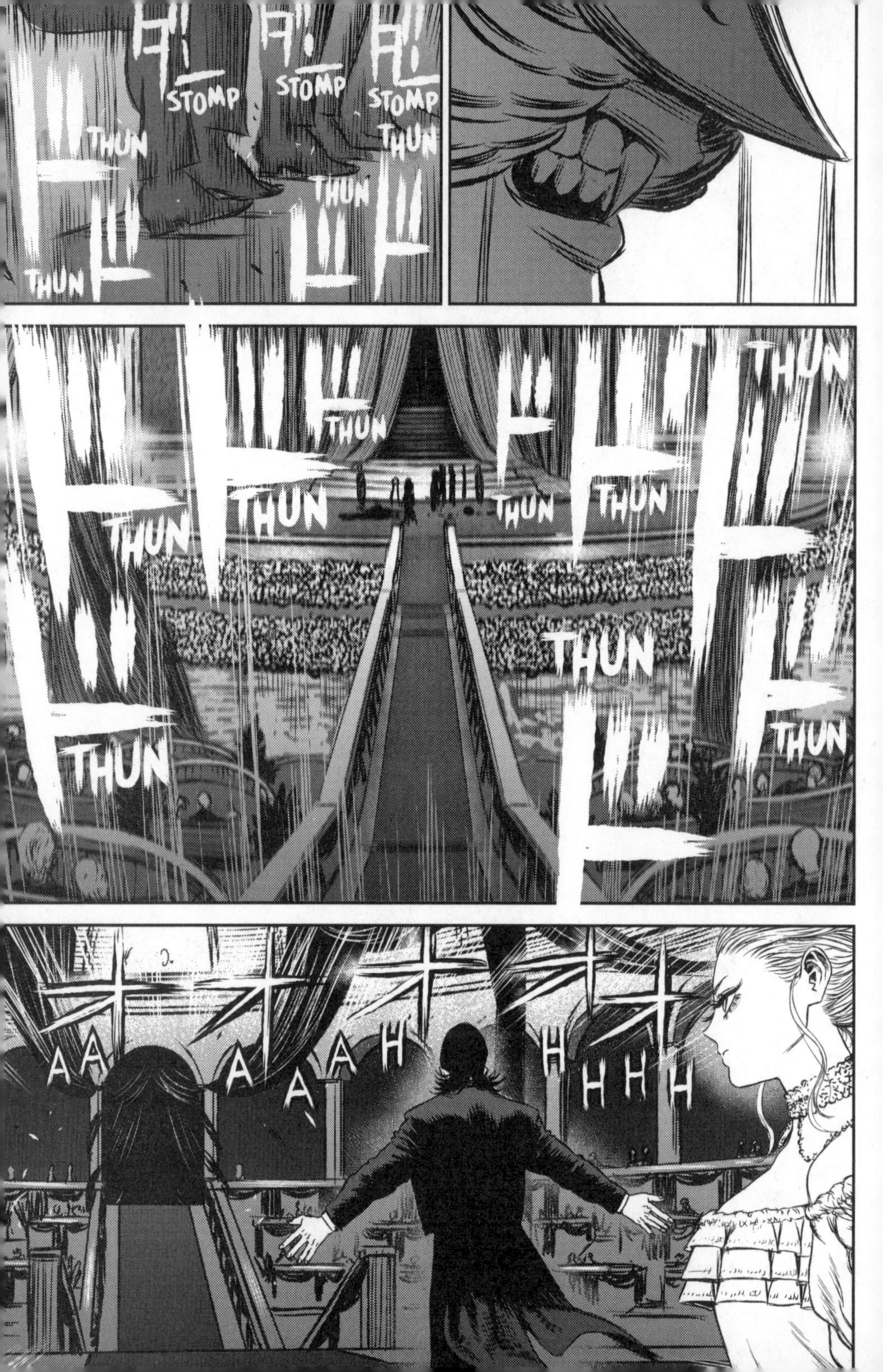
STOMP
THUN
STOMP
THUN
STOMP
THUN
THUN
THUN
THUN
THUN
THUN
THUN
THUN
THUN
THUN
THUN
AAAAAHHHHHH

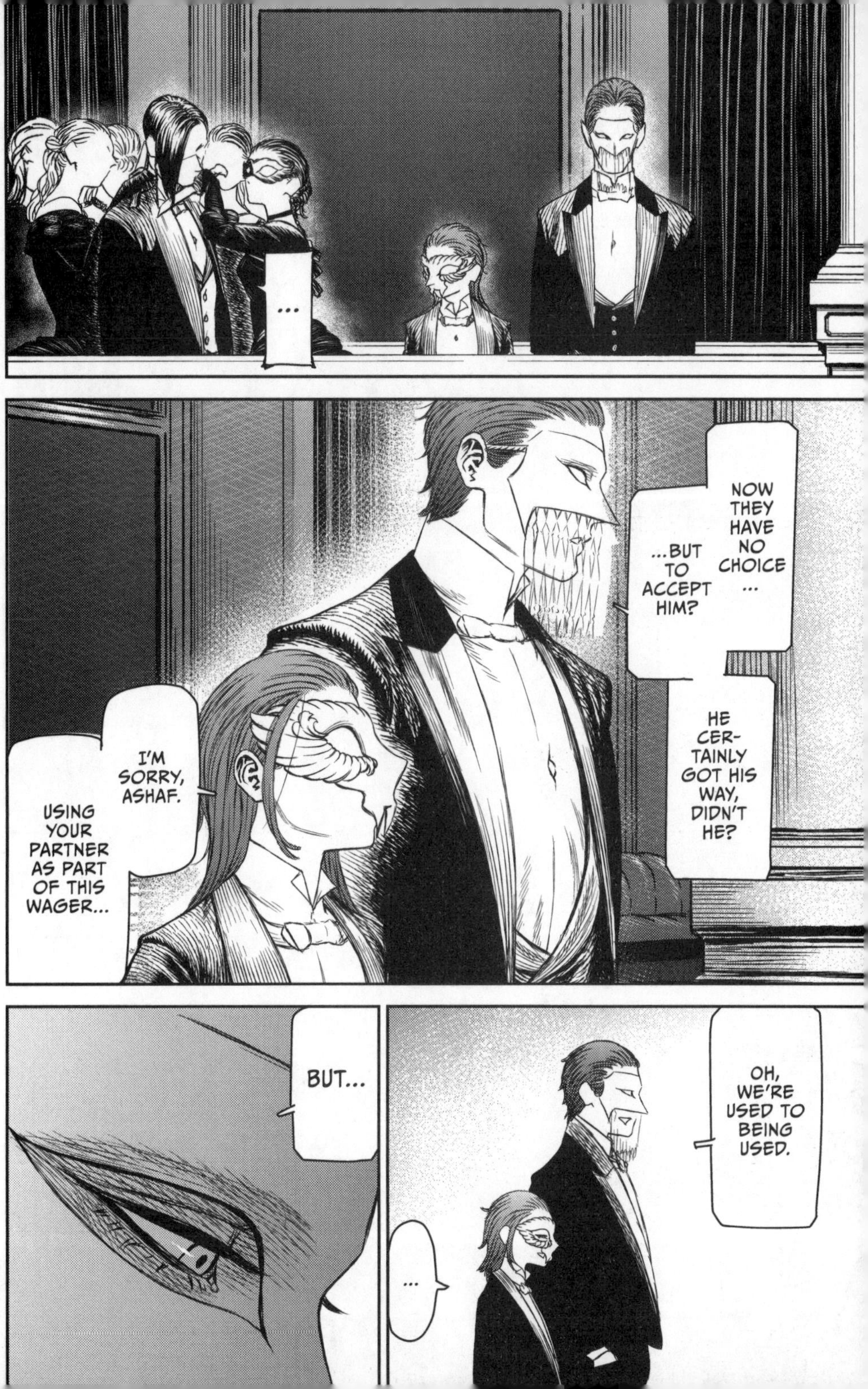
...
NOW THEY HAVE NO CHOICE ...
...BUT TO ACCEPT HIM?
HE CERTAINLY GOT HIS WAY, DIDN'T HE?
I'M SORRY, ASHAF.
USING YOUR PARTNER AS PART OF THIS WAGER...
OH, WE'RE USED TO BEING USED.
...
BUT...

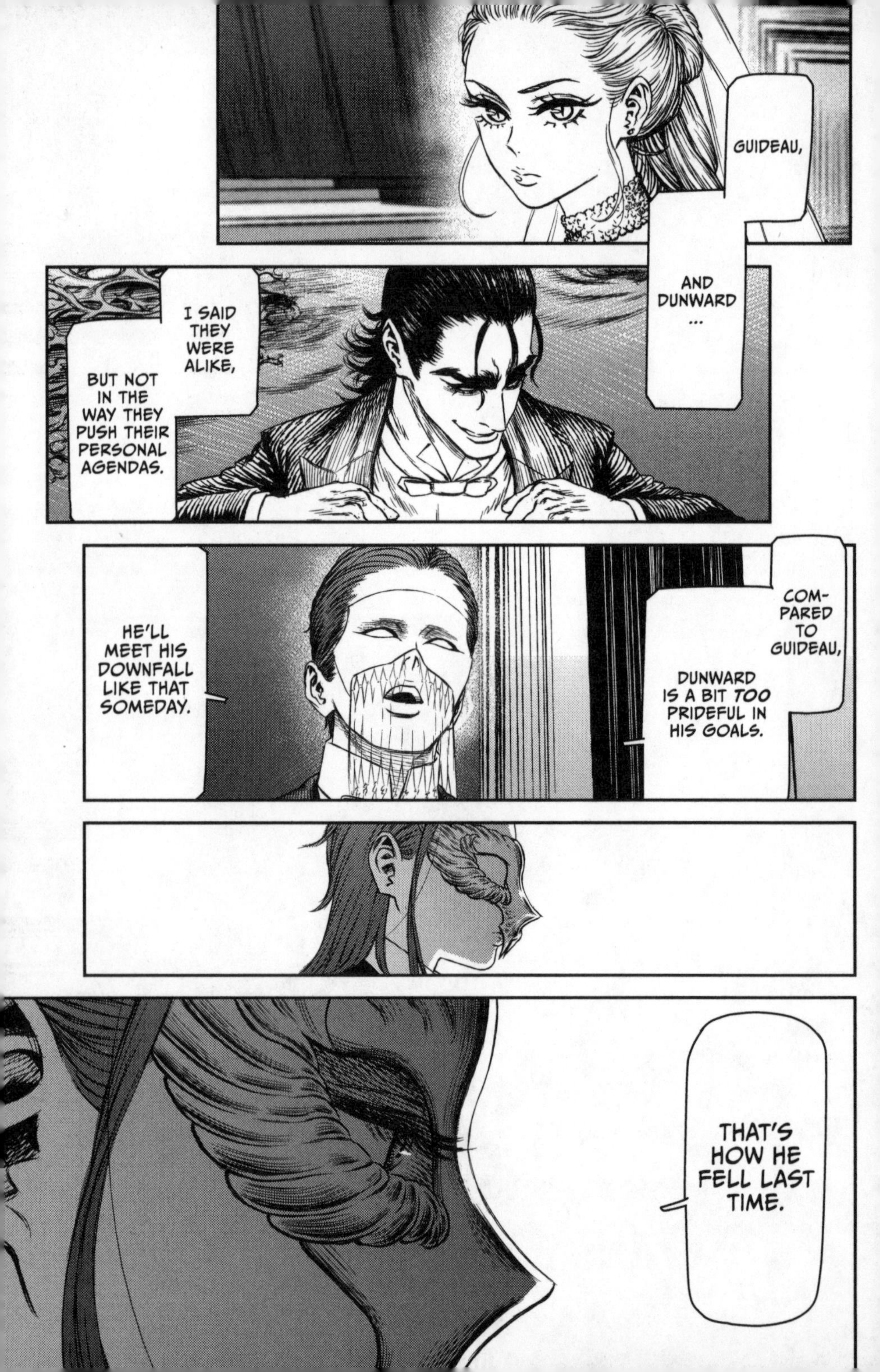
GUIDEAU,
AND DUNWARD ...
I SAID THEY WERE ALIKE,
BUT NOT IN THE WAY THEY PUSH THEIR PERSONAL AGENDAS.
COM-PARED TO GUIDEAU,
DUNWARD IS A BIT *TOO* PRIDEFUL IN HIS GOALS.
HE'LL MEET HIS DOWNFALL LIKE THAT SOMEDAY.
THAT'S HOW HE FELL LAST TIME.

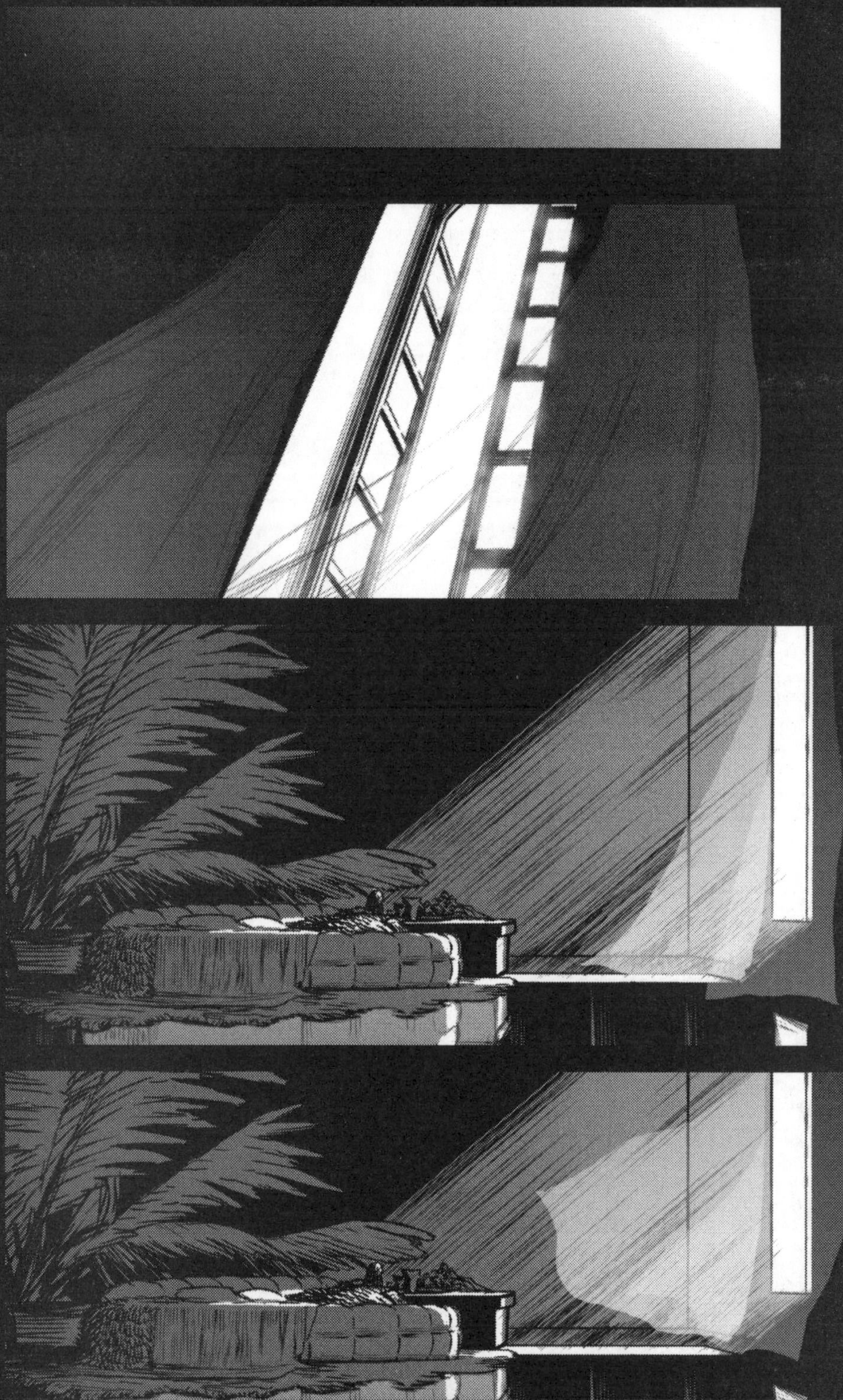

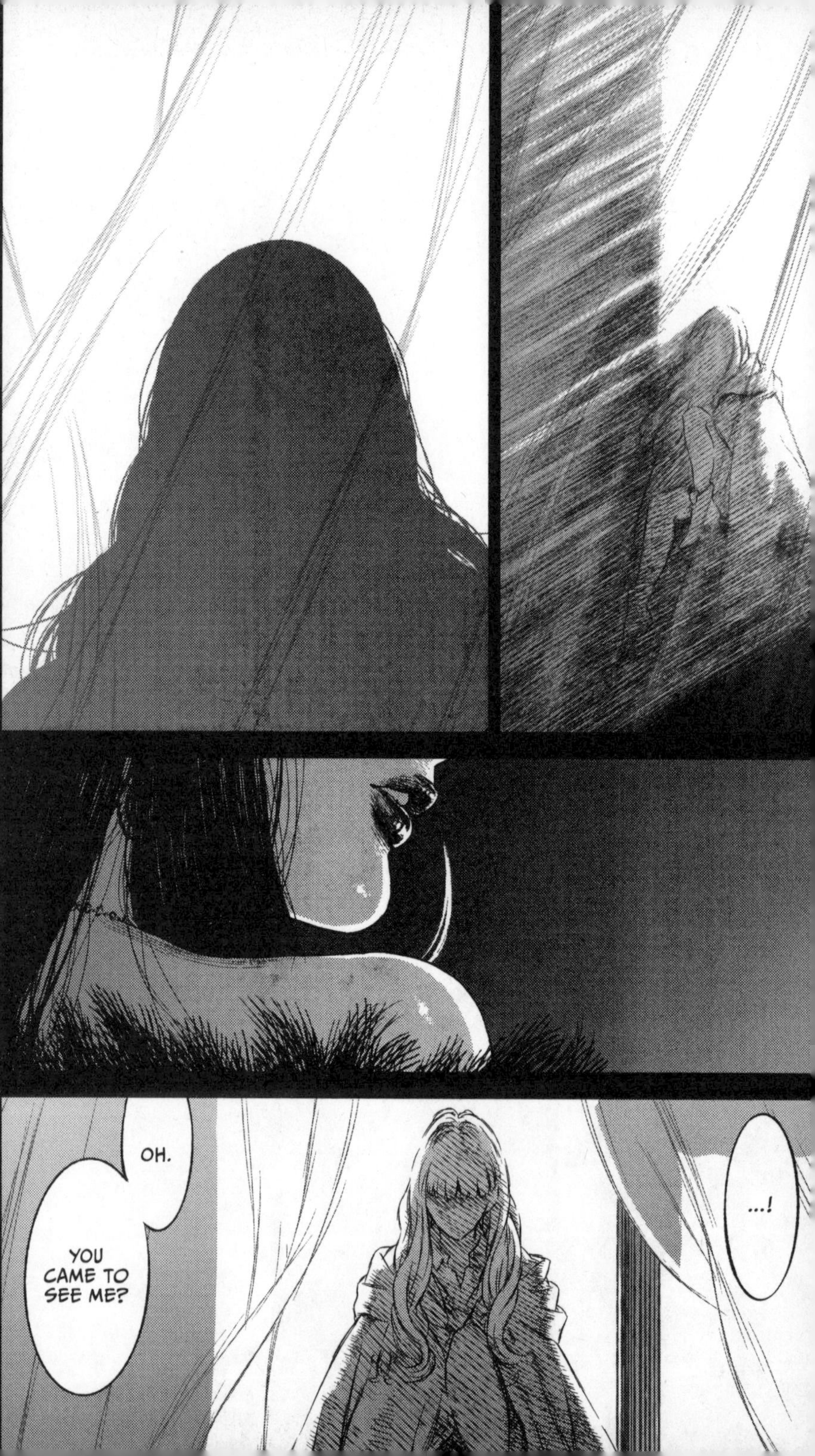
...!
OH.
YOU CAME TO SEE ME?

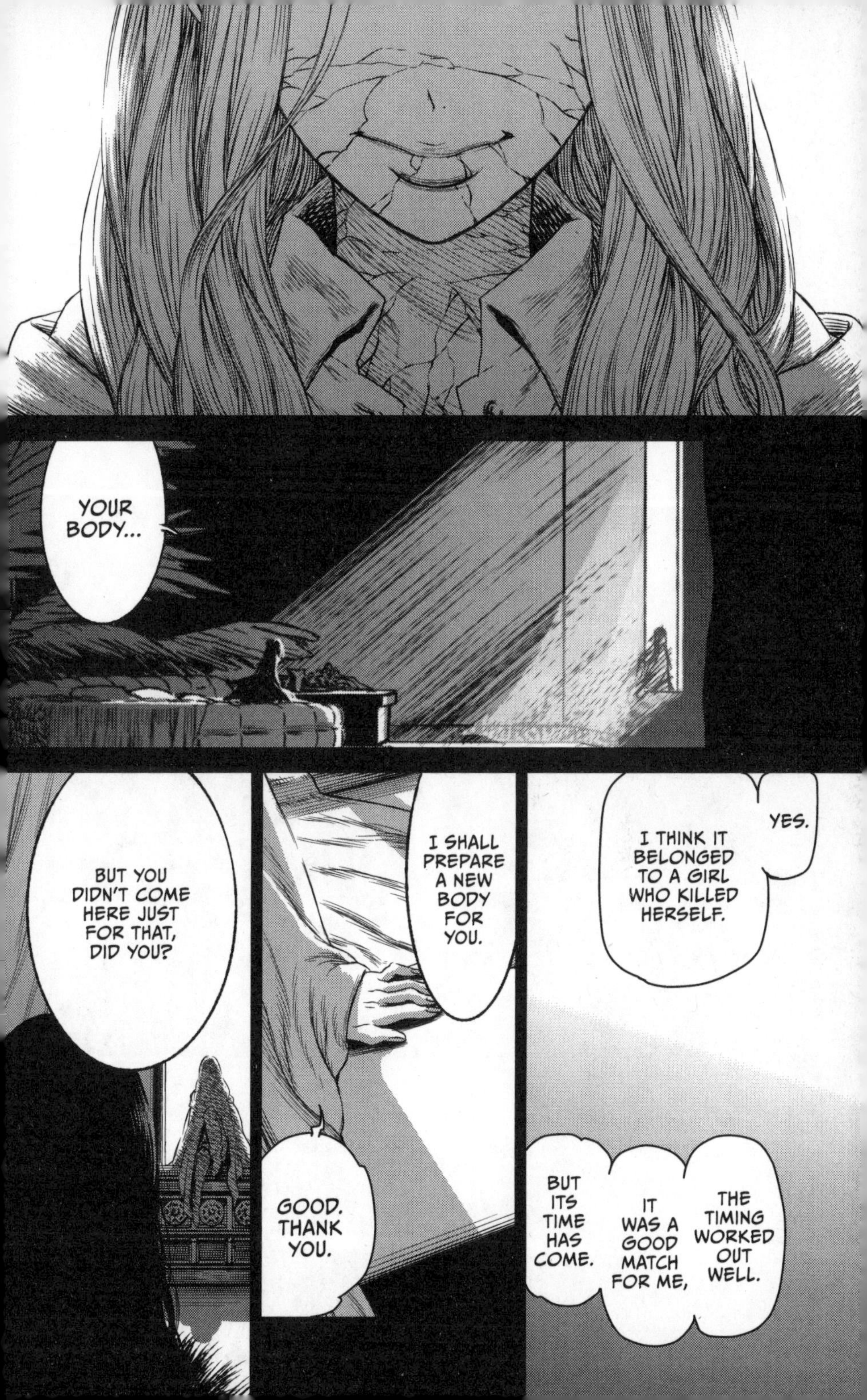
YOUR BODY...
YES.
I THINK IT BELONGED TO A GIRL WHO KILLED HERSELF.
THE TIMING WORKED OUT WELL.
IT WAS A GOOD MATCH FOR ME,
BUT ITS TIME HAS COME.
I SHALL PREPARE A NEW BODY FOR YOU.
GOOD. THANK YOU.
BUT YOU DIDN'T COME HERE JUST FOR THAT, DID YOU?

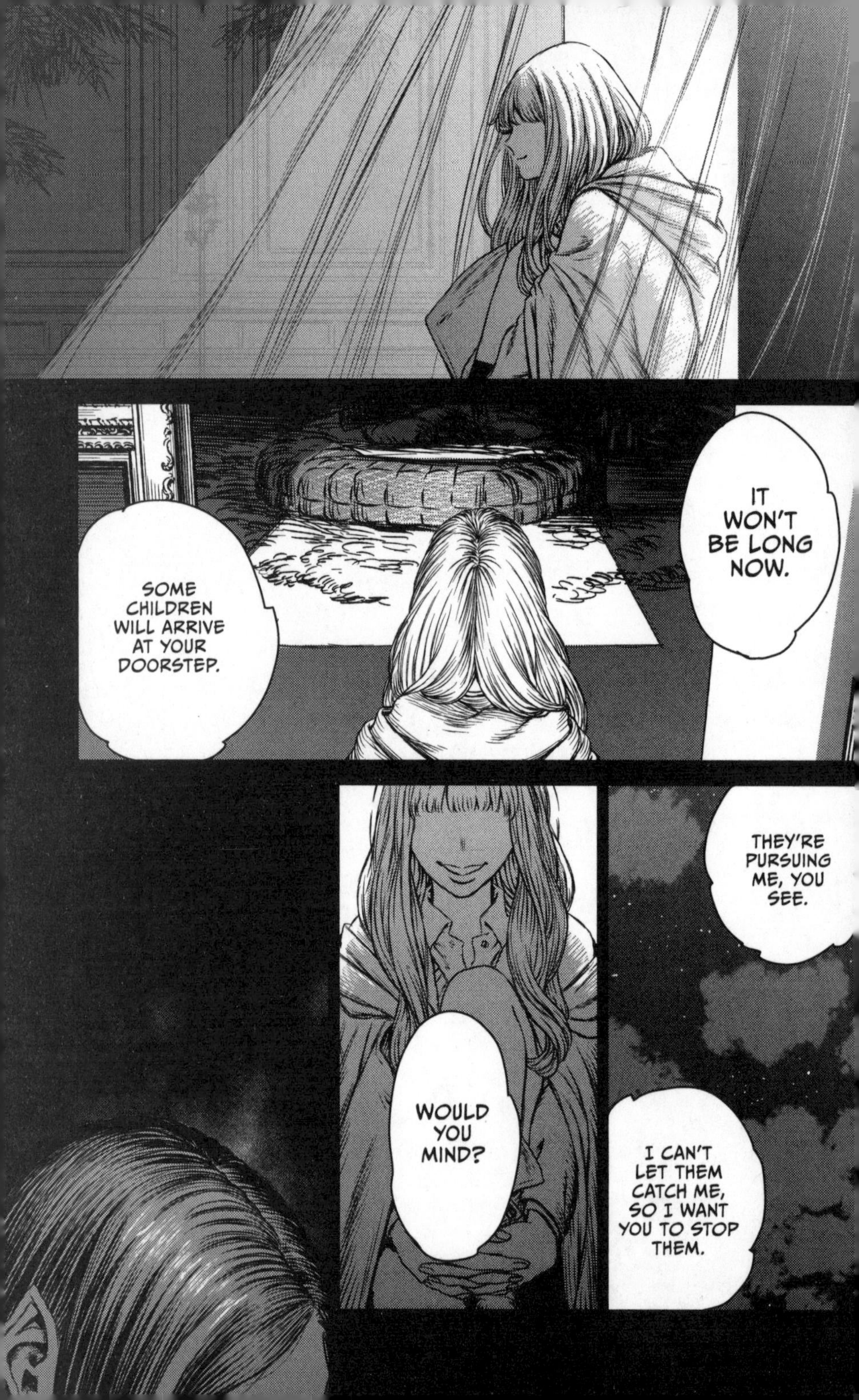
IT WON'T BE LONG NOW.
SOME CHILDREN WILL ARRIVE AT YOUR DOORSTEP.
THEY'RE PURSUING ME, YOU SEE.
I CAN'T LET THEM CATCH ME, SO I WANT YOU TO STOP THEM.
WOULD YOU MIND?

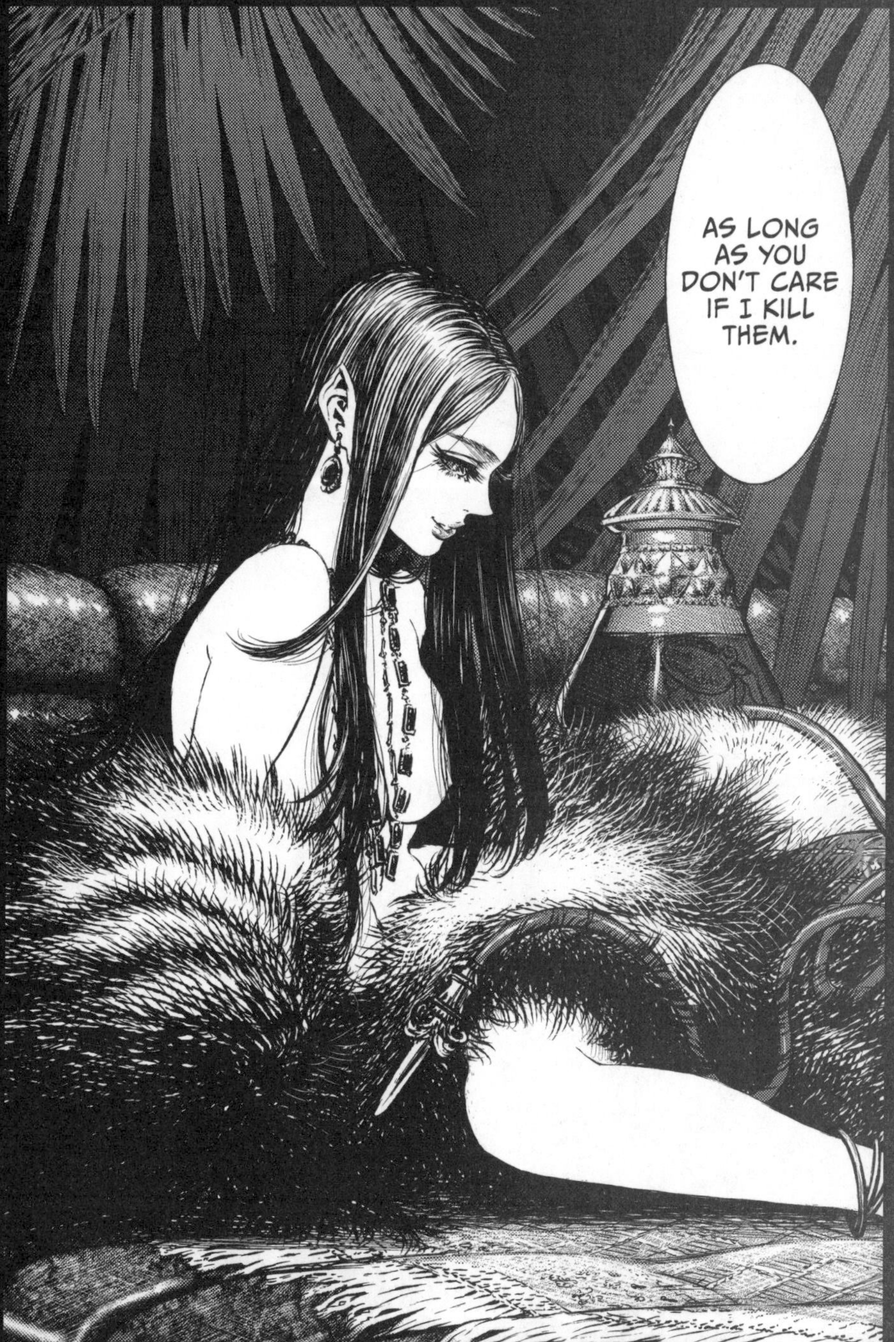
AS LONG AS YOU DON'T CARE IF I KILL THEM.

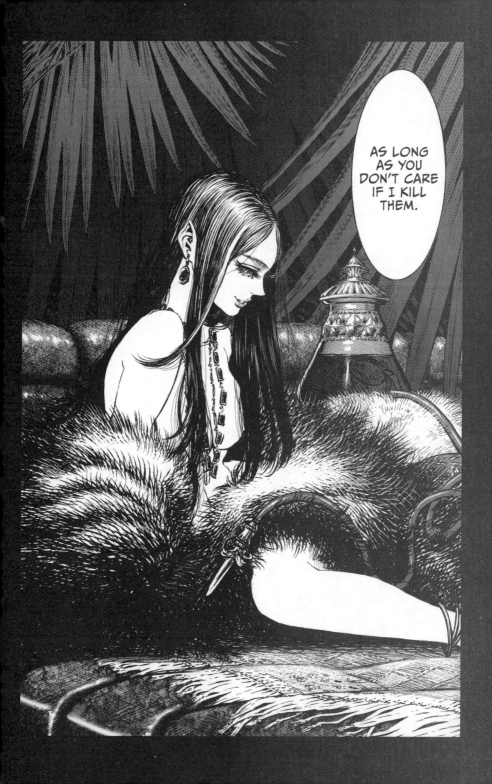

# THE WITCH AND THE BEAST

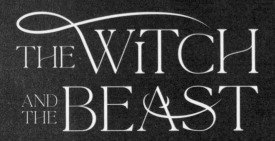

SPECIAL ONE-SHOT

CHAPTER 0:
# WITCH AND WHIM

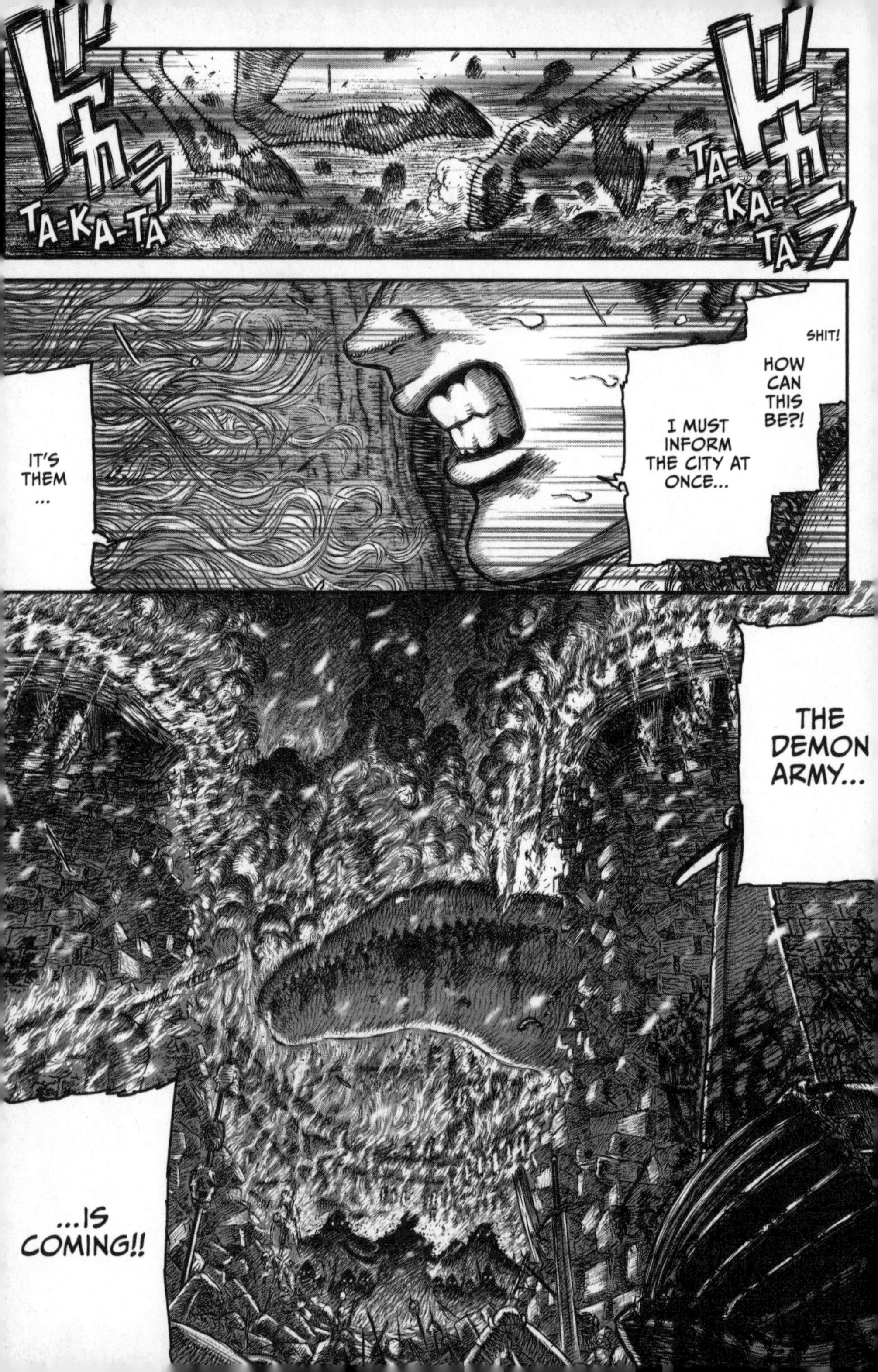
ドカラ
TA-KA-TA
ドカラ
TA-KA-TA
SHIT!
HOW CAN THIS BE?!
I MUST INFORM THE CITY AT ONCE...
IT'S THEM ...
THE DEMON ARMY...
...IS COMING!!

# 魔女ときまぐれ

Witch and whim

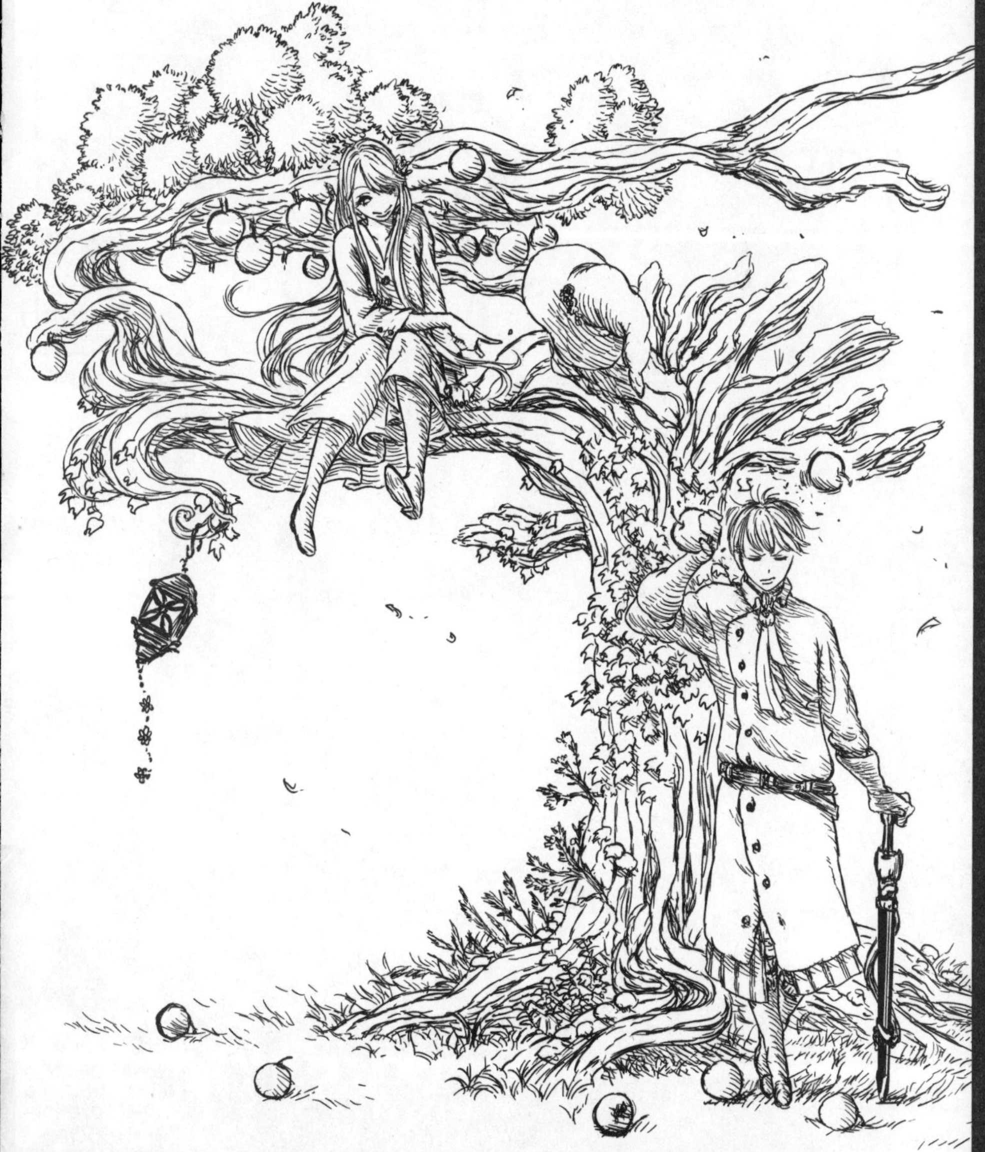

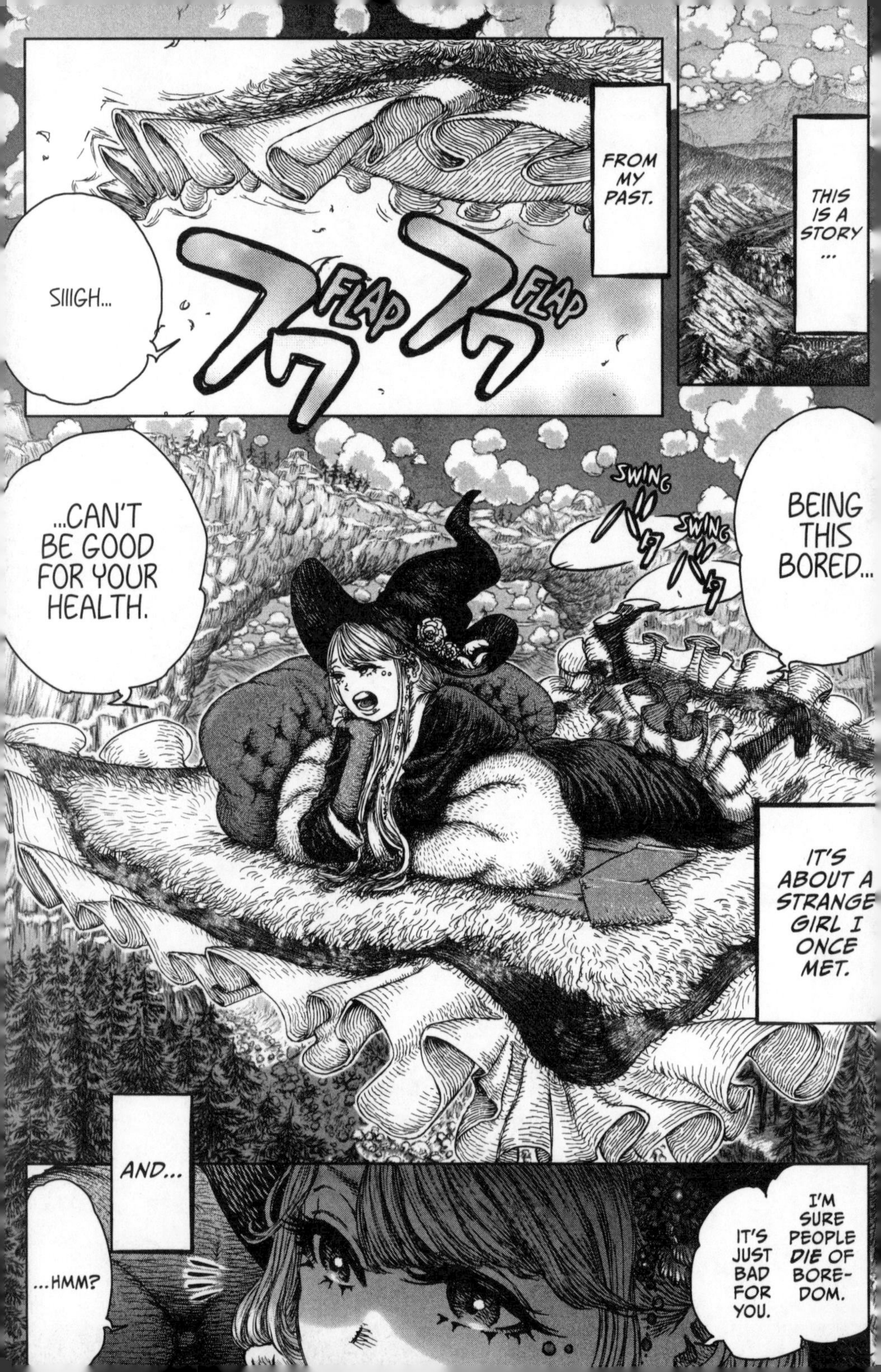
THIS IS A STORY...
FROM MY PAST.
FLAP
FLAP
SIIIGH...
BEING THIS BORED...
SWING
SWING
...CAN'T BE GOOD FOR YOUR HEALTH.
IT'S ABOUT A STRANGE GIRL I ONCE MET.
I'M SURE PEOPLE *DIE* OF BORE-DOM.
IT'S JUST BAD FOR YOU.
AND...
...HMM?

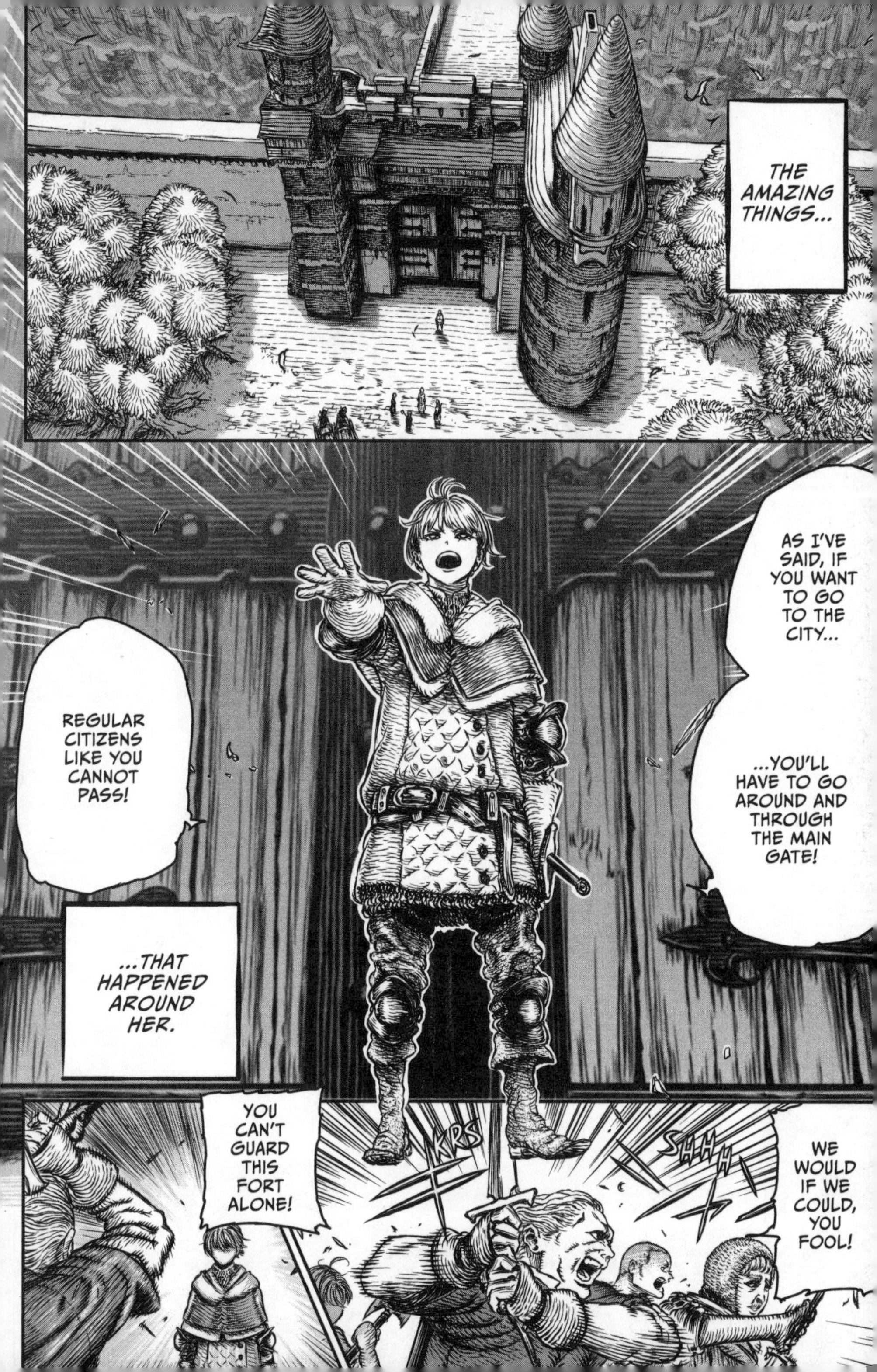
THE AMAZING THINGS...
AS I'VE SAID, IF YOU WANT TO GO TO THE CITY...
...YOU'LL HAVE TO GO AROUND AND THROUGH THE MAIN GATE!
REGULAR CITIZENS LIKE YOU CANNOT PASS!
...THAT HAPPENED AROUND HER.
SHHH
KRS
YOU CAN'T GUARD THIS FORT ALONE!
WE WOULD IF WE COULD, YOU FOOL!

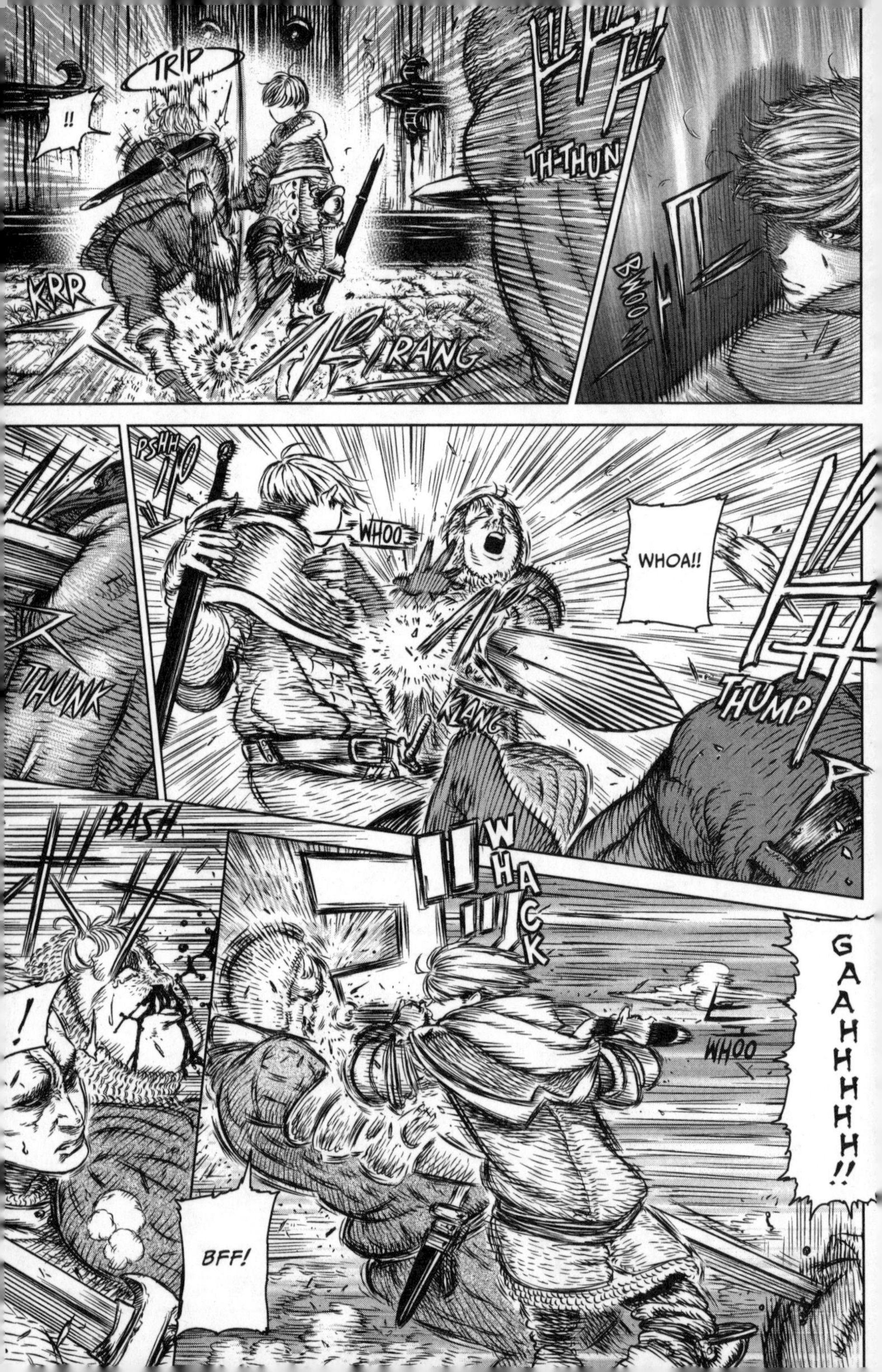

BWOOM
TH-THUN
TRIP
!!
RANG
KRR
WHOA!!
THUMP
WHOO
PSHH
KLANG
THUNK
GAHHHHH!!
WHOO
WHACK
BASH
!
BFF!

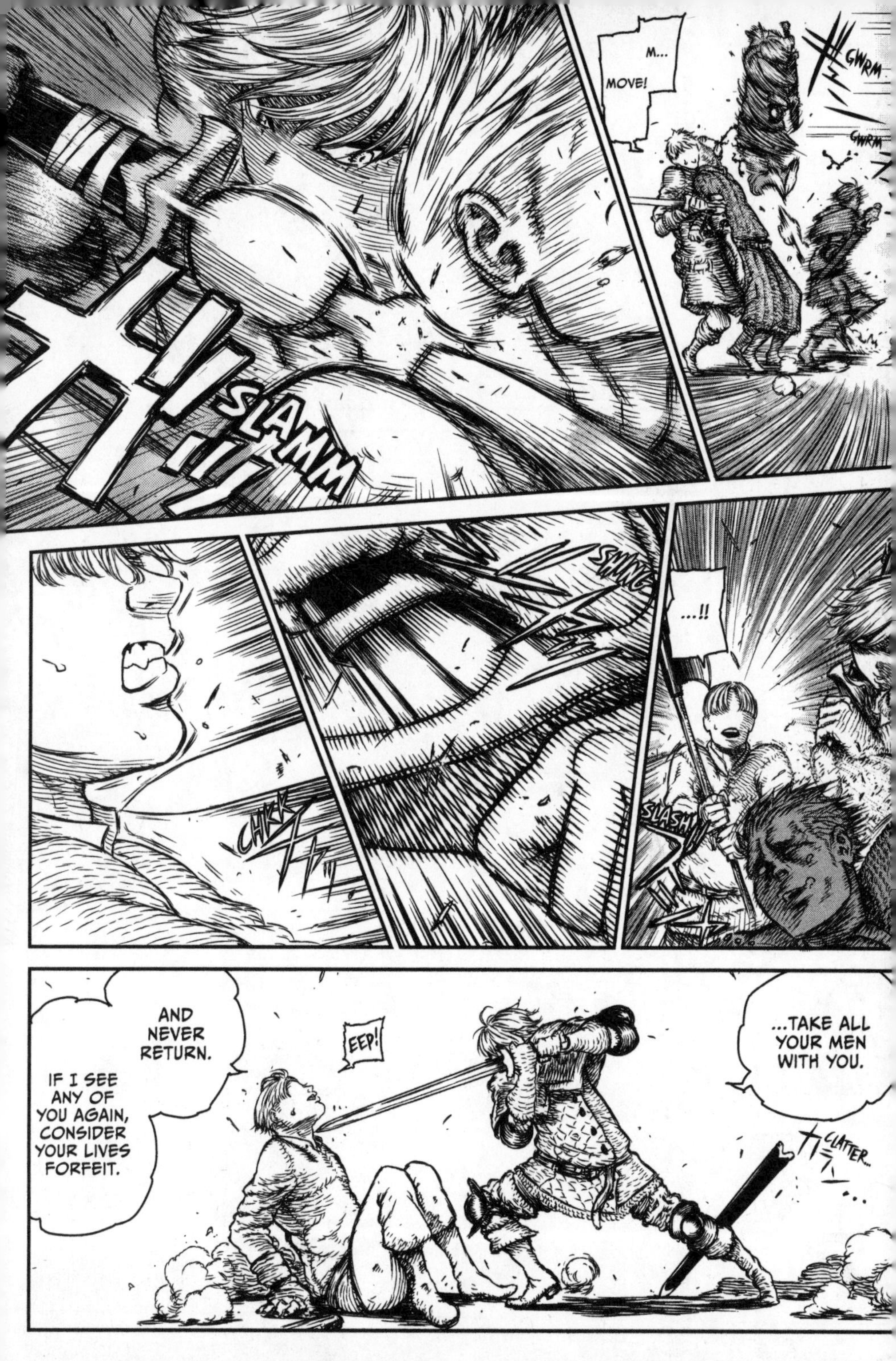
M...
MOVE!
GWRM
GWRM
SLAMM
...!!
SLASH
SHING
CHKK
...TAKE ALL YOUR MEN WITH YOU.
CLATTER...
EEP!
AND NEVER RETURN.
IF I SEE ANY OF YOU AGAIN, CONSIDER YOUR LIVES FORFEIT.

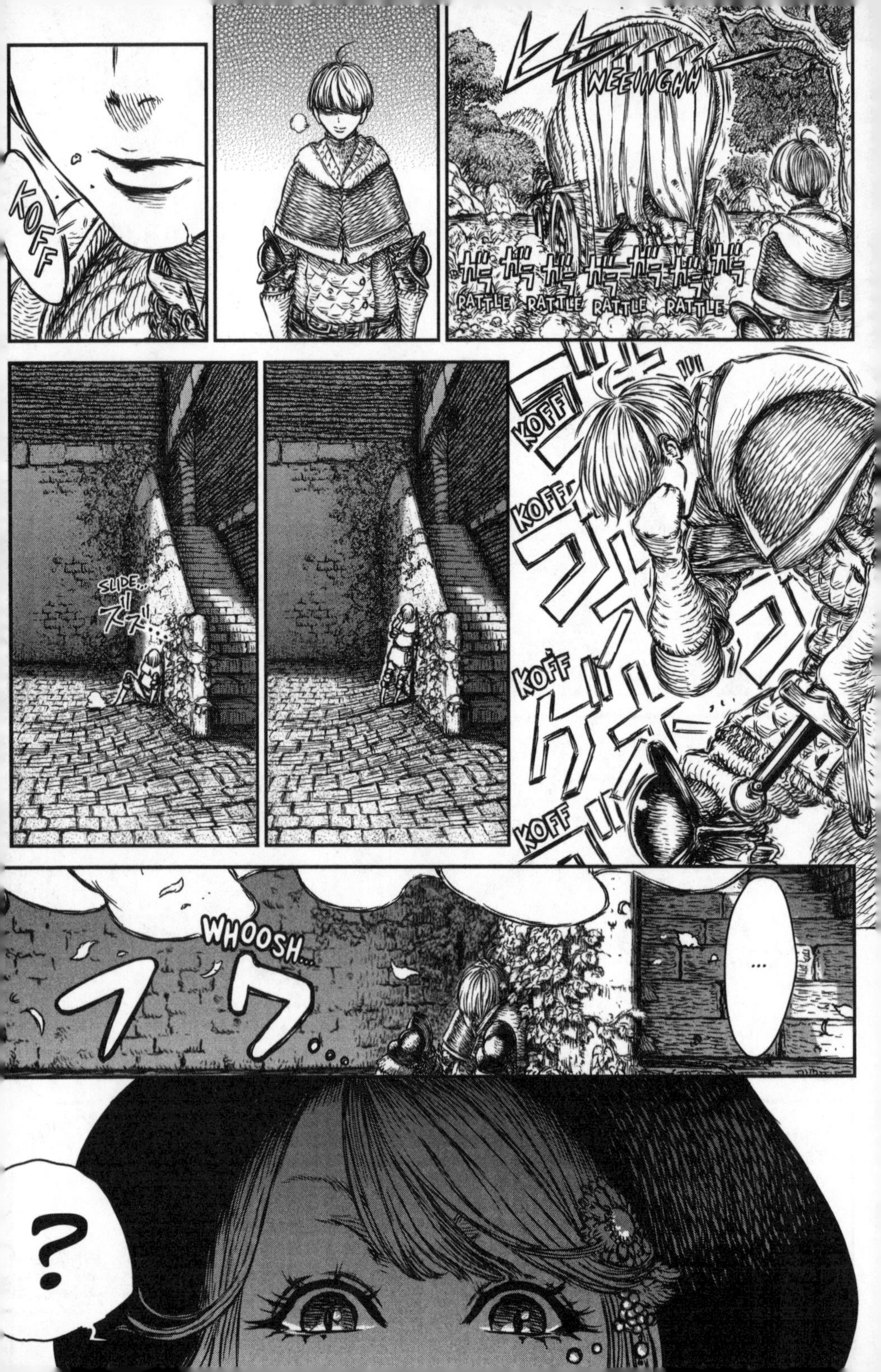
WEEIIIGHH
RATTLE RATTLE RATTLE RATTLE
KOFF
KOFF
KOFF
KOFF
KOFF
SLIDE...
...
WHOOSH...
?

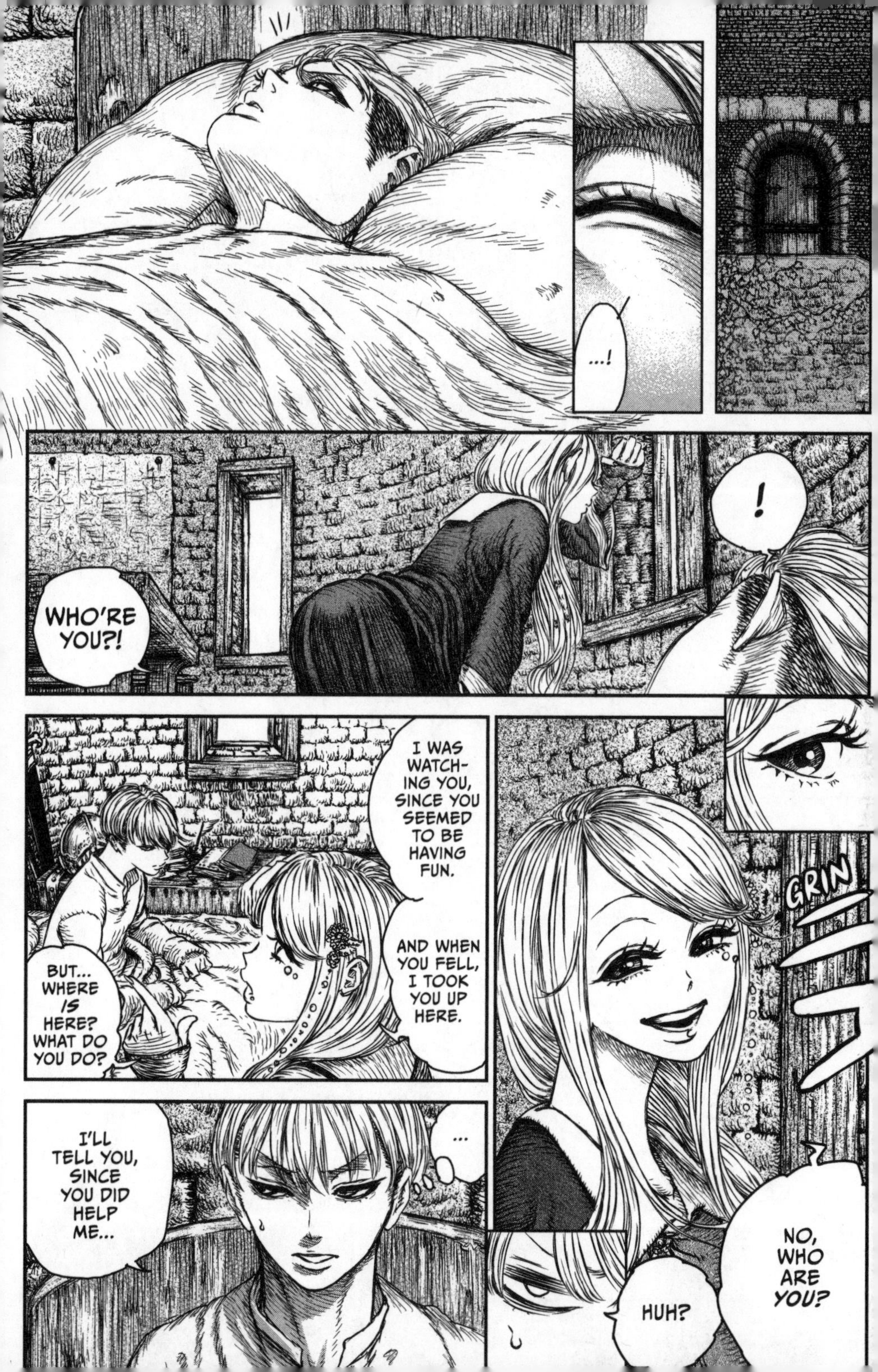
...!
!
WHO'RE YOU?!
I WAS WATCHING YOU, SINCE YOU SEEMED TO BE HAVING FUN.
AND WHEN YOU FELL, I TOOK YOU UP HERE.
BUT... WHERE *IS* HERE? WHAT DO YOU DO?
...
I'LL TELL YOU, SINCE YOU DID HELP ME...
GRIN
NO, WHO ARE *YOU*?
HUH?

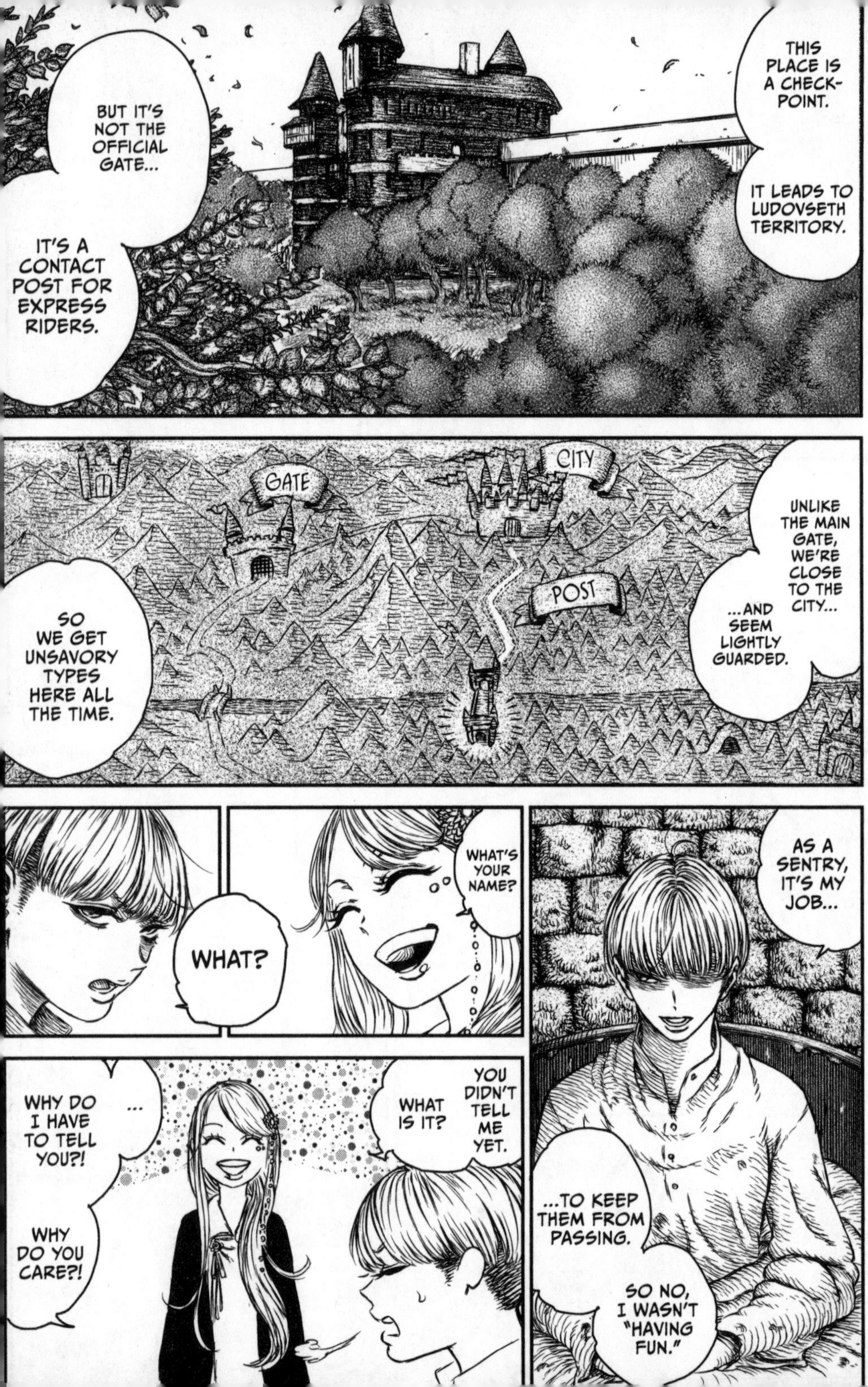
THIS PLACE IS A CHECK-POINT.
IT LEADS TO LUDOVSETH TERRITORY.
BUT IT'S NOT THE OFFICIAL GATE...
IT'S A CONTACT POST FOR EXPRESS RIDERS.
CITY
GATE
POST
UNLIKE THE MAIN GATE, WE'RE CLOSE TO THE CITY...
...AND SEEM LIGHTLY GUARDED.
SO WE GET UNSAVORY TYPES HERE ALL THE TIME.
AS A SENTRY, IT'S MY JOB...
...TO KEEP THEM FROM PASSING.
SO NO, I WASN'T "HAVING FUN."
WHAT'S YOUR NAME?
WHAT?
YOU DIDN'T TELL ME YET.
WHAT IS IT?
...
WHY DO I HAVE TO TELL YOU?!
WHY DO YOU CARE?!

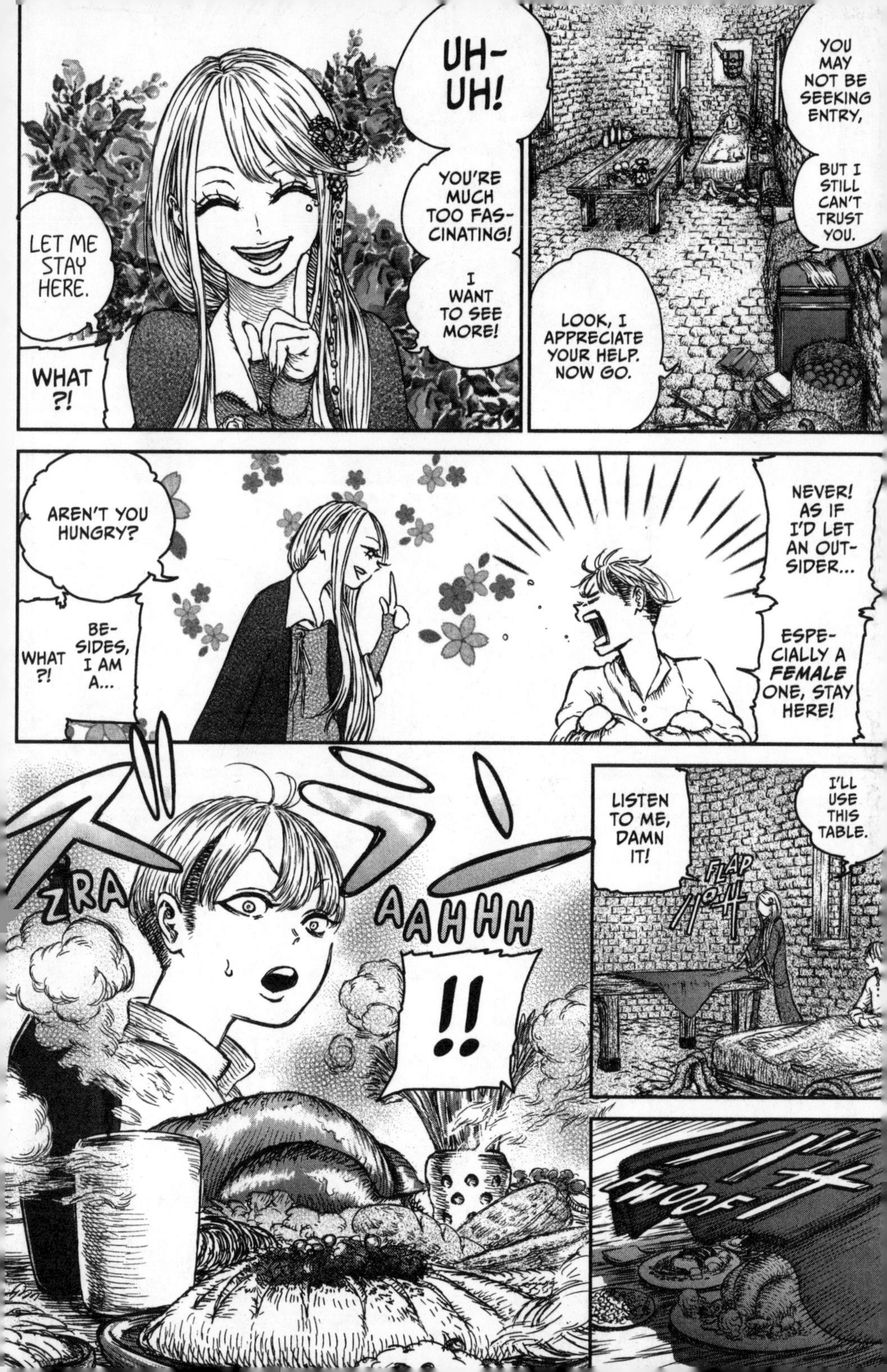
YOU MAY NOT BE SEEKING ENTRY,
BUT I STILL CAN'T TRUST YOU.
LOOK, I APPRECIATE YOUR HELP. NOW GO.
UH-UH!
YOU'RE MUCH TOO FASCINATING!
I WANT TO SEE MORE!
LET ME STAY HERE.
WHAT?!
NEVER! AS IF I'D LET AN OUTSIDER...
ESPECIALLY A *FEMALE* ONE, STAY HERE!
AREN'T YOU HUNGRY?
BESIDES, I AM A...
WHAT?!
I'LL USE THIS TABLE.
LISTEN TO ME, DAMN IT!
FLAP
FWOOF
ZRA
AAHHH
!!

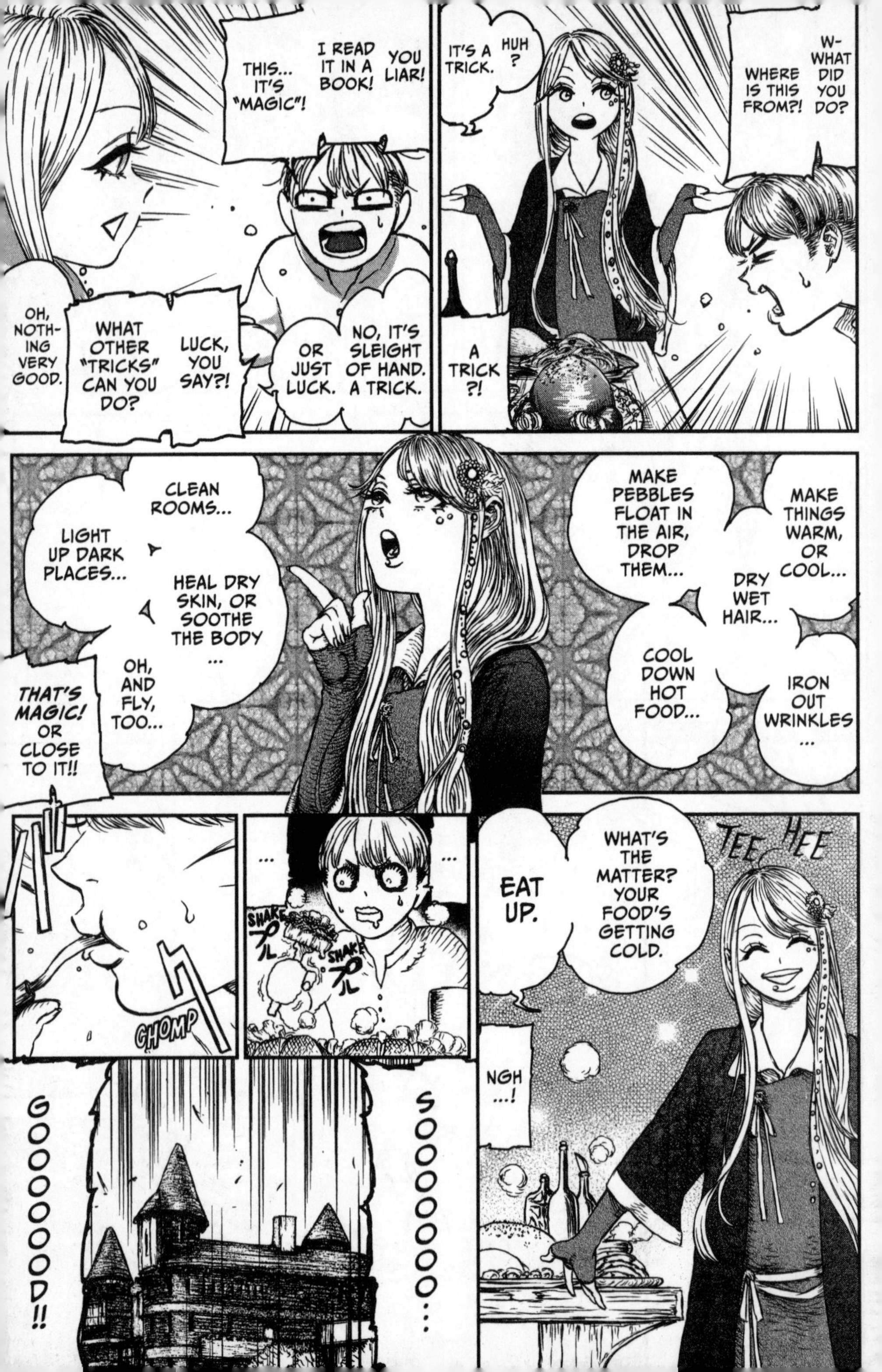
W-WHAT DID YOU DO?
WHERE IS THIS FROM?!
HUH?
IT'S A TRICK.
A TRICK?!
YOU LIAR!
I READ IT IN A BOOK!
THIS... IT'S "MAGIC"!
NO, IT'S SLEIGHT OF HAND. A TRICK.
OR JUST LUCK.
LUCK, YOU SAY?!
WHAT OTHER "TRICKS" CAN YOU DO?
OH, NOTHING VERY GOOD.
MAKE THINGS WARM, OR COOL...
MAKE PEBBLES FLOAT IN THE AIR, DROP THEM...
DRY WET HAIR...
IRON OUT WRINKLES...
COOL DOWN HOT FOOD...
CLEAN ROOMS...
LIGHT UP DARK PLACES...
HEAL DRY SKIN, OR SOOTHE THE BODY...
OH, AND FLY, TOO...
THAT'S MAGIC! OR CLOSE TO IT!!
TEE HEE
WHAT'S THE MATTER? YOUR FOOD'S GETTING COLD.
EAT UP.
NGH...!
...
...
SHAKE
SHAKE
CHOMP
SOOOOOOOO...
GOOOOOOOOD!!

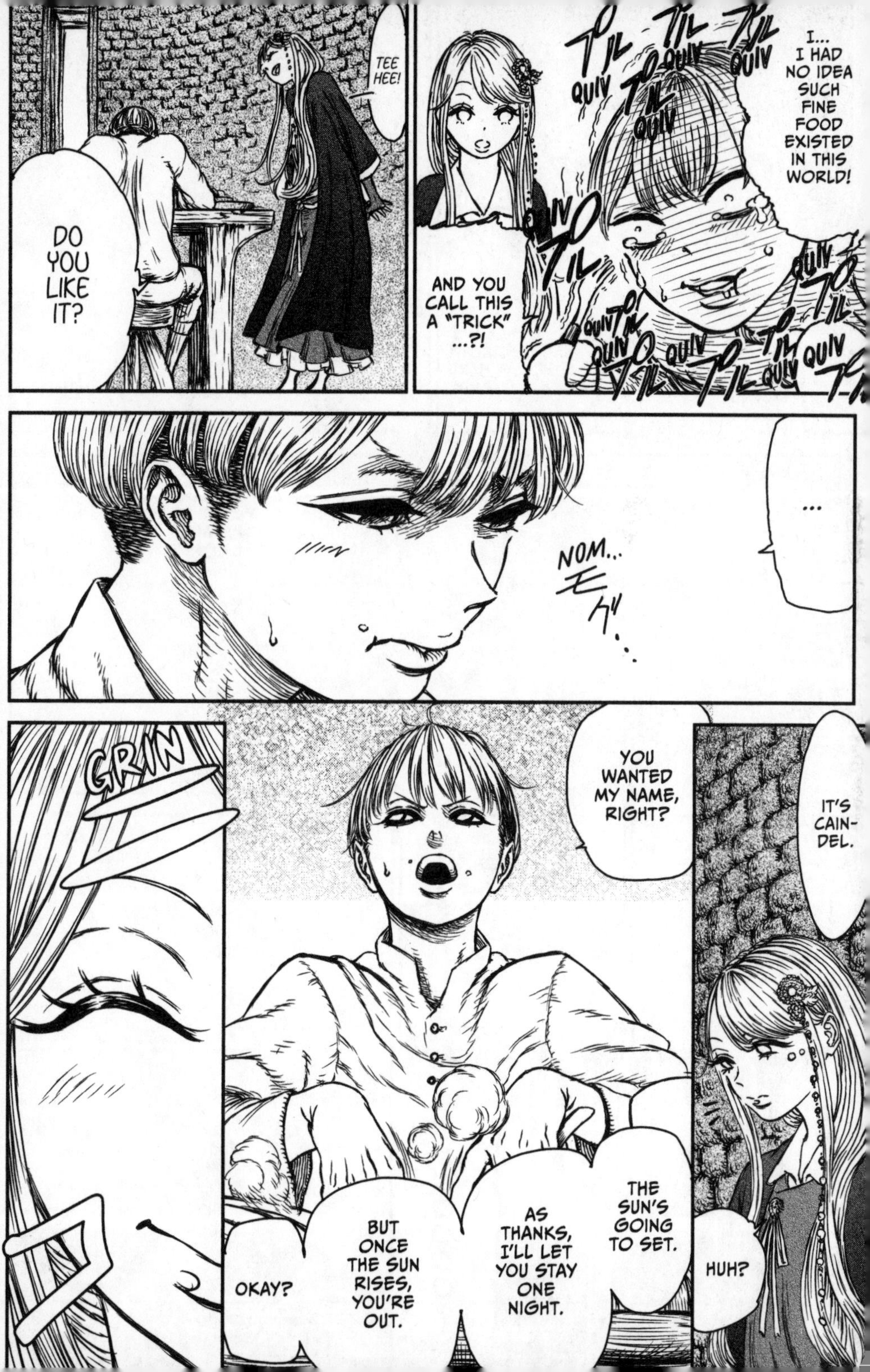
I... I HAD NO IDEA SUCH FINE FOOD EXISTED IN THIS WORLD!
QUIV QUIV QUIV
AND YOU CALL THIS A "TRICK" ...?!
TEE HEE!
DO YOU LIKE IT?
...
NOM...
YOU WANTED MY NAME, RIGHT?
IT'S CAIN-DEL.
HUH?
THE SUN'S GOING TO SET.
AS THANKS, I'LL LET YOU STAY ONE NIGHT.
BUT ONCE THE SUN RISES, YOU'RE OUT.
OKAY?
GRIN

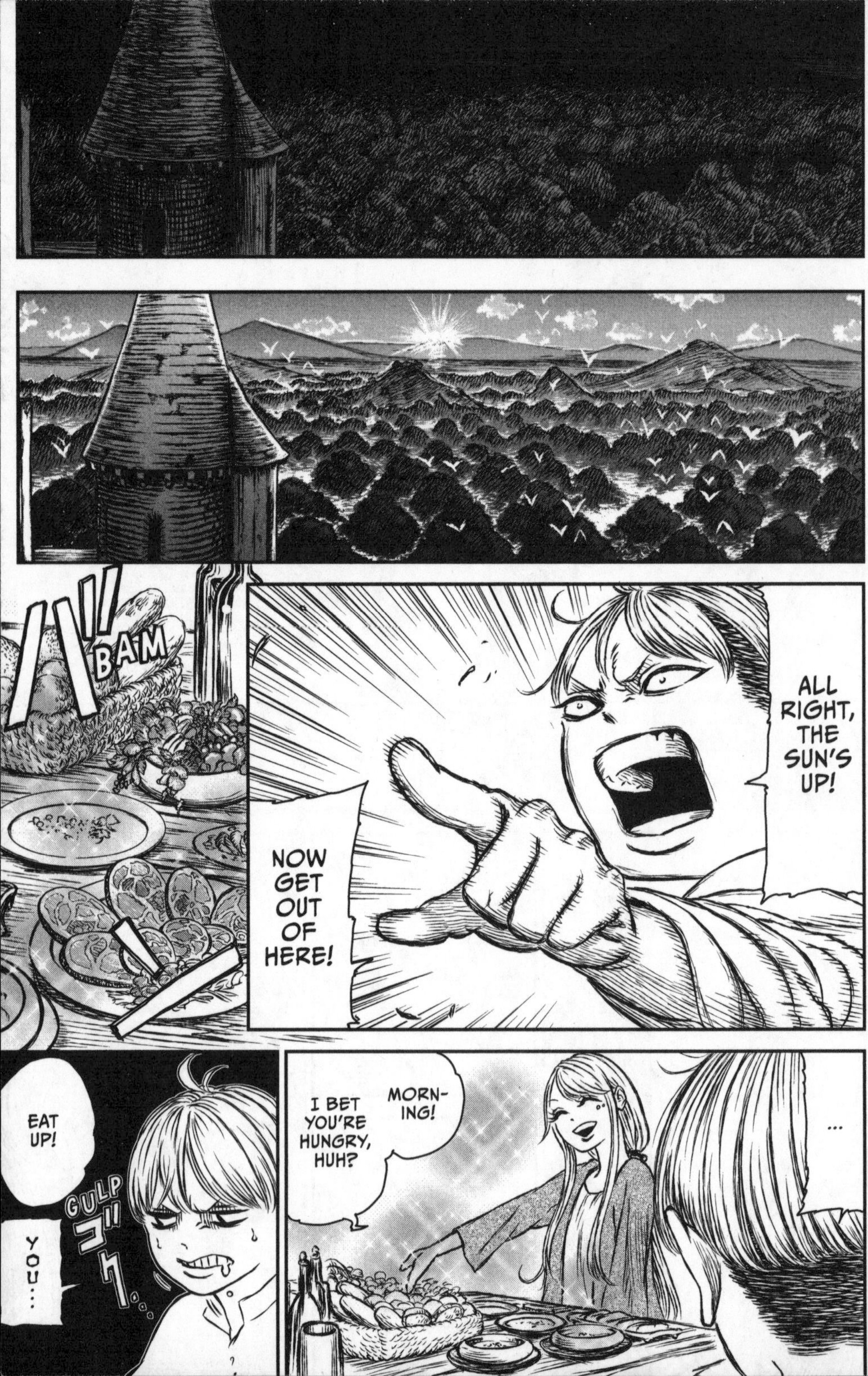
ALL RIGHT, THE SUN'S UP!
NOW GET OUT OF HERE!
BAM
...
MORNING!
I BET YOU'RE HUNGRY, HUH?
EAT UP!
GULP
YOU...

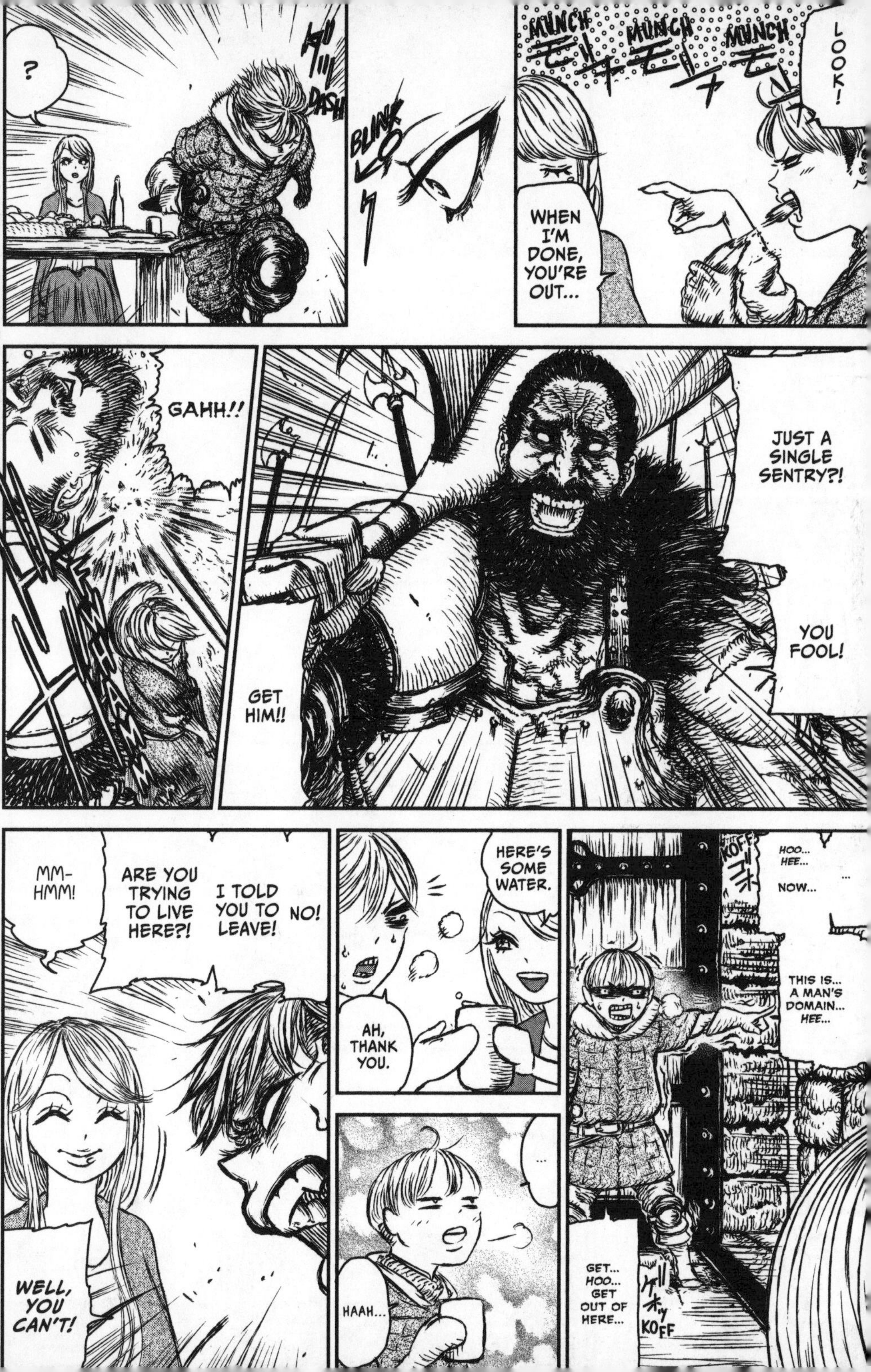
MUNCH
MUNCH
MUNCH
LOOK!
WHEN I'M DONE, YOU'RE OUT...
BLINK
DASH
?
JUST A SINGLE SENTRY?!
YOU FOOL!
GET HIM!!
GAHH!!
HOO... HEE...
...
NOW...
KOFF
THIS IS... A MAN'S DOMAIN... HEE...
GET... HOO... GET OUT OF HERE...
KOFF
HERE'S SOME WATER.
AH, THANK YOU.
...
HAAH...
NO!
I TOLD YOU TO LEAVE!
ARE YOU TRYING TO LIVE HERE?!
MM-HMM!
WELL, YOU CAN'T!

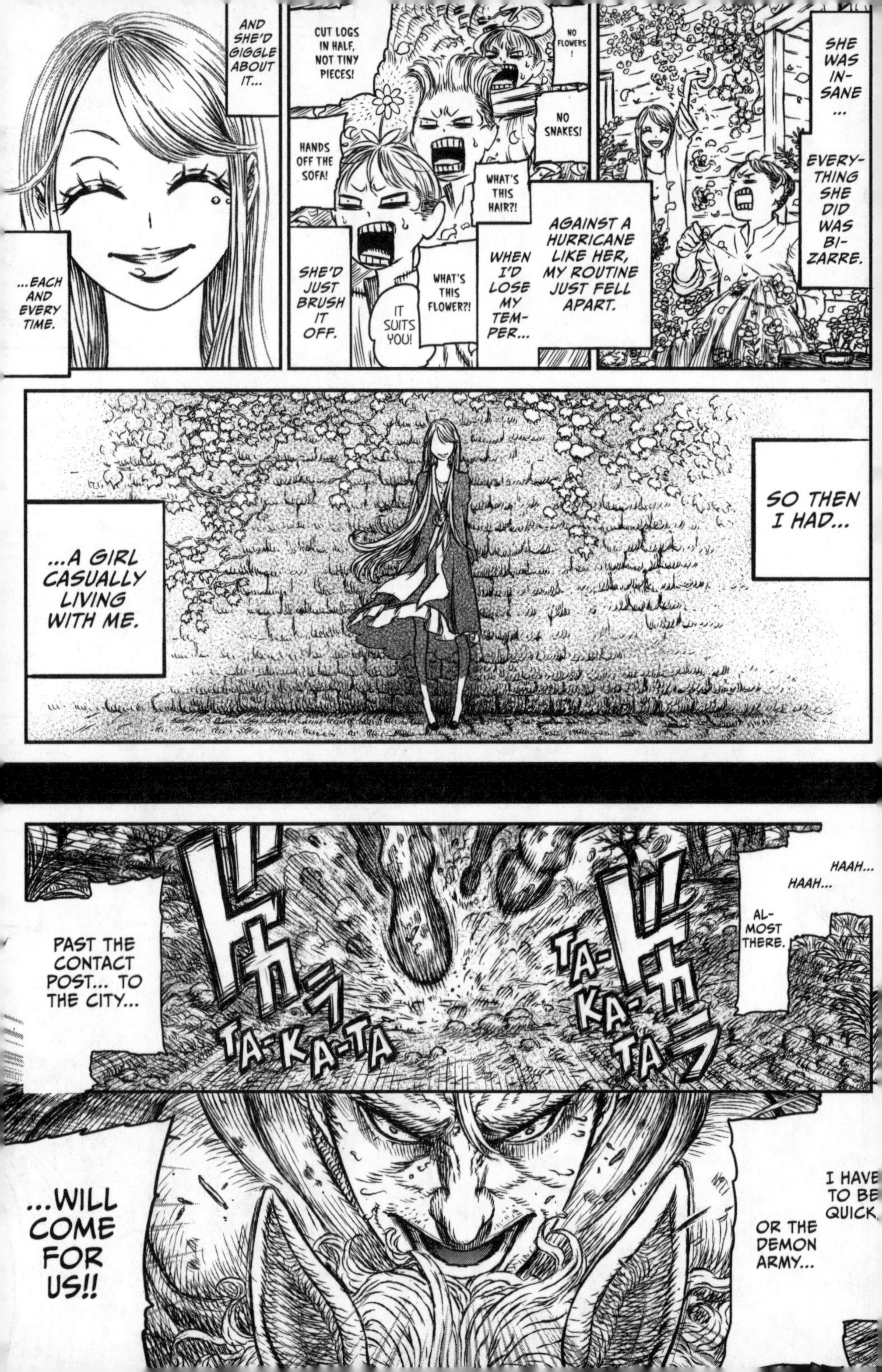
SHE WAS IN-SANE...
EVERY-THING SHE DID WAS BI-ZARRE.
NO FLOWERS!
NO SNAKES!
WHAT'S THIS HAIR?!
AGAINST A HURRICANE LIKE HER, MY ROUTINE JUST FELL APART.
WHEN I'D LOSE MY TEM-PER...
CUT LOGS IN HALF, NOT TINY PIECES!
HANDS OFF THE SOFA!
WHAT'S THIS FLOWER?!
IT SUITS YOU!
SHE'D JUST BRUSH IT OFF.
AND SHE'D GIGGLE ABOUT IT...
...EACH AND EVERY TIME.
SO THEN I HAD...
...A GIRL CASUALLY LIVING WITH ME.
HAAH... HAAH...
AL-MOST THERE.
TA-KA-TA
TA-KA-TA
PAST THE CONTACT POST... TO THE CITY...
I HAVE TO BE QUICK,
OR THE DEMON ARMY...
...WILL COME FOR US!!

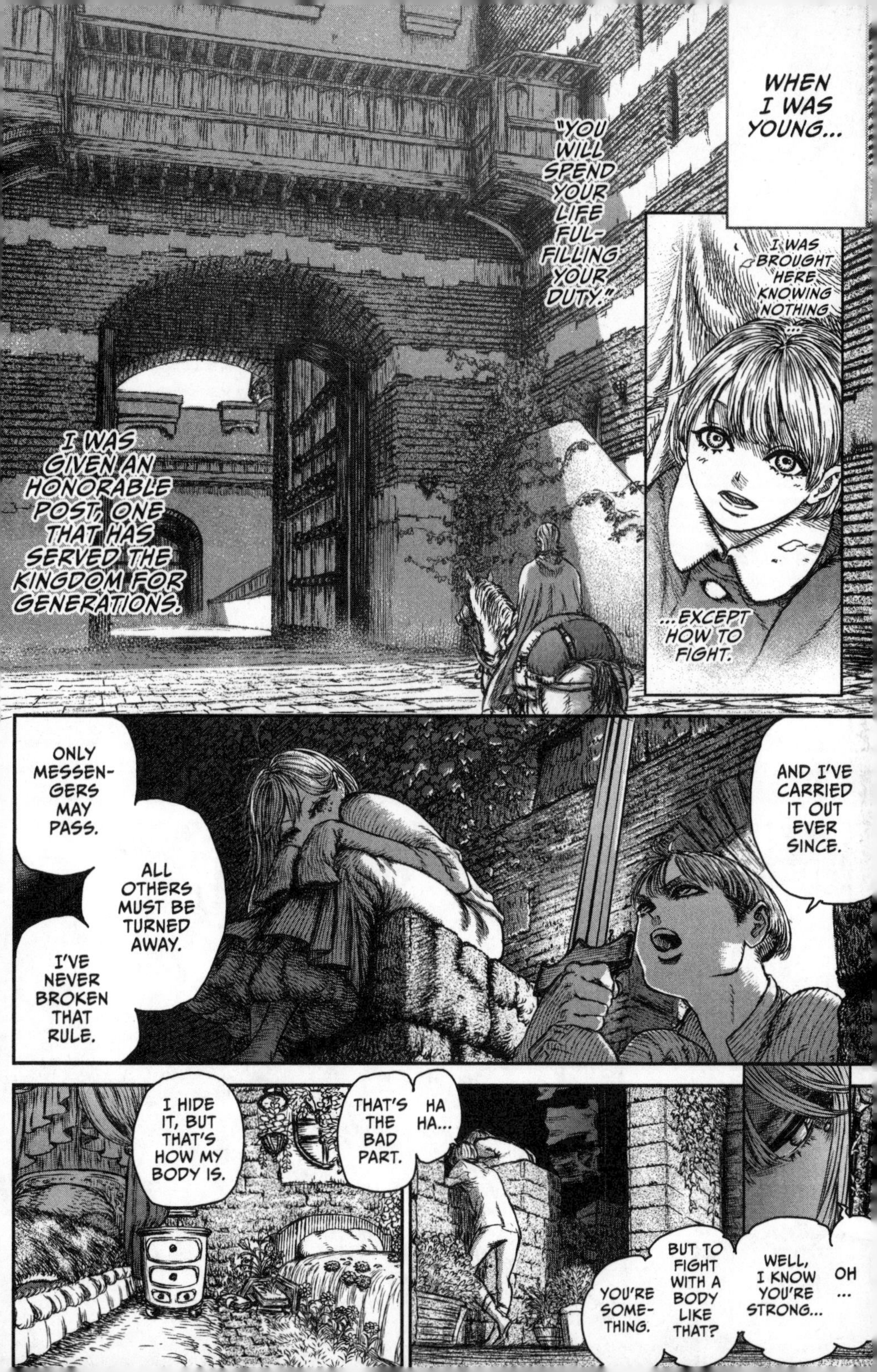
WHEN I WAS YOUNG...
"YOU WILL SPEND YOUR LIFE FUL-FILLING YOUR DUTY."
I WAS GIVEN AN HONORABLE POST, ONE THAT HAS SERVED THE KINGDOM FOR GENERATIONS.
I WAS BROUGHT HERE KNOWING NOTHING...
...EXCEPT HOW TO FIGHT.
AND I'VE CARRIED IT OUT EVER SINCE.
ONLY MESSEN-GERS MAY PASS.
ALL OTHERS MUST BE TURNED AWAY.
I'VE NEVER BROKEN THAT RULE.
OH ...
WELL, I KNOW YOU'RE STRONG...
BUT TO FIGHT WITH A BODY LIKE THAT?
YOU'RE SOME-THING.
HA HA...
THAT'S THE BAD PART.
I HIDE IT, BUT THAT'S HOW MY BODY IS.

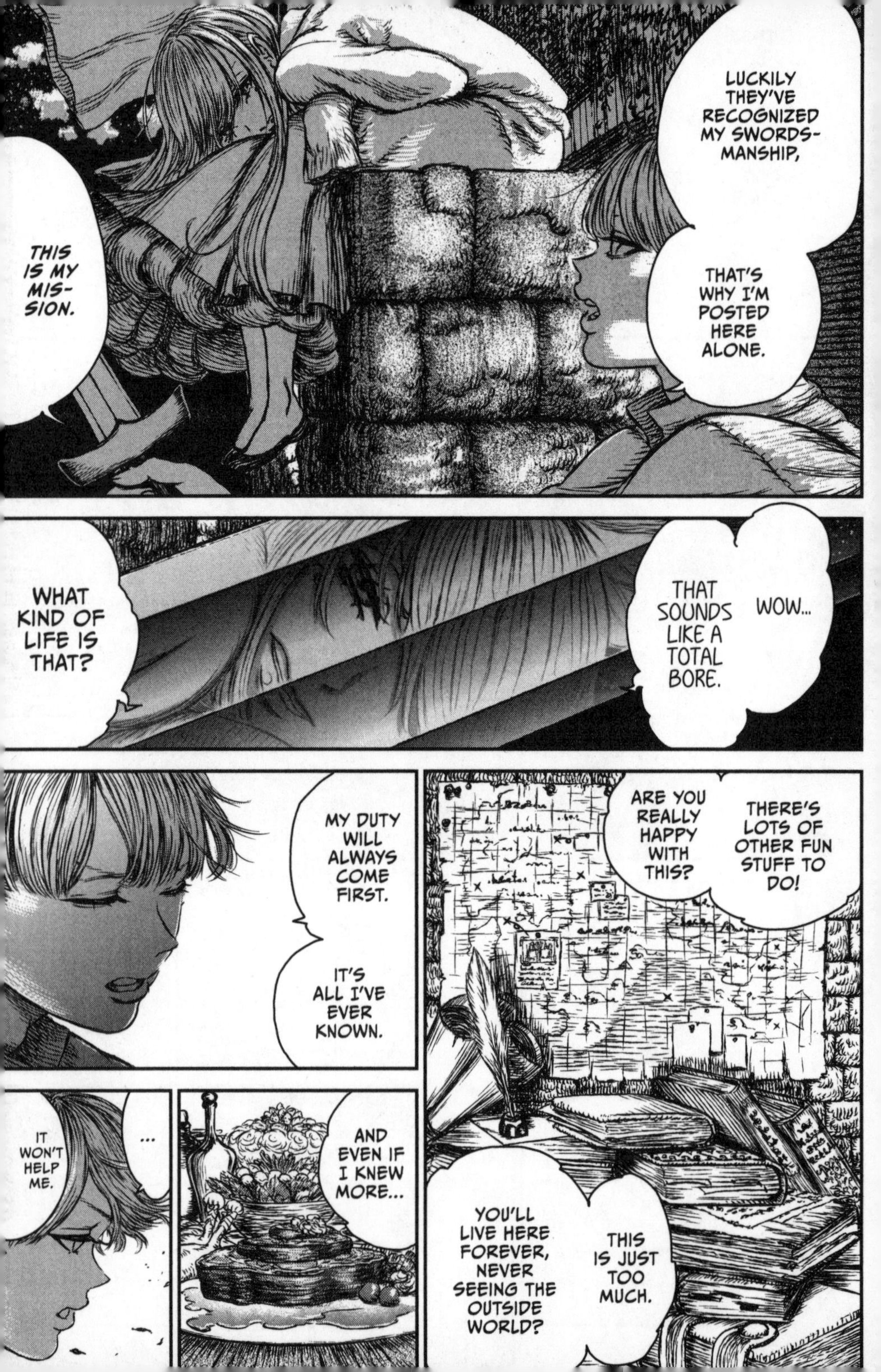

LUCKILY THEY'VE RECOGNIZED MY SWORDS-MANSHIP,
THAT'S WHY I'M POSTED HERE ALONE.
THIS IS MY MIS-SION.
WOW...
THAT SOUNDS LIKE A TOTAL BORE.
WHAT KIND OF LIFE IS THAT?
THERE'S LOTS OF OTHER FUN STUFF TO DO!
ARE YOU REALLY HAPPY WITH THIS?
THIS IS JUST TOO MUCH.
YOU'LL LIVE HERE FOREVER, NEVER SEEING THE OUTSIDE WORLD?
MY DUTY WILL ALWAYS COME FIRST.
IT'S ALL I'VE EVER KNOWN.
AND EVEN IF I KNEW MORE...
...
IT WON'T HELP ME.

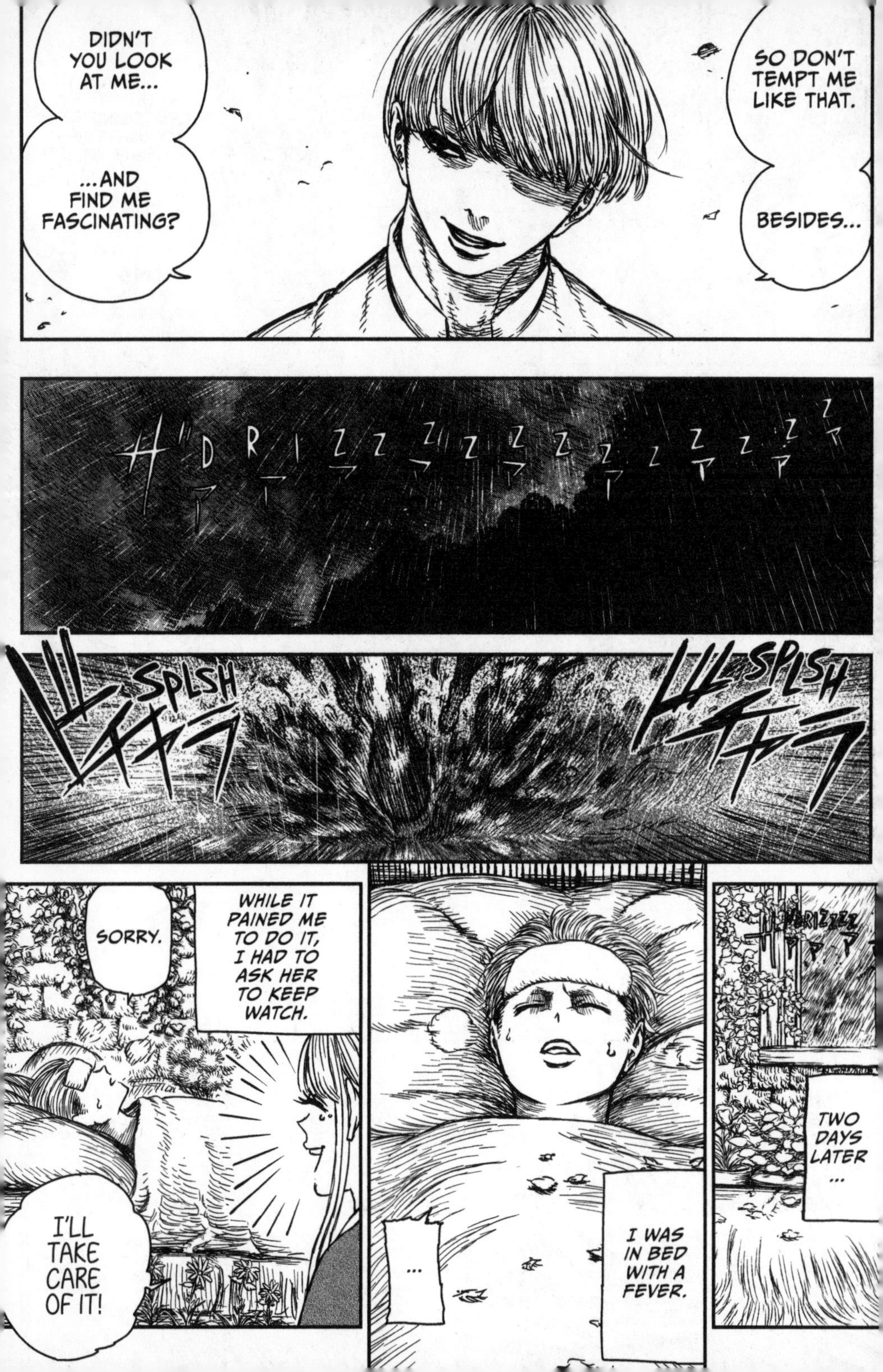
SO DON'T TEMPT ME LIKE THAT.
BESIDES...
DIDN'T YOU LOOK AT ME...
...AND FIND ME FASCINATING?
DRIZZZZZZZZZZZ
SPLSH
SPLSH
TWO DAYS LATER...
I WAS IN BED WITH A FEVER.
...
WHILE IT PAINED ME TO DO IT, I HAD TO ASK HER TO KEEP WATCH.
SORRY.
I'LL TAKE CARE OF IT!

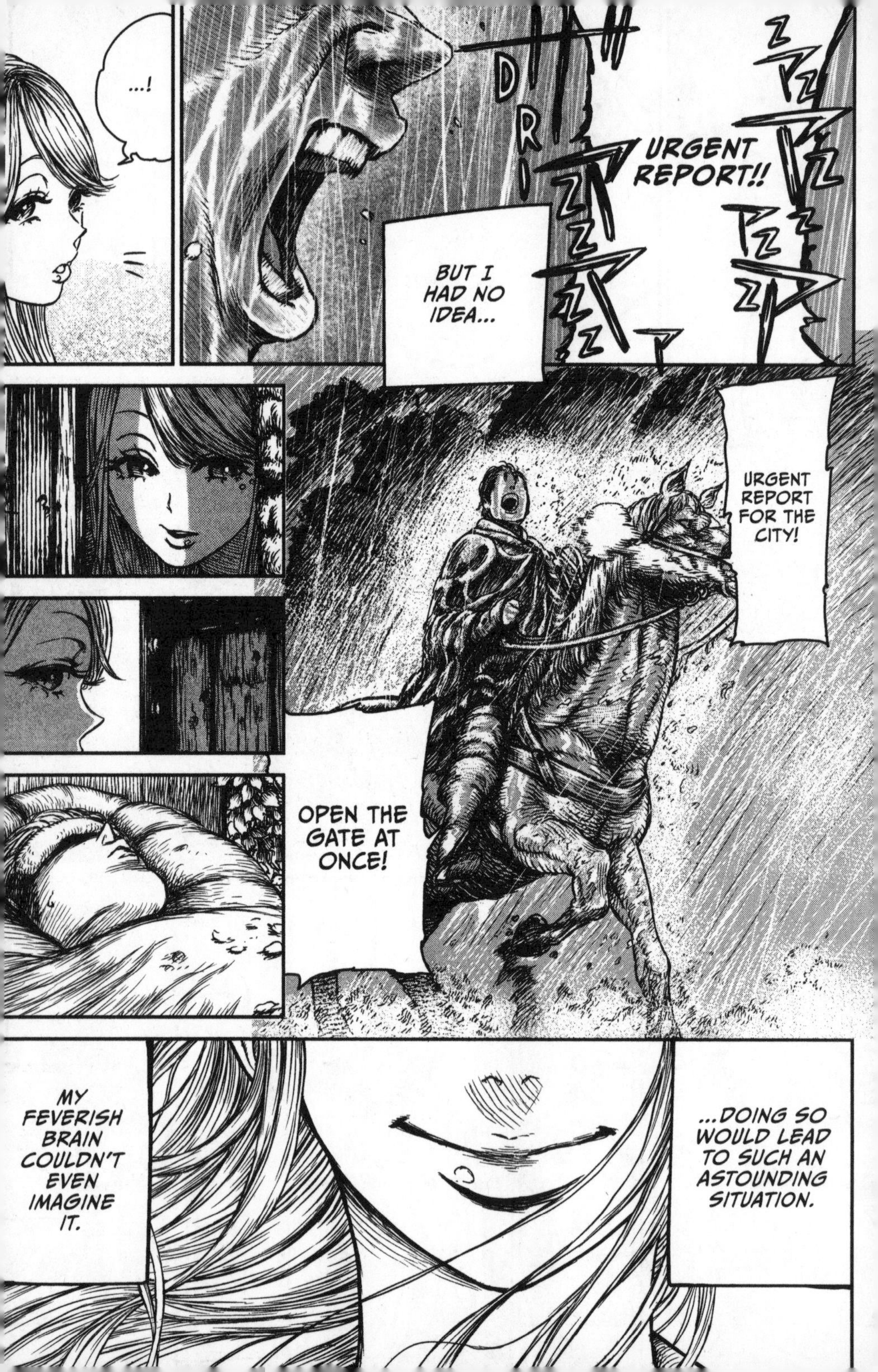
URGENT REPORT!!
BUT I HAD NO IDEA...
...!
URGENT REPORT FOR THE CITY!
OPEN THE GATE AT ONCE!
...DOING SO WOULD LEAD TO SUCH AN ASTOUNDING SITUATION.
MY FEVERISH BRAIN COULDN'T EVEN IMAGINE IT.

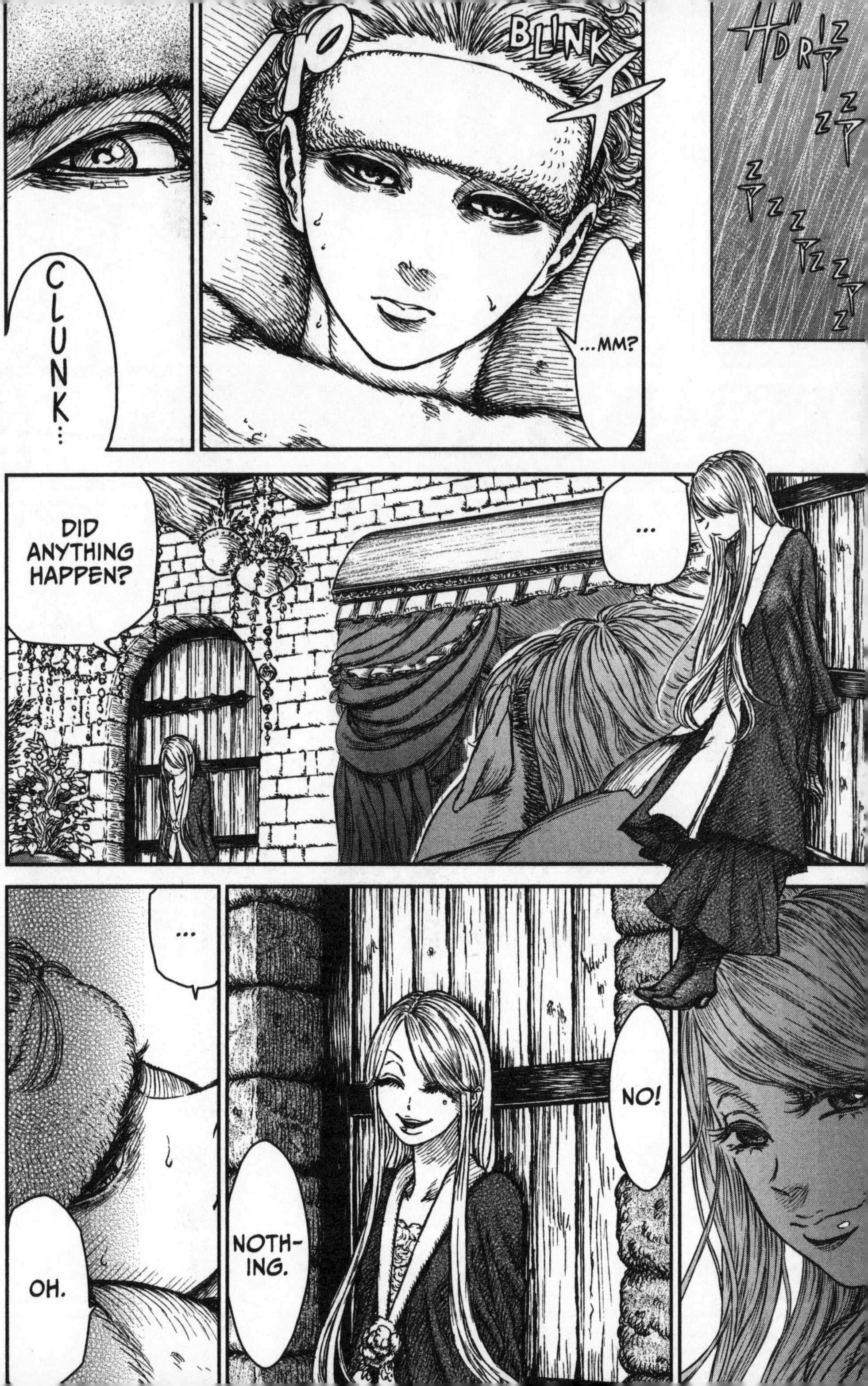
BLINK
...MM?
CLUNK...
...
DID ANYTHING HAPPEN?
NO!
NOTH-ING.
...
OH.

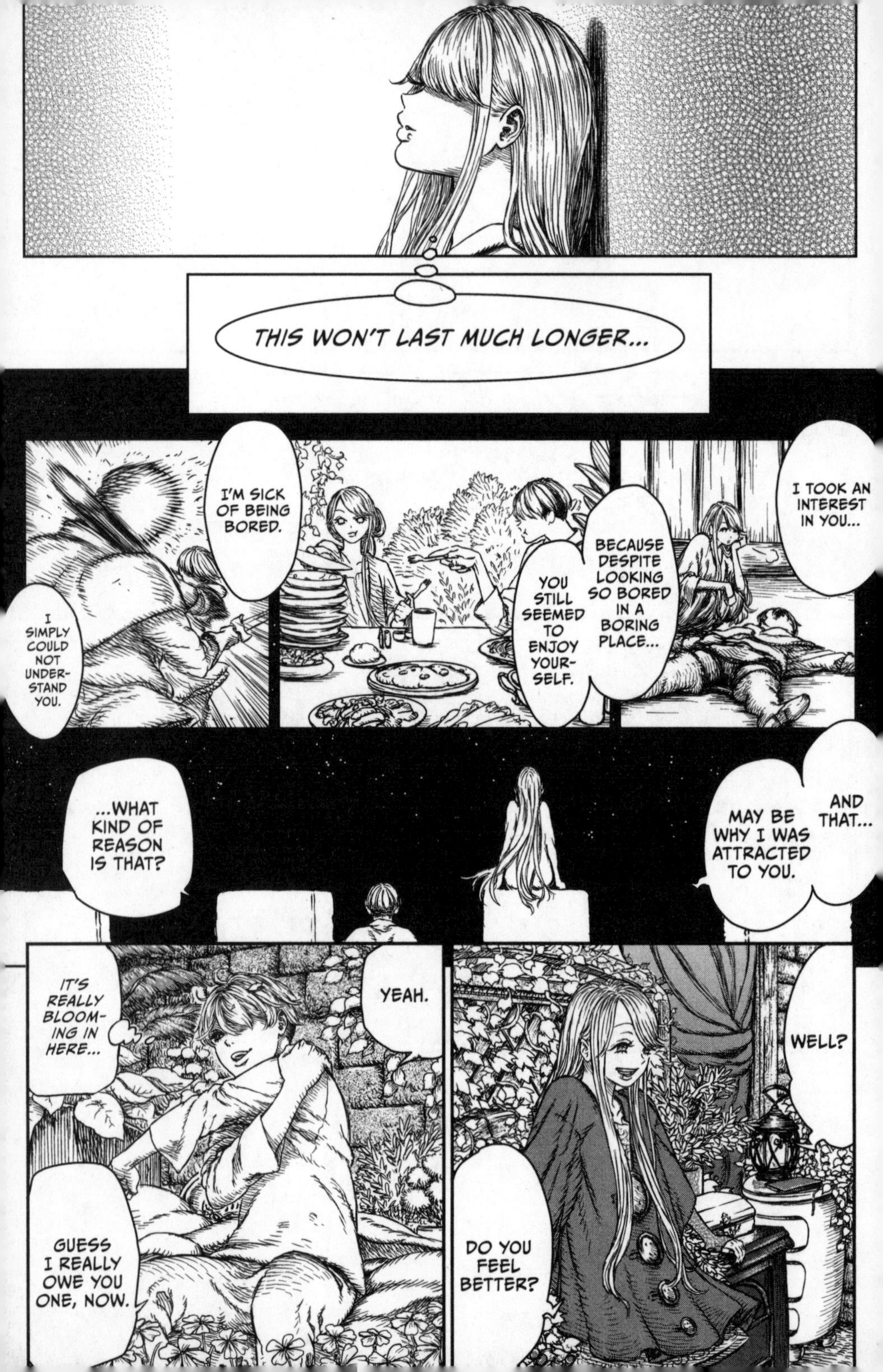
THIS WON'T LAST MUCH LONGER...
I TOOK AN INTEREST IN YOU...
BECAUSE DESPITE LOOKING SO BORED IN A BORING PLACE...
YOU STILL SEEMED TO ENJOY YOUR-SELF.
I'M SICK OF BEING BORED.
I SIMPLY COULD NOT UNDER-STAND YOU.
AND THAT...
MAY BE WHY I WAS ATTRACTED TO YOU.
...WHAT KIND OF REASON IS THAT?
WELL?
DO YOU FEEL BETTER?
YEAH.
IT'S REALLY BLOOM-ING IN HERE...
GUESS I REALLY OWE YOU ONE, NOW.

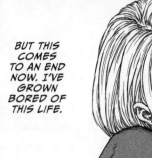

BUT THIS COMES TO AN END NOW. I'VE GROWN BORED OF THIS LIFE.

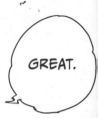

GREAT.

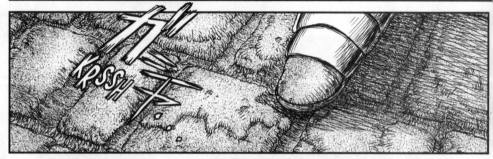

KRSSSH

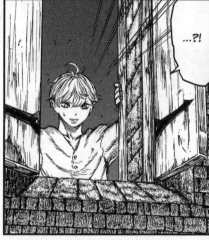

...?!

CAINDEL BICHON! ETERNAL SENTRY OF FORT SAISOYE!

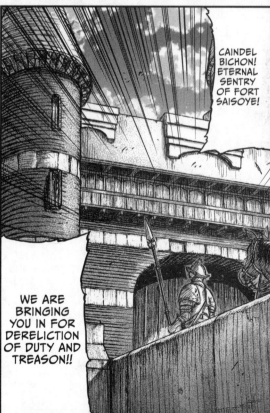

WE ARE BRINGING YOU IN FOR DERELICTION OF DUTY AND TREASON!!

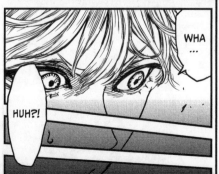

WHA...

HUH?!

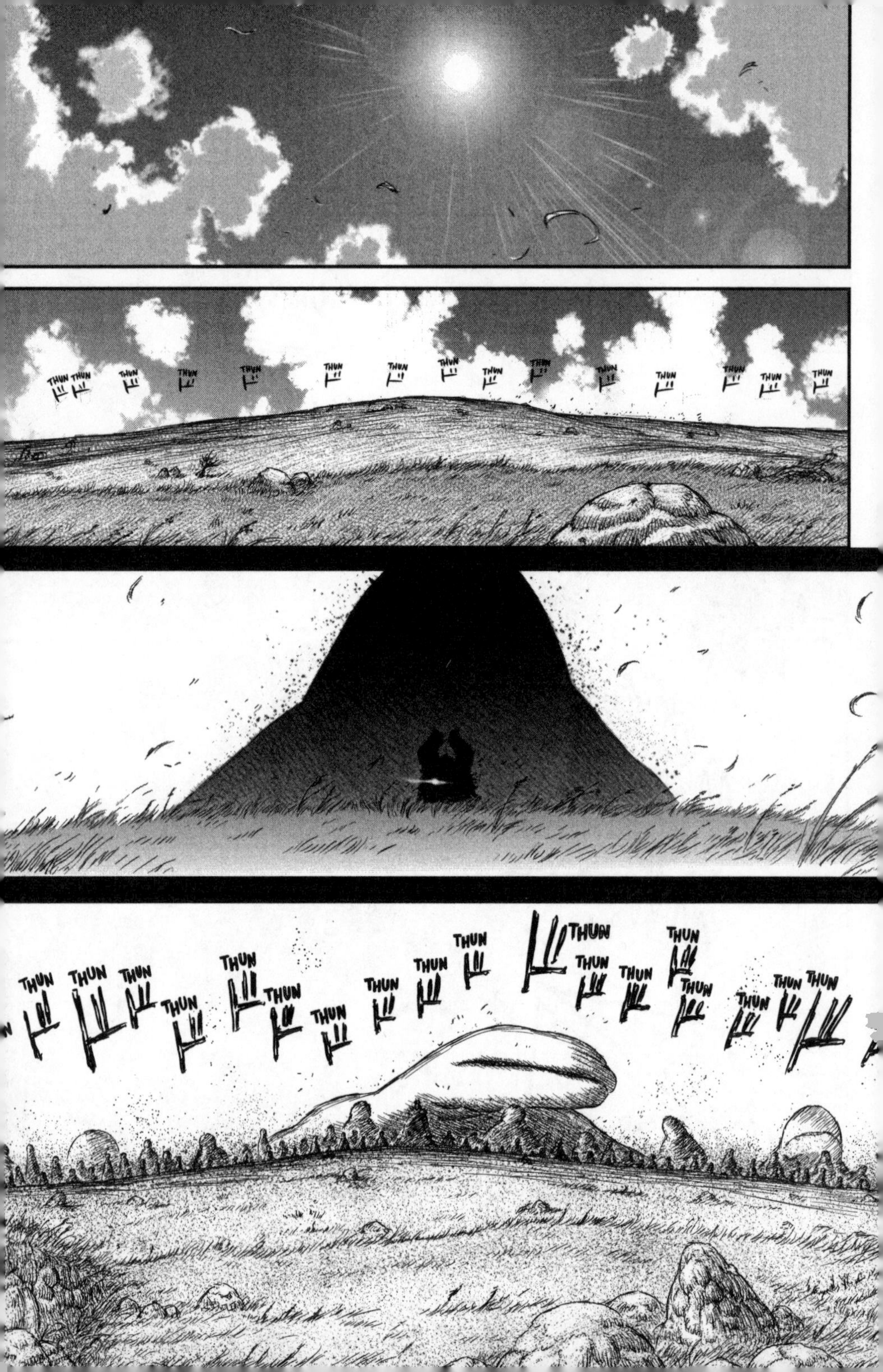
THUN THUN THUN THUN THUN THUN THUN THUN THUN THUN THUN THUN THUN THUN THUN
THUN THUN THUN THUN THUN THUN THUN THUN THUN THUN THUN THUN THUN THUN THUN THUN THUN THUN

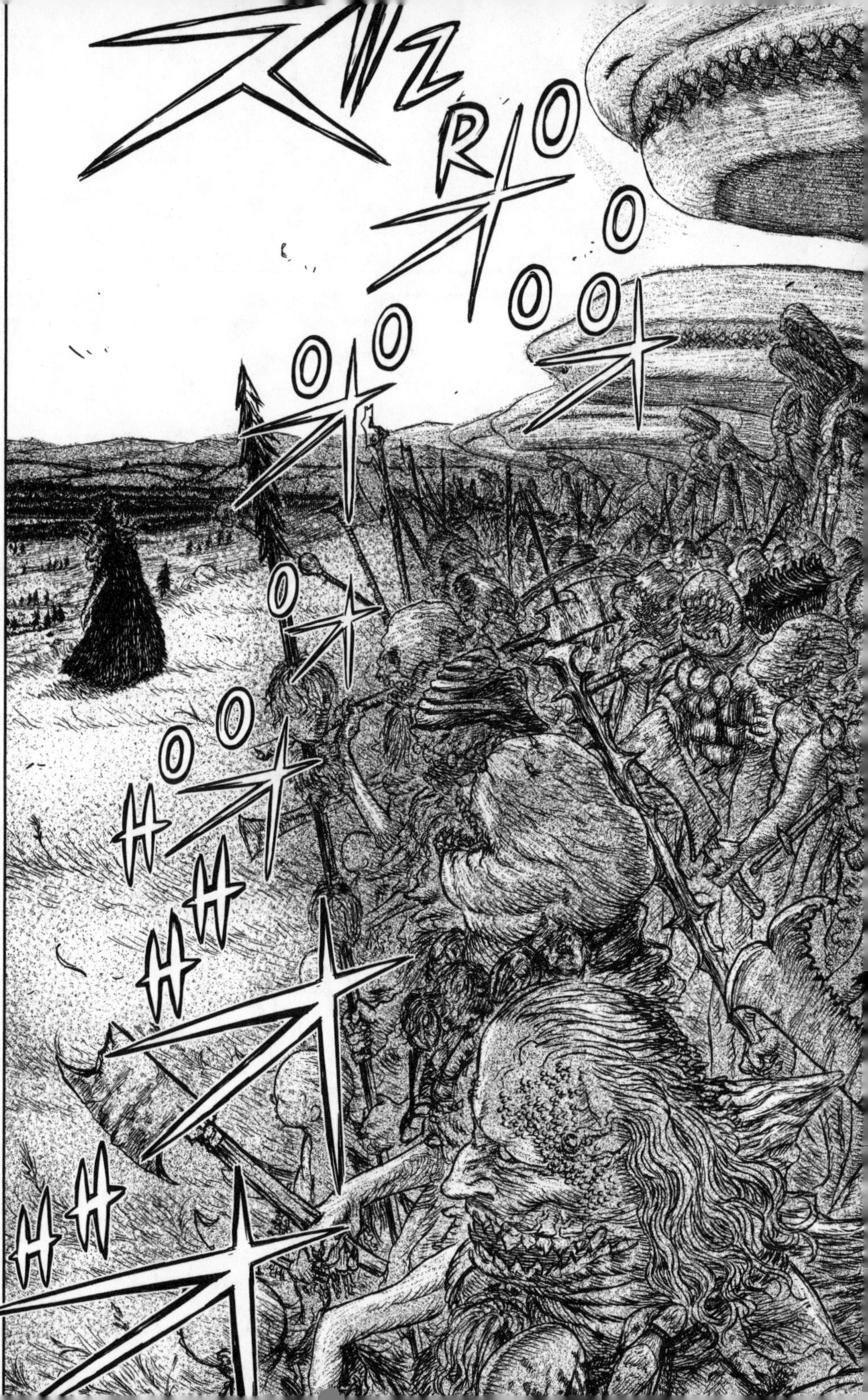
ZROOOOOOOOOHHHHH

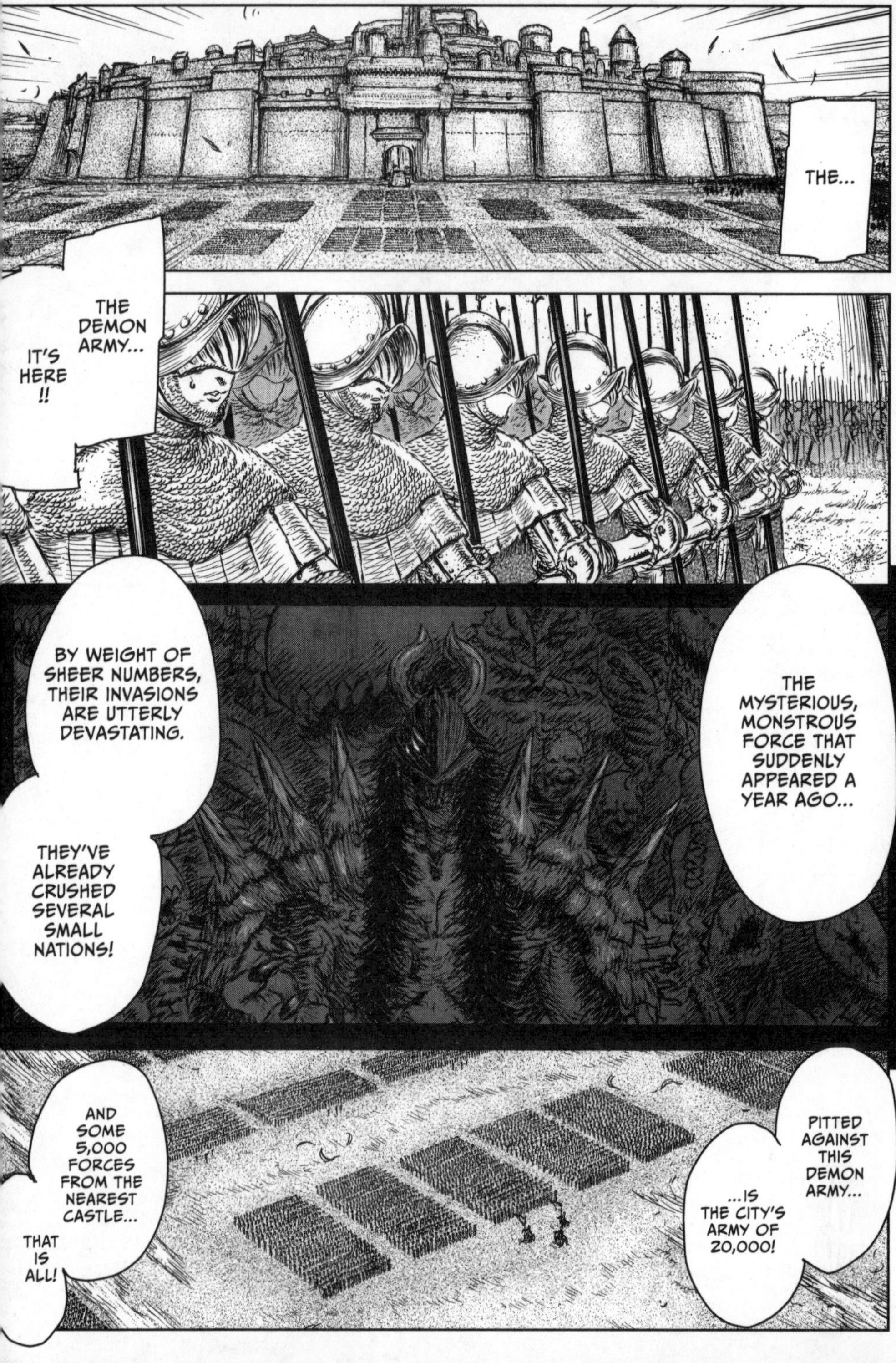
THE...
THE DEMON ARMY...
IT'S HERE!!
THE MYSTERIOUS, MONSTROUS FORCE THAT SUDDENLY APPEARED A YEAR AGO...
BY WEIGHT OF SHEER NUMBERS, THEIR INVASIONS ARE UTTERLY DEVASTATING.
THEY'VE ALREADY CRUSHED SEVERAL SMALL NATIONS!
PITTED AGAINST THIS DEMON ARMY...
...IS THE CITY'S ARMY OF 20,000!
AND SOME 5,000 FORCES FROM THE NEAREST CASTLE...
THAT IS ALL!

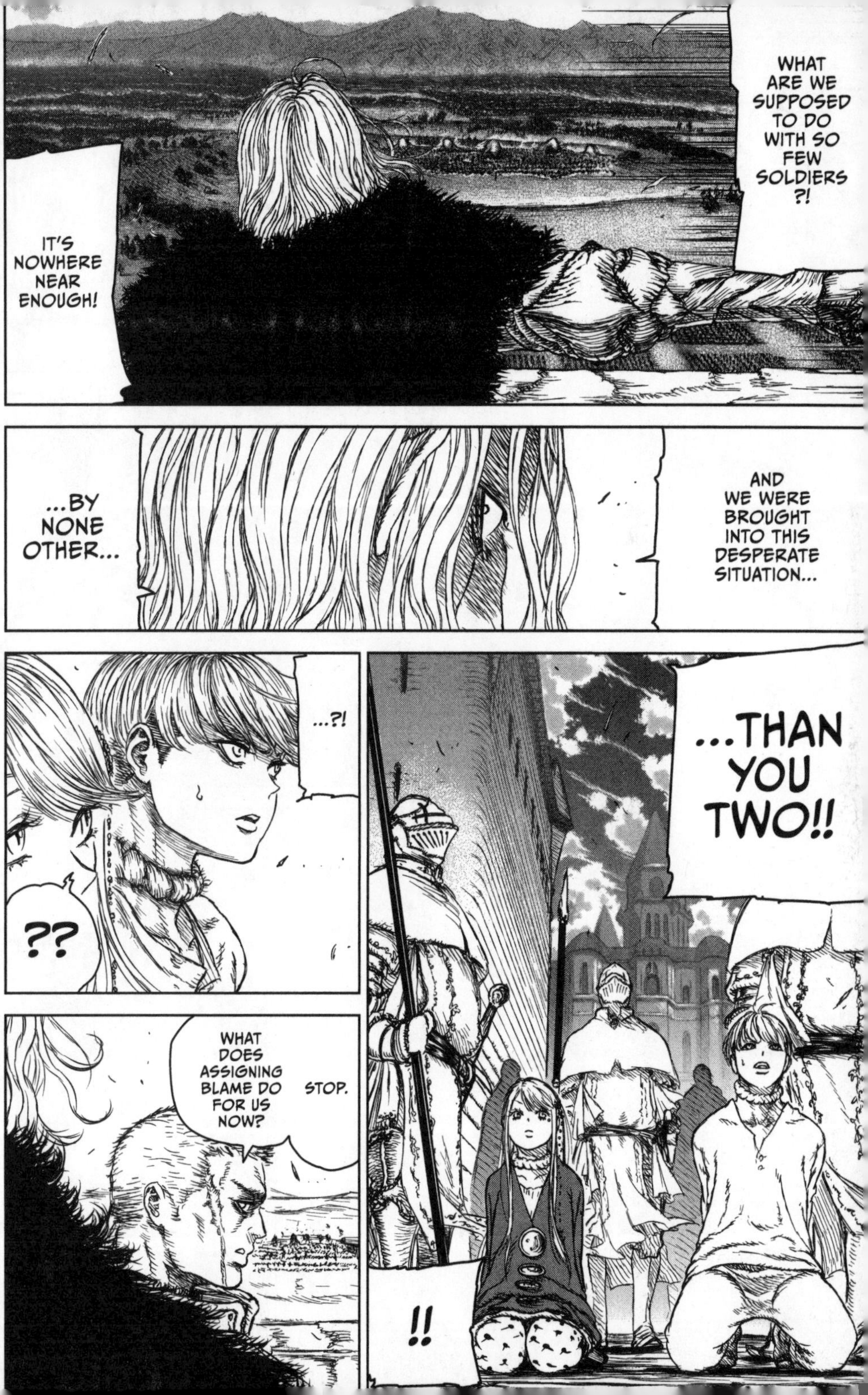
WHAT ARE WE SUPPOSED TO DO WITH SO FEW SOLDIERS?!
IT'S NOWHERE NEAR ENOUGH!
AND WE WERE BROUGHT INTO THIS DESPERATE SITUATION...
...BY NONE OTHER...
...THAN YOU TWO!!
!!
...?!
??
STOP.
WHAT DOES ASSIGNING BLAME DO FOR US NOW?

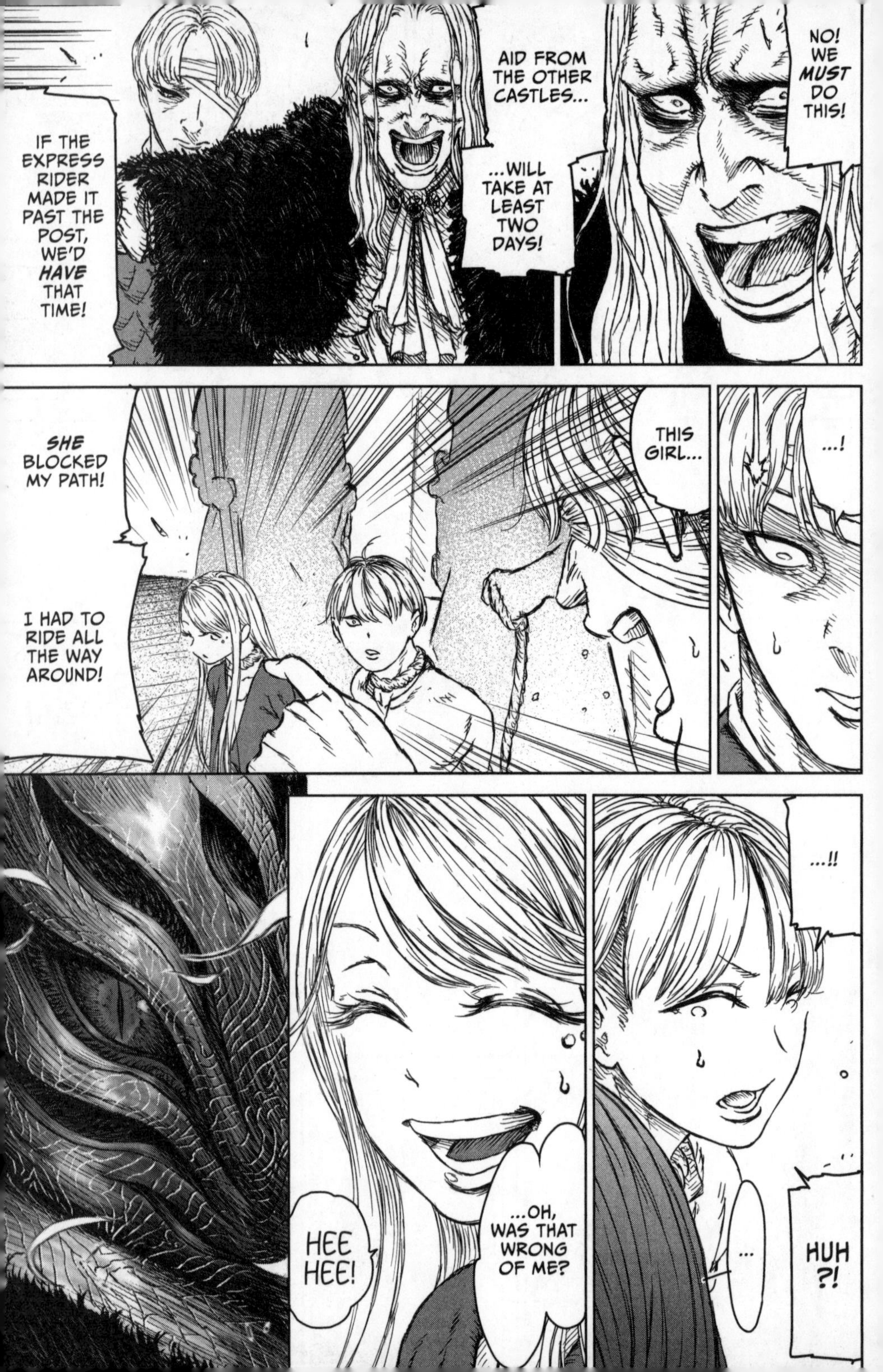
NO! WE MUST DO THIS!
AID FROM THE OTHER CASTLES...
...WILL TAKE AT LEAST TWO DAYS!
IF THE EXPRESS RIDER MADE IT PAST THE POST, WE'D HAVE THAT TIME!
...!
THIS GIRL...
SHE BLOCKED MY PATH!
I HAD TO RIDE ALL THE WAY AROUND!
...!!
HUH ?!
...
...OH, WAS THAT WRONG OF ME?
HEE HEE!

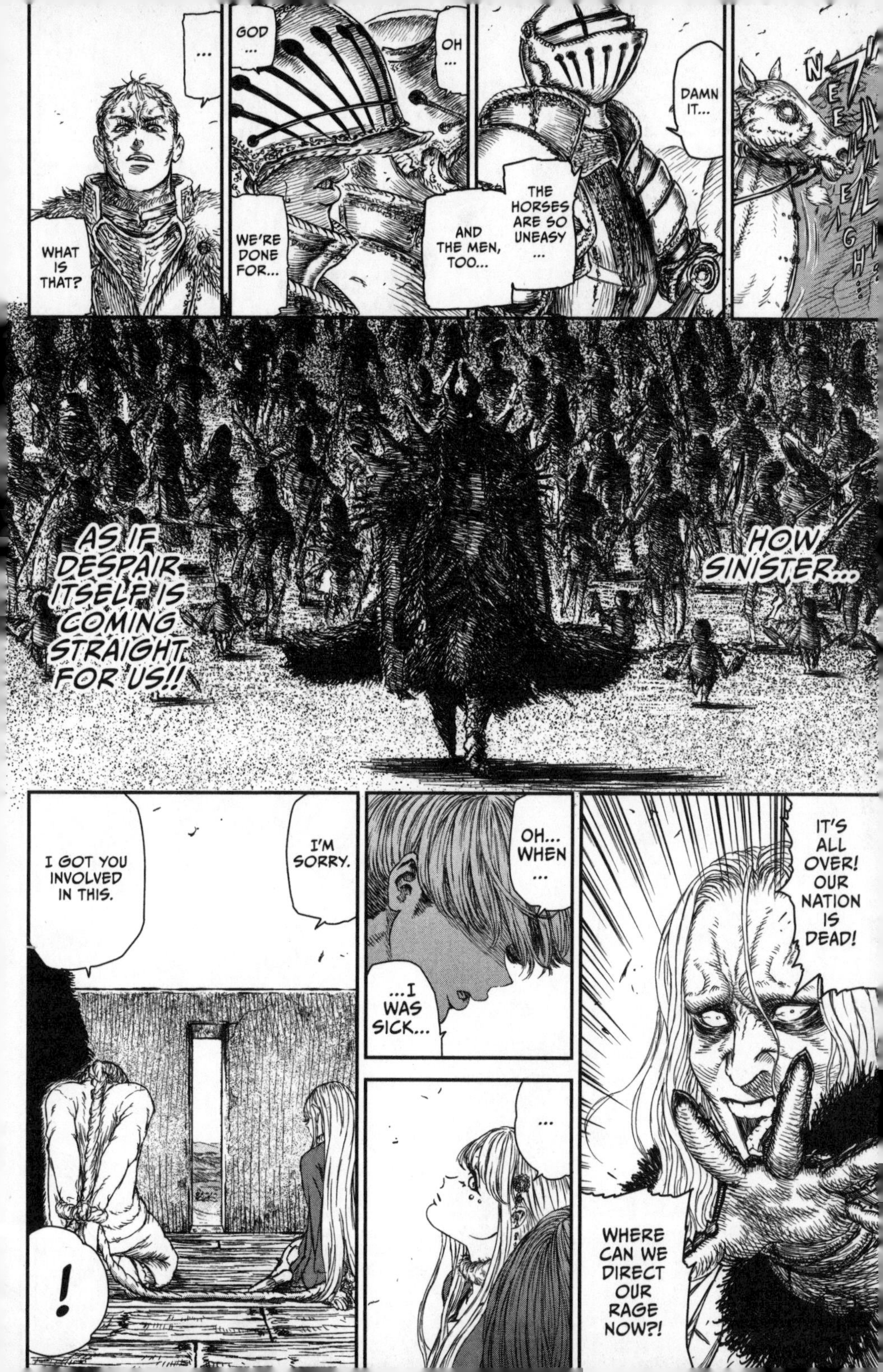
ÑEEEIGH...
DAMN IT...
THE HORSES ARE SO UNEASY...
AND THE MEN, TOO...
OH...
GOD...
WE'RE DONE FOR...
...
WHAT IS THAT?
HOW SINISTER...
AS IF DESPAIR ITSELF IS COMING STRAIGHT FOR US!!
IT'S ALL OVER! OUR NATION IS DEAD!
WHERE CAN WE DIRECT OUR RAGE NOW?!
OH... WHEN...
...I WAS SICK...
...
I'M SORRY.
I GOT YOU INVOLVED IN THIS.
!

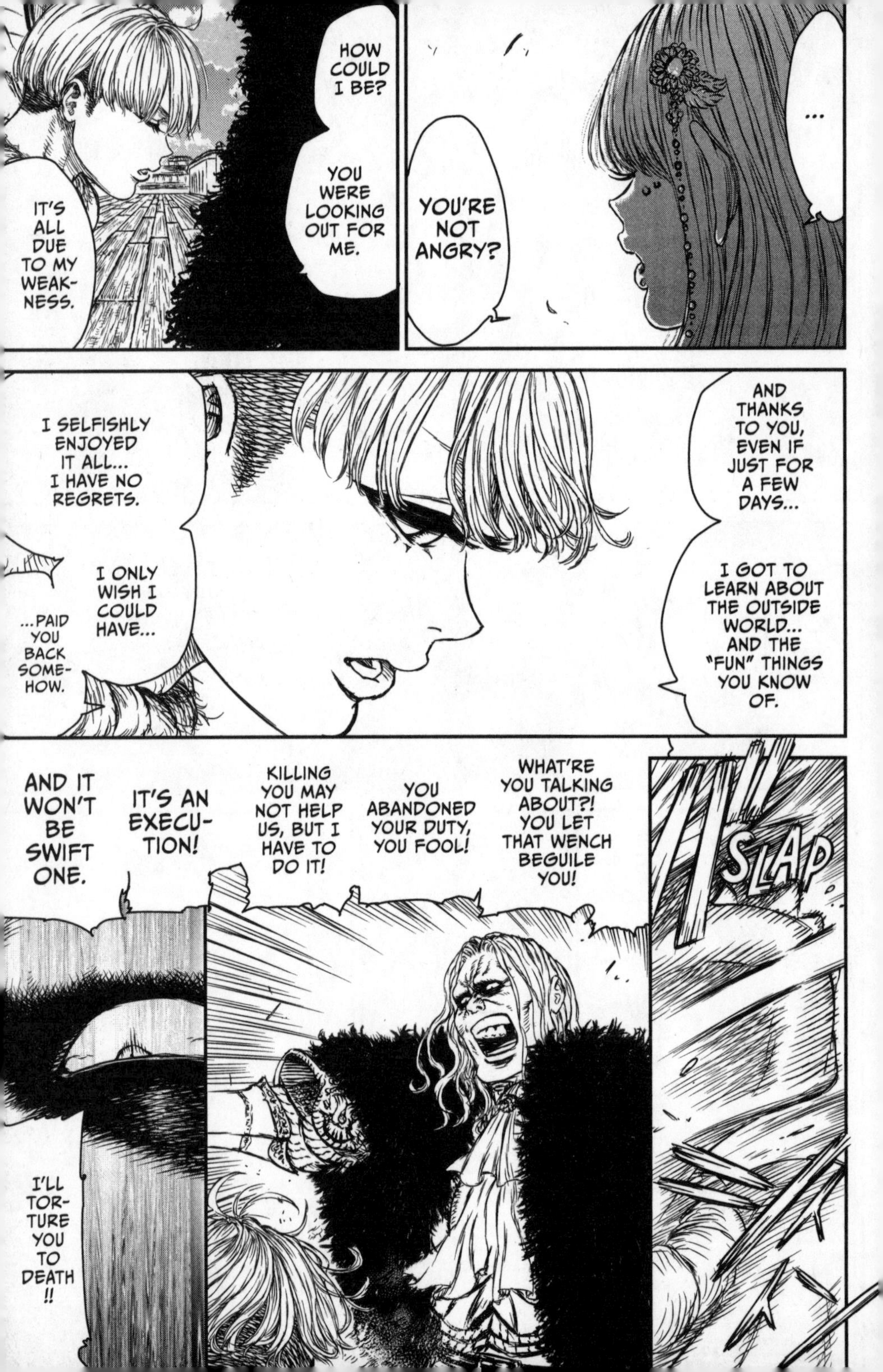
...
YOU'RE NOT ANGRY?
HOW COULD I BE?
YOU WERE LOOKING OUT FOR ME.
IT'S ALL DUE TO MY WEAK-NESS.
AND THANKS TO YOU, EVEN IF JUST FOR A FEW DAYS...
I GOT TO LEARN ABOUT THE OUTSIDE WORLD... AND THE "FUN" THINGS YOU KNOW OF.
I SELFISHLY ENJOYED IT ALL... I HAVE NO REGRETS.
I ONLY WISH I COULD HAVE...
...PAID YOU BACK SOME-HOW.
SLAP
WHAT'RE YOU TALKING ABOUT?! YOU LET THAT WENCH BEGUILE YOU!
YOU ABANDONED YOUR DUTY, YOU FOOL!
KILLING YOU MAY NOT HELP US, BUT I HAVE TO DO IT!
IT'S AN EXECU-TION!
AND IT WON'T BE SWIFT ONE.
I'LL TOR-TURE YOU TO DEATH!!

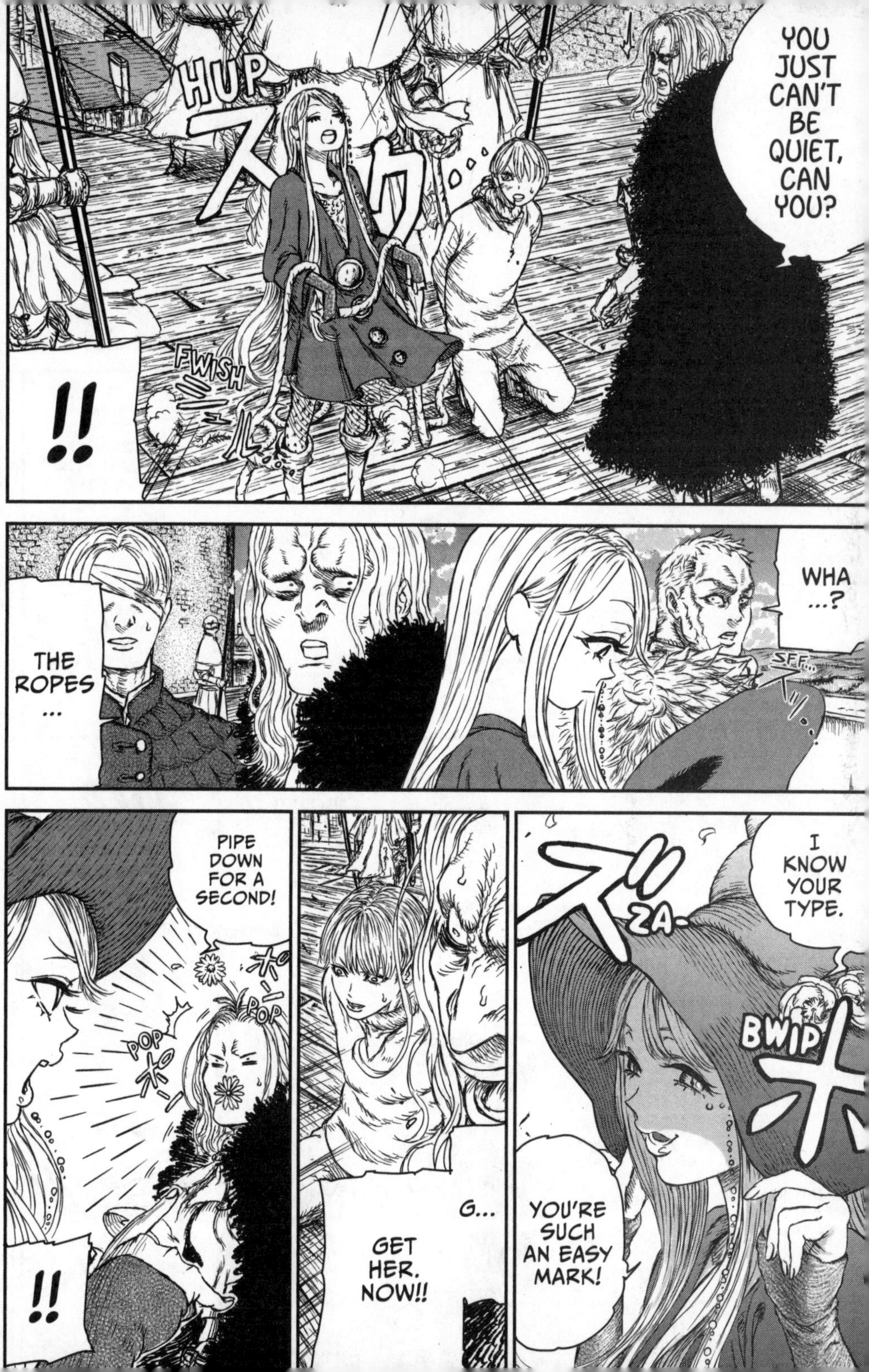
YOU JUST CAN'T BE QUIET, CAN YOU?
HUP
FWISH
!!
WHA ...?
SFF...
THE ROPES ...
I KNOW YOUR TYPE.
ZA-
BWIP
YOU'RE SUCH AN EASY MARK!
G...
GET HER. NOW!!
PIPE DOWN FOR A SECOND!
POP
POP
!!

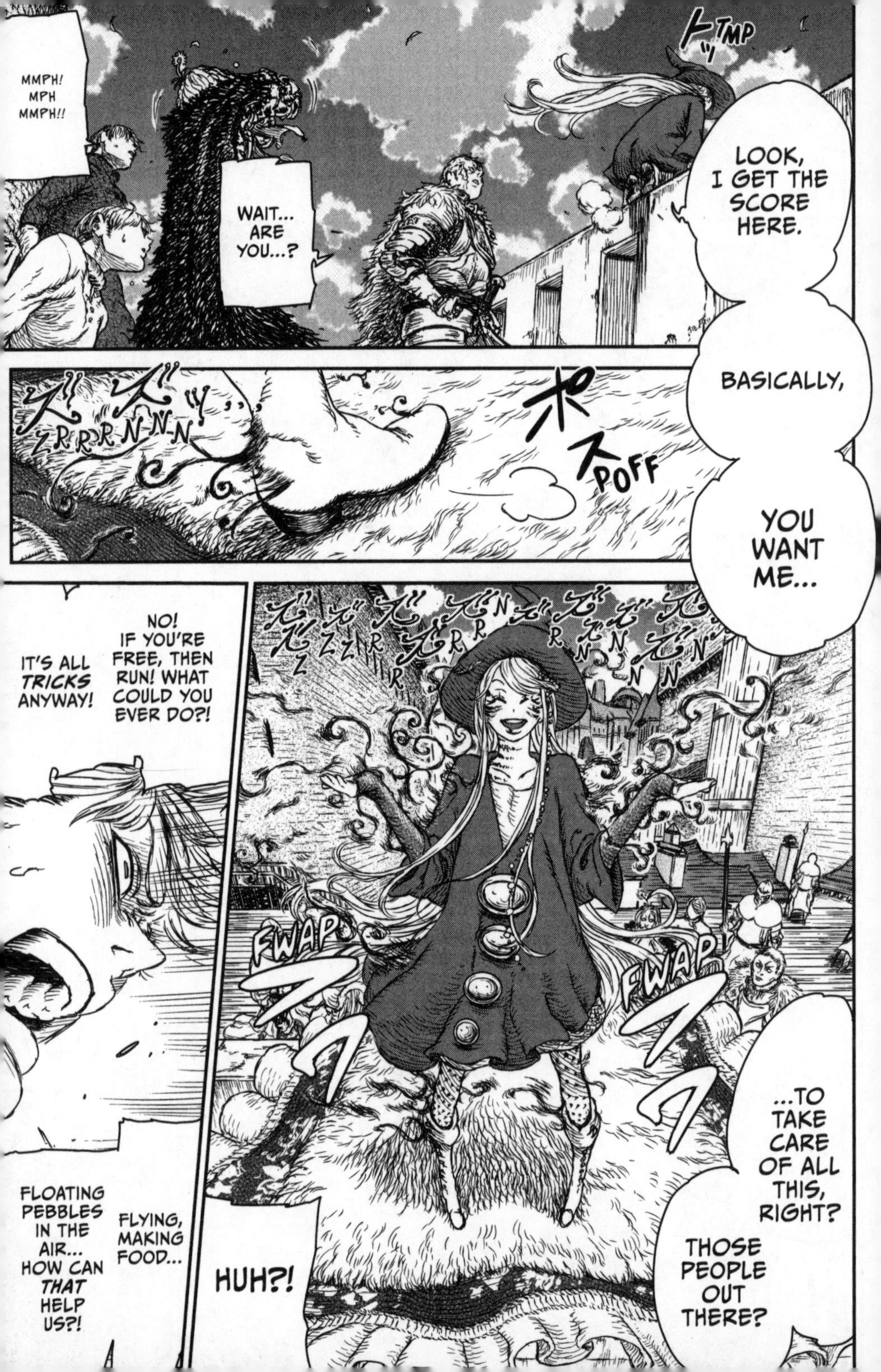
TMP
LOOK, I GET THE SCORE HERE.
WAIT... ARE YOU...?
MMPH! MPH MMPH!!
BASICALLY,
POFF
ZRRRNNN
YOU WANT ME...
FWAP
FWAP
...TO TAKE CARE OF ALL THIS, RIGHT?
THOSE PEOPLE OUT THERE?
NO! IF YOU'RE FREE, THEN RUN! WHAT COULD YOU EVER DO?!
IT'S ALL *TRICKS* ANYWAY!
HUH?!
FLYING, MAKING FOOD...
FLOATING PEBBLES IN THE AIR... HOW CAN *THAT* HELP US?!

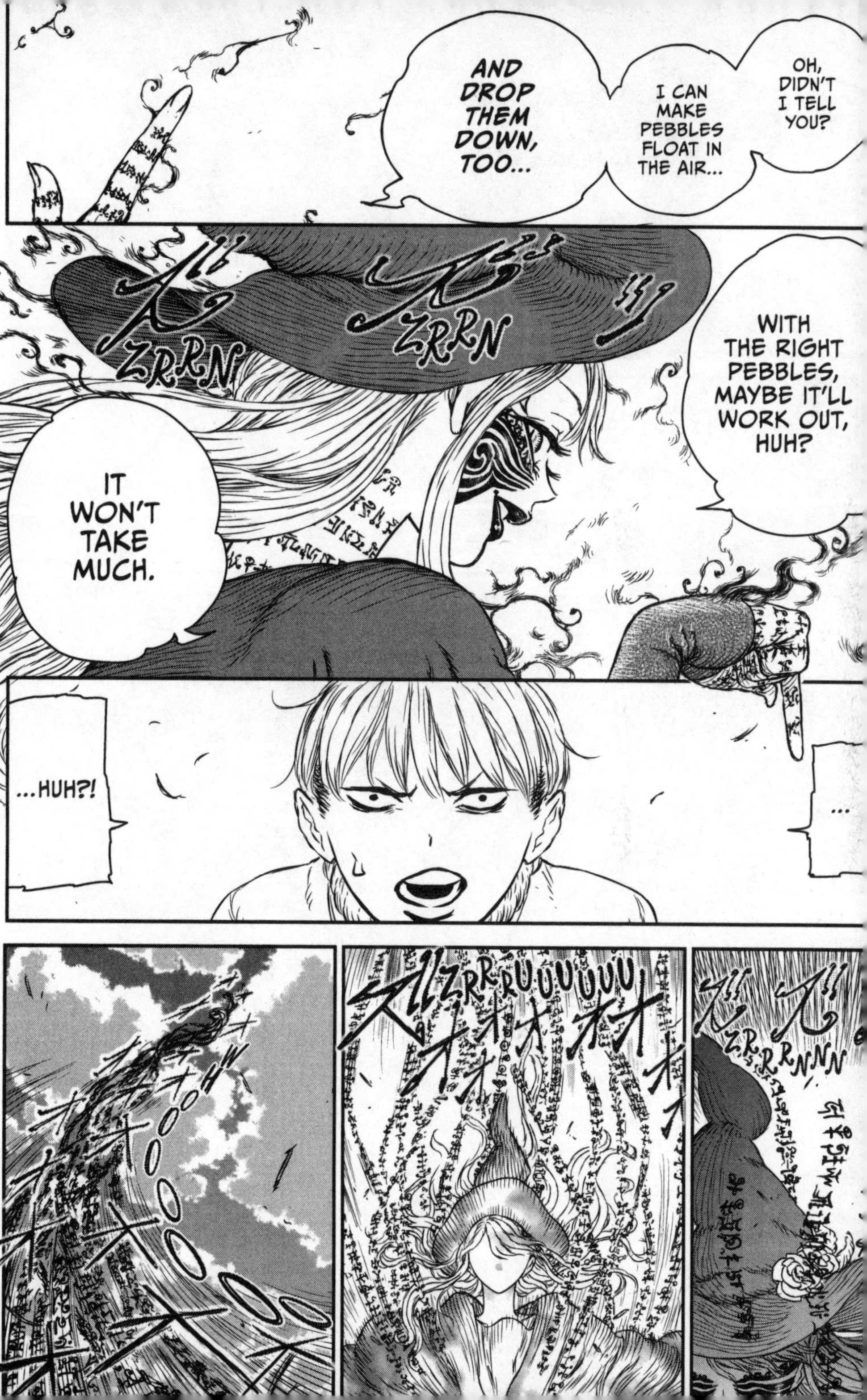
OH, DIDN'T I TELL YOU?
I CAN MAKE PEBBLES FLOAT IN THE AIR...
AND DROP THEM DOWN, TOO...
ZRRN
ZRRN
WITH THE RIGHT PEBBLES, MAYBE IT'LL WORK OUT, HUH?
IT WON'T TAKE MUCH.
...
...HUH?!
ZRRRRNNN
ZZRRRUUUUUU
WHOOOOOOO

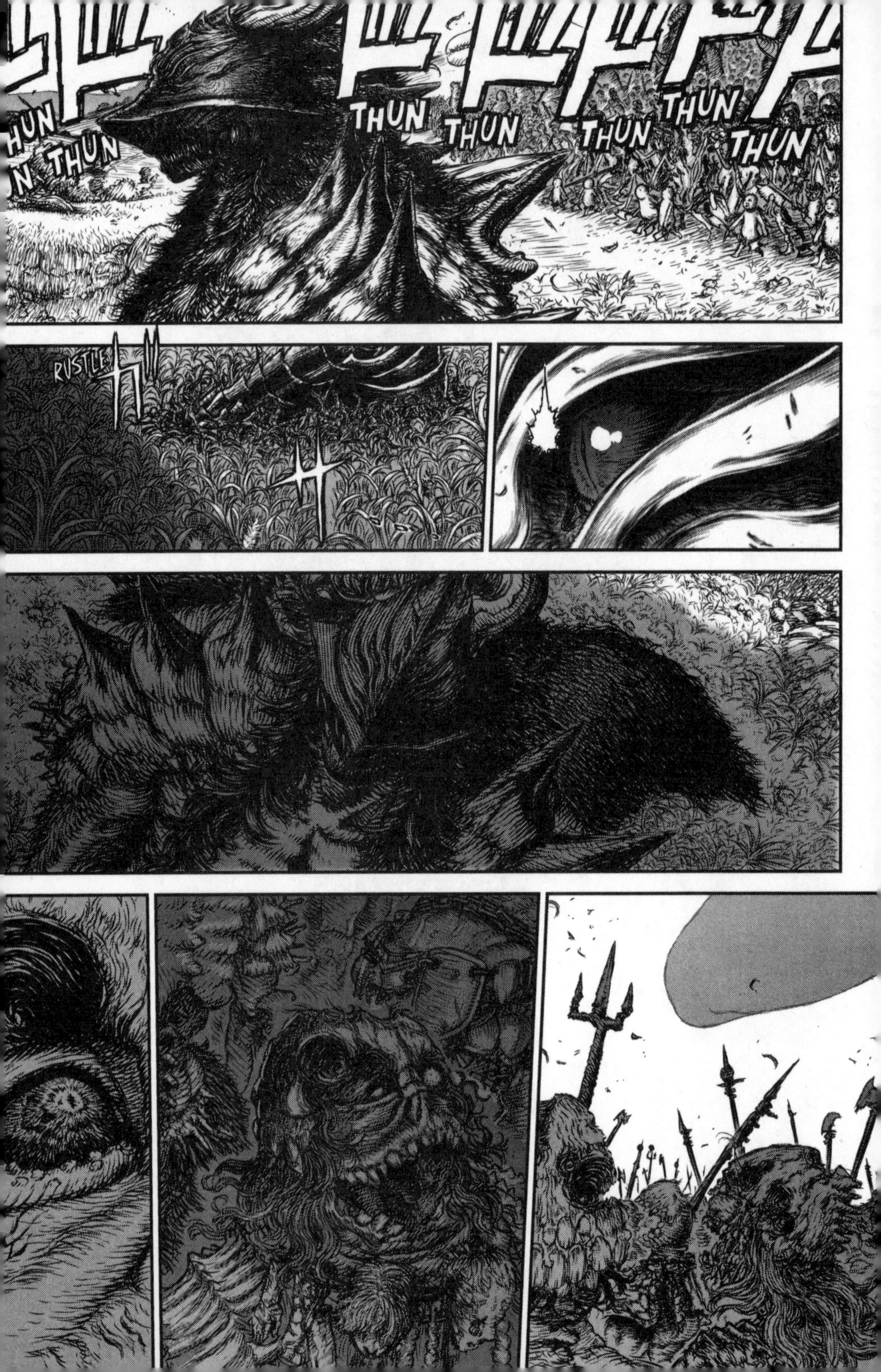

THUN
THUN
THUN
THUN
THUN
THUN
THUN
HUN
N THUN
RUSTLE

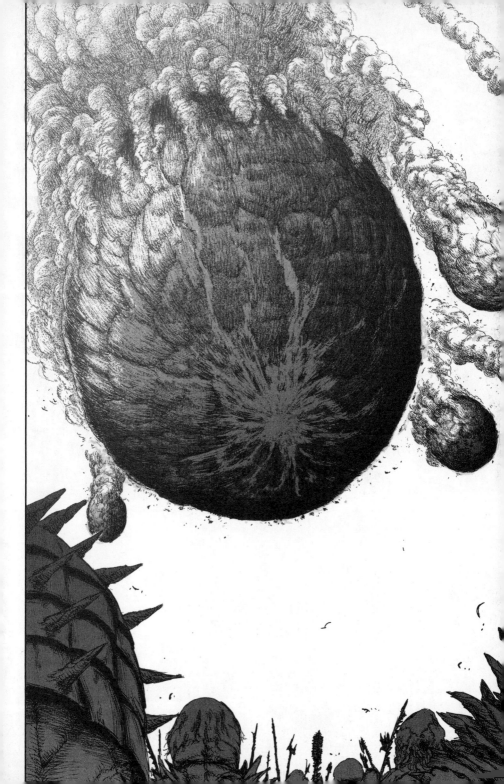

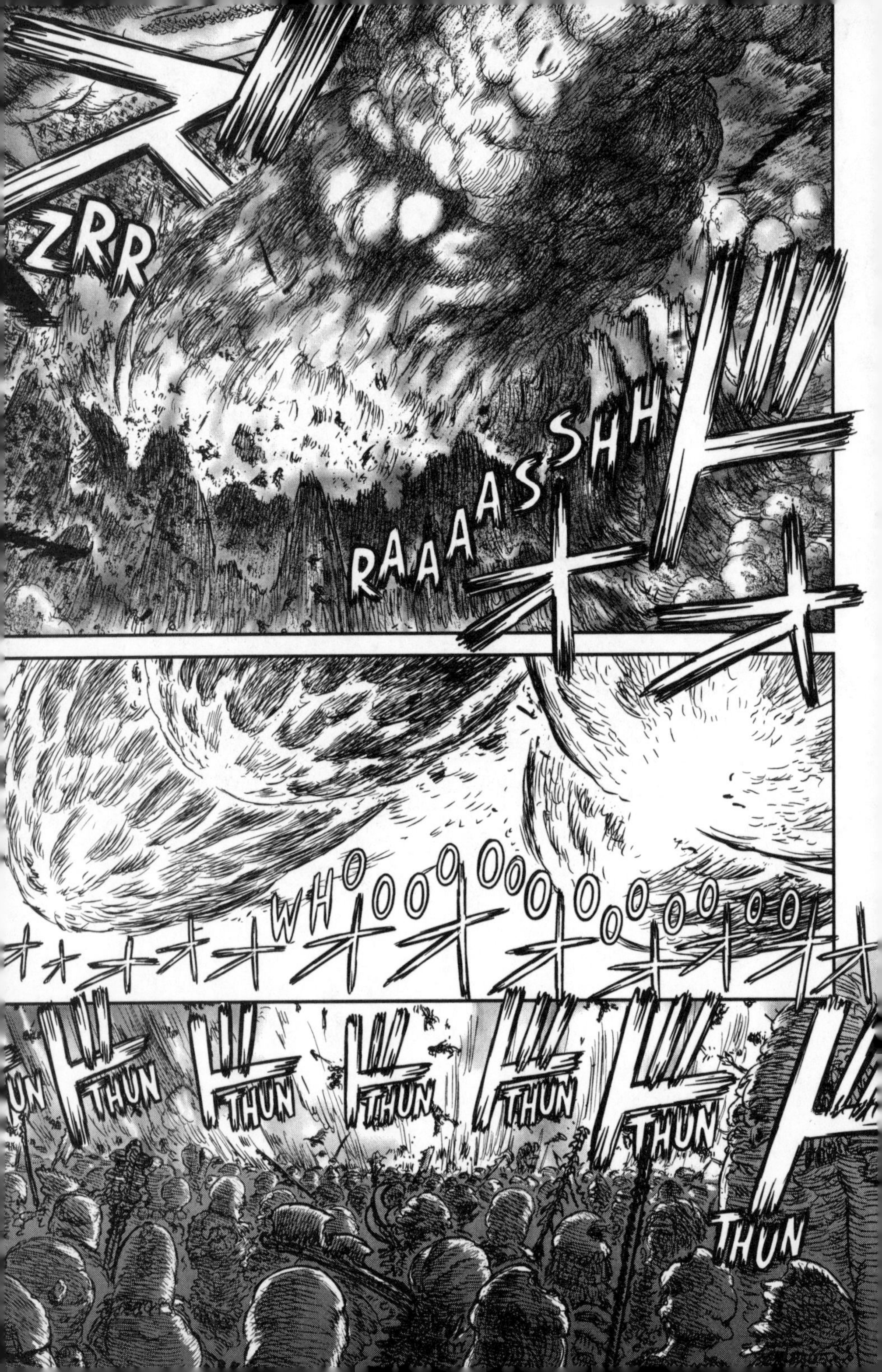
RAAAASSHH
ZRR
WHOOOOOOOOOOOOOO
THUN
THUN
THUN
THUN
THUN
THUN

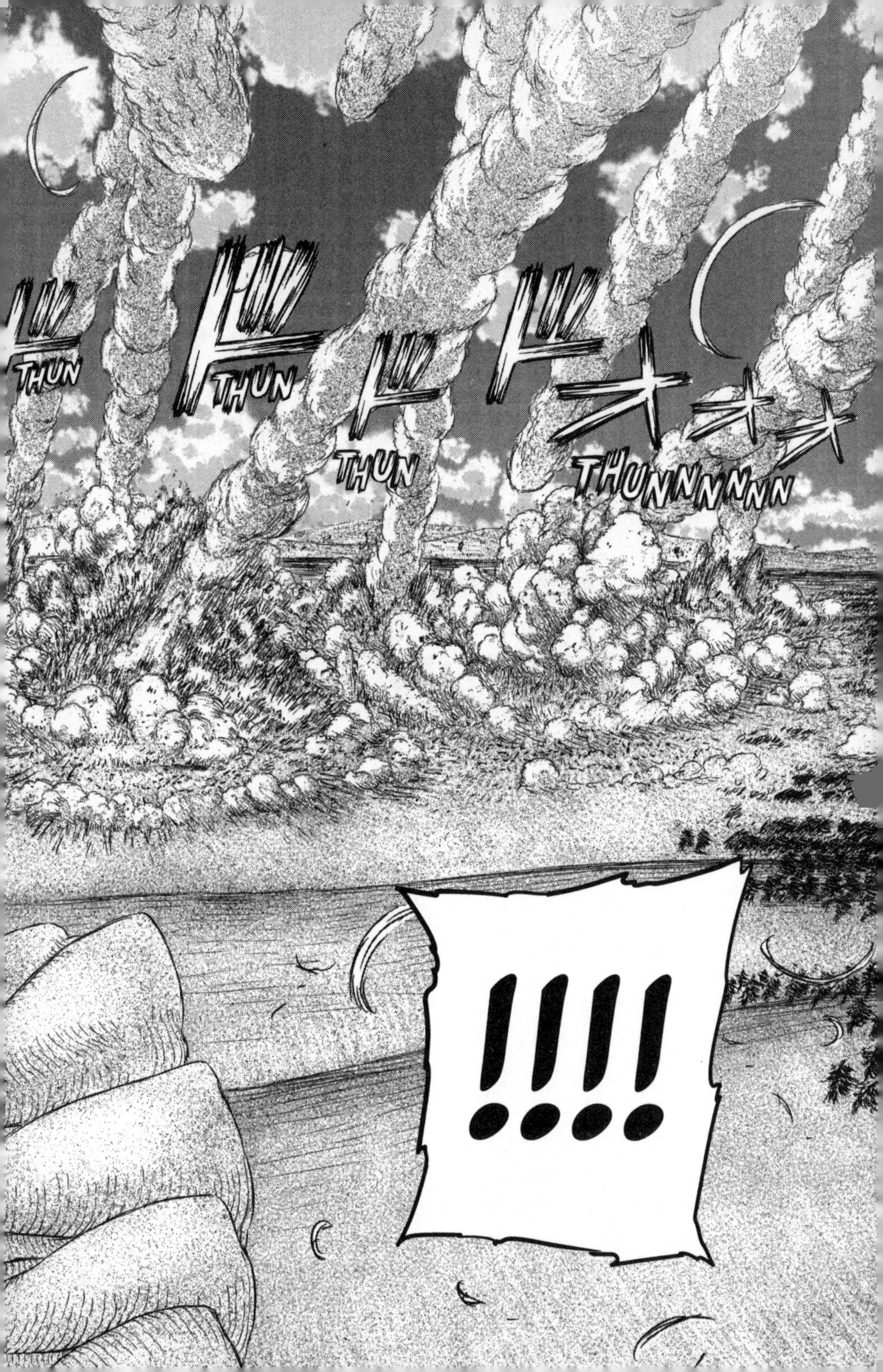
ドドドドオオオ
THUN
THUN
THUN
THUNNNNNNN
!!!!

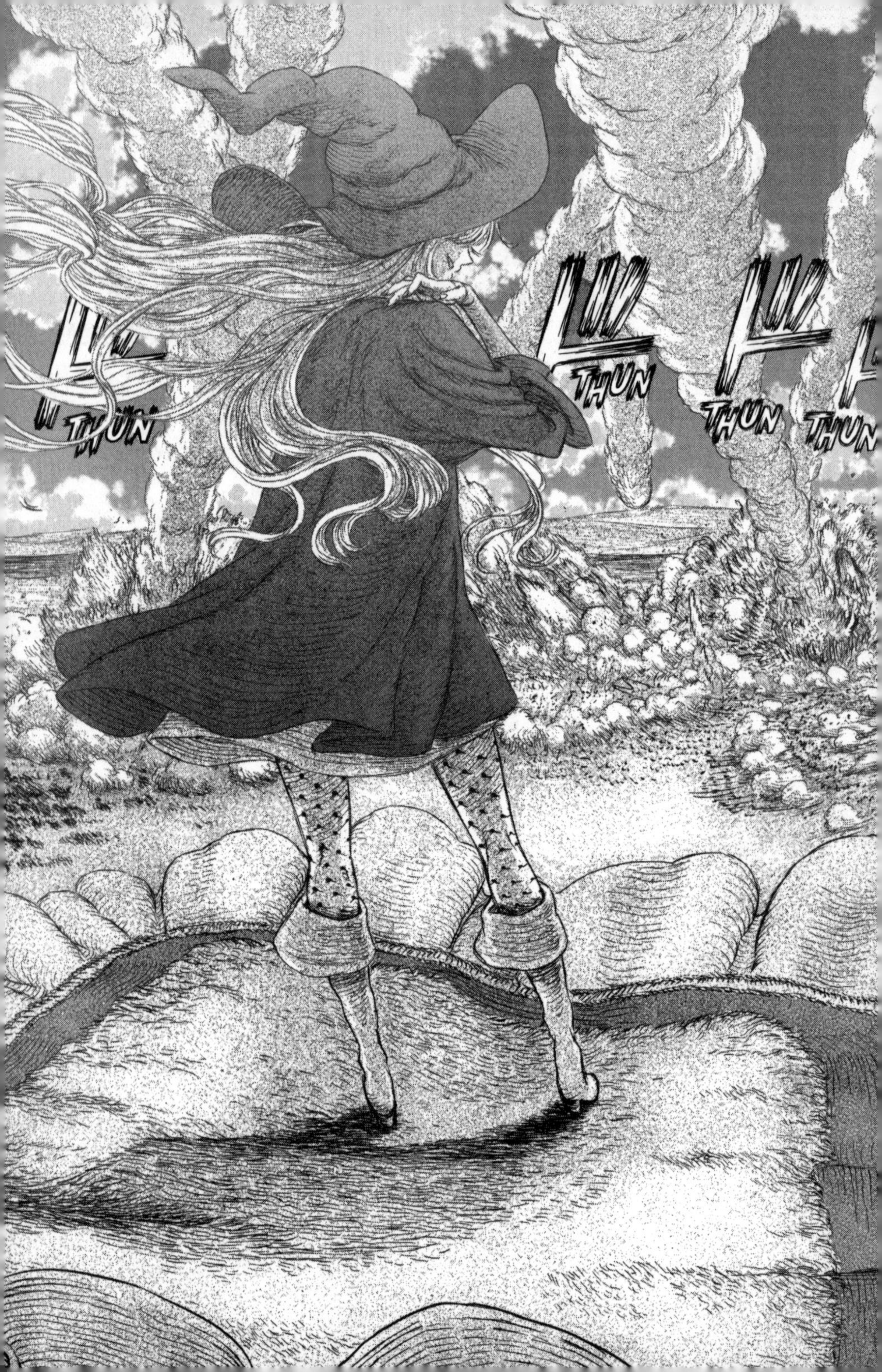
THUN
THUN
THUN
THUN

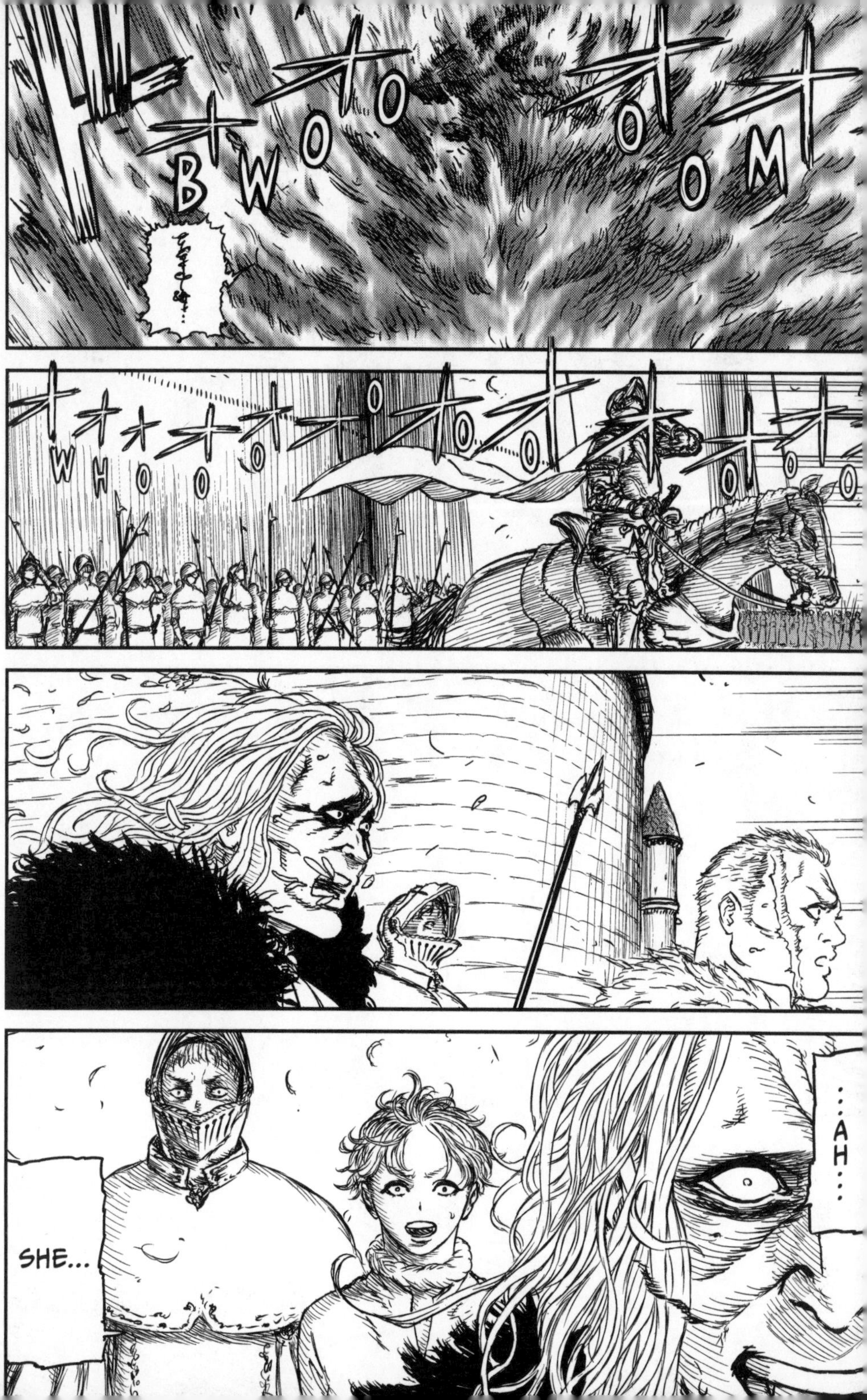
BWOOOM
WHOOOO
...AH...
SHE...

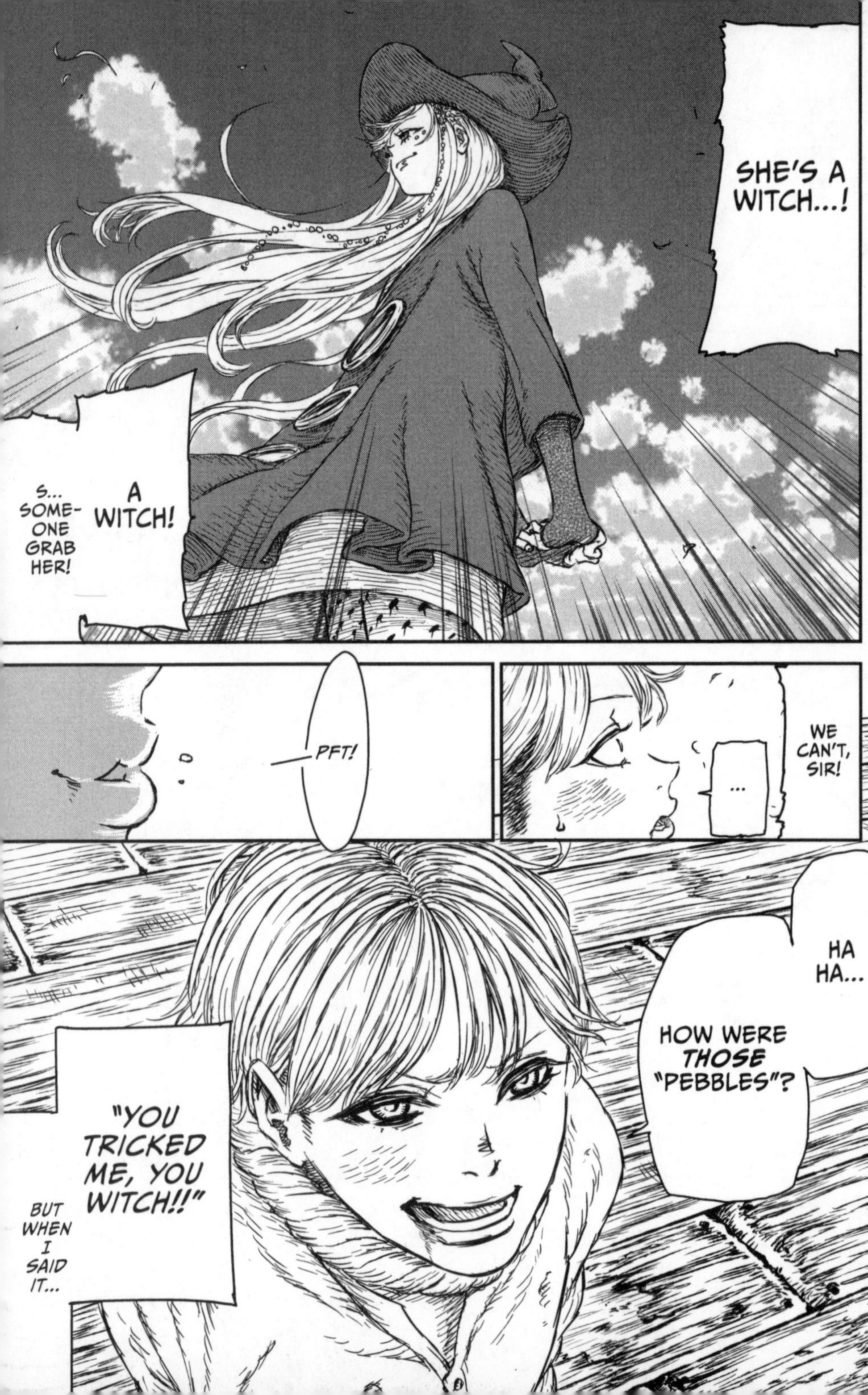

SHE'S A WITCH...!
A WITCH!
S... SOMEONE GRAB HER!
WE CAN'T, SIR!
...
PFT!
HA HA...
HOW WERE *THOSE* "PEBBLES"?
"YOU TRICKED ME, YOU WITCH!!"
BUT WHEN I SAID IT...

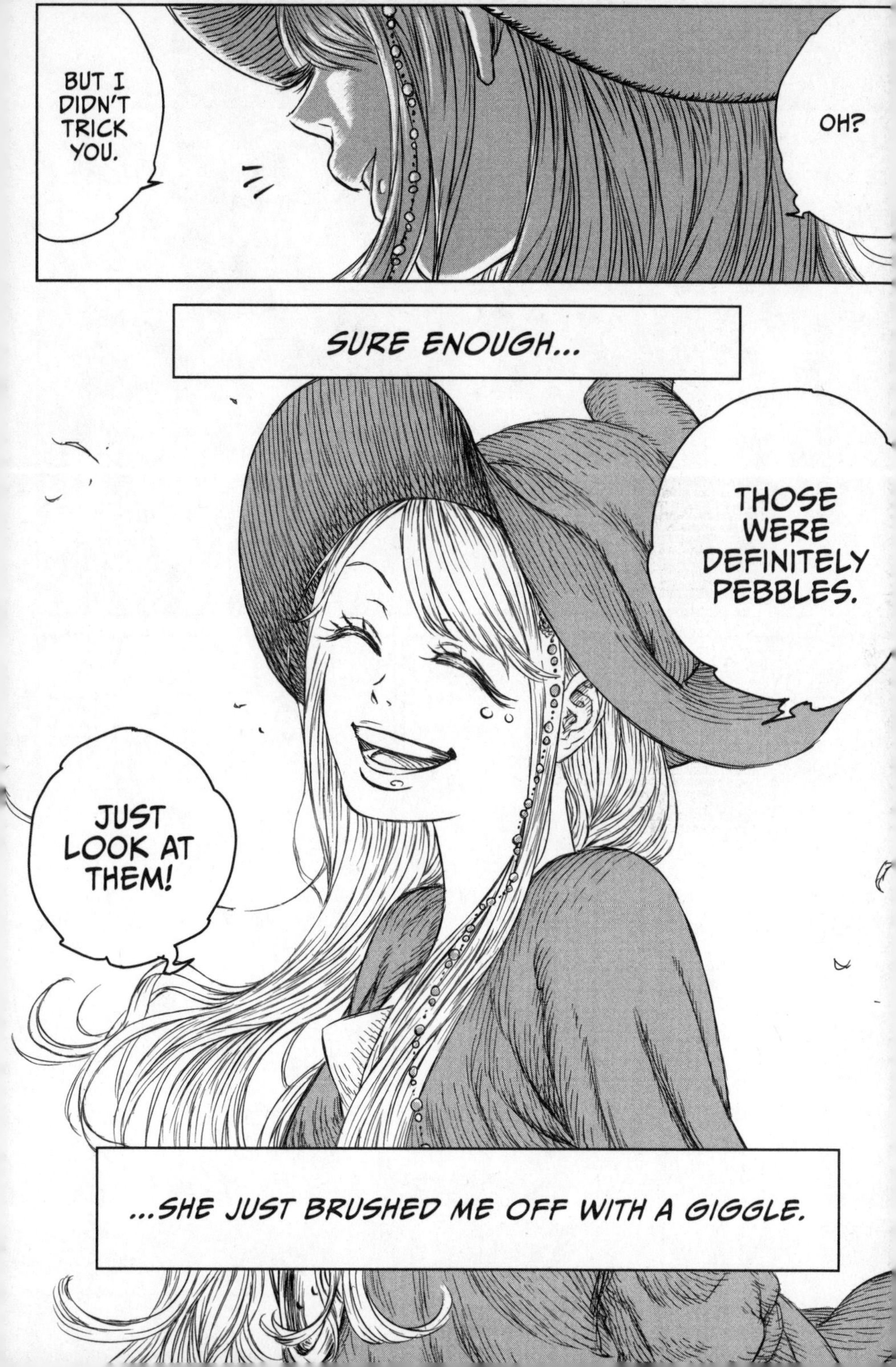
OH?
BUT I DIDN'T TRICK YOU.
SURE ENOUGH...
THOSE WERE DEFINITELY PEBBLES.
JUST LOOK AT THEM!
...SHE JUST BRUSHED ME OFF WITH A GIGGLE.

# THE WITCH AND THE BEAST

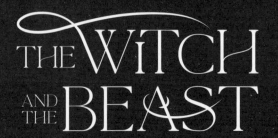

# THE WITCH AND THE BEAST

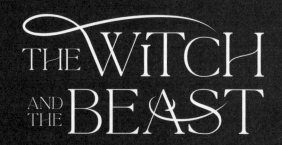

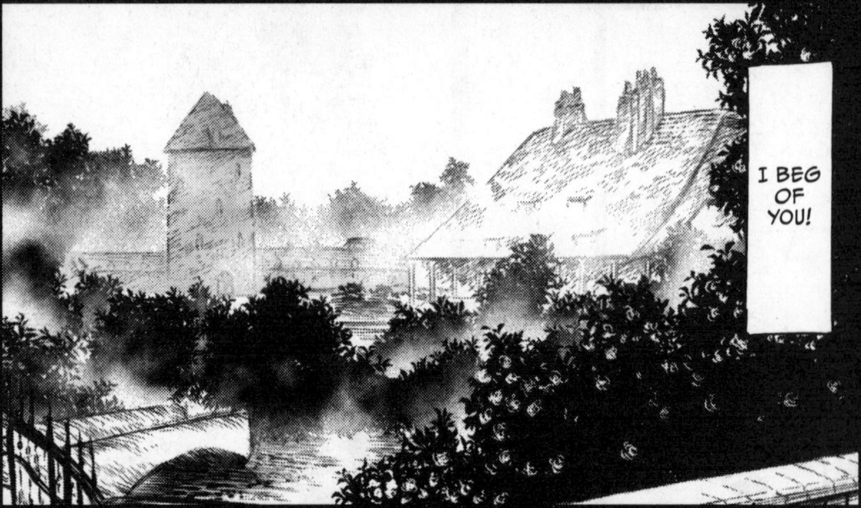
I BEG OF YOU!

## P.S. "BEYOND DEATH"

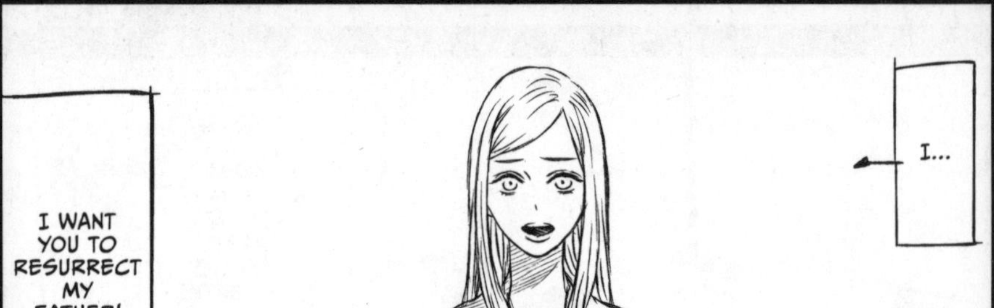
I...
I WANT YOU TO RESURRECT MY FATHER!

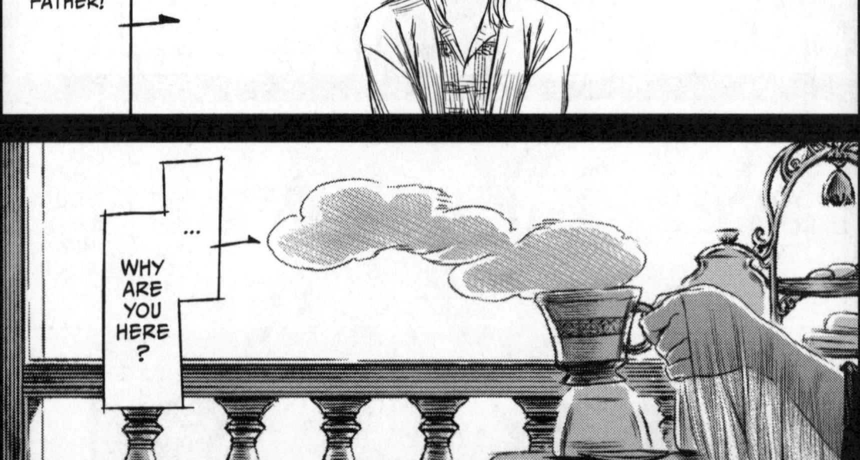
...
WHY ARE YOU HERE?

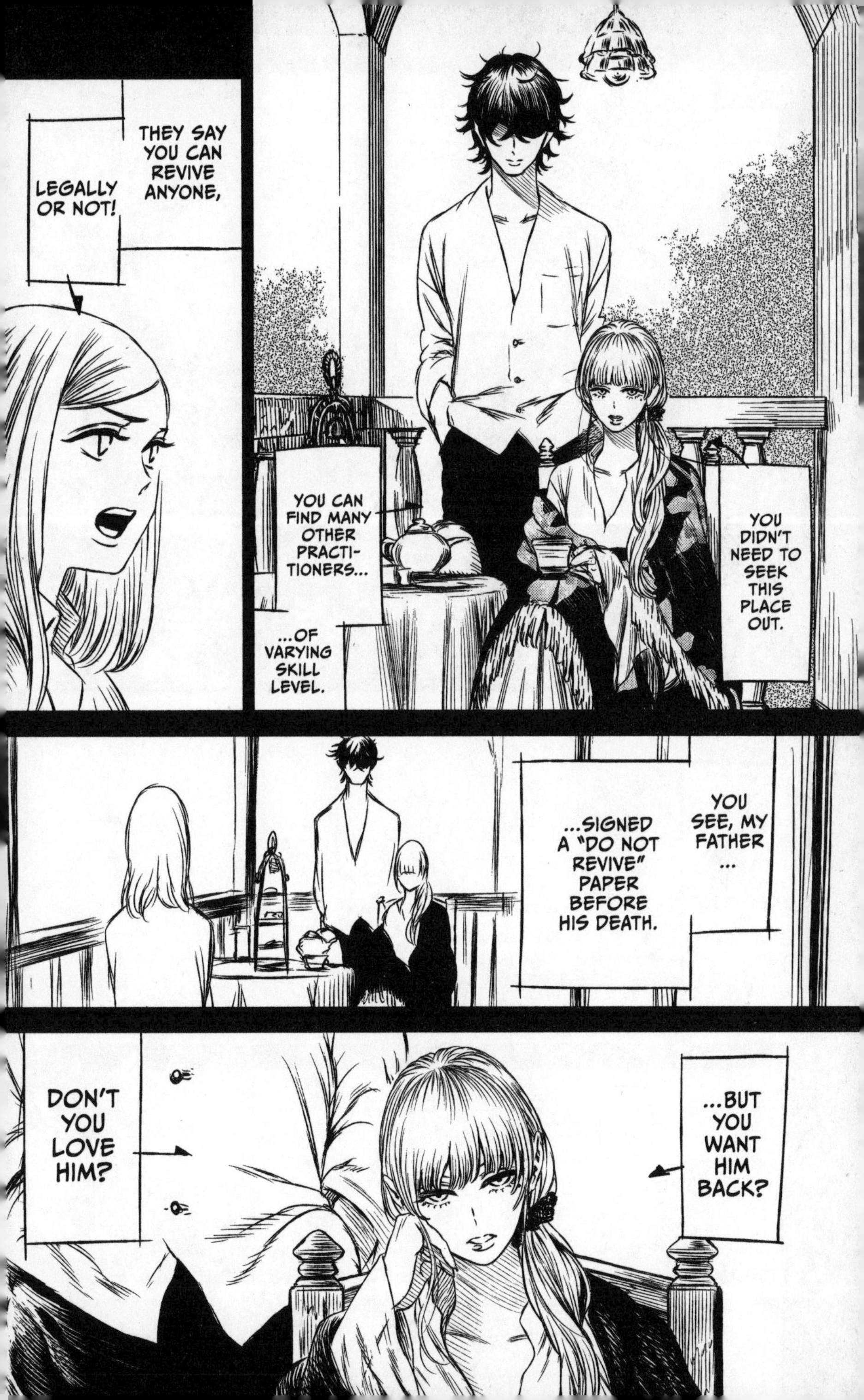
YOU DIDN'T NEED TO SEEK THIS PLACE OUT.
YOU CAN FIND MANY OTHER PRACTI-TIONERS...
...OF VARYING SKILL LEVEL.
THEY SAY YOU CAN REVIVE ANYONE,
LEGALLY OR NOT!
YOU SEE, MY FATHER ...
...SIGNED A "DO NOT REVIVE" PAPER BEFORE HIS DEATH.
...BUT YOU WANT HIM BACK?
DON'T YOU LOVE HIM?

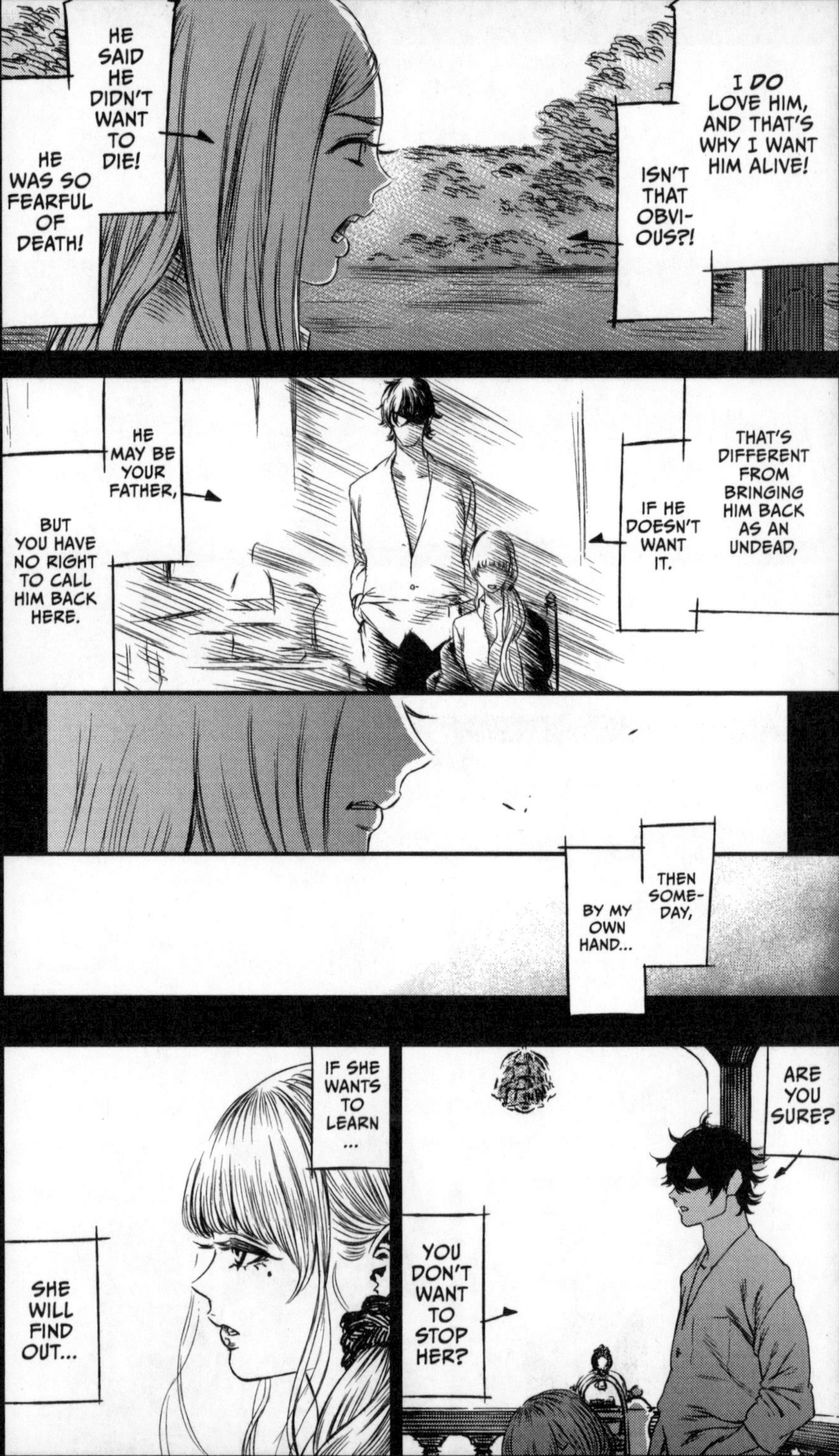

I *DO* LOVE HIM, AND THAT'S WHY I WANT HIM ALIVE!
ISN'T THAT OBVIOUS?!
HE SAID HE DIDN'T WANT TO DIE!
HE WAS SO FEARFUL OF DEATH!
THAT'S DIFFERENT FROM BRINGING HIM BACK AS AN UNDEAD,
IF HE DOESN'T WANT IT.
HE MAY BE YOUR FATHER,
BUT YOU HAVE NO RIGHT TO CALL HIM BACK HERE.
THEN SOMEDAY,
BY MY OWN HAND...
ARE YOU SURE?
YOU DON'T WANT TO STOP HER?
IF SHE WANTS TO LEARN ...
SHE WILL FIND OUT...

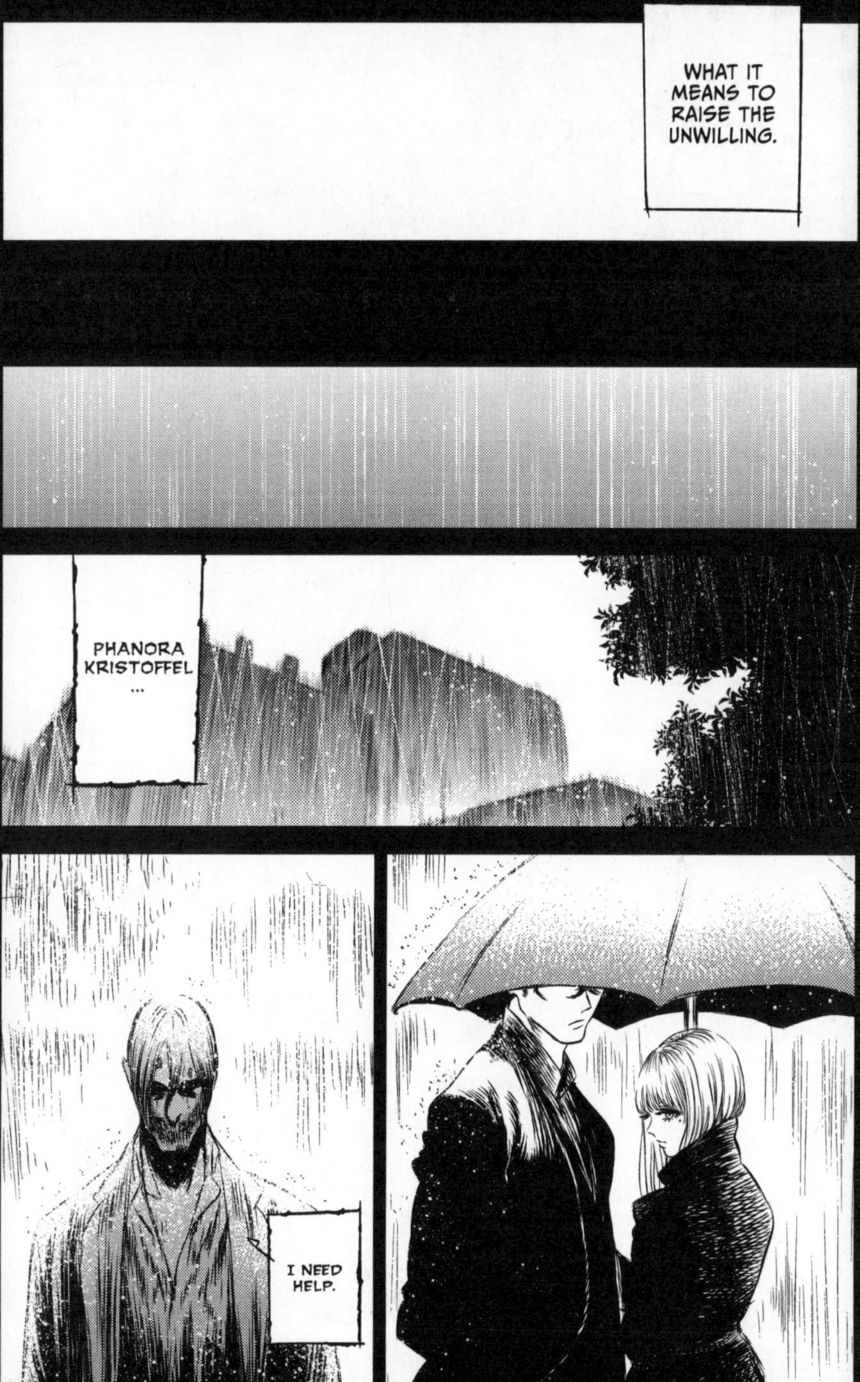
WHAT IT MEANS TO RAISE THE UNWILLING.
PHANORA KRISTOFFEL ...
I NEED HELP.

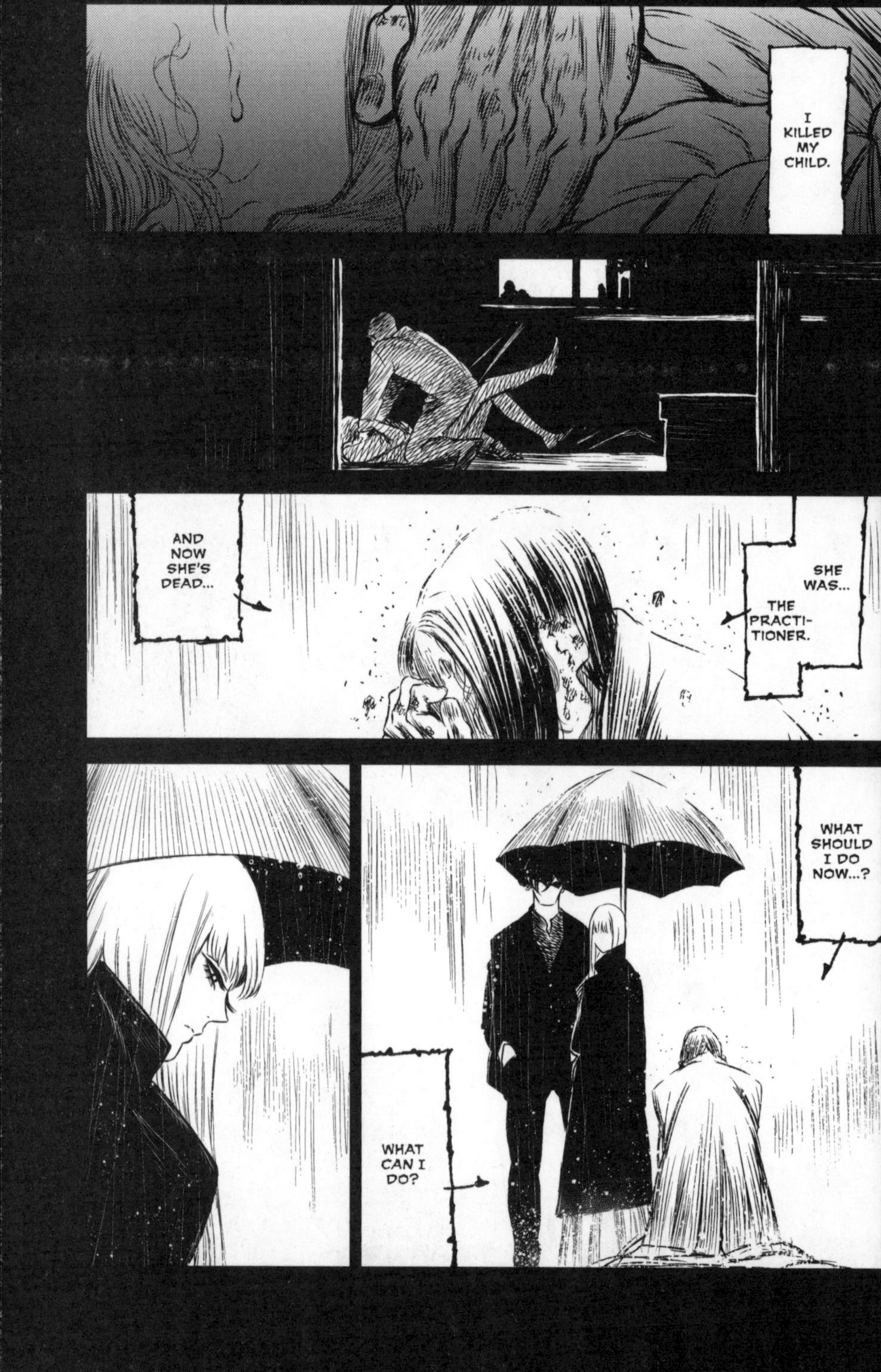
I KILLED MY CHILD.
SHE WAS... THE PRACTI- TIONER.
AND NOW SHE'S DEAD...
WHAT SHOULD I DO NOW...?
WHAT CAN I DO?

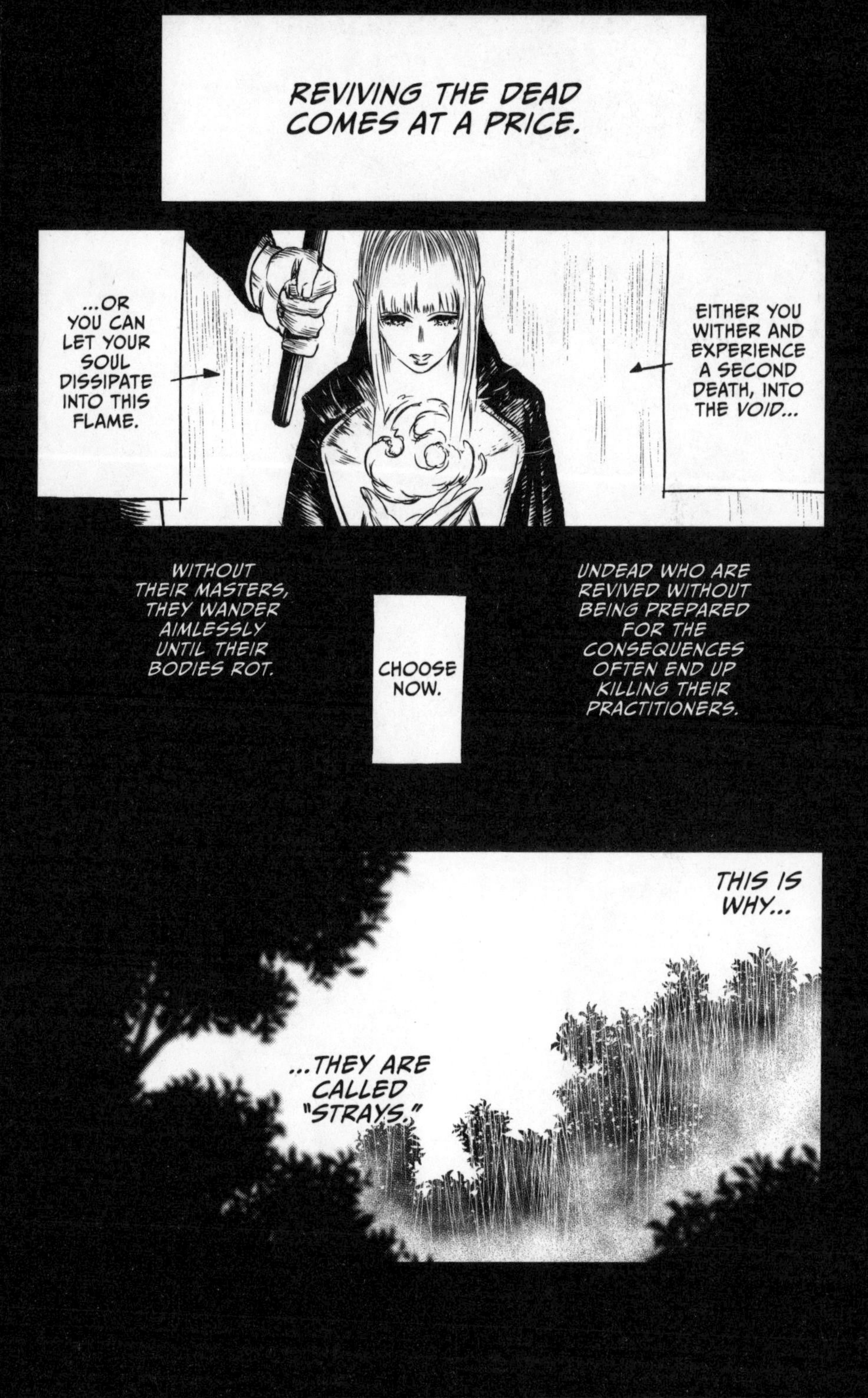
REVIVING THE DEAD COMES AT A PRICE.
EITHER YOU WITHER AND EXPERIENCE A SECOND DEATH, INTO THE *VOID*...
...OR YOU CAN LET YOUR SOUL DISSIPATE INTO THIS FLAME.
UNDEAD WHO ARE REVIVED WITHOUT BEING PREPARED FOR THE CONSEQUENCES OFTEN END UP KILLING THEIR PRACTITIONERS.
CHOOSE NOW.
WITHOUT THEIR MASTERS, THEY WANDER AIMLESSLY UNTIL THEIR BODIES ROT.
THIS IS WHY...
...THEY ARE CALLED "STRAYS."

# THE WITCH AND THE BEAST

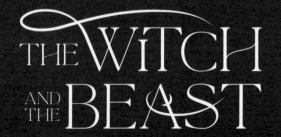

## The boys are back, in 400-page hardcovers that are as pretty and badass as they are!

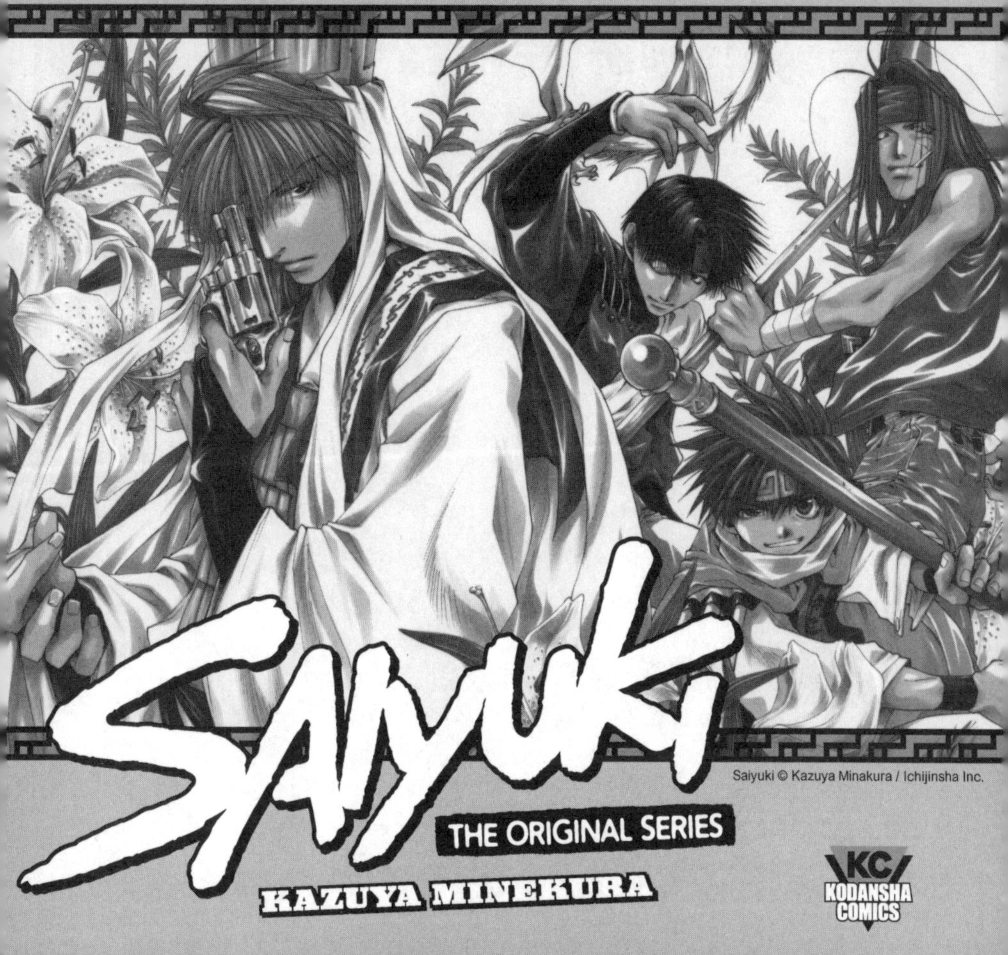
Saiyuki

Saiyuki © Kazuya Minakura / Ichijinsha Inc.

# Saiyuki
THE ORIGINAL SERIES

KAZUYA MINEKURA

KC KODANSHA COMICS

"AN EDGY COMIC LOOK AT AN ANCIENT CHINESE TALE." —YALSA

Genjo Sanzo is a Buddhist priest in the city of Togenkyo, which is being ravaged by yokai spirits that have fallen out of balance with the natural order. His superiors send him on a journey far to the west to discover why this is happening and how to stop it. His companions are three yokai with human souls. But this is no day trip — the four will encounter many discoveries and horrors on the way.

**FEATURES NEW TRANSLATION, COLOR PAGES, AND BEAUTIFUL WRAPAROUND COVER ART!**

# Young characters and steampunk setting, like *Howl's Moving Castle* and *Battle Angel Alita*

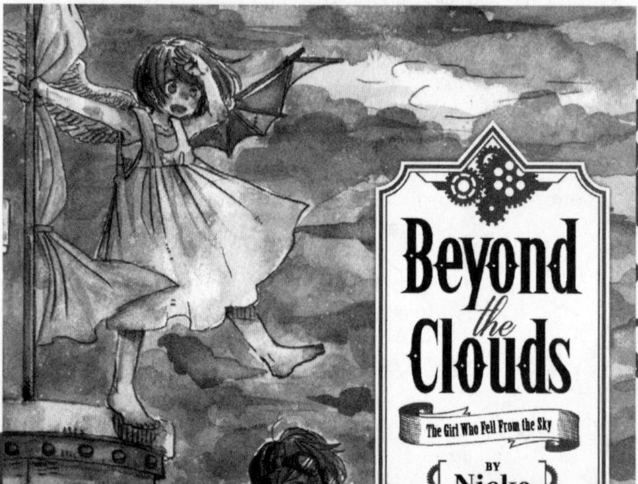
Beyond the Clouds
The Girl Who Fell From the Sky
BY Nicke
VOLUME 01

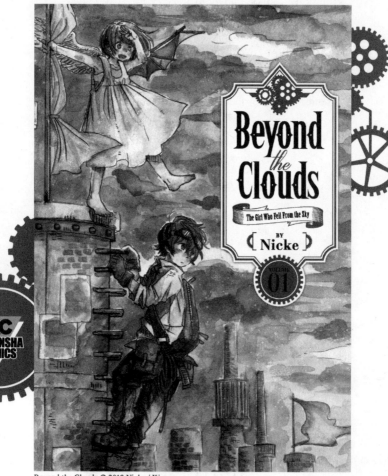

Beyond the Clouds © 2018 Nicke / Ki-oon

KC KODANSHA COMICS

A boy with a talent for machines and a mysterious girl whose wings he's fixed will take you beyond the clouds! In the tradition of the high-flying, resonant adventure stories of Studio Ghibli comes a gorgeous tale about the longing of young hearts for adventure and friendship!

A Kodansha Comics Trade Paperback Original
*The Witch and the Beast 6* copyright © 2020 Kousuke Satake
English translation copyright © 2021 Kousuke Satake

Published in the United States by Kodansha Comics, an imprint of Kodansha USA Publishing, LLC, New York.

Publication rights for this English edition arranged through Kodansha Ltd., Tokyo.

First published in Japan in 2020 by Kodansha Ltd., Tokyo as *Majo to yaju*, volume 6.

ISBN 978-1-64651-225-6

Original cover design by Yusuke Kurachi (Astrorb)

Printed in the United States of America.

www.kodansha.us

9 8 7 6 5 4 3 2 1
Translation: Kevin Gifford
Lettering: Phil Christie
Editing: Vanessa Tenazas
Kodansha Comics edition cover design by My Truong

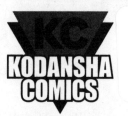

D0840897

Publisher: Kiichiro Sugawara

Director of publishing services: Ben Applegate
Associate director of operations: Stephen Pakula
Publishing services managing editors: Alanna Ruse, Madison Salters
Production managers: Emi Lotto, Angela Zurlo
Logo and character art ©Kodansha USA Publishing, LLC